SEND ME GOD

Brepols Medieval Women Series

SEND ME GOD

The Lives of
Ida the Compassionate of Nivelles,
Nun of La Ramée,
Arnulf, Lay Brother of Villers,
and Abundus, Monk of Villers,
by Goswin of Bossut

translated by, and with an introduction by
Martinus Cawley OCSO

and with a preface by
Barbara Newman

The Pennsylvania State University Press
University Park, Pennsylvania

Copyright © 2003, Brepols Publishers n.v., Turnhout, Belgium

Published in 2006 in paperback by The Pennsylvania State University Press.

First published in 2003 in a clothbound edition by Brepols Publishers
as volume 6 of the series Medieval Women: Texts and Contexts.

Library of Congress Cataloging-in-Publication Data

Goswin, of Bossut.
Send me God : the lives of Ida the Compassionate of Nivelles,
nun of La Ramee, Arnulf, lay brother of Villers, and Abundus, monk of
Villers / by Goswin of Bossut ; translated by, and with an introduction by
Martinus Cawley ; and with a preface by Barbara Newman.
p.   cm.
(Brepols medieval women series)
Includes bibliographical references.
ISBN 0-271-02683-9 (pbk. : alk. paper)
1. Ida, of Nivelles, d. 1231.
2. Arnulf, of Villers.
3. Abundus, of Villers.
4. Christian saints—Belgium—Biography.
5. Cistercians—Belgium—Biography. I. Title. II. Series.

BX4700.I26G67 2005
271'.12022493—dc22
2005027944

The Pennsylvania State University Press is a member of the
Association of American University Presses.

It is the policy of The Pennsylvania State University Press
to use acid-free paper. Publications on uncoated stock satisfy the minimum
requirements of American National Standard for Information Sciences—
Permanence of Paper for Printed Library Material, ANSI Z39.48–1992.

In loving memory of
Sister John Nepomucene RNDM
who taught me to read and to love stories
in Wagin, Western Australia, 1940–1942
and for whom we pupils became her own lifelong stories

Contents

Introduction to the Lives

The Life of Ida the Compassionate of Nivelles, Nun of La Ramée

The Life of Arnulf, Lay Brother of Villers

The Life of Abundus, Monk of Villers

Abbreviations

Abbreviations in bold denote works that are the subject of the translations here.

AASS   Acta Sanctorum (Antwerp, 1643–1770; Brussels, 1780–86, 1845–83, and 1894– ; Tongerloo, 1794; Paris, 1875–87)

Ab   Goswin of Bossut, *Vita Abundi*, ed. by A. M. Frenken, 'De Vita van Abundus van Hoei', *Citeaux*, 10 (1959), 5–33. [All references below are to the work, chapter, and paragraph, in the form, for example: *Ab* 2c, meaning *Vita Abundi*, Chapter 2, Paragraph c.]

Al   *Vita Aleydis Scarembecanae*, ed. by G. Henschen, AASS (Paris, 1867) June, II, pp. 471–77; trans. by M. Cawley (Lafayette, OR: Guadelupe Translations, 1987 and 2000). [Anonymous, but probably by Abbot Arnulf II of Villers]

Arn   Goswin of Bossut, *Vita Arnulfi*, ed. by D. Papebroeck, AASS (Antwerp, 1709) June, VII, pp. 606–31; (Paris, 1867), pp. 558–79. [All references below are to the work, book, chapter, and paragraph, in the form, for example: *Arn* II.2c, meaning *Vita Arnulfi*, Book II, Chapter 2, Paragraph c.]

Beat   *Vita Beatricis*, ed. by L. Reypens, in *Beatrijs van Tienen O. Cist., 1200–1268* (Antwerp: Ruusbroec-Genootschap, 1964); *The Life of Beatrice of Nazareth, 1200–1268*, trans. by Roger DeGanck and John Baptist Hasbrouck, Cistercian Fathers, 50 (Kalamazoo: CP, 1991)

Bern, *De grad*   Bernard of Clairvaux, *De gradibus humilitatis et superbiae*, ed. by J. Leclercq and H. M. Rochais, in *S. Bernardi opera*, vol. III (Rome: Editiones Cistercienses, 1963), pp. 1–59; *The Steps of Humility and Pride*, trans. by Ambrose Conway, Cistercian Fathers, 13a (Kalamazoo: CP, 1973)

Caesarius, *DM*   Caesarius of Heisterbach, *Dialogus miraculorum*, ed. by Joseph

Strange (Cologne: H. Lempertz, 1851; repr. Ridgewood, NJ: Gregg Press, 1966); *The Dialogue of Miracles*, trans. by H. von E. Scott and C. C. Swinton Bland (London: Routledge, 1929)

CCSL   Corpus Christianorum. Series Latina (Turnhout: Brepols, 1954–)

CF   Cistercian Fathers

Chronica   *Chronica Villariensis monasterii*, ed. by Édouard Martène and Ursin Durand, *Thesaurus novus anecdotorum* (Paris, 1717), vol. III, 1267–1310; ed. by Georg Waitz, MGH SS, 25 (Leipzig, 1925), 192–219 [a chronological series of abbatial portraits within the *Monumenta historiae Villariensis*]; see also *Gesta*, below

Cîteaux   *Cîteaux: Commentarii Cistercienses*

COCR   Collectanea Ordinis Cisterciensium Reformatorum

Conrad, *EM*   Conrad of Eberbach, *Exordium magnum Cisterciense*, ed. by Bruno Griesser (Rome: Editiones Cistercienses, 1961)

CP   Cistercian Publications

CS   Cistercian Studies (series)

CSQ   *Cistercian Studies Quarterly*

EC   *Exordium Cisterciense*, ed. by Jean de la Croix Bouton and Jean Baptiste Van Damme, *Les plus anciens textes de Cîteaux* (Achel: Abbaye Cistercienne, 1974); also ed. by Chrysogonus Waddell, *Narrative and Legislative Texts from Early Cîteaux* (n. p.: Cîteaux. Commentarii Cistercienses, 1999) [a historical preface to early redactions of the Cistercian Usages]

EO   *Ecclesiastica Officia*, ed. and trans. by D. Choisselet and P. Vernet, *Les Ecclesiastica officia cisterciens du XIIe siècle* (Reiningue: Oelenberg, 1989); trans. by M. Cawley, *Ancient Usages* (Lafayette, OR: Guadelupe Translations, 1998) [the 1185 edition of the Cistercian Usages]

GC   *Statuta Capitulorum Generalium Ordinis Cisterciensis (1116– 1786)*, ed. by J.–M. Canivez, 8 vols (Leuven, 1933–41)

Gesta   *Gesta Sanctorum Villariensium*, ed. by Édouard Martène and Ursin Durand, *Thesaurus novus anecdotorum*, III, 1309–74 (full text); ed. by Georg Waitz, MGH SS, 25 (Leipzig, 1925), 220–35 (selections) [a series of individual portraits of monks and lay brothers of Villers within the *Monumenta historiae Villariensis*]

Gob   *Vita Goberti de Asperimonte*, ed. by P. Dolmans, AASS, August,

IV, pp. 370–95; summarized in *Gesta*, ed. by Martène and Durand, III, col. 1318–1333 and ed. by Georg Waitz, MGH SS, 25 (Leipzig, 1925), 227–29

Gregory, *Dial*   Gregory the Great, *Dialogorum libri quatuor de miraculis patrum italicorum*, ed. by A. de Vogüé and Paul Antin, Sources Chrétiennes, 260 (Paris: Cerf, 1979); [Book II] *The Life of St. Benedict*, trans. by Hilary Costello and Eoin de Bhaldraithe (Petersham, MA: St Bede's Publications, 1993)

Gregory, *Mor*   Gregory the Great, *Moralia in Job libri XXXV*, ed. by Marc Adriaen, CCSL, 143–143B (Turnhout: Brepols, 1979–1985)

GT   Guadalupe Translations (Lafayette, Oregon)

Henriquez   Chrisostomo Henriquez, *Quinque prudentes virgines* (Antwerp, 1630)

Herbert, *LM*   Herbert of Clairvaux, *Liber miraculorum*, or *De miraculis libri tres*, ed. by Jean Mabillon, PL 185bis, 1271–1393. Much of its material is incorporated into Conrad of Eberbach, *Exordium magnum Cisterciense*, and a useful concordance in this regard is given in the Griesser edition in Corpus Christianorum Continuatio Mediaevalis, 138 (Turnhout: Brepols, 1994), pp. 36–37

Hugh, *Juet*   Hugh of Floreffe, *Vita Juettae reclusae*, ed. by G. Henschen, AASS (Antwerp, 1643), January, I, pp. 863–87; (Brussels, 1863) 2 January, pp. 145–69; trans. by Jo Ann McNamara (Toronto: Peregrina, 1999)

Isidore, *Etym*   Isidore of Seville, *Etymologiarum, sive Originum libri XX*, ed. by W. M. Lindsay (Oxford: Clarendon Press, 1911; repr. 1966)

Lew   *Vita Idae Lewensis*, ed. by R. de Buck, AASS (Paris, 1883), October, XIII, pp. 100–35; *Ida the Gentle of Lewis*, trans. by M. Cawley (GT, 1998), and forthcoming from Brepols

Lov   *Vita Idae Lovaniensis*, ed. by D. Papebroeck, AASS (Paris, 1866) April, II, pp. 155–89; *Ida the Eager of Louvain*, trans. by M. Cawley (GT, 1990; revised edn, 2000), forthcoming from Brepols

MGH SS   Monumenta Germaniae Historica Scriptores (Hannover, 1826–)

Niv   Goswin of Bossut, *Vita Idae Nivellensis*, in *Quinque prudentes virgines*, ed. by Chrisostomo Henriquez (Antwerp, 1630), pp. 199–297. [References are to the work, chapter, and paragraph, in the form: *Niv* 24f, meaning *Vita Idae Nivellensis*, Chapter 24, Paragraph f.]

Oig	James of Vitry [Supplement by Thomas of Cantimpré], *Vita Mariae Oigniacensis*, ed. by D. Papebroeck in AASS (Paris, 1867), June, V, pp. 542–72, with Supplement on pp. 572–81; trans. by Margot King and Marie Marsolais, 4th edn (Toronto: Peregrina, 1999) [includes translation by Hugh Feiss of the Supplement, and an anonymous History of the Church of Oignies]
PL	Patrologia Latina, ed. by J.-P. Migne, 221 vols (Paris, 1844–1866)
RB	*Regula Benedicti*, ed. by A. de Vogüé and J. Neufville, Sources Chrétiennes, 181–182 (Paris: Cerf, 1972)
Rit	*Rituale cisterciense*, ed. by. Jean Petit (1688; repr. Westmalle, 1949). [As with the Antiphonary and Hymnarium, my references are not to a particular edition, but to the fact that the rite or formula alluded to can easily be found in any edition.]
Sim	*Vita Simonis Alnensis*: in *La vie du bienheureux frère Simon, convers en l'abbaye d'Aulne*, trans. by Jean d'Assignies (Mons, 1603). The original Life survives only in fragments, including passages in Caesarius, *Dialogus miraculorum*, the *Vita Lutgardis*, and the *Vita sanctae Odiliae*. These were gathered in Brussels, Bibliothèque royale, MS 8965–8966, fols 209–24. The Life is not found in the AASS, but it was edited in Latin by Franciscus Moschus and put into French by Jean d'Assignies (see the notice on Goswin's *Vita Arnulfi*, p. xx, n. 3 below). A French translation of Moschus was put out by Lérins in 1875. In 1621, a remarkable series of illustrations was prepared for an edition of the Life of Simon that never appeared. Recently, however, the Baron de Dorlodot published the drawings, adding French captions drawn from Moschus and d'Assignies, and from a poet involved in their first preparation, *La vie du bienheureux Simon* (Tournai: Desclée, 1968)
Sulp, *VM*	Sulpicius Severus, *Vita Martini*, ed. by Jacques Fontaine, Sources Chrétiennes, 133 (Paris: Cerf, 1967)
Thomas, *BUA*	Thomas of Cantimpré, *Bonum universale de apibus*, ed. by Georgius Colvenerius (Douai, 1597)
Thomas, *Let*	Thomas of Cantimpré, 'Deux lettres inédites de Thomas, chantre de Villers', ed. by E. Mikkers, COCR, 10 (1948), 161–73; trans. by M. Cawley, in Appendix IV on Abundus, below
Thomas, *Lut*	Thomas of Cantimpré, *Vita Lutgardis*, ed. by G. Henschen, AASS (Antwerp, 1791), June, III, pp. 234–62; (Paris, 1867), ed. by G. Hendrix [*Vita Antiqua* and Old French Version], *Cîteaux*, 29

(1978), 153–206; ed. and trans. by M. Cawley (GT, 1987) [all three versions]; trans. by Margot King (Toronto: Peregrina, 1989) [English translation of AASS text]

UC   *Usus Conversorum*: in *Nomasticon Cisterciense*, ed. by J. Paris (Solesmes: e Typographeo Sancti Petri, 1892), pp. 234–41; also ed. by Chrysogonus Waddell, *Cistercian Lay Brothers: Twelfth-Century Usages with Related Texts* (Brecht and Cîteaux: Commentarii Cistercienses, 2000). [As with the Antiphonary, etc., reference is to customs common to all the early editions.]

VP   *Vita prima Bernardi*, ed. by J. Mabillon, PL 185, 225–466; trans. by M. Cawley (GT, 1990) [Book I of *VP* by William of Saint–Thierry and selections from the other seven books and the *Vita Tertia*, early 'fragments' penned by Bernard's secretary, Geoffrey of Auxerre.]

Select Bibliography

Since the present work is essentially a translation, with comment based almost exclusively on internal evidence from computerization of the original texts, this Select Bibliography is confined to core works and to the few secondary works actually consulted.

Section 1: The Latin Texts

Please note that the system of internal referencing for these works is explained in the Abbreviations above.

Vita Idae Nivellensis

The two extant manuscripts are Brussels, Bibliothèque royale, MS 8609–8620, fols 146^r–178^v (A) and MS 8895–96, fols 1^r–35^v (B). For more details, see *Catalogus Codicum Hagiographicorum Bibliothecae Regiae Bruxellensis*, 2 vols (Brussels, 1886, 1889), 2: 222–26 and 266. The manuscript B is earlier than A, and in the few divergences between them, B usually seems closer to the original (but see *Niv* 34g, n. 204).[1]

Codex B carries the title *Vita venerabilis Idae sanctimonialis de Rameya*. Since its only other content is a copy of the one other local Life, that of Ida of Gorsleeuw (Lewis, Léau), we may presume that it was commissioned for the house of La Ramée, where both Idas lived.

Codex A is said to be in a later hand. This is confirmed by its omission of remarks in which Goswin speaks of certain persons as being still alive (for example, fol. 166^v for *Niv* 24f). In a few instances A has a better reading than B, and so it was apparently copied, not from B, but either from the original or some other early copy.

---

[1] The first folio of both manuscripts is reproduced in *La Ramée, abbaye cistercienne en Brabant wallon*, ed. by Thomas Coomans (Brussels: Racine, 2002), pp. 36 and 39; see also pp. 33 and 35.

For example, in *Niv* 34b A has the meaningful *vigorem* (fol. 176^r) where B has the meaningless *pigorem* (fol. 33ra). Hence, in any given divergence, either manuscript could represent the original, especially since both seem to stem from copyists who understood what they were writing, and virtually all variants, apart from slips and matters of orthography, amount to unconscious substitution of synonyms. Thus, I usually try to provide a translation that embraces both variants; for instance, in *Niv* 33g, where B (fol. 32va) speaks of God's *dispositione*, A (fol. 175^v) perhaps absent-mindedly makes it God's *potestate*. Although I opt for B, I would be equally willing to follow A. However, in *Niv* 29b–1, where A (fol. 170^r) has the commonplace *omni custodia cor suum servans* (kept constant watch on her heart), B (fol. 26va) uses the term *scrutans*, whose daring echo of Ps. 7.10, surely stems from Goswin himself, and A's departure from this, if deliberate, would be a toning down of an adventurous idea. Hence my translation makes it 'scrutinizing her heart with all watchfulness'.

The first printed edition was made by Chrisostomo Henriquez, with Ida as the first of five female nuns in his *Quinque prudentes virgines* (Antwerp, 1630), pp. 199–297. In adapting the text to readers of his day, Henriquez made many omissions and changes. The text of his longer omissions is reproduced in the entry for Codex 8609–8620 in *Catalogus Codicum Hagiographicorum Bibliothecae Regiae Bruxellensis* (Brussels, 1889), 2: 222–26. A critical edition of two chapters (25 and 28) is given as an appendix by L. Reypens in his edition of the *Vita Beatricis*.[2] It was my perusal of this appendix that convinced me of the need to resort to the surviving manuscripts.

Divergences between the two manuscripts, graciously supplied to me in microfilm by the Brussels Royal Library, seemed so minimal in contrast to their often sharp difference from Henriquez's text, that in my original edition of *Ida*, I made no systematic distinction between the two. For this edition, however, I have collated the manuscripts against Henriquez and the extracts in the *Catalogus*, and have carefully identified all allusions to the manuscripts. While I speak of Henriquez as 'bowdlerizing', I should add that he deserves praise as an editor for taking out expressions that could have posed difficulty for his readers. Some of the expressions he thus suppressed were among Goswin's richest, and one happy result of his avoiding them was precisely to draw them to my attention.

Vita Arnulfi conversi Villariensis

Three manuscripts are noted by the Bollandist editor, D. Papebroeck, AASS (Antwerp, 1709) June, VII, p. 607ef; one from Villers, one from Orval, and one in the possession of Miraeus (Aubert Le Mire). In addition, Moreau (pp. xxvii–xxviii)

---

[2] *Beatrijs van Tienen O. Cist., 1200–1268*, ed. by L. Reypens (Antwerp: Ruusbroec–Genootschap, 1964), pp. 218–20.

reports a fourth manuscript in what was then the Imperial Library of Berlin, and a fifth in the Bodleian Library at Oxford, neither of which has been collated with the first three. Moreau is nevertheless confident in the AASS text, and I agree with him, although I differ in explaining why Miraeus's text is shorter and more succinct than those of the other two from *Arn* II.9b onwards (or more precisely, *Arn* II.29 in the AASS reference system).

The Life is excerpted in the *Gesta Sanctorum Villariensium*, ed. by Martène and Durand, III, cols 1359–1362; and partially in MGH SS, 25, p. 234. It is sketchily summarized in several surveys of Cistercian saints from about 1600 onwards. There are extensive verbatim excerpts from Goswin in a volume edited by Franciscus Moschus,[3] in which he presented the two lay brothers, Arnulf of Villers and Simon of Aulne. Papebroeck studied Moschus's Latin text and found it very inferior to that of the manuscripts he used for the AASS edition.

My work on Arnulf is based on the text in AASS, which has the appearance of being virtually free from significant typographical errors. A system of square brackets in that edition enables the reader to choose between two texts for Arnulf, the shorter of which differs from the longer only by way of omission. The editor considers the short text Goswin's original and the long one a later revision, made by Goswin himself. Moreau (p. xxvii–xxviii) and Roisin (pp. 32–33) agree with him on this. They argue from the apparent date of the longer text's mention of the fulfilment of a prophecy (*Arn* II.20j; II.59). Not having access to the manuscripts, only hesitatingly do I disagree with them on this.

I appreciate the force of the argument from *Arn* II.20j, and I could cite others like it, but I am puzzled as to why the two texts do not diverge until *Arn* II.9b, almost seventy per cent of the way through the long text, and even closer to the end in the short. Also, why do the 'additions' get bulkier the closer we get to the end? It seems

---

[3] *La vie du bienheureux frère Simon, convers en l'abbaye d'Aulne*, ed. by Franciscus Moschus (Arras, 1603). Moschus was a secular canon of Armentiers and a parish priest at Seclin near Lille. He had previously published James of Vitry's famous *Historia occidentalis* and *Historia orientalis*. There is a list of his excerpts in the Bollandists' *Bibliotheca Hagiographica Latina Antiquae et Mediae Aetatis* (Brussels, 1898–99), I, p. 115. In his first twelve pages, Moschus completely re-cast, and greatly shortened, Goswin's Book I. Then on pp. 13–59 he reproduced many passages of Goswin with only minimal alteration. On his page 68 he again began making excerpts, and continued so until his page 79, but these later excerpts drop many of Goswin's phrases. The Bollandist listing also tells which passages of Goswin thus reappear in Moschus. More interesting is that he omits, or bowdlerizes: all of *Arn* I, and some of the anecdotes of Arn II: II.2ac (Pigs); II.9a–8c (Laughter and Demons); II.9a–14d (key examples of 'sending God'); II.16ae (Theophania of Paris); II.18a–29k (with the one exception of II.20de, an innocent tale of two clerics); II.21a (making the physician tell the truth); II.21h–end (death). Three years after Moschus's book appeared, the section on Simon, but not that on Arnulf, was put into French by a monk of Cambron named Jean d'Assignies, published at Mons, in 1603.

to me more natural to suppose that the long text is Goswin's original, and that a later copyist, on reaching II.9b, began to worry about running out of space or time, and started omitting unnecessary words, and eventually even whole paragraphs, including II.20j. Then, too, I do not see the mention of the 'decade' in II.20j as dating the text so much later.

All agree that the style of the long text is purely Goswinian. The short text, on the other hand, often 'truncates' a typical Goswinian word play or literary allusion. I point to a few instances of this in the notes (for example at *Arn* II.12e, 13ab). Beyond such notes, I see no point in burdening the English text with the square brackets of the AASS since all agree anyway that the long text is what Goswin intended us to have.

Vita Abundi

Just two manuscripts of this work are mentioned (Moreau, p. xxix–xxxi; Frenken, p. 5; p. 11, n. 27). The first, Brussels, Bibliothèque royale, MS 19525, is from Goswin's time and comes from Villers. The second, Vienna, Österreichische Nationalbibliothek, cvp 12854, seems to have been copied from the first, some time in the fifteenth century. Apart from selections in the *Gesta*, and from summaries in general surveys of Cistercian saints, the only extensive publication of the Life was the French translation of it by Jean d'Assignies at Mons in 1603. However, in 1846 the Royal Library printed the Prologue in Latin in its *Annuaire* (p. 96). Finally, the Brussels manuscript was published in *Cîteaux*, 10 (1959), 5–33, by Msgr A. M. Frenken, then a priest in Zeelst, near Eindhoven.

For the Life of Abundus, I simply reproduce Frenken's critical edition, correcting his many obvious misprints, a couple of which I indicated in the notes on *Ab* 2c, 14b. Also, I change Frenken's Latin orthography to what Cistercians are accustomed to from the Westmalle choir books in the use of 'i/j' and 'u/v'. The Brussels cataloguing of the manuscripts is given in Roisin (p. 14).

Section 2: Secondary Sources

BOUDREAU, Claire, '"With Desire Have I Desired": Ida of Nivelles' Love for the Eucharist', in *Hidden Springs, Cistercian Monastic Women*, Medieval Religious Women III, ed. by John A. Nichols and Lillian Thomas Shank, CS, 113a (Kalamazoo: CP, 1995), I, pp. 323–44.

BROUETTE, Émile, 'Villers', in *Monasticon Belge*, ed. by Ursmer BERLIÈRE (Liège: Centre national de recherches d'histoire religieuse, 1968), IV, pp. 341–405. This multi-volume dictionary of historic abbeys, launched in 1890, groups the abbeys geographically among the civil provinces of modern Belgium, and within these, it subgroups them by religious order. The Villers entry offers mainly an exhaustive bibliography about the abbey's cartularies. Only on pp. 354–55 does the survey focus on the literature of the saintly men of Villers, before moving on to such topics as the architecture and real-estate acquisition in the early years. The last forty pages offer bibliography on each of the successive abbots, including the four under whom Arnulf and Abundus served, namely Charles, Conrad, Walter, and William (pp. 369–74). This work, now sponsored by government endowment, seems designed primarily for regional historians, so that the author's few comments on Goswin's heroes are purely bibliographical. He is, however, somewhat more personal in his presentation of their abbots, seen as administrators. He frequently cites the work of Édouard de Moreau, listed below, who has been my principal guide throughout my study of Goswin's Lives. Brouette calls Moreau's work 'magistrale' and a classic (p. 359).

CAWLEY, Martinus, 'Ida of Nivelles, Cistercian Nun', in *Hidden Springs, Cistercian Monastic Women*, Medieval Religious Women III, ed. by John A. Nichols and Lillian Thomas Shank, CS, 113a (Kalamazoo: CP, 1995), I, pp. 305–21.
——, 'Our Lady and the Nuns and Monks of Thirteenth-Century Belgium', in *Word & Spirit*, 10 (1988), 94–128.
——, 'Four Abbots of the Golden Age of Villers', in *CSQ*, 27 (1992), 299–327.
——, '*Mulieres Religiosae* in Goswin of Villers', in *Vox Benedictina*, 9 (1992), 99–107, reprinted in *Vox Benedictina*, 11 (1994).

COOMANS, Thomas, *L'Abbaye de Villers-en-Brabant, Construction, configuration et signification d'une abbaye cistercienne gothique* (Brussels: Racine/Brecht: Cîteaux commentarii cistercienses, 2000). This tall volume of six hundred and twenty-two pages is lavishly illustrated and is unsurpassed for those interested in the architecture of the buildings Arnulf and Abundus would have frequented. It is difficult, however, to match the stages of their construction with those of these men's careers. In my footnotes I allude to several of Coomans's illustrations. Given his technical topic, Coomans names Arnulf and Abundus only in an endnote linked to p. 42.

COOMANS, Thomas, ed., *La Ramée, abbaye cistercienne en Brabant wallon* (Brussels: Racine, 2002). In its two hundred and thirty-one pages it offers nineteen essays on aspects of the convent's history. Three are by Coomans, and four by Marie-Elizabeth Henneau. Ida of Nivelles is discussed mainly by Henneau (pp. 18–31), who situates her within community life in the early years, and by Thomas Falmagne (pp. 32–40), who brings Ida of Nivelles into a discussion of nuns as copyists of manuscripts. On p. 33 a text on the scribal activity of Ida of Gorsleeuw is mistakenly attributed to Ida of Nivelles. Readers will enjoy the images reproduced of both Idas and of the manuscripts of their Lives.

DEGANCK, Roger, *The Life of Beatrice of Nazareth, 1200–1268*, CF, 50 (Kalamazoo: CP, 1991).
——, *Beatrice of Nazareth in her Context* (Kalamazoo: CP, 1991)
——, *Towards Unification with God*, CS, 121–122 (Kalamazoo: CP, 1991).
These volumes provide an annotated translation of Reypens's critical text, followed by two erudite tomes on the spiritual life, in the course of which Ida of Nivelles is often mentioned.

GILLES, Henri, *The Abbey of Our Lady of Villers in Brabant* (Villers-la-Ville, 1990). This ninety-six page well-illustrated guidebook offers the serious tourist an initial orientation (pp. 1–12), followed by a tour and interpretation of the buildings and surroundings (pp. 13–75). A quite readable survey of the abbey's history (pp. 78–82) has just one column on the golden age, with no mention of Arnulf or Abundus. The ruins and their preservation are given in some detail (pp. 83–91).

HUYGHEBAERT, N., 'Arnould ou Abond? A propos d'une épitaphe de Villers-en-Brabant', *Cîteaux*, 33 (1982), 392–96. Concerning this work, see the introductory note to Appendix II on Abundus.

MCGUIRE, Brian Patrick, 'Self-Denial and Self-Assertion in Arnulf of Villers', *CSQ*, 28 (1993), 241–50. This is a very interesting study, first of Arnulf's self-flagellation, seen from a psychological point of view, and then of his social contact, inside and outside the cloister.

MISONNE, Daniel, 'Office liturgique neumé de la bienheureuse Marie d'Oignies à l'abbaye de Villers au XIIIᵉ siècle', in *Album J. Balon*, ed. by J. Balon (Namur: Les anciens établissements Godenne, 1968), pp. 171–89. This Office is said to have been composed by Goswin when the body of Mary of Oignies was brought to Villers in view of her possible canonization.

MOREAU, Édouard de and René MAERE, *L'Abbaye de Villers-en-Brabant au XIIᵉ et XIIIᵉ siècles, études d'histoire religieuse et économique* (Brussels: Dewit, 1909). For readers interested in Villers's hagiographical literature, this remains the handiest introduction. On pp. xvii–lxxii Moreau guides us into what would otherwise seem a bewildering maze of early literature in successive editions. He then, as historian, offers an account of the abbey, from its beginnings and up through its golden age (Book I). After that, as theologian he surveys every aspect of the religious life of Villers (Book II). Finally, as economist, he tells us all about the business life of the abbey and its granges (Book III). To all this he appends helpful lists and a detailed table of contents (though no alphabetical index). Canon Maere then adds an archaeological study. Much has since been learned about Villers in many fields, but I know of no work better suited to orienting an inquirer about its saints.

ROISIN, Simone, *L'Hagiographie cistercienne dans le diocèse de Liège au XIIIe siècle* (Leuven: Universiteitsbibliotheek, 1947). What Moreau does for the hagiography of Villers and for all other aspects of that house, Roisin does just for its hagiography, and for that of other Cistercian houses in its immediate milieu. After her Introduction and Select Bibliography, she dedicates some fifty pages to presenting such literature from two male houses (Villers and Aulne) and from eight female houses (including La Ramée). It is these first seventy pages that are most useful to the beginner. The three sections that follow are, indeed, interesting, but, like any such synthesis, they are personal and dated, and English-speakers may prefer to build equivalent syntheses of their own, guided by works available in English.

SIMONS, Walter, *Cities of Ladies: Beguine Communities in the Medieval Low Countries, 1200–1565* (Philadelphia: University of Pennsylvania Press, 2001). Just as Roisin extends Moreau's study to all the Cistercian houses of the diocese of Liège, so Simons extends it to all female houses of the whole of the Southern Low Countries, bounded in the north and east by the Maas (Meuse) river. More specifically, he presents all communities composed of beguines or having dealings with them, including the La Ramée of Ida of Nivelles. Simons has almost nothing to say about the male Cistercians, Arnulf and Abundus, but much to say on their home towns and on some of their friends, be these female or clerical. Numerous passages mention each of the Idas of La Ramée, and also Goswin as a biographer. The book has seventeen pages of maps, charts and illustrations; seventy-three pages of endnotes, twenty-eight pages of bibliography, sixty pages of appendices (with paragraphs on each of well over a hundred houses), and an index of twenty pages.

WADDELL, Chrysogonus, 'Pseudo-Origen's Homily on Mary Magdalene at the Tomb of Jesus', in *Liturgy OCSO*, 23 (1989), 45–65. Under discussion here is the text of the vigils readings for an Office put together by Goswin for welcoming the relics of Mary of Oignies to Villers for honourable burial. This was in 1228, when her cause for canonization was pending. The first eight pages explain how Fr Chrysogonus traced the text to its pseudo-patristic source, and the remaining twelve provide a translation.

Autour de Villers-la-Ville (Fondation Roi Baudouin: Équipe 'Des pierres pour le dire' n.d.). This forty-six-page guidebook, being from a series with governmental support, is understandably more elegant than Gilles's locally produced monograph. It gives an excellent idea of the kind of terrain through which Arnulf drove his wagon, and of the kind of buildings he stopped off at en route.

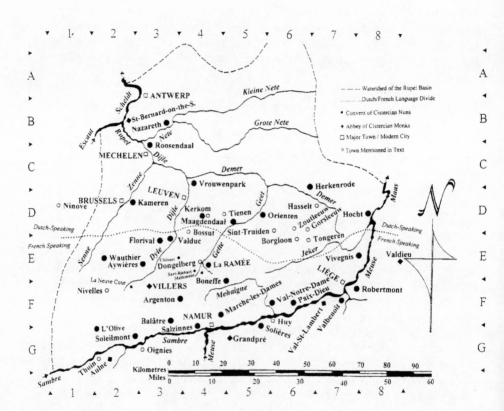

Villers and its Environs

INDEX TO THE MAP

The dates indicate the approximate year of foundation or transfer to a new location.

Preface

Goswin of Villers and the Visionary Network

by Barbara Newman

Medieval hagiography, or the writing of saints' Lives, is at once the most conventional and the most revealing of genres: tantalizing in its representation of profound inner experience, maddening in its historical vagueness and formulaic style.

What any saint's Life or *vita* reveals is not the factual 'truth' that a biographer today might strive to reconstruct, but a potent amalgam of cultural ideals, individual aspirations, communal pride, and sacred propaganda. Though the narrative voice of hagiography may sound naive, especially to novice readers, it is in fact deeply layered. In the case of historical saints (as opposed to purely folkloric figures), the core of the Life might derive from the saint's own observed and remembered experience, sometimes retrievable with difficulty, sometimes not. This experience is filtered by what is loosely called 'oral tradition', that is, the reminiscences of loving friends, clients, superiors, and confessors, transmuted over the course of time into a rich store of inspiring vignettes and stylized tales. If these anecdotes seem impressive enough to suggest the need for a Life, or if the saint's community decides to commission one, a hagiographer must be found, preferably a cleric with a reputation for learning and a respectable Latin style.[1] Personal acquaintance with the saint is desirable, but by no means indispensable. This cleric prepares for his task by gathering all the material he can find: from his own memory, if he happens to have known the saint in the flesh; from interviews with people who did; from their written

---

[1] Evelyn Birge Vitz, 'From the Oral to the Written in Medieval and Renaissance Saints' Lives', in *Images of Sainthood in Medieval Europe*, ed. by Renate Blumenfeld-Kosinski and Timea Szell (Ithaca, NY: Cornell University Press, 1991), pp. 97–114.

notes, including vernacular texts that seldom come down to us; and not least, from other saints' Lives, which supply not only stylistic models and structural patterns, but also specific episodes that may be adapted or even borrowed verbatim. So, if we read the whole corpus of saints' Lives from a given time and region, what we see is like a row of stained glass windows high in the clerestory of a Gothic church. We may be struck by the 'dim religious light' they cast or the play of rhetorical colours, but the average viewer will come away with an aesthetic impression of the whole rather than a distinct view of any individual figure. To see more closely, we must climb the often rickety scaffolding of historical research.

The Lives stemming from the thirteenth-century southern Low Countries, an area corresponding roughly to modern Belgium or the medieval diocese of Liège, form a canon probably unique in the annals of hagiography.[2] The first remarkable feature we notice about this canon is the exceptional prominence it accords to women and others of comparatively low status. According to Donald Weinstein and Rudolph Bell, who conducted a statistical analysis of 864 saints' Lives written between 1000 and 1700, only 17.5% of the saints in their sample were women. For the thirteenth century, this figure rises to 22.6%.[3] Of the twenty-four southern Netherlandish Lives, however, well over half celebrate female holiness.[4] Seven of the fourteen women commemorated in these Lives spent much or all of their religious careers as Cistercian nuns, while the other seven were beguines, recluses, or 'irregulars', like

---

[2] The choice of terminology for this region is politically sensitive. In the Middle Ages an east–west political boundary divided Flanders and Artois, which were fiefs of the French crown, from Brabant, Hainaut, and other principalities that owed fealty to the German emperor. Both eastern and western regions were bisected by a north–south language border that separated the Dutch-speaking north from the French-speaking south (the ancestors of 'Flemish' and 'Walloons' in modern Belgium). Finally, while most of the municipalities mentioned here belonged to the diocese or prince-bishopric of Liège, a few lay within the smaller neighbouring dioceses of Cambrai and Tournai. The most accurate term for the entire region is 'southern Low Countries'. The adjective 'Netherlandish' properly refers to the Low Countries as a whole, including the present-day Netherlands and parts of northern France, so I have here used the term 'southern Netherlandish'. I thank Walter Simons and John Van Engen for their helpful explanations. For more on the demographics of the region see Walter Simons, *Cities of Ladies: Beguine Communities in the Medieval Low Countries, 1200–1565* (Philadelphia: University of Pennsylvania Press, 2001), pp. 1–19.

[3] Donald Weinstein and Rudolph M. Bell, *Saints and Society: The Two Worlds of Western Christendom, 1000–1700* (Chicago: University of Chicago Press, 1982), p. 220.

[4] See the list below, pp. xlviii–xlvix. The exact figures would vary depending on whether one counted only self-standing Lives or also the short Lives embedded in longer sources, such as the chronicle of Villers, Caesarius of Heisterbach's *Dialogus miraculorum*, and Thomas of Cantimpré's *Bonum universale de apibus*. Several of the male Lives are fragmentary. For accounts of the female canon see Simons, *Cities of Ladies*, 37–48, and Brenda Bolton, '*Vitae matrum*: A Further Aspect of the *Frauenfrage*', in *Medieval Women*, ed. by Derek Baker (Oxford: Blackwell, 1978), pp. 253–73.

the unclassifiable woman whose biographer called her Christina the Astonishing (*Mirabilis*). Christina was rejected by her neighbours as a mad woman or demoniac,[5] while the nun Alice ended her days as a miserably secluded leper.[6] Of the men in this group, several were lay brothers or *conversi*, men who joined a monastery in adulthood and worked at manual labour, lacking the literate skills of professed monks. Only four of the Lives, apart from those embedded in the chronicle of Villers, honour religious superiors. These are John, founding abbot of Cantimpré; Werric, second prior of Aulne; the nun Beatrice, prioress of Nazareth; and the canoness Juliana, who was prioress of a hospital community at Mont-Cornillon (near Liège) until she was exiled in the midst of civic strife, only to spend the rest of her life on the run from one monastery or beguinage to another.[7]

In short, and in sharp contrast to the hagiography of earlier centuries, these saints were collectively celebrated not for their outstanding leadership, brilliant preaching, or stupendous miracles, but for the intensity of their inner Lives. In a classic study now almost sixty years old, Simone Roisin highlighted the most salient features of this interiority: a willing acceptance of suffering, often embraced vicariously for the good of others; affectionate devotion to the humanity of Christ, especially his infancy and passion; contemplative absorption in the mysteries of the Trinity; fervent longing for the Eucharist; victorious combat with demons; and a strong predilection for experiences of the kind that used to be slightingly called 'paramystical' – visions, ecstasies, clairvoyance, even levitation.[8] These were the traits that hagiographers and their public found compelling, despite the reservations of contemporary churchmen or modern scholars. Unlike the Lives of more public saints, such as Bernard, Francis, Dominic, and Catherine of Siena, these Lives were written chiefly for local consumption, not for the benefit of authorities in Rome. In fact, none of the southern Netherlandish saints were ever canonized, although several are liturgically honoured as 'blessed'.

The two most 'successful' Lives in this corpus – that is, the most widely read, copied, translated, and imitated, were the works of comparatively famous authors. James of Vitry was a celebrated preacher, crusade promoter, bishop of Acre in the

---

[5] On demoniacs see Barbara Newman, 'Possessed by the Spirit: Devout Women, Demoniacs, and the Apostolic Life in the Thirteenth Century', *Speculum*, 73 (1998), 733–70.

[6] *Alice the Leper: Life of St. Alice of Schaerbeek*, trans. by Martinus Cawley (GT, 2000). A revised edition of this text will appear in a sequel to the present volume, along with the anonymous Lives of Ida of Gorsleeuw (Lewis) and Ida of Leuven.

[7] *Life of Juliana of Mont-Cornillon*, trans. by Barbara Newman (Toronto: Peregrina, 1988).

[8] Simone Roisin, *L'Hagiographie cistercienne dans le diocèse de Liège au XIIIe siècle* (Louvain: Bibliothèque de l'Université, 1947). For more recent, sympathetic accounts of these women's spirituality see Simons, *Cities of Ladies*; Caroline Walker Bynum, *Holy Feast and Holy Fast: The Religious Significance of Food to Medieval Women* (Berkeley: University of California Press, 1987); and Roger DeGanck, *Beatrice of Nazareth in her Context*, 2 vols. (Kalamazoo: CP, 1991).

Holy Land, and ultimately cardinal bishop of Tusculanum. His high standing in the Church lent considerable weight to his championship of the incipient beguine movement, which he defended both in person and in his well known Life of Mary of Oignies (d. 1213). In a Supplement to that Life, Thomas of Cantimpré, a protégé of James, would audaciously chide his famous mentor for betraying Mary's ideals of humble service in order to seek wealth and glory in the curia.[9] Yet the Dominican Thomas attained his own share of fame as a preacher, theologian, and hagiographer. In addition to the Supplement he composed four original Lives, of which the most celebrated is his Life of Christina the Astonishing (d. 1224).[10] Interestingly, each of Thomas's hagiographic subjects represents a different religious status: John of Cantimpré founded the house of Augustinian canons where Thomas was first professed, while Mary was a beguine, Margaret of Ieper (Ypres) a Dominican tertiary, Lutgard of Aywières a Cistercian nun, and Christina a devout if eccentric laywoman.[11] Two other clerics wrote the Lives of female recluses who practised exceptional piety in their own homes. Hugh of Floreffe, a Premonstratensian canon, celebrated a young widow and mother, Yvette of Huy,[12] while the monk Philip of Clairvaux memorialized Elizabeth of Spalbeek, famous for the remarkably literal re-enactments of Christ's Passion that she performed in trance before an eager public.[13] Several other Lives in this canon are anonymous, though hidden female authorship lurks behind at least two of them. Beatrice of Nazareth's hagiographer apparently destroyed her Dutch spiritual diary after translating it into a formal Latin Life; only a short treatise, Seven Manners of Love, can now be ascribed to the nun with some confidence.[14] The life of Juliana, herself a gifted liturgical poet, was first written in

---

[9] Jacques de Vitry, The Life of Marie d'Oignies, trans. by Margot King, and Thomas de Cantimpré, Supplement to the Life of Marie d'Oignies, trans. by Hugh Feiss, in Two Lives of Marie d'Oignies (Toronto: Peregrina, 1993).

[10] Thomas de Cantimpré, The Life of Christina the Astonishing, trans. by Margot King, 2nd edn (Toronto: Peregrina, 1999).

[11] Robert Godding, 'Une oeuvre inédite de Thomas de Cantimpré: La Vita Ioannis Cantipratensis', Revue d'histoire ecclésiastique, 76 (1981), 241–316; Thomas de Cantimpré, The Life of Margaret of Ypres, trans. by Margot King, 2nd edn (Toronto: Peregrina, 1995) and The Life of Lutgard of Aywières, trans. by Margot King, 2nd edn (Toronto: Peregrina, 1991).

[12] Hugh of Floreffe, The Life of Yvette of Huy, trans. by Jo Ann McNamara (Toronto: Peregrina, 1999).

[13] For a Middle English translation of this Life see Carl Horstmann, 'Prosalegende: Legende des MS. Douce 114', Anglia, 8 (1885), 102–96. See also Walter Simons and Joanna Ziegler, 'Phenomenal Religion in the Thirteenth Century and its Image: Elisabeth of Spalbeek and the Passion Cult', in Women in the Church, ed. by W. J. Sheils and Diana Wood (Oxford: Blackwell, 1990), pp. 117–26.

[14] Roger DeGanck, trans., The Life of Beatrice of Nazareth, 1200–1268, with a reprint of the Latin edition by Léonce Reypens (Kalamazoo: CP, 1991). A forthcoming article by Wybren Scheepsma casts slight doubt on the authenticity of Seven Manners of Love: 'Beatrice

French by her close friend, the recluse Eve of Saint-Martin; but again, this vernacular source was lost or discarded once it had been 'superseded' by an official text in Latin.[15]

Goswin, author of the three Lives translated in this volume, is perhaps the least familiar of the named hagiographers. Born in the French-speaking hamlet of Bossut, he became a monk and cantor at the great abbey of Villers, which had been founded as a daughter house of Clairvaux in 1146/47 at the height of St Bernard's fame, and reached its apogee under a succession of effective, charismatic abbots in the first half of the thirteenth century.[16] The office of cantor was an important one, perhaps third in rank only to the abbot and prior, for this monk ideally possessed a high degree of rhetorical as well as musical skill. The cantor (or *cantrix* among nuns) was not only responsible for training and directing the monastic choir, which included all professed members as well as novices, but also for assuring that the liturgy was performed in a reverent fashion and the service books corrected and re-copied as needed. Other duties included assigning the monks' weekly chores, choosing seasonally apt readings for the refectory, and writing occasional pieces such as obituaries. In a flourishing and liturgically creative monastery such as Villers, the cantor might well try his hand at composition, as evidenced by the verses Goswin appended to the life of Ida of Nivelles and the office he composed for the feast of Mary of Oignies. Writing Lives of saintly members of the community could be seen as an ambitious extension of such tasks.

Only one manuscript of Arnulf's Life actually bears Goswin's name, but the Lives of Ida of Nivelles and Abundus of Huy have been convincingly ascribed to him on stylistic grounds.[17] If we accept these attributions, the three Lives can be read as a kind of trilogy. Just as the historical writings from Villers commemorate lay brothers along with abbots and monks,[18] so Goswin's three Lives, probably all

---

of Nazareth: The First Woman Author of Mystical Texts', in *Seeing and Knowing: Women and Learning in Medieval Europe, 1200—1550*, ed. by Anneke Mulder-Bakker (Turnhout: Brepols, forthcoming).

[15] On Juliana and Eve of Saint-Martin, see Anneke Mulder-Bakker, *Lives of the Anchoresses* (Philadelphia: University of Pennsylvania Press, forthcoming), Chapters 4–5.

[16] Édouard de Moreau and René Maere, *L'Abbaye de Villers-en-Brabant au XIIe et XIIIe siècles* (Brussels: Dewit, 1909); Thomas Coomans, *L'Abbaye de Villers-en-Brabant: Construction, configuration et signification d'une abbaye cistercienne gothique* (Brussels: Éditions Racine and Cîteaux, 2000); Martinus Cawley, 'Four Abbots of the Golden Age of Villers', *CSQ*, 27 (1992), 299–327.

[17] Roisin, *L'Hagiographie cistercienne*, pp. 35–38, 56–59.

[18] Editorial titles for this corpus vary. The older edition, entitled *Monumenta historiae Villariensis*, appears in *Thesaurus novus anecdotorum*, ed. by Edmond Martène and Ursin Durand (Paris: Delaulne, 1717), III, 1267–1374. In the more recent edition by Georg Waitz the work is divided into three components: *Chronica Villariensis monasterii* (MGH SS, 25, pp. 195–209), including Lives of 13th-century abbots; a continuation of this chronicle (pp. 209–

composed in the 1230s, honour three different religious vocations within the
Cistercian Order. Ida (d. 1231) was a nun at La Ramée, one of several women's
monasteries supervised by Villers, while Arnulf was a lay brother (d. 1228) and
Abundus a monk (d. 1239). Goswin wrote the first two of these Lives on
commission not long after their protagonists died, but since Abundus's Life lacks an
account of his death – otherwise an essential component of hagiography – we can
assume he was still living at the time of composition. The motive for writing in this
case seems not to have been a superior's commission but, as Martinus Cawley
suggests, a personal desire to commemorate the life of an intimate friend. Like his
contemporary, Thomas of Cantimpré, Goswin may also have intended to praise the
unity of divine grace as manifested through a diversity of vocations.

Both the southern Netherlandish canon as a whole and the three Lives by Goswin
reflect a milieu in which celibate men and women were able to cultivate friendships
with unusual freedom. Far different was the Cistercian 'Golden Age' in which
Villers was founded. The great spiritual writers of the twelfth century, Bernard of
Clairvaux, William of Saint-Thierry, Aelred of Rievaulx, Isaac of Stella, had
inhabited a male homosocial world in which women figured as patrons to be
honoured respectfully, sisters to be instructed at a distance, or (most often)
temptations to be avoided, but never intimate friends. In contrast, the first half of the
thirteenth century represented an apogee of what Jo Ann McNamara has termed
'syneisactism', the willing collaboration of the chaste in a spiritual project
understood to transcend, if never obliterate, the difference of gender.[19] One reason
for this short-lived blossoming was the sheer number of women now flocking to
forms of religious life, in part because in this era European women significantly
outnumbered men,[20] while the proportion of marriageable males steadily dwindled as
the ranks of clergy expanded (university students and their teachers were also
considered clerics and thus required to be celibate). It has been customary among
historians to regard this state of affairs as a problem, whether it is described in
thirteenth-century pastoral terms as the *cura mulierum* (care of women) or in
twentieth-century academic terms as the *Frauenfrage* (women question). Like most
problems, however, this one was also an opportunity, and our hagiographers clearly
saw it as such. Although the Cistercian General Chapter in 1228 banned the
incorporation of any more nunneries into the order, this legislation was widely

---

19); and the later *Gesta sanctorum Villariensium* (pp. 220–35), a compendium of abridged
Lives of monks and lay brothers.

[19] Jo Ann McNamara, *Sisters in Arms: Catholic Nuns through Two Millennia* (MA,
Cambridge: Harvard University Press, 1996); see especially Chapters 9–11.

[20] Numerous reasons have been proposed to explain this demographic imbalance, including
the number of men killed in war or absent on crusade as well as improvements in agricultural
production, which reduced the number of female deaths due to malnutrition or anaemia during
pregnancy and childbirth.

flouted as the white monks experienced what Brian McGuire describes as a new 'opening to women'.[21] McGuire shrewdly notes that, once the numbers in the great abbeys had increased from one or two dozen monks to a hundred or more, it was no longer possible to maintain the idealized male intimacy of earlier days, and gradually 'friendships at a distance', including cross-gender friendships, 'came to be seen as more accessible and desirable than friendships within the same monastery.'[22] Thirteenth-century Cistercians also mingled more freely with the laity in general, abandoning their earlier emphasis on strict claustration for a kind of apostolate that included the spiritual direction of beguines and recluses, although by mid-century their role as confidants of religious women would be eclipsed by the newer mendicant orders. Pastoral interactions between men and women are evident not only in the hagiographic corpus, but also in contemporary collections of exempla (edifying tales), such as Thomas of Cantimpré's *Bonum universale de apibus* and the German monk Caesarius of Heisterbach's *Dialogus miraculorum*.[23]

Not coincidentally, the early thirteenth century was also a high-water mark of female mysticism. In the same decade that Goswin wrote his Lives, the mystical theologian Hadewijch, living at a beguinage in Antwerp or perhaps in Brussels, was producing a remarkable body of visions, poems, and letters that constitute one of the earliest monuments of Dutch literature.[24] In Germany, the beguine Mechthild of Magdeburg may already have begun her own visionary text, *The Flowing Light of the Godhead*.[25] Among her acquaintances in that town was probably the recluse Margaret the Lame, subject of yet another Life.[26] Nor were these spiritual currents confined to northern Europe, for the same religious impulses we observe in the beguine movement of the southern Low Countries and the Rhineland were embodied just as fully by Franciscan and Dominican tertiaries in Italy. The so-called evangelical awakening of the twelfth century, epitomized by a quest for what contemporaries called the 'apostolic life', continued into the thirteenth with the rise

---

[21] Brian McGuire, 'The Cistercians and Friendship: An Opening to Women', in *Hidden Springs: Cistercian Monastic Women*, ed. by John Nicholas and Lillian T. Shank (Kalamazoo: CP, 1995), I, pp. 171–200. See also Brenda Bolton, '*Mulieres Sanctae*', in *Women in Medieval Society*, ed. by Susan M. Stuard (Philadelphia: University of Pennsylvania Press, 1976): 141–58; Sally Thompson, 'The Problem of the Cistercian Nuns in the Twelfth and Early Thirteenth Centuries', in *Medieval Women*, ed. by Baker, 227–52.

[22] McGuire, 'Cistercians', 189.

[23] Thomas of Cantimpré, *Bonum universale de apibus* (Douai: Beller, 1627); Caesarius of Heisterbach, *Dialogue on Miracles*, trans. by H. von E. Scott and C. C. Swinton Bland (London: Routledge, 1929).

[24] Hadewijch, *The Complete Works*, trans. by Columba Hart (New York: Paulist, 1980).

[25] Mechthild of Magdeburg, *The Flowing Light of the Godhead*, trans. by Frank Tobin (New York: Paulist, 1998).

[26] Mulder-Bakker, *Lives of the Anchoresses*, Chapter 2.

and fall of numerous religious movements, including several that straddled the permeable boundary between orthodoxy and heresy.[27] Competition between old and new orders, and between regular and semi-regular forms of religious life, had the paradoxical effect of fostering both a strong sense of communal identity and a high degree of fluidity. Goswin, for example, is self-consciously, proudly Cistercian, if one can say this with due respect for a monk whose order prided itself on humility. Yet his Lives reveal a world in which Cistercians and other religious shared warm friendships as well as spiritual ideals. Ida of Nivelles became a nun after a girlhood spent among beguines, and the recluse Elizabeth of Spalbeek also joined a Cistercian monastery at a later stage of her career. Alice of Schaarbeek, on the other hand, left her nunnery for a recluse's cell when leprosy made communal life impossible for her,[28] and Juliana was at various points a canoness, a beguine, a Cistercian, and finally a recluse. Thomas of Cantimpré migrated from the Augustinians to the Dominicans, yet revered his Cistercian friend Lutgard of Aywières as a spiritual mother, and near the end of his life he returned to complete a Life of the Augustinian John of Cantimpré, begun perhaps forty years earlier. In this context, the era's relatively free exchanges between male and female religious can be seen as one aspect of a broader openness to new spiritual trends, which coexisted with intense and even violent competition.

Nowadays we speak somewhat glibly of 'spiritualities', Benedictine, Cistercian, Franciscan, and so forth, meaning by that term the whole complex of beliefs, attitudes, and practices that shape an individual's or community's response to God and the world. There is no close medieval equivalent of this word. Hagiographers spoke on the one hand of virtues (charity, humility, obedience) that were ideally the same for all, and on the other hand of religious vocations, each with its own distinctive calling. In the thirteenth-century canon we are considering, they also said much about graces, or divine favours, bestowed on the saints either gratuitously or in response to prayer. Visions, prophecies, and even illnesses could fall into this category. So, in our efforts to discern the 'spirituality' of Goswin's hagiographic subjects, we must bear in mind that his criteria for holiness were first universal qualities, and second, those he viewed as suitable to a particular vocation. Only in the third place were they traits specific to an individual. Thus Ida of Nivelles

---

[27] Herbert Grundmann, *Religious Movements in the Middle Ages: The Historical Links between Heresy, the Mendicant Orders, and the Women's Religious Movement in the Twelfth and Thirteenth Century*, trans. by Steven Rowan (Notre Dame: University of Notre Dame Press, 1995); M.-D. Chenu, *Nature, Man, and Society in the Twelfth Century*, trans. by Jerome Taylor and Lester K. Little (Chicago: University of Chicago Press, 1968), Chapters 6–7; Giles Constable, *The Reformation of the Twelfth Century* (Cambridge: Cambridge University Press, 1996).

[28] Edith Scholl, 'The Golden Cross: Aleydis of Schaerbeek', in *Hidden Springs*, I, pp. 377–93; Edmund Mikkers, 'Meditations on the *Life* of Alice of Schaerbeek', in *Hidden Springs*, I, pp. 395–413.

represents what Goswin and his public would have considered the archetype of a holy nun, Arnulf a holy lay brother, and Abundus a holy monk, in the way those vocations were understood at Villers and surrounding communities. The saints' individual personalities emerge more faintly: Martinus Cawley's introduction brings them out with extraordinary nuance. Yet readers must be aware that, when Goswin presents detailed accounts of the inner experience of Ida (whom he had never met) or Arnulf (whom he knew only slightly), the spirituality we are encountering is chiefly the writer's own, building on the reports of others and his own empathetic knowledge of his contemporaries.

Another salutary caution holds true for saints' Lives as a literary genre.[29] Given a choice between natural and supernatural explanations for an event, a hagiographer will almost always prefer the latter. Thus, if a saint's death is prophesied, yet she recovers and lives for thirteen more years, it is not because the prophecy was mistaken, but rather because God listened to the community's urgent prayers. Illness and healing, the unexpected visit of a friend or stranger, the sudden arrival of a priest at the precise moment a nun is pining for the Eucharist, even the silence that falls when pigs in a farm wagon stop their grunting[30], these are not chance events, but answers to prayer or revelations of God's providence. It should go without saying that one who criticizes a saint's behaviour, no matter how inconvenient or odd, is motivated by some vice. This convention, which we might call vertical as opposed to horizontal reference, is one distinguishing feature of hagiography. Others include hyperbolic praise, an extensive pattern of biblical and liturgical allusions, and direct exhortations to the reader. These generic traits, while hardly unique to Goswin or his milieu, remind us that the historical questions we pose most urgently to his Lives may be at best tangential to the writer's purpose, which was to glorify God and the saints and to reaffirm the Cistercian ideal.

With these preliminaries, let us turn to the individual Lives and the specific patterns of holiness they represent. Ida of Nivelles was a middle-class girl whose father died when she was nine. After this bereavement, Goswin says, she ran away from her family home to escape an arranged marriage (*Niv* 1e), in accord with a hagiographic convention that would have been familiar to readers from the virgin martyr legends of antiquity. But, since the girl's relatives allowed her to spend the rest of her childhood undisturbed among the beguines of Nivelles, Ida may well have obtained their consent to her plans. At sixteen she joined a community of Cistercian nuns at Kerkom, moving with them soon afterward to their new monastery at La Ramée. As a teenager there she formed a close friendship with another young nun, Beatrice, who displayed such intellectual promise that she was sent from her own monastery, Nazareth, to study calligraphy at La Ramée. Although the two girls were

---

[29] For more on the genre see René Aigrain, *L'Hagiographie: ses sources, ses méthodes, son histoire* (Brussels: Société des Bollandistes, 2000).

[30] *Arn* II.2.

about the same age, Beatrice's Life represents the 'venerable' Ida as the older and more experienced of the two, and it was Ida who initiated her friend into the visionary and ecstatic spirituality so prized by the women of this milieu. Beatrice outlived Ida by many decades and went on to become a spiritual writer and prioress of her community; Goswin indicates that she was still alive and fairly young at the time of his writing (*Niv* 25c). Ida, on the other hand, seems to have been only marginally literate. An anecdote early in her Life says that she loved Scripture, but showed this affection by hugging the books to her breast rather than reading them, since she could just barely pick out the words 'God' and 'Christ' (*Niv* 2e). Later on, however, Goswin recounts a dream vision in which Ida reads the names inscribed in the Book of Life, charmingly presented as a deluxe illuminated manuscript (*Niv* 18a). If Ida did report such a vision, she must have acquired greater literacy in the course of her religious life, at least in her dreams. Whatever the state of her Latin skills, we know she was bilingual in the vernacular. French was her native tongue, but early in her religious life she mastered the language Goswin calls 'Teutonic', the form of Dutch native to Beatrice (*Niv* 2e).

One of the most significant facts about Ida's life is its brevity: she died at the age of thirty-two, probably of tuberculosis, for Goswin frequently mentions her vomiting blood. In each case, however, he ascribes these attacks to her compassion for sinful or tempted souls, making her bouts of illness into excruciating bodily prayers. Instead of praying for her own health, Ida prays for further sickness, each time offering her pain for the salvation of someone else: a lustful priest, an incestuous father, a nun tempted to blasphemy. We cannot know if this interpretation was Goswin's or Ida's own, or perhaps most likely, an understanding shared within their milieu, for vicarious suffering was one of the most important ways that believers could imitate Christ and unite themselves with his sacrifice as co-redeemers.[31] In studied contrast to Ida's redemptive blood, Goswin presents sinners vomiting up their filth in confession, while demons vomit purgatorial fire.[32]

The motif of orality runs throughout Ida's Life: what goes into the mouth is just as important as what comes out of it. Ida's hunger for the Eucharist is so great that she habitually swoons after receiving it and trembles at the mere sight of a pyx where the sacrament is reserved (*Niv* 29b–4). On one occasion she even resorts to a pious subterfuge, proposing that her sisters visit a dying woman in the hope of receiving communion when the priest comes to administer the last rites (*Niv* 20c). These eucharistic ecstasies are inconvenient, provoking ill-tempered complaints

---

[31] Catholic readers may be reminded of St Thérèse of Lisieux, another adept in the art of vicarious suffering, who died of tuberculosis in 1897 at the age of twenty-four. On co-redemption in Ida's milieu see Barbara Newman, 'On the Threshold of the Dead: Purgatory, Hell, and Religious Women', in *From Virile Woman to WomanChrist* (Philadelphia: University of Pennsylvania Press, 1995), pp. 108–36.

[32] For Ida's vomiting blood see *Niv* 6a, 7a, 9a, 11a, and 13b. A confessing nun vomits up the filth of her sins in 13c; demons vomit fire in 14a.

when her sisters have to sidestep her prostrate body in order to return to their choir stalls; yet Ida protests that she has absolutely no control over her sudden swoons. In this respect her devotion exemplifies the characteristically female pattern so memorably outlined by Caroline Bynum in *Holy Feast and Holy Fast*.[33] Neither Arnulf nor Abundus display the same ardent eucharistic piety. Although Goswin does not stress Ida's fasting, her fainting spells and consumptive fits keep her physical presence constantly before the reader's eye, as her spiritual strength is revealed in bodily weakness.

A still more remarkable and distinctive theme is that of shared ecstasies, a leitmotif that sharply challenges our notion of 'mystical experience' as something deeply private, if not ineffable. Time and again Ida will fall into rapture, experience a vision of Christ or the Virgin, and send her divine visitor along to a close friend, or conversely receive such a vision sent her way by another friend. This is the practice referred to in the title of this volume as 'sending God'. Some of these incidents illustrate the extraordinary trust shared between women and men within this milieu. On one occasion, an abbess sends a sceptical priest to visit Ida, which he does three times without resolving his doubts about the genuineness of her sanctity. After the third visit, however, he sees a vision of Ida's face while celebrating mass and hears her praises sung by Christ himself. Returning to La Ramée, he sees Ida a fourth time, but at this meeting both priest and nun fall into ecstasy side by side, conversing not in audible words but 'in the honey-laden whisper used in heaven by the souls of the saints' (*Niv* 26e). The priest awakens first and departs while Ida is still entranced; she wakes soon afterward. Questioned separately by the nuns, both confirm their celestial conversation.

A similar anecdote features another devout priest and the abbess of Maagdendaal (Val-des-Vierges), a Cistercian convent across the language boundary on the Dutch side. As these two religious are conversing the priest suddenly swoons and, on recovering, tells the abbess in jest, 'Had I bow and arrow at hand, I'd shoot her back for shooting me!' (*Niv* 27b). He then explains that Ida, having fallen into a eucharistic ecstasy 'as usual', has prayed that he might share her grace. Returning to his rapture, the priest now experiences a vision of Christ in heaven along with 'his bride Ida'. As the priest falls on his knees to receive the Lord's blessing, Ida draws near and kisses him. On Goswin's account, which must be elaborating on either the priest's tale or the abbess's, or both, 'this kissing was a pressing of spirit to spirit, not of mouth to mouth, since the vision was spiritual, not corporeal. At that moment it seemed to the man of God that his own spirit became so inseparably joined to Ida's spirit as to become . . . one single spirit in the Lord' (*Niv* 27c). A later inquiry by the abbess confirms that Ida was indeed in rapture that day.

---

[33] Bynum, *Holy Feast and Holy Fast*, pp. 77, 115; Claire Boudreau, '"With Desire Have I Desired": Ida of Nivelles' Love for the Eucharist', in *Hidden Springs*, I, pp. 323–44. Two later nuns from this milieu, Ida of Gorsleeuw and Ida of Leuven, are even more extravagant in their eucharistic piety.

This extraordinary tale links eucharistic communion to the 'communion of saints' that transcends space and time, marking Ida's visionary experience as no less social than her mundane life. The abbess witnesses the priest's ecstasy; he in turn witnesses Ida's conversation with Christ in heaven; Christ witnesses the spiritual union of Ida and the priest; and Goswin finally bears witness to his audience of the whole event. In addition, the priest's allusion to 'bow and arrow' places this ecstatic kiss in the surprising context of courtly love, or *fin' amors*. Devotional writers of the early thirteenth century eagerly adapted the idioms of secular love literature, imagining Christ in the guise of Cupid with his quiver, or Lady Charity as a Christianized goddess of love.[34] Ida is here implicitly compared to a poetic lady whose entrancing eyes launch the arrows of love at her suitor's heart.

Brother Arnulf's Life seems at first to stem from an utterly different world. The novel Cistercian institution of lay brothers (also known as *conversi* or converts) had been introduced in the twelfth century, partly as an apostolate to the laity, but mainly as an efficient means of farming the monks' extensive property. Working under the supervision of masters, some *conversi* were stationed on the abbey's granges or farms, where they cultivated the land, while others worked in the abbey outbuildings at such trades as carpentry and blacksmithing. Arnulf, lacking any specialized skills, was assigned to make delivery runs between Villers and its granges, transporting grain to the monastery's mill to be ground into flour and returning with bread and other goods for the farm workers. Along his wagon route he also distributed alms to the monks' welfare clients, lay persons who depended on Villers for material as well as spiritual succour, requesting prayers and religious guidance as they accepted gifts of food. Goswin shows no special concern for the monastic economy, but he is deeply interested in intercessory prayer, so he fills this Life with intriguing stories about Arnulf's relationships with the laymen and women he came to know in the course of these duties.

But it is not this aspect of Arnulf's life that first attracts the reader's or the writer's attention. Lay brothers, like beguines, occupied an intermediate status between full monastic profession and ordinary secular life. Since they were not literate, they could not read Scripture or chant the Divine Office as monks did, but they attended services when their duties permitted, especially on feast-days. To compensate for their lack of learning they were encouraged to practise other devotions, such as frequent repetitions of the Lord's Prayer and Hail Mary, and some adopted severe forms of bodily penance. Arnulf and his contemporary, Simon of Aulne, were particularly known for their hair-raising ascetic feats. In fact, Book One of Arnulf's two-part Life is a virtual catalogue of self-torture. This brother was not

---

[34] Barbara Newman, 'Love's Arrows: Christ as Cupid in Late Medieval Art and Devotion', in *The Mind's Eye: Art and Theological Argument in the Medieval West*, ed. by Jeffrey Hamburger and Anne-Marie Bouché (Princeton: Princeton University Press, forthcoming), and *God and the Goddesses: Vision, Poetry, and Belief in the Middle Ages* (Philadelphia: University of Pennsylvania Press, 2002), Chapter 4.

content to wear an ordinary hair shirt, a penitential garment woven of rough animal hair and infested with lice and fleas. Instead he stitched his own special garment of hedgehog pelts, which he wore quill side in over a coat of chain mail, then covered the ensemble with a hair shirt and bound it with iron chains (*Arn* I.12a). No hedgehog was safe in Arnulf's vicinity, for he persuaded shepherds to skin the harmless animals wherever they found them so he could wear their pelts (*Arn* I.6b). One of his favourite penitential activities was self-flagellation, for which he preferred either a cane enhanced with quills or a scourge of thorny branches; sometimes he aggravated the wounds after a session by rolling naked in a patch of nettles (*Arn* I.4c). If we take his Life literally, which is probably unwise, Arnulf engaged in this discipline for hours on end. During Lent he is said to have spent every weekday scourging himself without a break from terce (around 9 a.m.) until vespers in the early evening (*Arn* I.11a).

But to what end? Goswin refers to Arnulf in Book One as an athlete, a soldier of God, and a latter-day martyr, all terms that recall the heroic era of the early Church. In the ancient martyr legends that were staples of monastic reading, the saints suffered any number of torments at the hands of their pagan persecutors, while the fourth- and fifth-century heroes of the Lives of the Desert Fathers castigated their flesh with ferocious self-denial. In more recent history self-flagellation was a specialty of male hermits. This discipline had been popularized in the eleventh century by St Peter Damian, who adopted it as one element of a severe penitential regimen. By flogging himself, Damian believed, the hermit not only imitated Christ in his passion, but anticipated Christ's judgment on his sins: only by offering himself to God as a living, bleeding sacrifice could he face the Last Day with confidence.[35] Some of Arnulf's practices sound so much like those described in Peter Damian's hagiographic writings that these might have supplied Goswin with a literary model.[36] One of Arnulf's motives was also penitential: when a monk asks why he is so determined to martyr himself, he replies that he is killing not himself but his sins (*Arn* I.3d). Yet more often Goswin represents Arnulf's flagellation, like Ida's sickness, as a form of vicarious suffering. While the lay brother beats himself he chants rhythmically in time with the scourging, 'Got to be braver, got to be manly, manly I've got to be! Friends need it badly: this stroke for this one; that stroke for that one; take *that* in the name of God!' (*Arn* I.11b).[37] In other words, every stroke of the lash represents a prayer: with each blow to his wounded flesh, Arnulf pounds the heart of God with his petitions.

---

[35] Rachel Fulton, *From Judgment to Passion: Devotion to Christ and the Virgin Mary, 800–1200* (New York: Columbia University Press, 2002), pp. 97–106.

[36] Peter Damian, *Vita S. Rodulphi et S. Dominici Loricati* (Letter 109 to Pope Alexander II), PL, 144: 1007–24.

[37] For the Latin see *Arn* I.11b n. 52. As Cawley points out, Goswin is presumably translating Arnulf's vernacular scourging song.

Goswin's attitude toward his hero's self-torture seems to have been ambivalent. Noting Arnulf's lack of discretion and the outright horror his practices inspired in others, he anticipates that some of his readers might criticize the abbots of Villers for permitting such excess (*Arn* I.6c). More often, though, Goswin praises Arnulf's behaviour in the most florid rhetorical style, assigning to it only impeccable motives. Soon after his conversion, for example, the brother manages to wind a knotted rope around his waist so tightly 'that the flesh began to rot and wriggle with worms. And what a stench all this belched forth!' (*Arn* I.2e). The writer purports to see in Arnulf's rotting flesh a sign of immense divine favour: 'Oh, the happiness of this newborn child, for whom Mother Grace is so solicitous that she not only nourishes him with the sweetness of her milk but . . . there in his infant cradle, she swaddles him in the bands of these piercing cords, and with so sharp a flint-knife, she circumcizes away any lewdness in his flesh' (*Arn* I.2f). Here Goswin tries to mitigate the horror by invoking a feminized, nurturing deity, whose role is paradoxically to validate the same self-martyrdom that Arnulf himself, in his flogging bouts, described as 'manly'.

The repression of 'lewdness', or sexual desire, was a motive central to the asceticism of the desert fathers and still more to that of Peter Damian, well known for his misogyny. But here is where Arnulf surprises us, for chastity is not a major concern of his Life. Despite one encounter with demons in the guise of women (*Arn* II.8c), he appears generally to have enjoyed close and trusting relationships with the opposite sex, just as Ida did. One of the most interesting cases involves a recluse who was on such intimate terms of friendship with Arnulf that she called him 'dearest father', although he was not a priest (*Arn* II.11a). This recluse was herself the spiritual mother and mentor of a young student. Eventually she noticed that the lad was spending so much time with her that he had fallen behind in his classes, so she exhorted him to stay away for a whole month. Reading between the lines, we might wonder if the recluse herself had concerns about chastity, since literature for recluses invariably warned them against conversations with men. Aelred of Rievaulx, in his twelfth-century 'Rule of Life for a Recluse', had advised his sister never to teach, allow children to approach her cell, or speak with any man at all save her confessor, except in the presence of a third party. Above all she was to 'avoid all conversation with young men'.[38] So, by conventional standards, the recluse was doing exactly as she should in attempting to cool her friendship with the boy. But Arnulf sees the matter quite differently: he goes to visit the woman, finds her sick with a fever, and tells her this is her just punishment for 'senselessly rebuffing . . . one whom you had mothered in Christ' (*Arn* II.11c). 'Informed of this from on high', Arnulf adds that God had been planning to punish the recluse even more harshly with a withdrawal of his grace, but through his own prayers, he enabled her to escape with a mere fever.

---

[38] Aelred of Rievaulx, 'Rule of Life for a Recluse' I.7, trans. by Mary Macpherson, *Treatises and The Pastoral Prayer* (Kalamazoo: CP, 1971), p. 52.

Another remarkable tale concerns the landlady of a student hostel in faraway Paris. This woman has the unusual Greek name of Theophania: was she the widow of a Byzantine diplomat, or perhaps born on the feast of the Epiphany (6 January)? Or could Theophania (revelation) have been a pet name given by the students to their mystically-minded hostess? The lady hears from her Brabantine lodgers about their local holy man and sends him a messenger, asking for prayers. Arnulf graciously promises to 'send her God' on a designated date, and when that day arrives she experiences such a sudden, powerful ecstasy that 'her soul [was] totally liquefied and poured out into the embraces of her Beloved' (*Arn* II.16c). This event marks the beginning of a long-distance spiritual friendship. Although Arnulf and Theophania never met face to face, students continued to carry their messages, and the devout woman thus forged a link between the Parisian schools and the unlearned but saintly virtuoso of Villers. The anecdote also gives us valuable information about Goswin and his audience, for he notes that Theophania 'is still alive and is in the city of Paris to this day', so readers there can seek her out for themselves (*Arn* II.16e). Since Goswin seems to have written his account from personal acquaintance, he might well have studied in Paris before entering Villers. It could even have been from Theophania that he first heard of Arnulf, perhaps by serving as one of her messengers.

Goswin's third Life, the unfinished life of his friend Abundus, brings us closest both to the author himself and to his subject, since the two monks had occasion to converse as often as they liked about the intimate details of their spiritual lives. Not surprisingly, this Life also evokes the arch-Cistercian rhetoric and spirituality of Bernard of Clairvaux. Its predominant theme is the monk's devotion to the Virgin Mary, whom Cistercians venerated as the patroness of their order. What eucharistic ecstasies were to Ida or flogging sessions to Arnulf, Marian visions are to Abundus. Although the Virgin appears briefly in the Lives of Arnulf (*Arn* II.15a) and Ida (*Niv* 23b, 25d), her presence to Abundus seems so constant that other monks use him as a go-between when they want to secure some favour from her (*Ab* 9b). One conspicuous and touching feature of these visions is that Abundus does not see Mary in heaven on her throne of glory. Rather, she appears to him in the midst of the community, chanting along with the choir, bowing at the proper moments (*Ab* 8b), censing the monks (*Ab* 20a), cooling their sweat-drenched faces at harvest time (*Ab* 14b), and offering her child, the light of the world, as her 'candle' during a liturgical procession (*Ab* 11e). Once, as a special grace, Abundus prays for permission to kiss Mary's hand, and she exceeds his request by kissing his mouth, a favour that reminds Goswin of miracle stories about pious men who are supposed to have sucked her breast (*Ab* 10ab).[39] Although Abundus sees other visions as well, among them the prophet Elijah (*Ab* 13c), it is the Virgin who clearly dominates his inner

---

[39] The legend of St Bernard's own lactation, a popular subject in Baroque art, post-dates the literary career of Goswin.

life, her benign and familiar presence casting a soft glow around the rituals of everyday life. In marked contrast with the sickly Ida and the self-punishing Arnulf, Abundus seems to have lived out his days in singular happiness and calm, especially under the reign of Abbot Walter. Most unusually for a saint's life, suffering plays little part in this narrative.

Like Goswin's other Lives, however, this one is filled with vignettes that reveal the intimate exchanges between men and women in a milieu where the spiritual and the social were indissolubly linked. Before entering Villers, the teenaged Abundus asked his friend and fellow townswoman, the recluse Yvette of Huy, for advice about which monastery to join (*Ab* 4b), although in this case he chose not to take it. Another of his friends was Master John of Nivelle, famed as a confessor and adviser to religious women. John's soul appears to Abundus in a posthumous vision, revealing that he is especially glorified among the saints for his ability to preserve perfect chastity while listening to women's confessions. No matter how salacious their sins, he 'stood amid this conflagration of the flesh [and] was never scorched by its flames' (*Ab* 15c). This revelation reminds Goswin of another anecdote about John, how once upon seeing a prostitute he paid her price simply to give her a night off from sinning (*Ab* 15d). His act of charity scandalizes bystanders, but deeply impresses the writer.

If there is anything to scandalize a modern reader in this Life, it is the tale of how Abundus won his sister to religious life. The monk stemmed from a bourgeois family of a type not uncommon in southern Netherlandish Lives. His pious mother, aptly named Mary, strove with all her zeal to compensate for her lost virginity by giving as many sons and daughters as possible to God, over the helpless protests of her merchant husband (*Ab* 12e). Three brothers and two sisters of the household eventually became Cistercians, while a third daughter remained in her parents' house as a virgin recluse until her early death (*Ab* 1b). Only one sister is known to have married (*Ab* 16b). Some time after Abundus entered Villers he learned, ostensibly by divine revelation, that his parents were arranging the marriage of his sister Mary. As Goswin tells the story, the monk's response was to hasten at once to La Ramée, telling the abbess urgently 'of his sister's peril' in order to secure a place for her among the nuns (*Ab* 12b). Successful in this goal, Abundus next hastens to his family home to dissuade his sister from marriage. Goswin places a formulaic sermon in his mouth, echoing countless treatises on virginity. Abundus tells Mary that her father's love for her is carnal, but his own is spiritual, for he has already arranged her marriage to a celestial bridegroom far superior to the 'fleshly husband' she was about to wed (*Ab* 12c). Mary's response is no less formulaic. Just as she had earlier consented to marriage (for Abundus knows 'that the will of your heart and the will of your father are agreed') she now blandly consents to virginity. 'Dear brother', we are to imagine her saying, 'if the thing for me to do is to reject secular life and wed myself to Christ, to leave the world and enter the cloister, . . . then be it done to me according to your word.' Their mother rejoices, while their father is furious but ultimately forced to yield, thanks to the Virgin's timely suasion.

How are we to interpret this narrative? Was Mary a helpless pawn bandied about between competing male wills, or did her brother's intervention give her a choice she might not otherwise have had? What did she *really* think? Was the abbess a willing accomplice in a plot arranged beforehand, perhaps with Mary's secret consent? Did her jilted bridegroom revolt like Burthred, the husband of the English visionary Christina of Markyate, who tried to preach virginity to him on their wedding night?[40] Or did he take it in stride and resolve to find a richer, prettier wife somewhere else? (We can be fairly sure he did not become a Cistercian, for Goswin would not have neglected to mention such a triumphant outcome.) This is one case where we would dearly love to hear the real conversations buried beneath the pious clichés, and some such conversations must actually have occurred, for Mary did enter La Ramée. As it stands, the story can bear as many interpretations as a tale by Chaucer. It bears witness to the intractable difficulty of extracting history from hagiography, reminding us that, no matter how compelling the female voices we hear in this canon, all have come to us refracted through the words of men.[41] Conversely, however, the title of this series (*Medieval Women: Texts and Contexts*) reminds us that, even in a monastic milieu, women's Lives cannot be fruitfully studied apart from men's Lives. We learn at least as much about the devout women of the southern Low Countries from the richly textured Lives of Arnulf and Abundus as we do from Ida's.

What finally, are the distinguishing marks of Goswin's Lives? In the first place his three protagonists, different though they are, all share an intensely *focused* sense of divine presence. For these saints, or at any rate for their publicist, God is not in the least remote or difficult to encounter, nor is he merely 'within' the faithful in some theoretical sense. Rather, he is visibly, audibly, tangibly present in specific events and places. For Ida this divine presence is most deeply concentrated in the Eucharist, for Abundus in the Virgin, and for Arnulf in the physical pain he so avidly seeks. But the presence of God is also concentrated and embodied in other people, especially in the network of devout monks, nuns, *conversi*, and recluses who constitute the wider Cistercian world. This experience of an immanent God goes a long way to explain why hagiography was such a privileged genre in the thirteenth-century religious movement. A second distinctive feature of Goswin's Lives, which they share with all the Lives in this canon, is his conviction that suffering has a point, not just vaguely in general, but in each concrete instance. Just as devotional writers found inexhaustible saving power in every one of Christ's wounds, so Goswin finds mercy and deliverance for some particular sinner in each spurt of blood that issues from Ida's tubercular lungs or Arnulf's tortured limbs.

---

[40] *The Life of Christina of Markyate: A Twelfth-Century Recluse*, Chapters 10–12, ed. and trans. by C. H. Talbot (Toronto: Medieval Academy of America, 1998), pp. 50–53.

[41] On this problem see *Gendered Voices: Medieval Saints and Their Interpreters*, ed. by Catherine M. Mooney (Philadelphia: University of Pennsylvania Press, 1999).

Beyond this insistent localizing of grace, Goswin's Lives reveal three rather astonishing convictions about the spiritual life, which are not unique to his writings but may perhaps be more pronounced in them than anywhere else in the canon. To sum up, we may say that the inner life, in Goswin's view, is characterized by its *sublimity*, *transparency*, and *community*.

(1) *Sublimity*, because our author displays an exceptional optimism about the soul's capacity for God on the one hand, and God's yearning to be known on the other. In Goswin's world there is no need for apophatic theology, no divine darkness, no desperate trembling before the Unknown. When Arnulf 'ardently yearn[s] for the blissful vision of the Holy Trinity', God simply grants it to him (*Arn* II.6b, 6e), and when the young Abundus begs 'with every fibre of his heart' for a vision of God 'in the fullest measure ever granted to mortals' (*Arn* 6a), that too is given. Nor does anyone seem to worry that such visions might be false. Although demons may intervene to confuse matters, their wiles are quite easily discerned and defeated.[42]

(2) *Transparency*, because just as God withholds no revelation from his lovers, the devout withhold no secrets from their friends. They do not even require words to communicate, for the minds of the blessed stand wholly open to one another, barriers of time and space notwithstanding. The story of Ida and the sceptical priest is a case in point: conversation between them would be superfluous, for one saint in ecstasy can know exactly what another saint in ecstasy is seeing. Gifted with a kind of spiritual telepathy, Ida can also read the consciences of others in order to counsel them, before or apart from sacramental confession. Even death is no obstacle to clear vision: the living routinely make pacts with the dying, who return to them in apparitions to reveal their blessed or purgatorial state.[43] This transparency is a special boon to the hagiographer, for Goswin himself shows no misgivings about his ability to supply precise accounts of his subjects' visions, as if he too were graced with clairvoyance.

(3) *Community*, for the God of these Lives is not only willing, but downright eager to be 'sent' hither and yon at the desire of his chosen ones. It is not enough that one devout person can *witness* the mystical experience of another, as if seeing from within the other's mind. What is more, the devout can actually *cause* such an experience to befall another through prayer, as Ida of Nivelles does for Beatrice of Nazareth,[44] Arnulf for Theophania (*Arn* II.16), and Abundus for the lay brother

---

[42] On the unproblematic distinction between true and false visions, see *Niv* 17d and *Ab* 9a. Demons appear in *Niv* 13a–d and *Arn* II.8a–d and II.19a. They take various forms (a small bird, an old hag, a monkey, a dwarf, seductive women, a black child, a tomcat), but never do Goswin's saints encounter a demon disguised as a holy person.

[43] For pacts of this kind see *Niv* 8ab and 10ab; for other posthumous apparitions see *Ab* 15bc and 16g. On women's purgatorial piety see Newman, 'On the Threshold of the Dead'.

[44] *Niv* Appendix III, I.10–11, pp. 107–16 below.

Baldwin (*Ab* 19cd). This kind of exchange involves not only visions and graces, but also temptations. Ida once frees a sister from her impulse to blaspheme by volunteering to suffer the temptation in her place, and thus for three days endures the 'smuttiest of thoughts' that a demon can inflict (*Niv* 7a). It would be true but vapid to characterize all three of Goswin's saints as virtuosos in intercessory prayer. This statement gains its full force only when we realize that, within this religious milieu, 'intercession' meant not the rapid-fire recitation of a list of names, but direct intervention in the most private recesses of another's heart.

Such is Goswin's mystical theology, revealed through his trilogy of Lives. By no means all hagiographers, let alone all contemporary theologians, would have shared these convictions, any more than they shared Goswin's confidence in the value of spiritual friendships across gender lines. This soaring intensity, overcoming the more cautious, not to say fearful proprieties observed by other monastic writers, is an attitude historically specific to Villers and the fervent communities within its ambit in the early decades of the thirteenth century. Whether we find this canon of saints' Lives attractive or alien, annoying or enticing, will depend very much on our own sensibilities. But the cantor of Villers confronts us with a distinctive, hitherto little known voice that deserves at last to be heard.

Canon of Thirteenth-Century Southern Netherlandish Saints' Lives[45]

by James of Vitry, bishop and cardinal (ca 1170–1240)
      Mary of Oignies, beguine (ca 1167–1213)

by Thomas of Cantimpré, Augustinian canon, later Dominican (ca 1201–ca 1272)
      Supplement to the Life of Mary of Oignies
      John of Cantimpré, Augustinian abbot (d. ca 1210)
      Christina of Sint-Truiden (Christina Mirabilis), freelance holy woman (ca 1150–1224)
      Margaret of Ieper (Ypres), Dominican tertiary (1216–1237)
      Lutgard of Tongeren, Cistercian nun of Aywières (1182–1246)

by Hugh of Floreffe, Premonstratensian canon
      Yvette (Juetta, Jutta) of Huy, widow and recluse (1158–1228)

by Goswin of Bossut, Cistercian monk and cantor of Villers
      Ida of Nivelles, Cistercian nun of La Ramée (1199–1231)
      Arnulf, lay brother of Villers (d. 1228)
      Abundus of Huy, Cistercian monk of Villers (1189–1239)

by Thomas, Cistercian monk and cantor of Villers
      Godfrey Pachomius, monk of Villers (ca 1200–1262)

by Henry, Cistercian monk of Saint-Bernard-on-the-Scheldt
      Peter, lay brother of Villers

by Philip, Cistercian monk of Clairvaux
      Elizabeth of Spalbeek, recluse, later Cistercian nun of Herkenrode (d. ca 1304?)

---

[45] Data in this list are compiled from a variety of sources; I have relied most on Simons, *Cities of Ladies*, pp. 37–48, and Roisin, *L'Hagiographie cistercienne*, pp. 28–73. I have anglicized personal names and left place names in their French or Dutch forms according to current local usage. Dates marked 'circa' should be taken with a grain of salt. The historiography reveals considerable variance in the dating of several saints, but the documentary basis for these dates is seldom discussed.

Anonymous Lives

> Godfrey the Sacristan (d. ca 1200), monk of Villers
> Werric (d. 1217), prior of Aulne (in verse)
> Odilia of Liège (d. 1220), widow and beguine
> Simon of Aulne, lay brother (d. 1229)
> Alice of Schaarbeek (Schaerbeek), Cistercian nun of La Cambre (d. 1250)
> Juliana of Mont-Cornillon, canoness, later beguine, Cistercian nun, and recluse (1193–1258)
> Gobert of Aspremont, knight and crusader, then lay monk of Villers (1189–1263)
> Franco of Archennes, knight and crusader, then monk of Villers (in verse)
> Beatrice of Tienen, Cistercian nun, prioress of Nazareth (1200–1268)
> Ida of Gorsleeuw (Lewis, Léau), Cistercian nun of La Ramée (d. ca 1270?)
> Ida of Leuven, Cistercian nun of Roosendaal (d. ca 1290?)
> Catherine of Leuven, Cistercian nun of Vrouwenpark (d. ca 1300?)

Other sources including brief Lives

> Caesarius of Heisterbach
> *Dialogus miraculorum* (Dialogue on Miracles), ca 1220–37

> Thomas of Cantimpré
> *Bonum universale de apibus* (Book of Bees), ca 1256–63

Anonymous

> *Chronica Villariensis monasterii* (History of the Monastery of Villers): Lives of the thirteenth-century abbots

> *Gesta sanctorum Villariensium* (Deeds of the Saints of Villers): a compendium of abridged Lives of monks and lay brothers

Introduction to the Lives

In January 1983 I was asked to translate the Lives of the early Cistercian nuns. Over the next four or five years, while groping for an approach, I circulated drafts, gave talks, wrote articles and developed a desktop publishing service, known as 'Guadalupe Translations'. By 1990 my focus had widened to all the biographical literature of Villers, with the present trilogy as its centrepiece. This trilogy brings together one outstanding female Life and two male Lives, all of the same ambience and by the same author, Goswin of Bossut, cantor of Villers. More or less definitive translations of all three Lives were ready for publication by 1993, but various setbacks caused delay until Guadalupe Translations brought them out as three pamphlets, between July 1998 and May 2000. This edition reproduces these earlier publications, with minor revisions.

Villers: The Geography and History of Goswin's World[1]

Much has been written in recent decades to identify the place names in these Lives, and readers well acquainted with the Low Countries may wish for great detail.[2] The following paragraphs offer them a short cut to the lay of the land. My description will be easier to follow if read in conjunction with the map on p. xxvi.

Modern Belgium is traversed by two great rivers, the Maas (Meuse) in the east and the Scheldt (Escaut) in the west. The Maas enters Belgium from France due south of Namur. At that city it is joined from the west by the Sambre. There also it takes a sharp turn east, along the foothills of the Ardennes, as far as Liège, where it swings sharply north into the panhandle of Dutch Limburg, eventually entering the sea just south of the Rhine delta. The deep valley of the Maas, from Namur to the Dutch border, roughly defines the south and east boundaries of the little world of Goswin and of Villers.

---

[1] I use spellings suggested by Walter Simons, *Cities of Ladies* (see Select Bibliography).

[2] The most comprehensive and easily accessible works of recent date on this are included in *Monasticon Belge*, ed. by Berlière (see Select Bibliography).

Over the ridge from that deep valley, to the west and to the north, lies a shallower, fanlike basin, all of whose gentle streams unite in the northwest to form one short river, called the Rupel, which joins the Schelde a little south of Antwerp. The basin of the Rupel forms the rest of Goswin's little world, and Villers itself nestles close to the watershed between it and the Maas.

Politically, Goswin's world corresponded largely to the duchy of Brabant, centred at Leuven (Louvain). Ecclesiastically, Villers itself belonged to the diocese of Liège, though a few kilometres west and north of the abbey ran the boundary of another diocese, that of Cambrai. Ida's home town of Nivelles likewise lies near the watershed, some twenty kilometres west of Villers. Her convent of La Ramée lies similarly some thirty-eight kilometres to Villers's east. Arnulf's home town of Brussels was already rivalling Leuven as the principal town of Brabant. It lies low down in the Rupel Basin, some fifty kilometres north of Villers. Abundus's home town of Huy lies on the Maas itself, where it long served as a military stronghold for an important stretch of that river. It lies some eighty kilometres east-south-east of Villers, midway between Namur and Liège.

The countryside around Villers is surprisingly hilly, and is today well wooded on the steeper slopes. Already in Goswin's day its rich agricultural lands were thickly populated, and transportation by road and river was well established. So great a surplus of young folk was then flocking to the monasteries that admission as a candidate was an enviable privilege (*Arn* II.20de; *Ab* 4bc, 12b, 18a).

Goswin's Brabant was split by a language frontier, which has scarcely fluctuated to this day. A Germanic language, an early form of Dutch, was spoken to the north, and a Romance language, an early form of French, to the south. These language groups also had important cultural differences, but the ecclesiastical and civil jurisdictions straddled the language divide, and did so with an ease that is a credit to the leadership. Villers happened to be on the French-speaking side, but bilingualism shows up often in its literary corpus.

Villers was founded from St Bernard's abbey of Clairvaux in 1146–47.[3] For some twelve years prior to that, Clairvaux foundations had remained behind something of a northern frontier that ran from Eberbach in the east (near Mainz) through Himmerod, Orval, Signy, Foigny and Vaucelles, to Ter Duinen (near Dunkerque).[4] St Bernard's preaching of the Crusade to the north of this line prompted him to break through it and found in rapid succession Villers, Aulne, and Cambron. A few other abbeys were added in later decades.

The first five decades of Villers were marked by agricultural consolidation and

---

[3] The early history of Villers was assembled in 1909 by the learned Jesuit, Édouard de Moreau, with an architectural appendix by R. Maere. More recent work is summarized by Émile Brouette in the *Monasticon Belge* (1968). A monumental study of the architecture was put out in 2000 by Thomas Coomans (*L'Abbaye de Villers*).

[4] Data gathered from maps, tables and index of Fredrik Van der Meer's *Atlas de l'Ordre Cistercien* (Paris: Sequoia, 1965).

spiritual fervour, but without much building activity at the abbey itself. Then, in 1197, came the bold step of electing as abbot a saintly man from Cologne named Charles,[5] then prior of Heisterbach, a house known to us from the famous *Dialogus miraculorum* of its Caesarius (1222). Charles would be at the helm of Villers until 1209, a total of twelve years, during which he would give it a tone like Heisterbach's, of warm friendship and sensible austerity. This would be the ambience into which Arnulf would enter in 1202 and Abundus in 1206.[6]

Charles, for all his popularity inside and outside the cloister, felt keenly that he lacked the sacred learning needed for his job, and he eventually managed to resign in favour of his prior, the learned and rather imperious nobleman, Conrad of Urach (1209–14). This is the same Conrad who is known to have long admired a saintly lay brother, Simon, over at nearby Aulne (*Sim,* pp. 29, 41–44),[7] and he now conceived a similar admiration for a fervent lay brother of his own, Arnulf. Not only did Conrad allow Arnulf space to cultivate friendships inside and outside the cloister; but he also allowed him to undertake extraordinary intercessory penances on their behalf. It was not long before tales about Arnulf were rivalling those about Simon himself, although some more practical souls at Villers would soon come to regard him as a crazy spendthrift.

Conrad, after barely five years as Abbot of Villers, was promoted to the mother house, Clairvaux, and later to Cîteaux itself, and finally to the cardinalate. His place at Villers was taken by an older man of considerable learning, quite open to mysticism, whose name was Walter of Utrecht (1214–21). What the ascetic Arnulf owed to Conrad, the mystic Abundus would now owe to Walter, as would the compassionate Ida. Walter not only promoted the kind of prayer life on which these latter two souls thrived; he was also a great one for incorporating women's communities into the Order.

Walter died while still in full vigour, and was succeeded in office by a man of like mind, William of Dongelbert[8] (alias, of Brussels), whose tenure (1221–37) was to mark the apogee of the golden age of Villers. What Arnulf, Abundus, and Ida owed to the earlier abbots, Goswin himself would owe to this William, who made him his cantor and seemingly something of a private confidant. In William's later years, however, as illustrated in certain episodes in Arnulf's Life, those in charge of

---

[5] Caesarius tells a story of Charles's devout father as living in Cologne, in Caesarius, *DM* 8.48.

[6] On Charles and the other abbots, see Cawley, 'Four Abbots of the Golden Age of Villers', in *CSQ*, 27 (1992), 299–327.

[7] My references to the Life of Simon are to the edition of the Baron de Dorlodot, *La Vie du Bienheureux Simon* (Tournai: Desclée, 1968).

[8] So spelt in Brouette's text, though his footnote is all about the Dongelberg family and its dealings with Villers. I presume William's birthplace corresponds to the modern village of Dongelberg, just twenty-five kilometres north-east of Villers.

finances at Villers were at odds with his abbatial policies. After sixteen years in office, William too was promoted to Clairvaux. In leaving Villers he was deeply concerned for the nuns he had befriended, and so he took the radical step of bequeathing paternity over several of their houses, not to his successor at Villers, but to himself as Villers's new higher superior at Clairvaux.[9] From that wealthy and populous house, he doubtless intended to serve the nuns better than ever, but things worked out differently, for very soon he was imprisoned by the emperor and, though he was later released, he died shortly afterwards, and his successors at Clairvaux seem never to have achieved the influence with the Brabantine nuns that Villers had once enjoyed. Instead, we soon find a new generation of nuns looking mainly to non-Cistercian clergy for friendship and support.

We can hardly exaggerate the importance of these four abbots for Goswin and for the heroes of his Lives, but literary convention usually obliged him to conceal their names, as well as the names of many other persons mentioned, especially if still alive (*Niv* 16e). This leaves our knowledge of the epoch much the poorer.

Villers: The Literary Corpus

The literature of the golden age of Villers contains nothing like the hortatory sermons and treatises of earlier Cistercian generations. Apart from legal documents, it is entirely narrative, consisting on the one hand of two systematic collections, known as the *Chronica* and the *Gesta* of Villers, and on the other, of Lives such as the present three. Even within the narrative genre, Villers shows an equally sharp contrast with earlier times, when storytelling was used only for idyllic accounts of the rugged early days of a monastery, or for miracle-laden biographies of abbots in line for canonization. In a broader sense, a number of other Lives of the same time and region share the genre used at Villers, and could be thought of as part of a greater Villers corpus.

Both the *Chronica* and the *Gesta* went through more than one early edition. The former work briefly presents the abbots of Villers in chronological order, up to the time of the current compiler, while the latter gives fuller accounts of brethren remembered for their holiness, whether or not they were abbots. The two editions of the *Gesta* group the heroes differently: one intersperses monks and lay brothers, while the other assembles the two categories in separate books. The *Chronica* and *Gesta* were first printed in Paris in 1717 by the Maurist scholars Édouard Martène and Ursin Durand. In 1925, Georg. Waitz published a more critical edition in Leipzig, which explains well the genesis of the texts, but scarcely differs in wording from the earlier edition, except in omitting large parts of the collection.

---

[9] In the *Chronica* the transfer is ascribed to Walter, but in my 'Four Abbots of the Golden Age of Villers', pp. 316–17 and 323, I argue that it was William's doing.

Though the *Chronica* and *Gesta* are the primary literary context for our trilogy, they are not yet available in translation, and even the critical Latin text must be used with caution. For instance, the *Gesta* includes summaries of Arnulf and Abundus, which show poor perception of their specific charisms and make major blunders in transcription.

In contrast with these schematic and often disappointing collections, Goswin's Lives are lively, homely and uniformly enjoyable. They spring from the edifying conferences which marked the hospitality the assembled community showed to visiting abbots.[10] The same anecdotes would be told and retold, not only in such public conferences but also in intimate exchanges of confessor and penitent, master and novice. Typically such anecdotes concern colourful characters, with reputations for mystical revelations and intercessory influence with heaven. At the death of Goswin's heroes, there might he pressure to put their anecdotes into writing, for reading in private and also at meals and before compline, both at home and in other nearby monasteries.

These anecdotes of Goswin are close in genre to those of his contemporary, Caesarius of Heisterbach, and to *exempla* literature in general. Perceptive storytellers with a sharp eye for a moral in a story, and a keen memory for detail, would assemble whole chains of anecdotes into anthologies, which they would offer to preachers and confessors as stimulating 'examples' to include in their exhortations. Caesarius's best known work, the *Dialogus miraculorum,* was published just a decade before Goswin started his trilogy. It contains many references to Villers. Caesarius is quite playful in his skilful marshalling of his materials into twelve themes or distinctions, of interest to confessor and penitent; and Goswin finds similar delight in mapping his own anecdotes within a catechetical framework (see the notes on *Niv* 29–32).

More surprising is the openness of Villers to poetry. For instance, almost the only thing known about Abbot William's immediate successor is a Latin rhyme he composed in his last illness (*Chronica* 7, ed. by Martène and Durand, III, 1285–88). And the next abbot, upon retiring, is granted a little private cell (*scriptorium*), where he hears confessions, and while waiting, recasts the text of a popular moral manual into Latin verse (*Chronica* 8, III, 1292). Quite a number of entries in the *Chronica* and *Gesta* carry poetic epitaphs (for example Abbot Conrad, *Chronica*, III, 1276); Abbot William (*Chronica* 6, III, 1285) and Gobert of Aspremont (*Gesta* 2, III, 1332–33), to say nothing at this point of the epitaphs attached to Goswin's own Lives and arguably composed by himself. Perhaps many more epitaphs were composed than have survived, though rarely, if ever, would they have been inscribed on stone. See especially the second appendix on Abundus, below.

---

[10] Such conferences are often alluded to by Caesarius. A particularly striking example is Caesarius, *DM* 7.38. He also repeatedly alluded to the swapping of conference stories among abbots at the General Chapter at Cîteaux (for example Caesarius, *DM* 7.59; 9.38)

Another poetic form is found in a number of Lives more or less connected with Villers, namely, the devout jingle, Latin or vernacular in language and often Marian in theme, which less erudite souls use as part of their prayer life (for example, *Oig* 98; *Lov* I.10d, II.6b; II.13a–14a, and above all Caesarius, *DM* 7.38). The death of one particularly colourful monk is recorded not merely with an epitaph, but with an outright ballad, namely that of the ex-knight Francon, preserved in full in *Gesta* 3, III, 1333–1339. It is a sheer delight to the ear and we can imagine it being sung to the assembled community on a feast-day afternoon. Other ballads survive only to the extent that the compiler of the *Gesta* became careless in his summarizing, with the result that line after line of his unformatted prose remains in rhythm and rhyme (for example *Gesta* 2, III, 1322A).

So much for the various authors, but did the heroes of Goswin's Lives enjoy poetry? Of these Abundus seems to take as much pleasure in the liturgy's melody and lyricism as does his cantor friend, Goswin (*Ab* 7ab). Even the rugged Arnulf, engaged in his rhythmic self-flagellation, accompanies it with what sounds like a poetic chant. Ida has to feel her way in a bilingual community, whose liturgy was in Latin, and so there is little trace of poetry in any utterance attributed to her, except that the saving word she offers to console a grieving client, often involves a vivid image that could be called a mini-poem, concrete, and capturing at once the inner distortion of the client as well as Ida's divine compassion in that regard (*Niv* 7b, 12c).

Goswin of Bossut, Cantor of Villers

Modern readers, plunged without introduction into female saints' Lives from the thirteenth-century Low Countries, will surely be bewildered by their strangeness. There is, however, one exception. No open mind can fail to be charmed by Ida the Compassionate of Nivelles. Her biographer, who also wrote the two male Lives, is fairly forthright about his witnesses and his commission to write. He is silent over his own name, as was more or less mandatory in his day, but after his death a friendly hand jotted it on a manuscript that has come down to us, Goswin of Bossut, cantor of Villers. Indeed, between the lines we can also often learn more about the witnesses and protagonists, discerning, if not their names, at least their gender and function in the monastery. It is in this way that we learn that Goswin's literary patron was none other than Abbot William, and that it was he who insisted on a simplicity of style (*Niv* Prol. b). This simplicity, which minimizes the strangeness of Ida's life, also reveals Goswin's own personality and almost allows us to hear the nuns from whom he first received the anecdotes.

The manuscript bearing Goswin's name is a copy of the Life of Arnulf. His authorship of the other two Lives is learned only from the evidence of a sameness of style and expression. Goswin was first proposed as author of the Life of Abundus on these grounds by Moreau in 1909 (pp. xxx–xxxi). The same was done for the Life of

Ida of Nivelles by Roisin in 1947 (pp. 55–58). What these scholars presented hypothetically, can now be taken as proven, as a result of my working on a critical text of the Life of Abundus, on both manuscripts of the Life of Ida, and on the excellent Bollandist text of the Life of Arnulf. My computer work on all three texts over several years has revealed far more similarities of phrasing and style than those two pioneers were equipped to notice, and I have found nothing at all to contradict their hypothesis. Many of the comparisons in question are indicated in my notes.

While the personal name of Goswin is certain, the surname 'of Bossut' has only the support of a vaguely known oral tradition at Villers (AASS, 607E). There is, however, no reason to doubt it, and a small French-speaking village still thrives under the name of Bossut-Gottechain, just twenty kilometres north-north-east of Villers. Beyond this, within the Lives themselves there are a number of topographical references, in which a reader may or may not catch an echo of the author's personal familiarity with the lay of the land, as if he had visited the place, or even been born or educated there (*Niv* 1a; *Ab* 2a).

As for Goswin's date of birth, Moreau hazards a guess that he was still young and enthusiastic when he first wrote about Arnulf (p. xxx), and my own spontaneous image of Goswin has always made him young, as if recruited as late as the time of Abbot William himself (1221–37). If this is valid, Goswin would be a decade or so younger than Abundus, whose birth was in 1189. Goswin's ease in dealing with scholarly matters certainly suggests some higher education, and his references to Paris (*Arn* II.16ae; *Ab* 13e) could well reflect his having received part of it in that city. We can be sure that his boldness in chiding deviant priests reflects his own sharing in their sacramental dignity. He obviously loved the priestly role in the silent canon of the mass (*Niv* 6c, 20e; *Arn* II.13d).

What we know best about Goswin is that he held at Villers the office of cantor, an office described in detail in the *Ancient Usages* (*EO* 115, etc). The cantor was expected to be at home with pen and ink, and skilled at writing up ordinary death notices; hence he would be an obvious choice for any more extended biographical work. Goswin's cantorial delight in the liturgy shows up in the many liturgical passages found in the Life of Abundus, and in the few found in the Lives of Ida and Arnulf. I also sense a cantor's embarrassment when anyone is absent from the common prayers or exercises (*Niv* 19def; *Arn* 11c; also *Ab* 7c).

Goswin undertook to write the Life of Ida only at William's behest (*Niv* Prol. b). The same may be true for that of Arnulf. But in the case of the monk Abundus, the initiative was his own, and William intervened only by way of permission (*Ab* Prol. c). Goswin claims no personal acquaintance of Ida at all. With Arnulf, he claims nothing more than the acquaintance of one living under the same roof for the saint's final years.[11] But with Abundus he claims intimate friendship, a friendship nourished by the liturgy and expressed most intensely in those afternoon sessions on major

---

[11] See *Arn* I.5f, n. 31; also such passages as *Arn* II.21ef.

feast-days when friends were often allowed to pair off and share the news of each other's inner life (*GC* 1233.6, as alluded to in *Niv* 17c, 23a; 27a; *Arn* I.7b; 12a). Goswin knew well what it was to look forward to a feast-day and to the spiritual lift afforded by its solemn chant (*Niv* 35[ii]; *Arn* II.15a; *Ab* 20b). He must have found it very rewarding to reminisce of an afternoon on the morning's choral experience with someone as like-minded as Abundus. While Goswin in his role as priest readily engages in harangues against his negligent colleagues (*Niv* 6c, 20e; *Arn* II.13d), as a cantor he never takes advantage of his captive readership to complain about the choir's performance. He simply lets the joy overflow.

We know nothing of Goswin's later life, except that another monk, named Thomas, was cantor around the year 1260. One might speculate, on the basis of the opposition towards the mystics, which Goswin often reflects in the Lives (*Niv* 17e; *Arn* I.10e; *Ab* 9d), that after William was promoted to Clairvaux, there was a gradual purge of his close associates, including the replacement of Goswin as cantor. If that is the case, his words at the end of the Prologue to Abundus take on added poignancy, replete with Benedictine humility: 'Let those willing to accept what I write of [Abundus] accept it in the Lord's name and in good faith. As for those unwilling, let them rest assured that no one will be forced to accept my contribution' (*Ab* Prol. d).

Ida the Compassionate of Nivelles

As is usual in any pre-modern Life, chronological sequence is followed in Goswin's *Ida* only in the opening and closing chapters, and only to that extent does the Life represent her career. The four opening chapters cover her childhood and early years in the convent; and the final three cover her last months and her posthumous miracles. One other chapter has a chronological reference, an episode in which her age at the time is implicitly mentioned (*Niv* 10f). The remaining twenty-seven chapters ignore chronology and follow a purely thematic arrangement.

The last three of these non-chronological chapters systematically study key virtues attributed to Ida (*Niv* 30–32). Just before them comes a long didactic chapter, offering to survey the key themes of her inner life (*Niv* 29). While this survey is somewhat *a priori,* the sequence of its items is in fact remarkably parallel to the sequence of themes in the anecdotes of the main body of the book (*Niv* 5–28). Interestingly, Goswin provides a little preface for that survey, and in it he expresses his delight in arranging the harmonious layout (*Niv* 29a).

In all those central anecdotes (*Niv* 5–28), we often glimpse between the lines Ida's role within the community of La Ramée, and so we have a clue to what we might call her career. Most of the anecdotes imply an authoritative role behind the respect shown to her by the protagonists, and the anecdotes themselves can be grouped by the kind of authority each one implies. Three anecdotes have purely catechetical themes, as when Ida appears as tutor of a catechism class among the young girls or the novices, speaking about cardinal virtues (*Niv* 8), The Book of Life (*Niv* 18), or The Seven Gifts (*Niv* 28). Ida appears in a similar role in the Life of Beatrice (*Beat* I.10–11, 50–58). In other stories Ida exercises a right to summon her clients and to bid them give an account of their actions, even if they are secular adults, as in a story about the incestuous man (*Niv* 11). See also the blasphemous sister (*Niv* 7).

In still other cases Ida has no official jurisdiction, but her clients admire her and are eager to have her pronounce on their spiritual state: as in stories of a priest in temptation, whom she has no way to summon, but for whom she effectively prays (*Niv* 6); a girl who is not allowed access to her at the parlour and promptly falls, but is safe again as soon as she gets back to Ida (*Niv* 12); a nun scarcely open to her, to whom Ida's only suggestion is sacramental confession to a priest (*Niv* 13); a canon regular whose conscience Ida relieves (*Niv* 16); a fellow mystic in another house, to whom Ida makes a daring and effective revelation (*Niv* 17).

Elsewhere, others ask Ida about the status, not of themselves but of a deceased relative. Ida then focuses her mind and her prayer on that person, until she can finally reply, as in stories about a sister's deceased father (*Niv* 5) and about the deceased kinswoman of a fellow nun, whom the latter has neglected (*Niv* 14). In yet other instances, admiration and spiritual influence are manifest without any exercise of authority or any mention of sin, as in stories of a night at Liège (*Niv* 22); a man's vision of Ida and the Christ Child (*Niv* 24); a friend's prayer life dominated by admiration for Ida (*Niv* 25); a doubting priest who comes to believe in Ida's gifts (*Niv* 26); two priests who have ecstasies in which Ida figures (*Niv* 27). Sometimes Ida interacts confidently with authoritative priests, or superiors, in various contexts, some of which involve the Eucharist (*Niv* 19, 20, 21 and 23). Finally there are two scenes where Ida's authority seems ineffective, as in stories of a woman at a bridge (*Niv* 9) and about an apostate canon, who yields to a rebuke, but is never heard of again (*Niv* 15).

In all these cases Ida's clients admire her insight and go away consoled or admonished. In some cases, what particularly touches them is a vivid image she offers them as a token to go with her reply. These are the 'mini-poems' mentioned above, which include the warped host (*Niv* 7b); the derelict toad (*Niv* 12c); the hand clinging to the sleeve and letting go of it (Niv 16d). To these we could add, in a more cautionary direction, Arnulf's image of the young cleric as an 'unrestrained stallion stumbling headlong into a pit' (*Arn* II.18ac).

While Goswin does not think to explain Ida's authority, he does give us to understand that the complaints against her were not a matter of authority, but rather of distrust of her sleep-like ecstasies. Ida seems to be at home with authority in general. Thus, in the few scenes where abbots, abbesses, or chaplains appear, she is at ease with them, and they fully endorse her forthrightness (*Niv* 15ab, 17abc, 23abc, 26a, 27abd, 33fgh, 34b). Her authority appears especially forceful in the remarkable chapter about her in the Life of Beatrice, where the two of them, still teenagers, openly hold daily conversations in a way inconceivable without official permission

(*Beat* I.10–11, 50–58). I present a translation of these and other relevant chapters from Beatrice as a third appendix on Ida. I suggest, therefore, that Ida's position at La Ramée was akin to that of St Thérèse, the semi-official novice-director in the Carmel of Lisieux. This hypothesis fits well with what we know of Ida's call to the Order. She had spent seven years with some beguines in Nivelles and had in effect become their errand girl (*Niv* 1). She had also formed a deep bond with a saintly woman among them named Helwigis, and this woman's death plunged the girl into a new maturity.

Twin events at this same time (1214) were to launch Ida into her Cistercian career: Villers had received a new abbot, in the person of Walter, and a group of devout women at nearby Kerkom were asking for incorporation into the Order, under Villers's authority. These nuns had been offered a better site for their convent (*Niv* 3a), but they were Dutch-speaking and the site was in the French-speaking area. The transition called for a bilingual chaplain (*Niv* 2c, 3b), and also a bilingual errand girl, or at least, a French-speaking one intelligent enough to become bilingual in short order. The choice of young Ida may have hinged on family bonds, or links with the late Lady Helwigis, or with the donor of the land, or even with Abbot Walter himself, or with the abbess or the chaplain. Possibly she already had a smattering of Dutch, especially if her infant nickname, 'Dutch Maid' referred to more than mere baby talk (*Niv* 1b). It does not occur to Goswin to enlighten us on any of this, and only between the lines do we perceive that she is playing the role as interpreter in anecdote after anecdote.

Ida's Compassion

The three Idas honoured in Brabant have traditionally been distinguished among themselves by mention of their home towns: Nivelles, Gorsleeuw (often called Léau),[12] and Leuven. Though each Ida differs greatly in her personality and in the style of her biography, casual readers find it hard to remember which is which. Hence I give each an epithet suggestive of her most memorable charism: Ida the Compassionate of Nivelles, Ida the Gentle of Gorsleeuw (Léau), and Ida the Eager of Leuven. When Goswin wrote of Ida of Nivelles he was clearly alert to her compassion. He brings it out not only in his chapter on her charity (*Niv* 30), and in his poetic appendix, but in some fifteen other passages throughout the Life, where he explicitly uses the term *compati/compassio*.

Compassion also has its place in Chapter 29, where Goswin offers that overview of Ida's inner life as a sequence of her typical themes. Thus in speaking of Ida as

---

[12] The Latin uses the name 'Lewis', which French-speaking scholars used to translate as 'Léau', a town known today as 'Zoutleeuw'. However, recent research has identified this Ida's birthplace as Gorsleeuw, now part of the municipality of Gors-Opleeuw, centred about seven kilometres north-west of Tongeren (Tongres).

'helping others out of their sins' (in *Niv* 29b–2), he is echoing themes of *Niv* 4b–18g, chapters in which anecdotes of explicit compassion abound. Even as late as *Niv* 26b, her compassion remains central; indeed, it is commented upon by Jesus himself. Here, however, there is a subtle difference: whereas earlier instances envisaged individual compassion, here a public-spirited compassion embraces 'all the calamities of the world'. True, this is immediately balanced with stress on individual beneficiaries, persons whom Ida 'relieves with suitable consolations', but the bold generalization does draw attention to the fact that, in the anecdotes themselves, Ida almost never looks to large-scale issues of Church or world. As we shall see later, in this bilingual convent, Ida is the all-purpose interpreter, and the bulk of her dealings are with the down-to-earth souls of the novitiate and the farmyard. The needs of such persons as these are very concrete and very local.

Another limitation of Ida's compassion is that it regards spiritual rather than physical sufferings. In *Niv* 5–16, we meet temptations, scruples, moral disgrace and prolonged purgation, loneliness, and disappointment, but no medical pains or economic setbacks. This limitation to the spiritual matches the nature of Ida's contacts and ministrations. She has many a chance to offer a kind word or to give of her time, but little chance to do infirmary chores or to distribute alms.

Five different elements can be noted in the anecdotes about Ida's compassion. Firstly, since the sufferings which Ida identifies with are spiritual rather than physical, it is important to notice how she learns that the sufferings exist. Goswin sometimes alludes to her being informed 'by a revelation', but at other times he puts it down to simple God-given shrewdness of observation. At times, too, she simply feels divine assurance that she is called to make a given suffering her own. This variety of divine invitation will be matched, later on, when she becomes convinced that her prayer has been heard and the suffering she prayed about is at an end, or nearly so. These successive intuitions of Ida's are akin to another certitude often attributed to her, namely the instinct by which she becomes aware of the state or standing of an individual, be it the state of grace in a living person, or the 'measure of purgation' in someone deceased.

Secondly, there is Goswin's rich vocabulary for the suffering itself, and for Ida's co-suffering. Particular interest attaches here to one theme, that of fatigue and of subsequent quiescence. Ida's compassion takes a toll, not only on her sleep but also on her health. She even bargains with God to send her some illness as a suffrage for the sufferer. This is particularly interesting when the sufferer is out of reach, such as a cleric unconnected with the convent. Ida will never have a chance to inform such a person of the prayerful service she is rendering him; it suffices that their common Lord should know it (*Niv* 6a). On the other hand, when she has direct access to the sufferer, her dealings take on the intimacy, tenderness, constancy and strength of a veritable mother (*Niv* 7a).

Thirdly, there are the metaphors and gestures, not only those for what is suffered, but also for the liberation from that suffering. Sometimes Ida conveys this sense of liberation by a physical gesture, as when, without violating the silence of the novitiate, she sits beside a gloomy novice and lets her own sunny disposition cheer her by osmosis (*Niv* 2e). Again, she offers an insecure soul a feel for security by letting him grip the sleeve of her cowl (*Niv* 16d). More often she offers her client a new self-image in the form of those 'mini-poems', such as the eucharistic host clearly marked with the name of a deeply shamed client. Mere mention of so touching a symbol is enough to convince the timid client that her God is inviting her to accept his embrace (*Niv* 7b). Then there is the female toad, abandoned by its wanton mate, but finding refuge in the folds of Ida's robe (*Niv* 12c). 'Mini-poems' of this kind are not confined to Ida, but are used by contemporaries of hers, such as *Arn* II.10c and especially *Oig* II.77–79, in which Mary of Oignies often asks a client to allow her a period of prayerful delay, precisely so that she can await the gift of such an image.

Fourthly, there is Goswin's sense of measure in Ida's compassion. We have already seen him inclined to measure some of her consolations in terms of their duration in time, but what measure can he apply to her compassion? Some of Ida's contemporaries engaged in a good deal of mathematics to measure their suffrages, especially recitations of prayers accompanied by prostrations or self-flagellations (*Arn* II.1b), or perhaps prolonged abstinence from food or drink. At Villers and its dependent monasteries, permission was rarely given for such athletic undertakings, especially on the part of women in poor health, such as Ida. Any extraordinary suffering had to be God-given, and the most obvious form for it to take was a providential setback in physical or psychic health. Readers will readily notice how Ida, while not scourging herself to the traditional point of drawing blood, has compassion for various clients to the point of vomiting blood (*Niv* 6a). Some modern readers see this as a question of tuberculosis, but equal importance should go to those non-medical campaigns of compassionate intercession in which Ida bargains with God to let her client's horrid temptations be transferred to her own soul (*Niv* 7a).

Fifthly, since Ida's compassion so often involves strenuous entreaty of God for her client, the reader should notice Goswin's rich vocabulary of entreaty, including metaphorical references to the bodily postures assumed by the suppliant Ida, or even by the God who leans down and hears her. She is very alert to any sign of response from God, be it a prolonged silence, a sense of futility, or some consoling 'revelation', such as the discovery of one of those 'mini-poems' mentioned above, in which she can offer her client an attractive new self-image.

Arnulf, Lay Brother of Villers

Whereas the memory of Ida has been blurred through confusion with her two namesakes, that of Arnulf has been distorted by another factor, an excessive stress on the austerities described in Book I of his Life, at the expense of the more attractive traits found in Book II. Even at Villers this distortion prevailed, as we can see in the

Gesta, which concentrates on his austerities (*Gesta*, III, 1359–62). It also goes on to make a major blunder, ascribing his death scene to someone else.[13] Whereas the austere Book I keeps dubbing him a martyr, athlete, and knight, the friendlier Book II describes his generous activities on his almsgiving rounds (see my notes on *Arn* I.2c, 5a; and also on *Arn* II.2a, 3e, 18c, 20g).

Comparing Arnulf with the dozen other lay brothers in the *Gesta*, one notices how few of them shared his permission to do extraordinary penances. The policy of Abbot Charles had been that all should be 'content with the simplicity of the regime' (Caesarius, *DM* 6.1), and any margin allowed for supererogatory austerity was always minimal. Goswin is alert to this local policy, and he repeatedly stresses Arnulf's compliance with his superiors in the matter (*Arn* I.2d, 6c). Even extra fasting from food was ruled out for Arnulf, and the most he ever did in that regard was to forego pittances (*Arn* I.8c) or, when he briefly had a kitchen job, to serve himself the least desirable foods (*Arn* I.8ab).

Only two other lay brothers are said to have worn a hairshirt, both of them while living on granges. First, there was Nicholas, tiny in stature and serving as shepherd, whose special schedule allowed him also to skip meals and to sleep in the open (*Gesta* III.3). Then there was the more refined John of Wiscrezees, who came to Villers under Abbot William, and who, while serving as grange master at Chênoit, wore a shirt and a pair of leggings made of sackcloth (*Gesta* III.5). For both of these it was the employment that opened the way to the austerities, and the same is true of Arnulf: all his instruments of penance are from sources connected with his wagon driving, obtained from the stable (*Arn* I.2ce), the barn, and winter work-room (*Arn* I.3ac), the smithy (*Arn* I.5e; II.20e) or the contacts along the road (*Arn* I.5d, 6b, 12a).

Goswin himself adds to the excess of limelight on Arnulf's penances when he gives the measure of time spent in self-flagellation. For two particular sessions he does give convincing measures (*Arn* I.3e; II.4g), but elsewhere he generalizes and has Arnulf flogging himself to exorbitant lengths. In Lent this amounts to virtually the whole day long (*Arn* I.11abc). In the notes I argue that Goswin is misinterpreting his oral sources. I understand these sources to reflect a single whipping, done daily after terce and lasting for about thirty minutes, but tripled in Lent by adding further sessions after sext and none. Aside from the element of time, however, Goswin conveys accurately two intentions that lay behind Arnulf's self-flagellation: a punitive/reformatory response to his own (unnamed) sins (*Arn* I.3d, 6e), and an intercessory aim on behalf of his friends (*Arn* I.7b, 11b; II.1be, 4f).

Arnulf's attraction to austerity was not acquired at Villers. He had learned it in devout circles of Brussels, during two years which intervened between his dissolute teens and his entry into the monastery (*Arn* I.1abc, 2b).

---

[13] The blunder is in *Gesta* II.10, partially ed. by Waitz, MGH SS, 23, p. 232, and fully ed. by Martène and Durand, III, 1352–54. The material on Arnulf is transferred to Abundus. Successive passages attributed to Abundus, beginning at 1352a, actually relate to *Arn* II.1c, II.3f, II.4e, II.14acd, II.20d, II.21a and the Epitaph.

Goswin singles out Arnulf's first seven years at Villers, and we might take that sacred number as an approximation, but it does happen that those seven years, 1202–09, were spent under Abbot Charles, who generally opposed individual additions to the regime, and under whom Arnulf felt frustrated. Goswin asserts, however, that even Charles recognized Arnulf's special call in that regard (*Arn* I.6c). At least initially, Arnulf felt doubly frustrated inasmuch as, besides the ban on extra austerities, he had no manual skill that could earn him an interesting job, into which he could channel his enthusiasm (*Arn* I.9a).

Liberation came through Conrad, who took office successively as prior (1206 at the latest) and then as abbot (precisely in 1209). Conrad had no qualms about austerity[14] and his admiration for the austere Simon of Aulne, already mentioned, surely left him wishing he had such a man on hand at Villers (*Sim*, pp. 29, 41–44). Conrad, being of the high nobility, was rather autocratic and had no difficulty assigning Arnulf to a grange and instructing the grange-master to give him *carte blanche* freedom to engage in long sessions of prayer and in specified penances, even during work time (*Arn* I.9a). To approve these penances in detail, Arnulf was also given a sympathetic confessor (*Arn* I.2d), doubtless hand-picked by Conrad and primed on what to do. This confessor was perhaps the monk Walter of *Arn* Pref. b and II.7a; perhaps also the friendly visitor of *Arn* I.7b and 11b. Either way, it was from this Walter that Goswin would receive the list of Arnulf's penitential instruments, a list upon which he would base Book I of the Life. Inasmuch as Goswin reveals the name, we can presume the witness was dead at the time of writing, and that Goswin was echoing what he had heard from him long ago. I suggest that he heard Walter at a public conference shortly after Arnulf's death, and, being already cantor, snatched up the details and stored them in his keen memory, and perhaps also in writing, for future use (*Arn* Pref. b).

Until Conrad's intervention, Arnulf was probably part of an unskilled labour crew, based at the abbey itself; but it seems that, as soon as he was assigned to a grange, he was given the job of wagoner, loading and carting sacks of grain from the storage barns at the grange in to the abbey mill, and from there bringing back baked loaves for the personnel of the granges and also for various devout persons outside, whom the abbey had undertaken to support. It was in the course of these charitable trips that he gathered intentions for his intercession. There is no mention of his interceding for cosmopolitan intentions, after the manner of a Lutgard, who consorted with prelates of cosmopolitan influence, or an Alice the Leper, but always for particular persons, after the manner of Ida the Compassionate.

In 1214, after five years as Abbot of Villers, Conrad was promoted to its mother house, Clairvaux. Arnulf was doubtless sorry to see him go, as it seems he had no difficulty getting a renewal of his appointments and his permissions from Conrad's

---

[14] Cawley, 'Four Abbots', pp. 307–14.

successor, Abbot Walter (1214–21).[15] At some stage, however, there was at least one change in the choice of grange from which Arnulf would do his wagon driving. After many years at Chênoit (*Arn* II.4d, 12e), there came a time when his alms had to be kept secret from overly zealous financial officers, and so he was stationed at Sart (*Arn* II.2a). This need for secrecy seems to have become acute in the time of William (1221 onwards), when the financial officers of the abbey were pressing for greater efficiency in almsgiving, in face of mounting debts. Strict limits were put on what enthusiasts such as Arnulf and Gobert of Aspremont could dispose of (*Gob* II.4.65).[16]

Discretion was also called for in that Arnulf's long years of austerity had taken a toll on his nervous system and had lowered the threshold of his laughter and his tears. At any moment, but especially during community assemblies, a spoken appeal to the emotions, however slight, could trigger in him mirth or grief beyond control (*Arn* II.7). William shrouded Arnulf's almsgiving in secrecy, to protect him from his opponents, but in the face of this hysteria he eventually had to yield to them and take him off the job.

This demotion involved eleven days of major excommunication (*Arn* II.3d), and forty days of a lesser disgrace (*Arn* II.3f), after the manner of the Rule of Benedict (44.10). I presume that, given the problem of his compulsive laughter, Arnulf was never reinstated in the wagon driving job, but for the remaining 'seven years' of his life was based mainly at the abbey itself. The 'seven years' of disgrace are perhaps not to be taken literally, since Goswin parallels them with a seven-year experience in the Book of Daniel (Dan. 4. 13, 22, 29). Arnulf was to die in mid-1228. If the seven years are taken literally, the demotion took place at the very outset of William's abbacy in 1221. In *Arn* II.19abc we find William sending a nobleman out to consult Arnulf at a grange. Some freedom of movement and employment is also implied when a family living adjacent to the grange of La Neuve Cour is watching out for his visits (*Arn* II.20ab). On the other hand, his conduct on both these occasions is admirably discreet.

Goswin's allusions to Arnulf's final years are vague. In the prime of life, one thing Arnulf had vehemently avoided was the infirmary (*Arn* I.10c, 12d), and so when, rather early in Book II, Goswin locates him squarely in that facility (*Arn* II.5c), we may take the episode in question to belong to those final years, in which uncontrollable laughter is a problem. The episode is a vision of our Lady, and if our dating is correct, its content is significant. Goswin presents Arnulf as engaging in one of the seven-piece devotions popular in those days, paralleling the seven

---

[15] Not to be confused with the biographical witness, Walter, already mentioned.

[16] On the financial officers under William, see Cawley, 'Four Abbots', p. 320. Interestingly, the Chronicle asserts that William's opponents all died untimely deaths (*Chronica*, I.12, ed. by Waitz, p. 201, lines 4–7; ed. by Martène and Durand, 1279D). These would be malicious opponents; but I suggest there was also a milder opposition, from monks of good will, experienced in the new mercantile economy and simply pressing for better management.

liturgical hours. This particular devotion consisted in meditating daily on our Lady's seven earthly joys, for which the apparition bids him substitute seven heavenly joys. Was meditation on these joys seen as a training in the control of laughter?

In his later years, some of the brethren thought ill of Arnulf and his handicap, but others understood him beautifully. One of these was Gombert, the grange master at La Neuve Cour, mentioned above. Gombert's calm enabled him to mediate between Arnulf and that distressed local family (*Arn* II.19ab). Human contacts of this kind must have been precious to Arnulf. Indeed, we know from Book I that, as late as a year or two before his death, he still had a chance to engage in vicarious penances, thanks to a nobleman's gift of shirt of mail for penitential use (*Arn* I.12a).

It was in these later years that Goswin himself gained his own small measure of acquaintance with Arnulf. One touching thing he noticed in the older man was how he economized on words, so as to minimize any triggering of his laughter. For instance, in consenting to a request for prayers, he would say: 'I'll do more than I'll promise' (*Arn* II.1b).

Goswin has few details to offer about Arnulf's final illness, but for his actual death he has some significant ones. Not only would Goswin have taken note of whatever the eyewitnesses reported at the conferences shortly after the death, but as cantor he would have had a privileged viewpoint during the last rites and the funeral. One thing he then noticed was the fervour in the singing during the burial ceremony. Also, as a cantor steeped in the liturgy, he was well able to couch these details with beautiful biblical overtones (*Arn* II.21).

Why Goswin Wrote Arnulf's Life

The distorted image of Arnulf picked up by so many readers was not something Goswin was deliberately trying to convey. But the question remains: why did he write this Life in the first place? Who were his anticipated readers? What was his message for them? What charism of Arnulf was he recommending?

Writing in Latin, he was certainly not addressing the lay brothers. Likewise, I see no evidence that Arnulf's friends, like Ida's, were pressing him to publish their tales about him, although Goswin does imagine possible readers as far away as a student hostel in Paris (*Arn* II.17c). As in Ida's Life, he addresses several harangues to his fellow clerics, and so I suggest it is primarily for them that he is writing (*Arn* I.10d, 12e; II.6f, 7d, 12d, 15d, 17c).

For Ida's Life, Goswin has an abbatial mandate. For that of Abundus he will have at least abbatial permission, but for that of Arnulf he invokes no abbatial intervention at all. I suspect Abbot William wished his own role in the composition to be kept secret, just as he did in Arnulf's giving of alms (*Arn* II.2bc). Goswin repeatedly says he is not calling for imitation of Arnulf's austerities, but simply for admiration (*Arn* Pref. a; I.6d, 12de; II.1e).

One might postulate a sisterly rivalry between Villers and Aulne, with Villers aiming to set up one of its own lay brothers to match Aulne's widely admired Simon, who died within a year and a half after Arnulf (*Sim*, p. 98). We do not know which of the two had his Life published first. Our only real clue to Goswin's aim is a word at the end of the Preface: 'to benefit both our contemporaries and readers of the future'. My personal suggestion is this. Abbot William was certainly faced with mounting pressures to allow the brethren a more lavish supply of consumer goods. He had also been pleased with the success of Ida's Life and now decided to have Goswin write the Life of Arnulf, intending the new work to promote the ideal of austerity. Indeed, the first thing noted in the Chronicle about William's immediate successor is his catering to the brethren's desire for a new stock of clothing (*Chronica*, ed. by Waitz, p. 22; ed. by Martène and Durand, III, 1285E–1286A). Brother Arnulf's tendencies had been in exactly the opposite direction (*Arn* I.10abc).

Arnulf's Counterpart, Simon of Aulne

My previous edition of Arnulf's Life carried an eleven-page appendix about his counterpart Simon, at the nearby abbey of Aulne. In his day, Simon seems greatly to have outshone Arnulf, but in our day it is hard to compare them, since Simon's Life survives only in disparate fragments. The fragments available to me were too chaotic to set alongside Goswin's orderly presentation of Arnulf. Moreover, what I had was mainly in French translations, though happily enhanced with some fifty drawings, made in 1621 to illustrate an edition of the Life which, alas, was never printed. In my appendix I took some fifty-five literary units and, without attempting a flowing translation, I regrouped them under several headings and sub-headings.

The chronology of Simon's Life is hard to establish, since several epochs of his Life are each given as multiples of the sacred measure, 'seven years'. Combining such approximations with a few established dates, it seems he entered Aulne about 1190, which is to say, about a decade before the encounter he was to have with Conrad, the novice from Villers. This would make Simon a dozen years senior to Arnulf in the brotherhood, but since he seems to have entered younger than Arnulf, Simon would be only about six years older than his counterpart. Both men spent their initial monastic years in obscurity, but again Simon seems to have assumed a public role earlier than Arnulf by perhaps a decade.

Simon had none of Arnulf's impracticality or compulsive laughter. On the contrary, he was a competent and respected grange-master, and on his travels he moved with ease among high-ranking clerics, even when in Rome, attending the Fourth Lateran Council (1215). The pope offered to ordain him on the spot, but he settled for a gift he had for listening in on confessions made to a priest, both as a stimulus to the penitent's memory and as an encouragement towards honesty. These traits of Simon certainly made him different from Arnulf, my impression is that these were not Simon's most typical traits. I would say rather that both men were most widely and thankfully remembered for more or less identical services, listening respectfully to troubled souls, giving them comfortable access to their official pastors, and thus enabling them to make a leap of conversion which they would otherwise have despaired of making.

There is no doubt that the friendship of Conrad of Villers was important to both of these lay brothers, but while there is ample evidence that it was central to Arnulf's career, the sources do not allow us to say how large it loomed in Simon's.

Abundus Monk of Villers

The Life of Abundus, unlike that of Ida, was not written under pressure from friends. Unlike that of Arnulf, it is not a propaganda piece. Ida's Life was composed shortly after her death (13 December, 1231), and Arnulf's not long before the end of William's abbacy (1221–37; *Arn* II.20j). For that of Abundus, however, it is difficult to suggest a sure date of composition.

In the Prologue to the Life of Abundus, Goswin speaks of being idle (*Ab* Prol. b). Does this reflect a recent removal from the busy office of cantor, without yet being assigned to some other employment? If so, a plausible date would be the early months under William's successor, the short-lived Abbot Nicholas (1237–40), a superior little known except for composing poetry on his deathbed. Certainly Goswin wrote part of Abundus's Life after 13 March 1233, since he mentions the death of John of Nivelle (*Ab* 15cd), which occurred on that day. Another clue is the dating of a nephew's death (see *Ab* 16d, n. 94), which places the composition after mid-August 1234. A *terminus ante quem* would be Abundus's death. That event is not mentioned in the Life, but the document presented in our Appendix I dates it to 1239. However, a more reliable document in our Appendix IV gives the impression that Abundus is still alive as late as 1260. My own guess is that individual chapters were composed shortly after the interviews involved, but that the process petered out at some turning point in Goswin's life, such as the accession of a new abbot. I suggest we think of it as written in the 1230s.

Abundus's Role within the Community

Goswin's intentions in writing about Abundus are beautifully explained in his Prologue. But unfortunately for us, just as he presents Ida and Arnulf without an outline of their career, so too with Abundus. As with the other two, we need to categorize the roles of Abundus within each anecdote. These can be grouped as follows. First there are six charming chapters on his individual life and his family: about his background (*Ab* 1); his schooling (*Ab* 2); his early devotional life (*Ab* 3); his vocation to Villers (*Ab* 4); his winning of his sister to La Ramée (*Ab* 12); his role in a nephew's deathbed conversion (*Ab* 16).

Next come five chapters of Abundus's more private experiences: a stereotyped account of his novitiate (*Ab* 5); an account of a lofty vision (*Ab* 6), compare *Niv* 28f, 29b–8 and *Arn* II.6e); his recognized role as intercessor with our Lady (*Ab* 9, 10);[17] outward details of a typical visionary experience (*Ab* 7). Six other chapters echo mystical themes familiar from Ida and Arnulf: visions showing the status of deceased friends (*Ab* 15); accompanying others through temptation and death (*Ab* 17, 18, 19, 20); a Marian revelation about a disturbing liturgical text (*Ab* 13).

We come closest to Abundus's heart, and to that of Goswin, in the visions experienced, not in private but in fullest awareness of the assembled community, whether standing still in choir, or on the march in procession, or out at work in the fields. We meet such scenes in the four remaining chapters: the Virgin chants along with the monks (*Ab* 8); Mary and her Son march in the Candlemas ceremonies (*Ab* 11); Mary and her escort make the rounds of the monks at harvest (*Ab* 14); Mary, her Son and St Bernard enjoy the festive vigils (*Ab* 20).

These visions imply an intense participation in the community exercises on the part of Abundus, an absorption that stands in sharp contrast with the more private piety of Ida. Goswin himself is aware of the difference, and seeks to reconcile it (*Ab* 6f; *Niv* 19, etc.). To my mind, these anecdotes suggest that the role of Abundus in the community of Villers is that of a father confessor (*EO* 70.96; 87.18). He is also a typical senior monk, of the kind that abbots wanted to have in residence, so that their very presence would have a formative impact on the juniors (*Chronica*, ed. by Waitz, I.10; ed. by Martène and Durand, III, 1277BC). Villers needed seniors, not only to make up for those sent out as chaplains to the nuns, but also those sent to the two new foundations, Grandpré and Sint-Bernards op de Schelde (I.12; 1279C).

In Appendix IV, 'The Letters of Thomas the Cantor', he is likewise seen as one to whose prayers any member of the community can have recourse in time of need (Thomas, Letters, I.57–86). After praying for such clients, he sometimes shares with them an oracle that he has received from our Lady. He may well be doing this in penitent-and-confessor exchange (I.57–86). The friendship of Abundus with John of Nivelles is very telling here (*Ab* 15c), for this John was indeed an outstanding confessor of the epoch (Thomas, *BUA* II.31.3). Elsewhere Abundus is seen in similar friendship with Emmeloth, a leading Béguine of Nivelles (*Gob* II.1.37).

Such a role suggests a measure of seniority, surprising in that Goswin depicts Abundus as childlike, with a 'good simplicity'. Happily in this regard, we have good chronological data. Abundus was born about 1189, and was a lad of seventeen when he entered Villers. His mystical life began about seven years after profession, when he was still only twenty-five. We may think of him as still a youngster in the later episodes, but by the time of John of Nivelle's death (1233) he was into his mid-40s, and would have been close to fifty when Goswin took to surreptitiously interviewing

---

[17] The same relationship to our Lady in comes up in the letters of Thomas the Cantor, in our Appendix: intercession for individuals and revelations about individuals, with the monastic community serving simply as a supportive context.

him for this biography. If his death was indeed early in 1239, he was then aged about sixty.

Although he seems to have been a confessor, there is no evidence that he was ordained a priest. He was probably a cleric, however, since he is paired with a 'lay monk' in a setting where one of the pair is supposed to be a cleric (*Ab* 7b; compare *EO* 108.6–8). Promotion to Holy Orders is mentioned in the scene at Liège in which Abundus first contacts the personnel of Villers (*Ab* 4c), but Goswin, ever so conscious of his own priesthood, never alludes to any specifically priestly experience of Abundus. Indeed, his explanation of why Abundus communicated on a certain weekday seems to rule out his ever celebrating mass (*Ab* 16d).

The Abrupt Ending of the Life of Abundus

It is clear that Goswin left Abundus's Life incomplete. Not only do both surviving manuscripts cut off abruptly with *Ab* 20f, but neither Table of Contents lists any chapters beyond that. There survives, however, an independent and somewhat detailed account of Abundus's death in a French Life of Abundus published in 1603 (our Appendix I). This is clearly taken from a Latin manuscript, which is said to have existed at the Abbey of Cambron. I do not notice any Goswinian traits in its style, and the lack of scriptural allusions makes it hard to attribute to him. But it certainly deserves respect.

In the *Gesta*, an Epitaph is assigned to Abundus (our Appendix II). Its style is close to that of Ida, and similar arguments would attribute both to Goswin as author (II.9, III, 1354B). However, if Goswin wrote Abundus's Epitaph, we would imagine that he outlived his hero, though his leaving the Life incomplete would seem to suggest the opposite.

The Title, *Send Me God*

The title I give to Goswin's collected works is drawn from *Arn* II.9b: 'the phrase some are accustomed to use when asking for prayers: "send me God".' In Goswin's day, such a request was readily put to a revered person, especially at the end of an edifying interview. It envisaged not just a generic inclusion of the petitioner in the revered person's prayers, but a specific request that a mystical consolation be granted in the foreseeable future. On accepting the request, the revered person would set a mutually convenient liturgical date, and both parties would then begin an intense 'countdown' towards that day in warm mutual awareness. When the appointed day came, the typical moment for the consolation to occur might be that of receiving the Eucharist (*Arn* 19abc; *Ab* 16d; *Niv* 27b, etc), or a profession ceremony (*Ab* 19e); but it could come any time on the appointed day, or even within the octave (*Arn* II.9ab, 16c; *Niv* 28g, etc.). Goswin often notes not only the onset of such a grace, but also its lingering, be this throughout the rest of the liturgical day or season, or for a determined number of weeks (*Niv* 21e, 28bd, etc.). One of the most vivid descriptions of such a countdown comes in the Life of Beatrice, where Ida is initiating the young Beatrice into the mystical life and is promising her an ecstatic experience 'at Christmas', or at least within the Christmas season (*Beat* I.10–11, 50–58).

It is not always the hero of a Life who does the sending; he (or she) is sometimes on the receiving end. Thus, in *Niv* 23b, when our Lady brings Ida the Christ Child, she announces that he has been 'transmitted' to Ida by a third party, a certain abbot, who had recently paid her a personal visit. Indeed, it is not only 'God' who is 'sent', not only consolations that are transmitted. Sometimes the revered person asks for the very opposite. Thus Ida effectively pleads to be sent an illness, that she might endure it as a suffrage on another's behalf (*Niv* 5a, 6a). Elsewhere she obtains the transfer of a sister's severe temptation to herself (*Niv* 7a). This 'sending of God' is analogous to the giving of 'signs', and there is pleasure for all concerned when, as in John 4.52–53, news is brought that the signs have come true. Such news reinforces trust in the reality of the mystical intercourse between earth and heaven (*Niv* 26e, 27g, 28h).

Essentially, these shared countdowns are instances of intentional partnership in the mystical life, and we find in Goswin's Lives quite a range of such partnerships, especially by way of involvement in one another's ecstasies. Thus, Arnulf perceives in detail the experience a recluse has one Good Friday (*Arn* II.17abc), and Ida knows all about the ecstasies at Beatrice's convent on the day the bishop consecrates some sisters there as virgins (*Niv* 28g). Oddly, this mutual involvement need not include reciprocal awareness; for in *Niv* 24b a man has a vision of Ida and the Christ Child, apparently without her knowing a thing about it until later, when he tells her about it in the parlour.

The reality behind the 'sending of God' is found even in intercession on behalf of the deceased, especially when a contract is made with a dying person, an invitation to come back a given number of days after death, so as to reveal the soul's status as regards purgation. (*Niv* 8a, *Ab* 20c). This kind of partnership in the mystical life is by no means confined to the works of Goswin, but his citation of the phrase 'send me God' gives him a right to it as a title for his works.

Such was the simple faith of these fervent forebears of ours. They understood their mystical experiences as direct interventions of heaven, and an objective interplay with others living under the same roof. We today still speak of an intervention of God in the Eucharist, and we still call a priest confessor a 'vicar of Christ', as Goswin does in *Niv* 13c, 29b–1, *Arn* I.1b and *Ab* 16e. But are we ever as acutely attuned to the liturgical year as were his heroes? Above all, what would we think of someone under our own roof, noted for a drowsy swooning, if he or she claimed that the drowsiness came from God himself? Would we bring our requests to such a comrade, as to an Abundus, to one who had a 'hot line' to our Lady? What would we say if someone like Arnulf claimed to have read our minds at some key moment of the liturgy (*Arn* II.15), or at some moment of mental prayer (*Arn* II.17)?

Or if a woman like Ida came up and told us point-blank that our 'state' was one of grace, of temptation, or of grave sin (*Niv* 4b, 9a, 10c, 11b, 17c, 18a, 21b, 22c, 28bg)?

Indeed, not only for us are such things difficult to conceive; they left even a Goswin full of wonderment, as he tells us on every page. It is, however, a bit amusing to watch how, at one moment, he will bid us marvel at what he is saying, and the next he dismiss it as 'small wonder!' For us, however, the greatest wonder here is how these mystics of Brabant were able to thrive and be applauded, when further south so many comparable mystics were being condemned as Albigensians. Certainly there was local opposition to Goswin's mystics, but never on any grounds of heresy. Their key difference from the Cathars lay in their solidarity with the clergy and the sacraments of the Church. Their 'sending of God' involved both a countdown to a liturgical feast, and usually a build up to the Eucharist. Moreover, providence had blessed the mystics of Brabant with able defenders in the higher ranks of the clergy. Lutgard's patron, James of Vitry, became a Roman cardinal, as did Arnulf's patron, Conrad of Villers. And besides these defenders in Rome, the Brabantine mystics had a whole network of friendships and mutual openness that wove them together among themselves and with their confessors and superiors. This friendly openness is as deserving of wonder as is the content of any of their heavenly revelations.

Finally, the 'sending of God' is not the only exchange of gifts in Goswin's milieu. Already in the Rule of Benedict (54.1), we read of the exchange of little sacramentals, called *eulogiae*. In *EO* 76.31 we read of pittances or small gifts of food which a superior sends to an honoured guest, or to a brother who seems to merit it (*Arn* I.8c). However, in neither of these instances does the gift spring from a request, as is the case with 'send me God.'[18] Yet among the lay folk of Brabant, one gift in particular does involve placing a request, namely, access to the Eucharist. This demanded a preliminary interview with a priest to set up an appointment for receiving. The request made at such an interview was not unlike asking the priest to 'send me God' (*Niv* 3abc, 20abc, and especially *Niv* 29b–4). Indeed, we read in several lives of a mystical communion, in which God bypasses the priest, and the host comes miraculously straight to mystic (for example *Niv* 8d). In giving the title *Send Me God* to Goswin's works, I mean to include this whole range of human partnership in the mystical experience as lived in Cistercian Brabant.

Translation Policy

When I was asked to translate the Lives of those early nuns, the first text readily available was that of Ida the Gentle of Gorsleeuw (Léau), whose strange content and

---

[18] The theme is frequent in Caesarius of Heisterbach and in Thomas of Cantimpré's *Bonum universale de apibus*, and in the whole Villers literature.

style demanded policy decisions on such points as verbosity, anonymity of protagonists and elaborate titles for the heroine. Verbosity is prominent in several of these Lives. No noun or verb is allowed to stand alone, but each is accompanied by a dignifying synonym or a modifier of some sort. Although initially repulsive to the modern ear, this ample diction can take on a charm for the familiarized reader. I try to gear down the verbosity, if this can be done without losing themes of theological value.

The anonymity of witnesses and protagonists is annoying, not only because it often makes it impossible to determine who is subject and who is object within a sentence, but especially because it precludes our knowing if the same witness or protagonist comes up again in later anecdotes. This impedes a serious study of an individual's relationship with persons of her entourage. Wherever a careful study of the context allows me to determine who is who, I replace the ambiguous pronouns with unambiguous nouns. The nature of English pronouns often demands that I determine the gender of the person. In the notes, I try to go a step further and determine the person's religious status, and whether or not he or she is the same as a corresponding person in other literary units.

Honorific titles for the saint are of theological significance, but the very repetition of them can annoy a casual reader. Thus, I often replace them with the simple name of the heroine, but when this is done at the expense of theological riches, I try to offer the reader an introductory survey of the titles used, with an indication of the frequency of each. I have not done this with Goswin's Lives, since he followed Abbot William's directive, and kept the style 'simple'.

I was initially hoping to establish a standard English equivalent for each key word of Goswin's Latin. When this proved impractical, I ran many computer searches for given roots throughout his works, and so determined the range of his meanings and overtones, and from that I sought the best English equivalent for the given context. The fruit of such searches often appears in the notes. While attaching great importance to Goswin's key words, and trying to include his every syllable in the English, I do not hesitate to adapt his syntax. Thus I frequently switch between the parts of speech, turning Latin nouns into English adjectives, phrases into adverbs, active verbs into passive. The aim is for the overall thrust of my English to convey that of Goswin's Latin as fully and enjoyably as possible. I attach importance to Goswin's word order, in the sense that I like to introduce the elements of his thought in the same sequence that he uses, setting a key word on a pedestal at the beginning, if that is what he does, or holding it in reserve as a trump card for the end, if that is his choice. In the notes I reproduce the Latin phrasing wherever it seems ambiguous, or where my translation seems daring, or Goswin's expression is particularly powerful.

On the other hand, I often radically change the chapter titles. To facilitate cross-reference, I have also subdivided each chapter into literary units, rarely more than one page in length, each of which bears the chapter number and a sequential letter. For some Lives I rely on the Bollandist edition, in which case my references are to the Bollandist divisions, rather than to the original chapters. Thus, the one thing I do not reproduce from the Latin texts is their chapter titles even though these can be of interest for their vocabulary, and sometimes for their re-phrasing of difficult expressions. Goswin is certainly responsible for the division into chapters, but I am not sure that the existing Latin titles come from him. They are often rather arbitrary, and sometimes lengthy. The titles I have created in their stead aim to provide effective previews of the content of each chapter. They offer a pinpoint reference system more convenient than a mere citing of the numeral of a chapter or page. I try to minimize breaks in the text and to match Goswin's own shifts from one literary genre to another, as when he passes, for instance, from narrative to commentary or to apostrophe.

Just as modern writers will spice their text with the playfulness of slang and humour, so Goswin likes to spice his with jargon and echoes of the liturgy. To convey this in translation is not easy, but wherever I spot a term or phrase which he is using in this way, I italicize it and immediately add the reference in parentheses. In more complicated situations, I resort to footnotes. For the jargon and liturgical background, I cite my own translation of the *Ecclesiastica Officia,* or *Ancient Usages of Citeaux.* This is all the more useful in that it is a manual for cantors, dear to Goswin's heart. I also cite the Rule of St Benedict for the same reason. For a strictly literary or episodic background, I often quote the two works that seem to me the closest parallels to Goswin: Gregory the Great's Second Book of Dialogues, which is his Life of St Benedict, and Caesarius of Heisterbach's *Dialogus miraculorum,* as mentioned above.

Acknowledgements

In the twenty years that I have worked on this project, many persons have been eager to help, and quite a number have followed the developments year after year. Teamwork on a task like this calls for easy exchange of information, and if not for a parity of expertise, certainly for a complementarity of viewpoint and a persevering commitment of time and interest. Frequent face-to-face consultation is the key to real teamwork, and it is only natural that my most enduring help has come from those I have lived with at Guadalupe Abbey. But very real encouragement has also come from many outside friends, who have borne with me for years on end, even despite adventurous approaches that led me into dead-ends. Some such friends, I believe, would prefer to go unnamed, but my debt to others is too great to leave unmentioned.

Beginning at home, I first thank my successive abbots, Bernard McVeigh and Peter McCarthy, for their generous provision of facilities for study and for desktop publication. Then there is our late Father John Baptist Hasbrouck, whose tireless proofreading and helpful suggestions continued until a stroke impaired his speech, and whose interest and encouragement was visible on his face until death. Next comes our computer expert, Brother Phillip Wertman, who has solved not only my everyday problems, but even somehow salvaged a decade's work when the computer and back-up machine were stolen. Our librarian Brother Patrick has retrieved books for me at all hours. And speaking of librarians, I can never sufficiently thank Father Augustine de Noble and his colleagues at our neighbouring Benedictine Abbey of Mt Angel, as also Father Chrysogonus Waddell and successive librarians at Gethsemani Abbey. I have also had much encouragement from Father Charles Cummings, longtime editor of *CSQ*, who opened his pages for me to air my views to the scholarly world.

Among religious sisters, I first thank Reverend Mother Provincial Catherine Brabender RNDM for welcoming my dedication of this volume to my first teacher, the late Sister John Nepomucene, of the same congregation. Then there is Sister Lillian Thomas Shank OCSO of Mississippi Abbey, the one who invited me to translate these Lives of her forebears in the first place. The late Sister Marietta-Juanita Colón OCSO of Wrentham Abbey enlivened early editions with delightful illustrations. Mother Marion Rissetto and Sister Kay Kettenhofen OCSO of Angels Monastery have shown as much sustained interest as any. Sister Marie Gregory Foster OSB of Jamboree Abbey near Sydney was the editor of my very earliest publication and has continued to befriend me to this day.

Unique among lay friends is Brian Patrick McGuire, currently of the University of Roskilde in Denmark, who has not only offered helpful advice but has recommended my translations in countless lectures and publications. Dr Margot King of Peregrina Publishing, has not only carried articles of mine in her *Vox Benedictina,* but also provided me with many a photocopy of essential texts. Dr Gertrude de Moor, a Cistercian oblate, made a special trip for me from her home in Delft, The Netherlands, to obtain scholarly tourist guides of Villers, Nivelles, Huy and Liège. These have greatly clarified my understanding of the physical setting of the Lives. Last but not least is Mrs Marcia Lee, illustrator of several of my recent publications, who kindly re-drew the map for this volume.

The late Mr Martin Kelly of the Guadalupe Institute, and his successor, Mr Michael Keleher, have paid for numerous journeys in which I did research, not only on our shared Guadalupan patroness, but also on the present project. Especially valuable were the opportunities they gave me to meet with leading scholars. I have incurred an immense debt of gratitude to Maryna Mews and Constant Mews for the countless hours they have spent in working on issues of consistency within the manuscript. Warm thanks also to Professor Thomas Coomans, the great authority on the architecture of Villers, for his spontaneous interest in the book and for his generously supplying and arranging for the beautiful photo on the cover, and the image of Ida of Nivelles. Finally I must express what a pleasure it has been to work with Barbara Newman my liaison with the Brepols Publishers. Her warm and pointed encouragement has been matched with promptness of answers and clarity of instructions.

Martinus Cawley OCSO, Guadalupe Abbey, June 2003.

B. Walterus de Traiecto
Abbas 10. Villar.

B. Willermus Abb. Villar. 11.
et postea Claraeuallis

D ſe eerwerdyghe maghet criſti
Ꝑde vā Niuele bekeerde hair
tot gode te dienen van ionghen kinde
Als andere ionghe maechdekēs ſpeel
den.ſoe bleefſe te hups bp harer moe-
der gode dienēde/ſeer oetmoedich wal
ſe.ſedich.en gheſegghelijck.Ooc waſ-
ſe ſeer goedtieren en ōtfermhertich dē

Top: Ida's patrons, Abbots Walter and William of Villers.
For illustration credit, see p. 122, below.

Bottom: Ida of Nivelles (Yden van Nyuele), woodcut in a late medieval printed chronicle of the duchy of Brabant: *Cronycke van Brabant*, Antwerp, Roland Van den Dorpe, 1497 (copyright: Brussels, private collection).

The Life of Ida the Compassionate of Nivelles

Nun of La Ramée

Prologue

Here begins the Prologue to the Life of Ida, a nun of La Ramée.[1]

(Prol. a) It is a glory for the Lord, an honour for the Almighty, to put into writing the story of the virtuous *conversatio*[2] of his chosen ones. It is like *putting a lamp on a candle-stand* (Matt 5.15), enabling all on whom it sheds its radiant light to strive and to progress towards loftier realizations of the virtues. Rash, however, very rash are those who attempt to write of the brilliant virtues and valiant deeds of saintly men and women when nature has not bestowed on them the imagination for it, nor has education afforded them the learning, nor has fluency equipped them with the clarity of style. Far from embellishing their great topic, such writers do but entangle it and end up displaying only the dryness of their own unrefined imagination. As Jerome put it to Bishop Heliodorus (Letter 60.1): 'A scant imagination will not hold up under grandiose materials; rather will it succumb in the very act of venturing upon a task beyond its strength.'

(Prol. b) Yet this is just what has happened to me. I confess it, and I do not blush. I have undertaken to write the Life of Christ's virgin, Ida, undistinguished though I am by any oratorical fluency and unaware of any imaginative subtlety adequately equipping me to couch it in fitting words. What largely excuses me is an order from my abbot, obliging me to set out the Life in a fairly simple style. In doing this, I have relied, not on my own limited imagination, but on that almighty Lord who *opens the dumb mouth and makes infant tongues fluent of speech* (Wisd. 10.21).

(Prol. c) Little wonder that my mind trembles to begin a task it can scarcely carry through, especially in that the admirable *conversatio* of this blessed one involves a saintly affectivity difficult to describe and those many kinds of luminous contemplations graciously lavished on her by her Bridegroom. Yes, her fruitfulness can deservedly be compared to that of *a tree planted by the running waters* (Ps. 1.3),

---

[1] The Prologue is omitted by Henriquez.

[2] *Conversatio*: an untranslatable synonym for 'disciplined conduct', usually in the sense of 'monastic living'. Like many translators, I leave it in Latin, trusting that Goswin's frequent use will accustom the reader to its basic meaning. For more detail see *Arn* II.10a, n. 127.

watered by streams of grace *and heaving itself aloft* (Ecclus. 50.11) to exude *a fragrance as agreeable as Lebanon's* (ibid. 39.18).

(Prol. d) So write I shall, write for the benefit of holy mother Church, write to confound that devil whom the Lord's handmaid so mightily overcame! Yes, I shall write down the things I have heard from persons worthy of trust, things they *had seen with their own eyes, heard with their own ears* (Mark 8.18). And I shall so write as to *stop up the mouths that speak wicked things* (Ps. 62.12), so write that God be glorified in this holy virgin's wondrous deeds. And once I have this *conversatio* of Christ's beloved committed to writing, I shall consign it to all her friends, that in it they may glimpse her afresh, as in a lucid mirror and as if brought back to life. May they but busy themselves in imitating her whom they have loved! And more especially shall I consign it to those who loved her more especially and those whom she herself more especially loved. To the readers accordingly I make this appeal: if you find anything included in our story unusual or unheard of, do not lightly take me to task for it, but thoughtfully attribute it to God, *for whom no such thing is difficult* (Jer. 32.17).

1. Ida's Parentage, Infancy, and Childhood

(1a) Ida, that venerable virgin of Christ *whose memory is in benediction* (Ecclus. 45.1), took her origin from middle-class parents in a town within the Liège diocese named Nivelles. It is well remembered that she was related by blood to various persons who resided there, good men among them, and religious women. For although that town does count inhabitants of both sexes who pine after earthly desires and make light of their souls' salvation, it also claims not a few menfolk respectful of God's law and numerous virgins who devoutly serve the Lord; recluses too, faithful to their *conversatio*, who shut out the whole world from themselves and shut themselves in, wholly for God. All of these God frequently refreshes with nutritious grace from on high, so that the town seems almost a *paradise of delights* (Gen. 2.8).[3]

(1b) While Ida was still a babe in arms, nursing at her solicitous mother's breast, women neighbours jokingly told the mother of their hunch that her daughter would turn out religious. They also nicknamed her 'Dutch maid', and for a long time to come, many kept on calling her 'Dutch Ida'.[4] And later events would, as we shall

---

[3] This paragraph is omitted in Henriquez. Goswin will name three churches in Nivelles: St Gerard, Holy Sépulchre and St Nicholas. St Gertrude's founded in 648, has had its present form since 1046, and in our day, no less than in Ida's, it marks the hub of the town, from which streets radiate out as in spokes in a wheel. The chapel which Goswin will call the 'Sépulchre' was presumably on the site of the present church of that name, some five hundred metres north-east of St Gertrude.

[4] There is no indication of why they called her *Theutonicam*. Did she have some Dutch

see, show her becoming a religious and eventually learning the Dutch tongue.

(1c) In her infancy, which includes the first seven years, Ida avoided playing out in the street among toddlers of the neighbouring houses. Indeed, even after her seventh year she avoided any worldly girls of wanton, unrefined behaviour. Being a good-natured child, she lingered at home with her mother and constantly drilled herself in disciplined conduct. In count of years, she was an infant still, but the Almighty had an eye on her, meaning her to become his *vessel of election* (Acts 9.15), inwardly all along teaching her how she should act and what she should shun.

(1d) At this stage too, she began her frequent trips to church for morning mass, dressed in a little cloak made by her father to fit her tiny stature. It was St Gertrude's church that she attended. In summer it was fairly easy for her to get there, since the sun dried up the wetter spots along the way. But in winter the path was all churned up and muddy, and her little feet so sank down in it that her meagre strength could hardly lift them out unless helped by someone else. Another deed of hers worth mentioning was this. Whenever she had on hand a piece of bread or something meant for her to eat, she would *withhold it from her own mouth* (*RB* 49.7) and give it to some passing traveller.

(1e) When her infancy was over and she was nine, Ida's father, a man faithful in his secular duties,[5] reached his end and passed from this life. The relatives, seeing Ida deprived of a father's support, planned among themselves how to marry her off to the son of a certain citizen of Nivelles. But she caught the meaning of their whisperings and, since she longed to serve God in chastity, she foiled the trap they were laying for her by secretly climbing out a window and fleeing from her father's home. *Nothing at all* (*RB* 33.3) did she take with her, but for the psalter she had recently begun to memorize and the plain dress she had on. As a clear token of how she gloried more in the poverty of Christ than in any abundance of passing goods or any fruitfulness of numerous offspring, she slipped off to an alley of the town alongside a tiny chapel called the Sepulchre. There, among virgins *dwelling* in religious poverty *under the aid of the most high*, Ida *lingered under the protection of heaven's God* (Ps. 90.1). Her relatives, though aware of how little she was still, and how far from the age of discretion, were unwilling to upset her. And so they left her in peace, to seek peace among those women of peace.[6] Living in this house she had

---

blood?

[5] *Vir quantum ad saeculum fidelis:* Henriquez skips this tricky expression. I read it in a laudatory sense, as in I Sam. 22.14, not in the pejorative sense of *RB* 1.7 *(servantes saeculo fidem).*

[6] *Quaerentem pacem cum mulieribus pacis in pace reliquerunt:* the triple use of 'peace' sounds awkward in English. In Latin the three distinct grammatical endings and the biblical echoes allow it a pleasing sonority: see *Niv* 33f, n. 188. The chapel was presumably on the site of the present large church of St Sépulchre, about five hundred metres north-east of St Gertrude's.

as comrades seven virgins, to whom she strove to adapt herself in *the measure of each one's conversatio* (*RB* 22.2), be it fervent or remiss. So diligently did she keep peace with them, and so gracious and sweet was she to them all, that all of them loved her quite as much as she loved them.

(1f) Some three more years went by and Ida's mother, who had also lived religiously, passed from this life. Still too young at this death to provide for her own livelihood, Ida was cared for with all kindliness by a kinswoman of her mother named [...][7] out of the hereditary endowments bequeathed by both parents.

(1g) Ida, like a good maidservant of Christ, *well knew that* humility was *the way along which* we head *towards God* (*RB* 71.2), and so *before God and neighbour* (Ecclus. 10.7) she reflected every aspect of humility: ever modest, ever open to persuasion, ever ready to agree with the best.[8] Her very gait was marked by *a head ever bowed* (*RB* 7.63). They still tell of a memorable saying she once came out with: 'How I'd love, if it were possible, to be going along somewhere, or just standing still, and the earth would open up under my feet and the lower part of my body would hide away in the earth and the upper part grow short and tiny.' Oh, what a word! Whose was the whisper that ever inspired such a thought? Surely it was Christ, the master of humility, the Spouse who had *set his heart upon her comeliness* (Ps. 44.12) and *had placed his throne within* her (Antiphon: Virgins).

(1h) Humility is what keeps God's servants and handmaids ever tranquil of heart. So it is that the recluse, Mary of Heylonbineth, who then lived some time with Ida, testifies even today how never once in their four years together did she see her moved to anger or spite.[9] Out of humility too, Ida wanted to wear only old and ragged clothing, so that people would treat her as unimportant, but her kinswoman guardian would suffer no such thing. Compassionate too, she was towards her feebler and needier comrades, like some new Martha, *doing the rounds of the streets and alleys* of the town (Cant. 3.2), begging now for clothing, now footwear, now bread, now meat, now cheese or other needed eatables; begging both from kinsfolk and from others and bringing the things back in bags to *distribute to all as each had need* (Acts 2.45; 4.35). At times, on getting home from such errands, she felt tired, and if a comrade then told her of such and such women being sick and needing wine

---

[7] B fol. 3[rb], has *quaedam mulier* [then a clean gap, followed by] *nomine, cognata ejus.* This suggests that the guardian's name was in the original but was being suppressed. A fol. 148[r] omits the gap and the word *nomine* (named), as does Henriquez (p. 202), another indication that B was copied earlier and perhaps more locally than A.

[8] *Modesta, suadibilis et bonis omnibus consentiens:* the adjective *bonis* is of indeterminate gender, making Ida 'open' to either 'all good persons' or 'all good projects' or both. See also *Niv* 23a, *Arn* I.5c, II.3d, 9a, 10a and 18c.

[9] The manuscripts differ in giving the surname and the emotions: B fol. 3[va] has *Heylonbinec* and *ira vel indignatione*, whereas A and Henriquez have *Heylonbineth* and the nouns *ira vel odio.* Walter Simons suggests the place name should be *Willambroux*, a part of Nivelles associated with Mary of Oignies.

or such items, Ida would be the ready handmaid of Christ and would promptly offer her Lord the irreproachable sacrifice of a goodly willingness. With tranquil mind and speedy gait, she resumed her kindly errands and diligently carried out the injunction. Did she bring this aid to the sick purely for God's sake? Or did she aim at flattery and show? To find an answer to this, a girl named Oda once played a trick on her. Oda was lying sick in hospital at St Nicholas, and from there she asked Ida to go and beg some needed food and drink. With no affectation at all, Ida replied: 'I do not want you, dear sister, enduring any need. Here I am, ready to beg for your needs, just as you wish.' At the chapter of faults she was so meticulous that she often confessed the slightest, tiniest things; so much so that her comrades often burst out laughing.[10] Equally eagerly she kept up her childhood practice of rising early to get to church and hear matins and mass. After divine service was over, she would have liked to linger on in church for leisurely prayer, but her comrades repeatedly fetched her back on the grounds of her tender years.

(1i) Thus was Ida exerting herself as best she could in these good works, but still *God had not yet rained* any shower of tears *on the soil* of her heart (Gen. 2.5), nor had she yet experienced what the psalmist calls *tasting and seeing that the Lord is good* (Ps. 33.9). But not to delay such saving showers any longer, the Lord visited her in the following manner. There was a woman of Nivelles named Helwidis, a woman of respectable *conversatio*. When she fell ill of some sickness and died of it, the Lord took occasion of her felicitous death to pay a visit to Ida his handmaid. Suddenly and unexpectedly *the floodgates* of Ida's eyes and head *burst open* (Gen 7.11) and out poured such a flood of tears that scarce could she hold back their onrush. And we may rightly suppose that these tears sprang, not from the woman's death, but from the wellspring of heavenly grace. Such was her first visitation. In it the Lord moistened the dryness of her heart with an outpouring as abundant as it was mild, an *irrigation* at once *from below and from on high* (Josh. 15.19). Such progress and growth did this bring her that from that day on her mind was deservedly called the *fountain of never-failing waters* (Isa. 58.11).

(1j) Such were the venerable beginnings of the devout *conversatio* which God's chosen one carried on, both in her infancy and in her girlhood, wherein she bequeathed to everyone, boys as well as girls, an example of how to strive by good works ever to preserve the cleanness which is chastity and to learn a heartfelt compassion for the neediness of others.

---

[10] *In facienda confessione:* presumably a public asking of pardon, equivalent to *EO* 70.54, commonly called 'the chapter of faults'. Private confession is mentioned in the text at *Niv* 11b (a confession made to Ida), 13c, 14b, 16a, 17a*b* (made *ex officio* to an abbot), 29b–1; *Arn* I.1b, 2d (to 'the monk confessor'); II.13b, 18bc, 19b; *Ab* 15c, 16eg. In four of these texts Goswin names the confessor a priest and a *vicarius Christi*, 'role-player of Christ': *Niv* 13c, 29b–1; *Arn* I.1b and *Ab* 16e.

2. She Enters the Order at Kerkom

(2a) Ida, in the meantime, like a *precious pearl* for Christ (Matt. 13.46), gave serious thought to how *the Jews have no dealings with Samaritans* (John 4.9) and *how burdensome it is for* daughters *of Israel to tarry with Egyptian* women (*Ab* 4). She considered also how she might express still more perfectly her abandonment of the world. Thus, at sixteen she bade her people farewell and entered a Cistercian[11] monastery named Kerkom. The community of nuns at this place was still only small. They had abandoned an earlier site and had transferred hither with their belongings.

(2b) While in this monastery, Sister Ida used to hear the sisters speaking words quite foreign and unfamiliar to her, since almost all of them spoke Dutch, and she did not understand their tongue. Yet despite her ignorance of it, there was one religious gentleman who used to preach the word of God in that tongue, and whenever she listened to him, the Holy Spirit breathed into her soul and tears flowed from her eyes, tears too copious for her to hold back, her heart being in the grip of so agreeable a savour.

(2c) Not understanding what her sisters were saying, Ida frequently conversed with herself and God alone, remarkably combining meditative prayer and prayerful meditation. In doing this, she would bring to mind[12] various visible, bodily creatures for consideration, and in admiring them she would contemplate *their Creator* (Wisd. 13.5), an exercise in climbing to higher things, one little step at a time. Amid the great variety of things to see and scenes to gaze upon, Ida avoided bringing before her mind's eye anything that would sully the cleanness of her heart. Not in vain did she undertake to contemplate human vanity, but she turned her gaze downwards only to surge loftier in her praise of the Creator. Thus would she rediscover him in his handiwork, as ever the more to be admired, to be praised, to be loved. She thus came to see her cloistered existence as set in a very *paradise of God* (Ezek. 28.13), whose customary observances she gradually made her own.

(2d) Ida used to name two motives for her transfer to the Order: to unburden herself of concerns by *possessing absolutely nothing as her own* (*RB* 33.3) and also to receive the holy Eucharist frequently from the priest at mass,[13] as do the monks and nuns of the Order. Another custom of the Order that she praised was how monks

---

[11] *Quoddam monasterium ordinis Cisterciensis:* Goswin never uses 'Cistercian' without adding 'Order': see *Arn* II.20a, n. 170. Kerkom would be near the modern village of the same name, about seven kilometres north-west of Tienen (Tirlemont) and about thirteen kilometres east-south-east of Leuven. See *Niv* 20.

[12] *Adducebat in considerationem mentis suae [...] ante mentis oculos reduceret [...] in laudem Creatoris:* Henriquez replaces *adducebat* with *considerabat*; likewise, *asurgens* with *ascendens*. He perhaps gives a more passive sense: Ida would be not so much conjuring up edifying thoughts as dwelling on what lay before her and so being wafted aloft. See *Niv* 29b–5; Wisd. 13.

[13] On eucharistic practice and spirituality, see the notes on *Niv* 29b–4

and nuns *cross their hands* when bowing for the *Gloria Patri* (*EO* 68.14–15). This she interpreted as calling on each monk and nun to embrace the Trinity in welcome.[14]

(2e) As for sacred Scripture, she loved it as a mirror for her soul. Of course, *the law of the Lord was in the heart*, not in the hardbound tome (Ps. 36.31),[15] but some volumes there were in which she could spot terms like *God* or *Christ*, or *Emmanuel*,[16] and other terms too, fragrant with spiritual sweetness. These volumes she would press to her chest and hug so tightly in her bosom that the books' rugged embossing left her bruised. And she so loved exterior bodily calm that she was quite put out whenever she had to shuffle around.[17] In taking this attitude, she was prompted mainly by the s*pirit of counsel* (Isa. 11.2). The result was an outward peace, which in turn enabled her the more easily to maintain inward peace of soul. There was one of her sisters[18] whom she would sometimes see unusually downcast, and, though unable to speak to her in Dutch, she would sit beside her and lend her at least the serenity of an outward good cheer to clear away the clouding of her face. Her visitors too, men or women, whether or not religiously inclined, used to get great consolation from her exemplary conduct and from the abundant grace they were confident she possessed. And in any case, she gradually mastered the Dutch language and became able to speak suitably to her sisters and to people of that tongue.

---

[14] *Cancellatis manibus*, see *EO*, p. 438, n. 123. To ensure uniformity in the depth of the bow, it was specified that the hands be crossed and rest on the knees.

[15] *Et quamvis lex Dei ejus esset in corde ipsius et non in codice.* Henriquez omits this delightful pun on the psalm verse.

[16] Henriquez here introduces the name *Jesus* (p. 207), as he does also in *Niv* 24 title (p. 258). Absence of the name in the manuscript is significant (B fol. 5ra; A 149^v^). The name *Jesus* is never used in *RB*, which forbids speaking of fellow monks with just their given name and no title or term of reverence or endearment *(puro nomine, RB* 63.11). Similarly, Goswin's fourteen uses of *Jesus* in *Niv*, are all imbedded in biblical or sacramental formulae, or have a reverential or affectionate qualification. See *Niv* 29b–3, n. 144.

[17] *Plurimum molestaretur quoties eam exterius moveri oporteret.* The passive infinitive, *moveri*, also used in the ecstatic scenes of *Niv* 4b, 20d and 30j, envisages a preference for total stillness, both of the whole body and of the individual members.

[18] *Si quando videbat aliquam sororum suarum:* literally this could be any sister, but, in view of Goswin's policy of anonymity, I often interpret such expressions as envisaging a particular person, whose name is being hushed up. This problem of Goswin's use of anonymity for persons within his anecdotes is discussed in notes on such passages as the following: *Niv* 1f, 15a, 16e, 17a, 18b, 20b, 25a (Beatrice?), 26a, 29b–Ida's tact), 33c, 33g (where Goswin accidentally betrays the identity); *Arn* II.3d (Abbot William), *Arn* II.14c, II.15a, II.18d; *Ab* 8b. In addition, Goswin himself three times makes explicit apologies for anonymity, in *Niv* 16e; *Arn* II.18b and *Ab* 9d. The similarity of these passages became a major clue in postulating Goswin as their common author; see Roisin, *L'Hagiographie cistercienne*, p. 58.

3. The Monastery Transferred; A Clandestine Communion

(3a) The same year that she entered this cloister, an influential gentleman named Gerard helped the nuns to move from that place, which was arid, and go to another place, alongside a stream, and to set up a monastery there. This they named La Ramée, since it was overgrown with ramifying bushes.[19]

(3b) The following took place when Sister Ida was already at La Ramée. She *desired* with a great *desire to eat* the flesh of the *paschal* lamb (Luke 22.15), but could not find anyone to enable her to satisfy this desire. Inasmuch as she was inwardly undergoing intense torment of spirit, she came to the monastery chaplain and pretended she was worn out with *acedia*.[20] 'Dear sir', she told him, 'I am being worn out with a great attack of *acedia*. A most bothersome passion has set my heart in torment. Whatever I look at becomes a burden for me and I cannot even hearken to the Lord's service[21] with any peace in my heart. Back in Nivelles I was told that those worn out with this kind of bother could have their heaviness of heart quickly put to flight if they were but given the body of the Lord. So I beg of you, please fulfill this desire of mine.' The priest answered: 'Just wait, daughter, till tomorrow, and in celebrating mass I shall gladly give you communion, if, as you say, this will effectively relieve your grief.' Ida replied: 'No, dear sir, I cannot wait till tomorrow. And besides, I ask that you act secretly, giving me communion without anyone's knowing.' So the next day the priest gave her communion, understanding her to be worn out with *acedia*. This he did while the professed nuns were at their chapter. Thus Ida had the joy of finding in the taste of this saving refreshment a long-desired relief for her sadness. Just as those labouring under the ills of *acedia* find fasting, vigils, prayers and any spiritual exercises quite *heavy and unbearable* (Matt. 23.4), so Ida gave the name of *acedia* to her torment over her prolonged deprivation of this lifegiving sacrament.

(3c) Likewise, each Sunday throughout her whole year of probation her heart was tormented as she watched the nuns go up to the altar to eat of that holy banquet, and so great was her anxiety that she would have preferred to have her head cut off a

---

[19] *Quia ramoso virgulto consitum erat, Rameyam nuncupaverunt:* the Dutch nuns confer a French name; but what they are naming is the monastery (neuter), not the locality (masculine; locus). The latter had doubtless already borne this name for generations. It is located near modern Jauchelette, on the Grande Gette, fourteen kilometres west-south-west of Tienen (Tirlemont). Abundus's sister Mary enters there, *Ab* 1b, 12bcdf. On this Gerard see Coomans, *La Ramée*, p. 21 where there is also a reproduction of his deed of donation.

[20] *Acedia fatigari:* the noun *acedia*, transliterated from the Greek, is a common monastic synonym for 'listlessness'. The verb *fatigari* (be worn out) is a favourite of Goswin's, ranging in sense from purely physical fatigue to purely spiritual weariness. It comes sixteen times in *Niv*, twelve in *Arn*, and two in *Ab*.

[21] *Auscultare servitium Domini:* she means the high mass, the time of day when fervour was most strongly expected.

hundred times rather than have her reception of so sweet a sacrament further delayed. After this, a full year passed, and some months more, until she would turn eighteen[22] and be able to enter the *probationary cell of the novices* (*RB* 58.5,11), to undergo the Order's customary full year of probation and, *after* the year's *cycle* (ibid. 9), to be made a nun.

4. A Financial Decision; An Early Revelation

(4a) Now, I would say, is the moment to mention a sum of forty pounds accruing to Ida from her patrimony, a sum which she *conferred on the monastery* (*RB* 58.24). This money had, in her estimation, been acquired by means scarcely justified, and so she was troubled in heart and she consulted certain reliable gentlemen among her friends about it, each of whom was fairly well acquainted with her father's *conversatio*. These were all for removing from her heart any such meticulous scrupling,[23] and all for reassuring her by saying the money had been accumulated, not by the anathematized means of the usurers, but by fully justified commercial efforts on her father's part, and that it was thus permissible for her to use that money so as to give an alms in any manner she wished. But she, scarcely trusting their words, held on to her heart's scruple and betook herself to him who is the *one counsellor in a thousand* (Ecclus. 6.6), Christ the Lord, and this is the pact she made with him: 'Sweet Lord, see how upset I am in my heart over this money! Please, in your unspeakable goodness, it would be enough if you would deign to do this one thing for me: increase within me the grace of your Holy Spirit,[24] and I shall no longer contend that the money was gained as *filthy lucre* (I Pet. 5.2). Short of that, my heart knows no way to accept consolation in its dilemma.'

What wondrous prudence! And how pleasing to God! Burdensome though it was for her to be detained in this wicked world and held back from the delights of glory on high, nevertheless, when put on the spot, *the one thing she asked of* the Lord (I Kings 3.11) was not to have her life happily over and done with, or to be free of delay in getting *to see the God of gods in Zion* (Ps. 83.8), but rather she kept the

---

[22] This age limit is mentioned for male novices sixteen times in *GC* 1195–1215, especially in 1201.4. It clearly applied also to nuns.

[23] *Meticulosam scrupulositatem:* Henriquez substitutes for this the word *ambiguitatem*. See *Niv* 16a, n. 65.

[24] Goswin's notions of grace and of the Holy Spirit deserve much study. It is striking how often he imagines grace as a heavenly fluid. See the notes on the following passages: *Niv* 4a, 22b, 30i, 31b; *Arn* II.6b; *Ab* 3c. He often personifies grace, especially as an enriching 'mother'. See the notes on *Niv* 22a; *Arn* I. Pref. b, 2f; *Ab* Prol. c. Grace 'smiles' in *Arn* I. Pref. a, and 'helps' in *Arn* I.12d. But the soul can also become active and 'find' grace, as in *Arn* II.12e and *Ab* 11e. It even 'allures' grace in *Ab* 3a. Attention is drawn to even further aspects of grace in other individual notes.

proper order and asked for an increase of grace in herself to enable her to persevere to glory. And the Lord showed how pleased he was with her praiseworthy attitude of heart by multiplying his grace in her until the *little spring grew into a great river* (Esther 11.10) and the small *spark* blazed up *as a fire* far from small (Ecclus. 11.34).

(4b) Thus did the Lord's *grace grow* in her (Luke 2.40, 52) during her time as a novice. Once too, when she was engaged intently in prayer, her desire blazed out so ardently that her *soul* suddenly began to *melt away* (Cant. 5.6) and she was bereft of all bodily strength and her *mind* passed over and was *beside itself* (II Macc. 5.17), wafted aloft in heavenly rapture. Up there, in her vision, she encountered her beloved lover, *the Lord of hosts and King of glory* (Ps. 23.10), and she began entreating him, in honeyed whispers, on behalf of a beloved sister of hers, who had told her of being burdened with some uneasiness of mind. The Lord answered: 'Why ask that, daughter? If what you mean is her sins, these are already forgiven.' Ida replied: 'Lord, that is not enough; but *if I have found grace in your eyes* (Gen. 6.8) show me a reliable sign that she will be saved.' Then came the Lord's sweet, warm, gentle reply: 'Let me show you the place I shall give her *at the end without end*, a place of unutterable glory and joy. Yes, and tell her on my account to trouble her conscience no more! Rather, let her carry on in all peace and goodwill that *conversatio* which is now hers! And let this be a token for her: there, at the door of the church, I have sent her[25] so copious a blessing of my grace that her body has fainted away and she has fallen so fast asleep in the arms of holy love, as to not be able to move from the spot.' Ida rejoiced to hear this. And along with this revelation she received another, all about the status of certain of her friends, and their future. And what she then foresaw in spirit did indeed befall them later on. Upon returning from *the region of the living* (Ps. 114.9) to this *valley of tears* (Ps. 83.7), Ida communicated the Lord's message to the sister, who in turn recognized how true were the signs the Lord had established. And she was notably comforted thereby.[26]

5. Praying for the Soul of a Sister's Father

(5a) A sister at La Ramée asked Ida *to pour out prayers*[27] to the Lord on behalf of her father's soul (Ps. 141.3). This Ida undertook to do with pleasure, making solicitation for the soul night and day, heaping prayer upon prayer. But she was getting no answer of any kind about the soul. One day later on, when the nuns were

---

[25] *Dic igitur ei [...] his intersignis quod [...] misi ei [...]:* who was this friend? The command, *dic* (tell), suggests someone at La Ramée. The perfect tense of *misi* (I have sent) suggests a sign already realized. On *intersignum*, see *Ab* 20c, n. 117

[26] The rest of the paragraph is omitted by Henriquez.

[27] *Ut funderet preces [...] vacaret orationi:* on prayer as 'poured out', and grace as a 'fluid', see *Niv* 4a, n. 24

all out in the fields, engaged together in *harvesting the crops* (*RB* 48.7), and were all pausing for a rest, Ida took her rest apart from the others (*Ab* 14a), over by a stack of sheaves. At that moment it was revealed to her that the soul she had been pleading for to the Lord had been awarded purgatorial chastisements.[28] Given this revelation, she so compassionated the soul's torments that she petitioned the Lord to inflict on her any infirmity he might wish, if only the soul's purgation would be alleviated. The Lord responded favourably to this prayer, and at that very moment a fever invaded Ida, a fever so potent that for six weeks to come she was racked with its sickening effects. Many days later, when at leisurely prayer in church, she had a vision. Standing before her was the man for whose soul she had been offering the Lord that prayerful *sacrifice, sprinkled with the oil* of her charity (Ps. 140.2; Lev. 2.4). There he stood, clad in white from the waist up, which she took to mean that his sins were partly purged and partly not. After this vision, the man *vanished from her* gazing *eyes* (Luke 24.31). In reporting *the vision she had seen* (Antiphon: Matt. 17.9), Ida reassured the sister of her father's salvation. After that, she enlisted many prayers for him so that, *with the intercessors multiplied* (Collect: All Saints), the Lord's mercy would the more quickly free the soul from the pains of purgatory and bring it to refreshment.

6. Two Priests Tempted to Fornication

(6a) A certain priest, a praiseworthy man of reputable *conversatio*, was showing affectionate familiarity to a woman of sorts.[29] And so he was enticed into loving her with a love no longer chaste or holy but carnal and seductive, constituting a temptation that wearied him considerably. Ida became aware of this through a revelation from the Holy Spirit, and she grew very sad, for in Christ she loved that priest. So vehement a grief did she conceive in her heart that it forced her to vomit blood.[30] So she prayed attentively to the loving-kind Lord that he inflict upon herself any kind of ill health he might wish, if only he would completely remove from the mind of the priest the lethal disease that *was spreading like a canker* (II Tim 2.17) and sapping his priestly vigour of mind and his vitality (*Ab* 17b). And what did the loving-kind Lord then do? Did he brush her prayer aside? No, he sent her as a pittance[31] the illness she desired, an intermitting quartan fever, by which he scourged

---

[28] *Purgatoriis esset deputata suppliciis:* this is good news, in that the pains assigned are not eternal; but it is stern news, in that Ida and her friends must share the pains. See the notes on *Ab* 9b, 20e–h, and *Arn* II.20c.

[29] *Mulierculae cuidam:* this diminutive is not vituperative; it simply gives the sex and absence of any special virtue or social standing: 'a woman of sorts'. See *Arn* II.8c, n. 115.

[30] *Vi doloris sanguinem vomere cogeretur:* one of the medical aspects of Goswin's Lives deserving discussion. Tuberculosis?

her tender frame for six months on end, scourged it sufficiently for the priest to be freed from his temptation and for herself not to be deprived of the merit for the compassion she had shown in coming down to his level.

(6b) There was a second priest also, one who used to put on an outward show of a religiosity which he did not inwardly possess. One day this priest had a talk with Ida at the parlour window, with gracious good cheer all over his face. He gave Ida a great display of love, as if they were familiar friends, and he boasted of readiness to do some great deed for her. On hearing this, Ida, like a *prudent virgin* (Matt. 25.2), lowered her head a little and began to think. She dwelt admiringly on the supremely great love the Lord and creator of the universe had deigned in his unutterable kindliness to show his creatures, and she contrasted it with this frail mortal's effort to show a love outwardly comparable![32] While she was thinking these things over, it was suddenly revealed to her that the love of which the priest was making an outward show was all empty pretence. Yet he had no idea that such was her opinion of him when he bade her farewell and left. But to Ida, the far-seeing bride of Christ,[33] it was soon revealed that this priest was overcome by temptation and that he had stumbled into the whirlpool of fornication.

(6c) And you priests, ever so irreverent, so unappreciative: what do you say to that? you who *see the thief,* the devil, thieving away the salvation of your souls, and yet *you run with him,* run down to hell (Ps. 49.18)! You who *seek what is your own, not what is Jesus Christ's* (Philem. 2.21)! How dare you so rashly put on this outward show of a religion you do not inwardly have? Rather you ought to know that, just as it has been said to you: *Cleanse yourselves, you who bear the vessels of the Lord* (Isa. 52.11), and again as it has been said to you: *You are the salt of the earth* (stressing wisdom; Matt. 5.13), and *You are the light of the world* (stressing cleanness; ibid. 14),[34] so also it has been said to you: *Your deeds should shine out in everyone's sight as being good* (ibid. 16). What are you going to say to the Lord on the day of judgement, when the faithful menfolk who are your parishioners are *ranged on the right hand* to reign endlessly with the Lord (Matt. 25.33), while yourselves are *on the left hand,* to be tormented for age upon age *along with the devil*

---

[31] *Pitantiam ei immisit:* Henriquez omits the word *pitantiam* and loses Goswin's vivid Cistercian metaphor, based on a gesture of a prior at table, who notices a monk's special need and signals to the waiter to bring him something extra (*EO* 76.31–36).

[32] *Quando quidem homo mortalis et fragilis potest alicui tam mirabilem foris amorem exhibere:* I read this as a question which Ida asks herself, though I would be more comfortable with this sense if the decisive verb, *potest,* were moved closer to the opening of the sentence. Henriquez recasts the whole clause, but his printer has apparently left out some words; and so his text makes no sense.

[33] *Speculativae Christi sponsae:* this is a favourite term of Goswin's. See *Ab* 8b, n. 44.

[34] *Mundamini [...] lux mundi [...] propter munditiam:* Goswin's logic is obscure, but seems to hinge on a feeble pun between the noun *mundus* (world) and the adjective/verb *mundus/mundare* (clean/to cleanse). Henriquez omits from here on.

and his angels (ibid. 41)? May the Lord of majesty avert this from you, he who deigned to die for us! *Blush and be confounded* over your detestable deeds (Isa. 41.11); do penance for your evils perpetrated in the past and take up every kind of safeguard against future evils!

7. Ida Frees a Sister from Blasphemy

(7a) One sister at the monastery was being worn quite weary by a wicked spirit of blasphemy. Sister Ida was aware of this and, thanks to her ever-familiar spirit of the Lord,[35] she knew just how vexing a temptation it was. She compassionated the sister with such heartfelt anguish that she herself had to take to her bed, where she vomited blood. This sister was always looking for solitude wherever possible and wanting to hide from every eye, since whatever she had to do, whatever she happened to see, felt to her like a hefty burden laid upon her. One day, when she had thus separated herself from the community and slipped off to a hideaway in some corner, she was stricken with so forceful a heaviness that she all but wanted to deny her Lord and saviour .Sister Ida was in the cloister at the time and was given a divine awareness of what was happening to that cozy denizen of the hideaways.[36] She sought her out, found her and set her own hand to gag her mouth, lest, if she start speaking, she become frenzied and blurt out some word of blasphemy or denial of God. All that day Ida stayed with her, until about compline time; and then she led her to the dormitory and put her to bed,[37] always with one hand immovably over the mouth, lest at the slightest withdrawal she again become prone to blaspheme.[38] All night long Ida sat at the bedside, from compline till the signal for vigils, praying with continual tears that the Lord deign to look on the poor sister's affliction and come to her aid in peril. But even after her many prayers and tears, no heavenly consolation was given her, and so at last she requested the merciful Lord to free the nun from that most evil temptation and not hesitate to lay it on herself instead! That very hour

---

[35] *Per familiarem sibi spiritum Domini:* Henriquez reduces this to *spiritu divino.* He does the same at *Niv* 18a and 26a, but he retains Ida's 'familiarities' with the heavenly Christ at 22b, 23c, 24b, 24c, etc. In Henriquez's day the term 'familiar spirit' was in use among necromancers.

[36] *In latebrosum angulum [...] latebras foventem:* the sister is named pejoratively: 'she who keeps the hiding places warm.' *Latebrae* is also pejorative at *Arn* II. 8c, and *fovere* is pejorative in *Arn* I.3h. Elsewhere *fovere* is favourable (*Niv* 19c, 22a; *Arn* II.10b; *Ab* 20b).

[37] *Collocavit eam super lectum suum, manum suam [...] super os ejus:* literally, Ida lays the girl on Ida's bed; but in the next paragraph, Ida is sitting at the girl's bed *(ante lectum ejus).* Goswin presumably meant the girl's bed both times.

[38] *Ne si forte paululum [...] retraheret, ad verba blasphemiae [...] pronior efficeretur:* the 'proneness' is important: Ida is not physically bottling up the blasphemy; she is lovingly 'holding hands' till the crisis passes and the 'proneness' subsides.

the Lord *bent his ear to her pleadings* (Ps. 87.3). Then, not just for one hour but for three whole days, Ida was worn weary and helpless, worn all but lifeless, from the violence, the bitter violence, of those smuttiest of thoughts which the tempted woman had had, thoughts to be anathematized and driven far from the hearts of the elect. Yet in this way the sister was set free from that deadly temptation! On that day and for ever after, thanks to God's mercy and Ida's intercession, she enjoyed both peace and tranquillity of heart.

(7b) Ida wanted to go beyond these initial, remedial consolations and to see the sister more cheerily consoled by way of a gratifying revelation. So she came and told her: 'Dear sister, while that wicked spirit of blasphemy was still embattling you, one day at mass I was praying to the Lord my God, when suddenly *there shone around me a great light* (Acts 22.6). Within that light there appeared to me a man, one serene of face, gracious and venerably grey-haired (*Ab* 13d). His right hand held a wafer of bread, like a host but warped slightly upwards, and inscribed on the host was a name, your own name! 'At the sight of it I was divinely given to understand that the warp[39] in the host meant you had thought that worst of thoughts, to despair of God's ability to save you. But the venerable gentleman addressed me with a different lesson: to have seen your name written on that host should be my assurance that your *name was written also in the book of life* (Philem. 4.3; Apoc. 13.8), and that you were to be lifted on high with the Lord in endless immortal glory.' On hearing this revelation spelt out for her, the nun so progressed as to regain entirely her recently lost hope of salvation and a great alacrity of heart besides.

8. A Deceased Nun Appears to Ida

(8a) One nun at La Ramée had long languished with an illness, and when it took a turn for the worse, she came close to her end. Ida, taking her turn to sit with the dying nun, made this request: 'Please, dear sister, if permitted, on the seventh night after you die, would you come back and inform me of what you have found?'[40] In due course the nun did *enter upon the way of all flesh* (I Kings 2.2), and she did come back to Ida, though not on that seventh night. Within the sixth month, nevertheless, she made her entry, and made it accompanied by a venerable throng, a train of virgins assigned her by the Lord as an escort for entering into heavenly repose.

(8b) There she stood, facing Ida, robed in a purple gown with a brilliantly radiant

---

[39] *Per hoc quod recurva erat hostia:* compare *EO* 114.25–29, where the sacristan culls defective pieces when baking hosts.

[40] *Septima nocte [...] quid inveneris renunties:* the seventh, also the third and thirtieth, days after a death were honoured in the Cistercian missal with special prayers. See also *Niv* 10ab for the seventh and twenty-eighth nights. But the sixth month, mentioned below, had no special honour.

crown on her head, into which four precious stones had been neatly set: one in front, one behind, one to the right and one to the left. Ida, not recognizing a face so brilliantly lit, asked who she was and, once given the name, she further asked: *'Why is your raiment crimson?'* (Isa. 63.2) The nun answered: 'Because for many a day I bore up patiently while being martyred under a severe feebleness of body and under the lash of my heavenly *Father* as he graciously *chastised* me, *his daughter* (Heb. 12.6), *that I might not die but live and go on to tell of the Lord's doings* to me (Ps. 117.17–18). Hence you may be sure that in God's kingdom I shall share the glorious lot of the holy martyrs, even as my purple clothing indicates.' Ida pursued her question and asked the meaning of the four precious stones in her crown, and she replied: 'Be assured that the four stones inserted in my crown signify the four principal virtues: *prudence, temperance, fortitude and justice* (Wisd. 8.7)'

(8c) Deservedly were these four symbolic stones set in the nun's crown, for they imply that she had been a woman of virtue.[41] Prudence, to begin with, is a knowing of *things good and evil* (Isidore, *Etym.* II 24.6), along with acknowledgement of the true faith. Hence, *'PRUDens'* amounts to *'PorRo ViDens'* (ibid. X.201), which means 'forward-seeing' in the sense of 'PRoViDent' and 'eRUDite'. Temperance is the mind's firm and moderate rational mastery over libido and other wayward impulses. Fortitude is the virtue that *tolerates adversity with equanimity* (ibid. II 24.6). Its subdivisions are generosity, confidence, patience and perseverance. Justice is the rightness of a will that neither loves sin nor consents to it but *distributes to each the rightful due* (ibid.). Not undeservedly have we run briefly through these virtues, hinting how the nun blossomed in them. But back to our topic!

(8d) At that time Ida had been *desiring with a great desire* (Luke 22.15) to partake of the holy body of our Lord Jesus Christ, and it so happened that, while she was still speaking to this nun, there suddenly *appeared to her a hand* (Dan. 5.5), which proffered to her that very Eucharist. While yet she had it in her mouth, she had an experience of the senses, or so it seemed to her, in which she melted away into such inner sweetness that she felt her own spirit being bonded to the divine spirit, bonded with a glue of love,[42] a glue so potent that she became *one spirit*, as it were, with God (I Cor. 6.17). As for the nun, she had already completed her purgation for sins committed and was now to be lifted away from Ida's eyes, escorted by that throng of virgins and wafted up to share their blissful mansions in heavenly light.

---

[41] For themes similarly catechetical, see the notes on *Niv* 29b–7; *Arn* II.5b.; see also Cawley, 'Ida of Nivelles, Cistercian Nun', pp. 313–15.

[42] *Valido glutino amoris:* for Goswin's various uses of 'glue' and its cognates, see *Arn* I.4a; *Niv* 20c, 28d, 35bx; *Ab* 10a, 16e.

9. Pleading for a Woman; A Purgatorial Bridge

(9a) No sacrifice pleases God more than zeal for souls. Accordingly Ida had long desired a certain woman's salvation and had *poured out* many a *prayer* for her to the Lord (Ps. 141.3). But in praying thus, her spirit became ever downcast, and she could draw no consolation, for the woman's state seemed indeed perilous. This drove Ida to conceive a grief so intense and to slip into such an undoing of her body in response to her anxiety of spirit that her very entrails jostled and, amid their jarring pain, she could no longer hold back a copious vomiting of blood. In the midst of all this she became *beside herself in mind* (Acts 11.5): her *spirit took leave of her body* (II Macc. 5.17) and she was snatched away to the purgatorial places. There she met with many souls, each paying a penalty of purgation, greater or less, to the measure of their own misdeeds. She felt the onset of trembling, afraid she would have to undergo those horrid torments herself: the stinking water, the flame-vomiting fire, the unbearable chill. But her dread was not realized, for she passed through those punishments unscathed. Next she saw before her a great river discharging dense clouds of stinking fumes, from which came plaintive voices, those, it seemed, of souls in lamentation. And, spanning the river in the foreground, she saw a bridge, narrow as the razor edge of a sword. And, behold, right at the bridge, who should appear to her but that woman, for whom she had so devoutly offered to the Lord of majesty all those prayers and tears!

(9b) Lifting her eyes across the river she saw a nicely level space with a wondrously delightful charm about it, like *a paradise of the Lord* (Gen. 13.10). And within that space stood her Lord and saviour ! It seemed to Ida, he had all heaven and earth in his hand, and every other power within the universe as well; but he sweetly beckoned to her, saying: 'Cross over, my friend; cross the river and come to me!' Ida at first shuddered at the narrowness of the bridge, but then she took confidence in the Lord's help, and so she clasped the woman's hand in her own, so as to draw her along too, and so as both to cross the bridge together. But the woman was extremely upset and terrified, and *so withdrew her foot* (Gregory, *Dial* II Prol. 1). *The Lord looked* indulgently *upon* (Luke 22.61) the woman and said to her: 'Suffer it,[43] sweet daughter, that a saving suffrage be thus invested on your behalf. And do not lose sight of all that I myself have suffered to redeem you from the everlasting torments of hell.' Thereupon Ida made two more attempts to drag her along, and she did gain some three or four paces of headway, but the woman still disdained to follow her lead. Beholding this, the Lord resorted to threats of what would happen if she did not budge and allow herself to be helped.

(9c) Thereupon Ida made one mighty effort to tug her along, but in vain, for she

---

[43] *Patere [...] ut salutare tibi suffragium impendatur:* the deponent imperative, *patere,* 'suffer' is commonly used in this strong sense of 'allowing an investment', but Henriquez tones *patere* down to the bland active imperative of the similar-sounding, but really unrelated verb, *pete* (from *petere,* to petition). Henriquez thereby weakens Goswin's wording.

stayed immovably put. Again the Lord looked on, but this time almost in anger, and now he bade his beloved Ida abandon the wretch to her own will and weary herself over her no more. So Ida launched out upon the bridge and crossed without hindrance. And the further she pushed her footstep forward, the broader did she find the bridge. And so she arrived right in front of her Beloved. And that most gracious and *comely of the sons of men* (Ps. 44.3), so overflowing with sweetness and mercy, now graciously bestowed on her his embrace and his kiss and *kept* with her *a day of festivity* (Ps. 75.11). Yes, and to think how often she too, in the past and within the secret chamber of her heart, had given him the kisses and embraces of her own ardent charity and her overflowing tears! Taking a look around, there on the river flat,[44] Ida saw a number of her friends, living or dead; and about each of them, she received the Lord's reassuring word that they would indeed come through to the kingdom of supreme bliss. Finally, after these sweetly whispered exchanges with the Lord, Ida, by his leave, *came back to herself* (Acts 12.11), seeming as she did so, to feel her spirit wending its way back into her entrails. From that day to the end of her life, Ida could never again compassionate that woman with the tender affection she earlier had, despite all efforts to recapture and endure anew the very frying pan of intense compassion she had once had for her.

10. A Deceased Sister Foretells Ida's Death

(10a) One sister, still a pupil in the monastery and only eleven years old, used to spend much time in prayer. Her name was Margaret of Avesnes. Struck by an illness and confined to bed, she grew weaker day by day, and no other outcome was expected but her death. Ida paid her a visit one day and said: 'Do me a favour, Margaret dear: on your seventh night come back and tell me how things stand with you!' She replied: 'I will gladly do so, if the Lord permits.'

(10b) So the sister died and her little body was commended to the earth. The seventh night passed without her returning to Ida, but on the twenty-eighth night, there she stood in apparition before her. Ida, following the Order's customary observance, said: *'Benedicite'*, and the sister answered: *'Dominus'*.[45] Then Ida asked: 'How is it with you, dear sister?' She replied: 'Up until now I have been assigned to the purgatorial places for having been reared on victuals acquired with

---

[44] *In praedicti planitie loci:* the choreography of the vision is surprising. Here 'on the level-ground of the aforesaid place', Ida seems to find persons both living and dead, both in need of purging or already purged. I would have expected her to see them segregated to one or other bank, or else plunged into the river, or fearfully risking the bridge.

[45] *Benedicite/Dominus:* this custom, never explicitly enjoined in *EO*, is taken for granted in *EO* 71.17, 86.9, 120.4, 15, etc. The one initiating speech asks the other's blessing with the polite plural imperative, *benedicite*! The response is simply to name 'the Lord' and defer to him for a blessing on the speech.

sordid funds, victuals that should have gone to the many persons my father often received at his hospice. Had this impediment not shut off my entry into paradise, my soul would doubtless have passed straight from death to blissful rest. But now my twenty-eight-day penance is over and, free of all impediment, I am on my way, sure and cheery,[46] to heavenly joy.'

(10c) Ida then asked her how her friends, living and dead, were faring. She replied: 'Of those still living, some are on the path to the kingdom and shall be saved; others are in a perilous state and it is to be feared they may eventually be excluded from entering the heavenly kingdom.' She went on to say: 'Your father and mother are still detained in purgatory: your father for greater punishment, your mother for less. Indeed, your mother's purgation is shortly to end, but your father's will take rather longer to complete.' Ida kept up her questions, asking: 'Do tell me: is God pleased with my own *conversatio*? And how are things between me and the Lord?' With a smile and great serenity of face Margaret answered: 'Oh, how well! How very well!'

(10d) Ida then asked: 'And how long am I linger in this exile?' The other answered: 'This very year you shall pass to the Lord.' And saying this, she vanished from Ida's eyes. Barely six months later, Ida grew seriously ill. She received the eucharistic body of Christ and was anointed with the oil of the sick. Her countenance paled to a deathly hue and nothing else was expected for her but an imminent death. There then arose among the assembled sisters a great lament, as they groaned, sighed and pleaded with the Lord in tearful soliloquies that he deign to prolong the life of his beloved, even though her agony had already begun; that he not take her so soon, not throw them into upheaval and desolation at losing her. Numerous other religious persons too *made prayers to the Lord* for this cause (Acts 12.5), waging, as it were, a whole campaign to urge the Lord gently to spare them. And little wonder that they did so, since their need was so pressing!

(10e) They prayed: '*All-dominant Lord God* (Exod. 34.6), how long will you suffer your daughters to torment themselves with this continual wailing? Kindliest lover of our race, how long will your clemency put on this show of harshness? *Look down from your sanctuary, from your lofty abode in the heavens, upon the prayers of your* handmaids (Antiphon: I Kings 8). You are by nature all good, and you have told us: *ask and it shall be given you* (Matt. 7.7). It is not just that you now repulse your handmaids, but rather that you respond favourably to them in their trouble. This is what our lyricist, *your* holy *servant-boy David* (Acts 4.25), testifies: how he was listened to when he cried to you in tribulation: *To the Lord in the hour of my distress, I called and he answered me* (Ps. 119.1).' What need to quote more? He who is *gentle to all* (Ps. 144.9), he *whose inclination is ever to pity and to pardon* (Collect: the Dead), he who *does the will of those who fear him* (Ps. 144.19), he who *responds favourably to* their *pleading* (Ps. 6.10), he would not suffer these maids of his

---

[46] *Secura et hilaris:* see *Niv* 16d, 34g; *Arn* II. 4b and Goswin's whole theme of 'smiling'.

household to endure tribulation any longer! Rather did he deign to wipe away from their eyes the tears expressive of such grief, using, as it were, the handkerchief of a consolatory promise, as follows.[47]

(10f) That very night, while all were anticipating Ida's passing over from this life, a sister named Sapientia, who had drunk deep of the sapiential spirit (Isa. 11.2), lay awake in bed, grieving intensely as she stayed alert for Ida's passing, which seemed so imminent. But then she heard the Lord's consoling voice: 'Assuage this sadness of yours, dear sister. Let the stream of tears cease flowing from your eyes. This is not the time for my beloved Ida to die. True, nothing in her displeases me and she has found grace in my eyes. Even now she is ready to come to me and take possession of the everlasting delights I have prepared for her. But I am under compulsion from so many prayers, I have been enticed by so many groans and sighs, been forced, as it were, by so many tears. And so I am granting her a *truce* (*RB* Prol. 36) and letting her live on for many a day to come. And this, even despite my recently signifying to another beloved of mine that Ida would pass from this world within the present year. I do this most of all because so many people will still be gaining manifold consolation from Ida's colloquies and from her *conversatio*.' Heeding the voice, the sister left her bed, came and found Ida already sweating and somewhat relieved. She did, in fact, recover from that illness and lived another thirteen years, to the praise and glory of our Lord Jesus Christ and for the edification of the faithful.

11. The Incestuous Man

(11a) One day Christ's far-seeing bride[48] was praying in church, intent as usual on contemplation of heavenly things. Then, by a revelation from the Holy Spirit, she inwardly heard a voice, the way one hears in the heart, and the voice was telling her that a man of her acquaintance had committed the heinous crime of incest with the daughter whom he himself had begotten. Revelation though it was, Ida put scant belief in it, hesitant lest it be an illusion of the devil, meant to rob her of her peace of heart. She was ashamed to mention so disgraceful a thing to the man himself; yet so severely was she afflicted with compassion over so horrible a violation that she was forced to shed abundant tears and to vomit blood from her mouth. Her spirit got no rest in this matter at all until one day when she was again praying in church. It was then that the divine spirit offered her certitude by asserting that the *vision she had seen* (Antiphon: Matt. 17.9) had not been a fantasy and by bidding her have the man fetched for her to confront him with the matter.[49]

---

[47] Sentence omitted by Henriquez. *Sudarium* (handkerchief or 'sweat cloth') is derived from *sudor* (sweat), as in John 20.7 etc; Goswin is punning on Ida's healing sweat.

[48] *Speculativa Christi sponsa*: see *Ab* 8b, n. 44

[49] *Ad se faceret accersiri eumque super hoc conveniret*: Ida's authority over the personnel

(11b) When he had been fetched, she came to the window to speak with him. When she asked how his life stood he began accusing himself of many things, confessing himself a sinner but his *heart was so straitened* and his *countenance so confused* that he cloaked over the sin mentioned above (II Cor. 2.4; Bar. 1.15). Whereupon Ida heaved a sigh and said: *'I grieve over you, my brother;* yes, I grieve severely (II Sam 1.26). Vehement grief is besieging my heart and tormenting it, but your own heart has not yet been touched by such grief!' (II Cor. 10.14). As she said this, two streams of tears began welling up from her eyes as from twin fountains, until the man was in wonderment. Then she told him outright: 'Numerous sins you confess, dear brother, but one still greater you have been too ashamed to confess, namely that, setting aside the fear of your Lord and judge, you do not shrink from wretchedly sinning with your own daughter.'[50] Her words confounded and astounded him, *piercing* his heart like the keenest of *swords* (Luke 2.35). Now he too dissolved into abundant tears and met her upbraiding and exhortation with gestures of repentance. He avowed his disillusionment[51] with that detestable sin and with his other sins too. Then he thanked her, bade her farewell, asked her prayers and blessing and so retraced his steps back where he belonged.

12. Ida's Vision of Two Toads

(12a) A girl who had for a time been living a religious life came to the parlour window at La Ramée and asked leave to speak with Ida. But alas, she did not obtain what she was after,[52] namely to get some consolation from Ida for her soul. The need she had for counsel and help will become clear in what follows. Ida, thanks to a revelation from the Holy Spirit, was aware of the temptation wearying the girl's heart, but she, seeing she could not get what she was after, simply went her way. Some time later, enticed by a shameless fellow, she was drawn away from the path of innocence and soon fell into fornication with him.[53]

---

of La Ramée, and the differing attitudes she takes in differing circumstances, are briefly discussed in the Introduction to the Lives, pp. 8–10 above.

[50] *Peccare non formidas:* was the incest ongoing, or a thing of the past? The verb tenses offer contradictory clues, and Goswin himself seems not to have known the answer. Two elements suggest it was of the remote past: no concern to have the sin confessed to a priest and no precaution against relapse.

[51] *Se resipiscere testatus est:* literally 'to wise up', but with no pejorative tone, more like 'to wax wise again', with overtones of humble repentance. Found in *Arn* II.13b and *Ab* 9c, but nowhere in *RB* and only once in the Vulgate (at II Tim. 2.26).

[52] *Non impetravit quod quaerebat, ut aliquam Ab ea reciperet [...]:* the wording is vague. Perhaps Ida was summoned, but a circumstance, such as a lack of privacy, precluded any intimate exchange. See 12d below.

[53] *Cum eodem in fornicationem lapsa est:* either as a single act or as a stable cohabitation (I

(12b) He was, mind you, numbered among those called ministers of the Lord. But can one really call them ministers of the Lord when *they minister, not to the Lord, but* to their own desires (Rom. 16.18)? To girls of religious life they make a show of loving them in Christ and, like scorpions, are outwardly all smiles, while their hushed whispers shamelessly inject into ears and hearts the poison of a lust that drags into sin.[54]

(12c) And Ida, what action did she take? Did so detestable a deed escape her mind's ever lightsome eyes? Not at all! Rather, by the Lord's revelation she *saw, and, behold,* (Apoc. 4.1), two great toads appeared, a male and a female, with the male visibly mounting the female. By this she understood that that sinful fellow and this sin-laden lass had reached the stage of fornication.[55] A short delay and the male toad went totally crazy, veered away and off he went; but the female, with unwavering gait, made her way to Ida, who tucked her about with her cloak.

(12d) The sequence in the vision was verified in the outcome: first the sinful man *turned aside to his own path* (Isa. 56.11), and then the girl returned to La Ramée and told Sister Ida the story of all that had happened. Ida, in her compassion, avowed that, had the girl spoken with her before sinning, she would never have stumbled into such a pit. Ida then nursed her on *the breast of salutary consolation* (Isa. 66.11) and heartened her for the penance to be done for the sin, though not without warning her to be cautious with herself against such a crime in the future. Greatly comforted, the girl most affectionately commended herself to Ida's prayers and then directed her steps back to her band[56] of religious girls, among whom she never again swerved from upright behavior and the service of the Almighty up to the day of her death.

13. Demons in the Dormitory and Infirmary

(13a) One night, Ida was resting in her dormitory bed, lying awake while the others slept. Suddenly she beheld a demon in the guise of a little bird. It kept diving at one nun in bed there, using every illusion to trick her and contrive some evil against her. Ida, on seeing this, promptly rose from bed and started chasing him about the dormitory; but he, the wretched foe of the human race, kept passing from bed to bed, nastily scrutinizing them all. When he could see no further escape from

---

Cor 5.1). Goswin sees *fornicatio* as a 'pit' (*Niv* 12d; *Arn* II.18a) and a 'whirlpool' (*Niv* 6b, 18a; *Arn* I.1f) and as morally self-perpetuating (*Ab* 15e), though each night's sinning is an evil in itself (*Ab* 18d).

[54] Both scorpions and toads were already famous for their courtship rituals.

[55] *Peccatorem illum cum peccatrice illa peccatum fornicationis admisisse:* the demonstrative adjectives suggest that Ida knew the identity of the male culprit.

[57] *Ad contubernium religiosarum regrediens puellarum:* her 'band' is literally a 'tentmate team' (*Niv* 29b–7; *Arn* I.1d; II.11a, 12a; *Ab* 6i, 14b).

his persecutor, he flew up beside the lamp on the beam, meaning to put out its light. But Ida, like a valiant *virago* (Gen. 2.23), raised her right fist and threatened him not to dare do any such thing. Powerless before her threat, he crashed from the beam to the floor, where she seized on him, trampled him down like worthless mud under her feet and smote away at him with her fist. There he was, evil as ever, but bound now as with a chain. He was impotent to take any form but that of a sorry old hag.[57] Nor could he escape Ida's hand until, after many a slap, he finally got her permission to turn and flee, adjured by the power of the Crucified never to enter the dormitory again.

(13b) Another time Ida was sick and bedridden in the infirmary, and a sister passed by her bed with a demon as companion at her side. At that it was revealed to Ida what kind of temptation that poor little soul was being malignly assailed with. On her way back out of the infirmary, that smutty creature gave the sister a hug, heaved her in the air, whisked her outside and there kept her company, as inseparable as ever. Ida looked on with such compassion that her tears flowed copiously and she vomited blood and her illness grew worse. She was praying for the sister with all her heart's ardent devotion, when the demon, all upset and furious, accosted herself and said: 'Why, oh my enemy, are you bent on taking my friend from me? If you are minded to free her from my snares, the capability is admittedly yours; but short of that, or apart from you, I'm not afraid of anyone's being *able to snatch* her from my *hand*' (John 10.28).

(13c) At this, Ida devoutly made the sign of the cross to rid herself of that turncoat, and, as for the sister, Ida had her summoned and told her of the awesome *vision she had seen* of her (Antiphon: Matt. 17.9). Then with a word of exhortation, in the same gracious style she used with everyone, Ida suggested that the sister, so severely entangled in the inward nets and snares of evil thoughts, not delay to confess her sins to Christ's vicar and cleanse her conscience thereby. Seeing herself found out, the sister did approach the priest. Confessing to him was like imbibing a wholesome potion. Thanks to this potion she could completely vomit up all the filth she had been heaping up in the bottom of her heart by her carelessness and by thinking perverse thoughts. It was in this way that she received healing for her ailing soul.

(13d) Note that the demon appeared often to this warrior-maid of ours, now in the form of a monkey, now of a dog, and in many other shapes besides; but he never managed to inflict any hurt. And little wonder, for the Lord had set Ida atop the citadel of the virtues and had equipped her with a spiritual armour, enabling her to *tread on serpents and scorpions and all the power of that* (Luke 10.19) perdition-bound apostate and *murderer* (John 8.44)! In fact, Ida always had the demon as fully subject and obedient to herself as any disciple to a master.

---

[57] *Neque formam ullam praeter formam vetulae, neque de manibus ejus effugere praevaluit:* a verb is missing after *vetulae*; Henriquez supplies *praetendit* (in the indicative) and similarly I supply 'to take' (in the infinitive).

14. A Departed Soul Freed from Three Demons

(14a) One night Ida was sitting up awake in bed, when suddenly she saw a great fire mounting up towards the dormitory door. She saw it, by God's gift, with her bodily eyes. And, behold, hastening ahead of that fire with rapid stride came a soul. It was a soul in bodily effigy, able to be seen and recognized. And it was hastening towards Ida's bed. She looked again and, behold, just outside the dormitory door, there stood three demons, horrible of appearance and stature, and they were chasing after that soul. Their mouths were open wide to an amazing degree and they were vomiting the terrifying fire mentioned above, which billowed forth as from a furnace. They were about to use the fire pitilessly to torment that pitiable wretch. But by now she had reached Ida's bed and was covering herself in Ida's garments, hoping so to hide somewhat from her malign pursuers. Ida gazed on her with pitiful eye and compassionate affection and said: 'Fear not, poor little soul! You will not *be betrayed into the hands of your foes* (Dan. 3.32)! They will not hurt you nor get the better of you!' Whereupon the victorious warrior-maid set a sign of the cross against those malignant foes, and commanded with all constancy that they not approach the poor trembling soul.

(14b) Then Ida questioned the soul: 'Who are you? and where do you come from?' She replied: 'I am a woman you once knew', (giving her actual name); 'a resident of such-and-such village. Just recently, however, I have *entered upon the way of all flesh* (I Kings 2.2).' Ida recognized her and asked: 'And me? What is it you would like from me?' She replied: 'After my death I was led to *the tribunal of Christ,* that awesome judge (Rom. 14.10, etc.), and, wretch that I am, I was sentenced to purgatorial punishment, with these three demons to torment me with all their harsh ill will. And if you ask why such a sentence, let me tell you it was for some money I once acquired. While still in the body, I purged myself of the acquisition by confessing it, and I began its restitution, but I was delayed awhile and death intervened before I had it restored in full. And, to tell the truth, dear lady, there was a time when I had quite a love for you in the charity of Christ and I took joy in your progress and your holy *conversatio,* hoping to be helped by the patronage of your prayers. This was true while I was in the flesh and it is true again now that I am free from mortal flesh. And the Lord, spotting in me this one trace of good, pronounced as my sentence: "If you can get away from these demons and reach my beloved Ida before they catch up with you, she will surely free you from them."'

(14c) Ida, wishing to avoid any *imputation of presumption* (*RB* 49.9) in undertaking a task so great, so arduous, so far above her religious measure, answered instead: 'Go to your kinswoman, the one sleeping in the third bed down from me, and ask her to pray for you, for she has what it takes to come to your aid.' The soul then passed to her kinswoman's bed and touched her side to rouse her. And she, awakening to the sight of one she knew to have recently died, took fright to her inmost spirit, gave one shout of dread, rolled to her other side and turned her eyes away. The soul took stock of this and, returning to Ida, said: 'You can see for yourself, milady, how my kinswoman cannot stand my presence! So do now, I beg, as the Lord promised me: let me experience you as my helper.'

(14d) Perceiving that this task had been assigned specifically to herself,[58] Ida now turned to the demons where they stood awaiting the outcome and she threatened them thus: 'Unclean spirits, I command you by the power of the Holy Spirit: quit this place and get straight down to hell.' Unable to bear so weighty an adjuring, the demons gave a howl and vanished that very moment, to be *drowned in hell* (Antiphon: St Andrew). As for Ida, she fell prostrate in prayer before the Lord of mercy, begging him in terms of that mercy, to condone whatever purgatorial torment yet remained for that soul. This prayer rose up and *reached the ears of the Lord Sabaoth* (James 5.4), and without delay the soul was freed, was borne aloft, winged her way and passed over to the starry mansions, there to be associated everlastingly with the angels' choirs. *By the Lord was this done,* through his handmaid, *and it is wondrous in our eyes* (Ps. 117.23).

15. Ida Unmasks an Apostate Canon Regular

(15a) *It came to pass on one of those days* (Luke 8.22) that a Cistercian abbess[59] and Ida were seated in a carriage on their way home from Leuven, when they were approached by a youth carrying a sword in his hand.[60] Coming to a halt, the youth engaged in conversation with the lad driving the carriage. Suddenly, with a light-minded gesture, he hopped up and sat on the tongue-beam and began to play the coachman, saying: 'What a charioteer I'd make! How I could drive this carriage!' If in saying such things he could have known the trap about to be set for him, he would not have stayed put!

(15b) Ida, meanwhile, had her eyes closed and her head lightly leaning upon the abbess. Thus, when she first heard the youth speaking and making his show of light heartedness, she had not yet set eyes on him.[61] She nevertheless said to the abbess: 'Milady, let me tell you: this youth was once a monk!' The abbess replied: 'Sister! Watch what you say! You might well regret uttering such a word so rashly!' But Ida insisted: 'Ah no, milady, he was a monk !'

---

[58] *Cernens beata Christi virgo specialiter hoc opus sibi deputatum;* on Ida's authority, see *Niv* 11a, n. 49

[59] *Cum abbatissa quaedam ordinis Cisterciensis et venerabilis Ida pariter [...]:* given Goswin's policy of anonymity, this is probably Ida's own abbess. See *Niv* 2e, n. 18.

[60] *Gladium portans in manu sua:* apparently a weapon, not a workman's blade, but it has no further role in the story.

[61] The carriage was a covered wagon, affording the nuns no view outside. When the General Chapter mentions the wagons of abbesses, it seems less concerned with their being personally out of sight than with the cart itself not being ostentatious: *GC* 1240.9, 1241.44.

(15c) Then she lifted her head, opened her eyes and said: 'Brother, you were once a monk.' But he, wanting a cloak thrown over the thoughtlessness of heart behind his apostasy, answered: 'Wrong! I've never been a monk!' What he had once been was a member of the canons regular under the rule of Saint Augustine, known in Dutch as 'the white monks'. But Ida proved he was lying when she added: 'Here is a sign to prove to you that what I say is true: when you were all lined up[62] to leave the monastery, you stealthily picked up some books and bore them away with you.' He was shocked to hear this and was drenched with shame and grief to be convicted of lying. So he answered: 'It is true, milady; what you assert is true. I and a companion I had, we followed the senseless instability of our hearts and so we left our monastery, that of Nineveh.[63] My companion later betook himself back, not to his own monastery but a cloister of nuns of your order. But myself, to this day, I'm a wayfarer, astray from the path of religion, following the drive of my own will, never ceasing *to wander* hither and yon' (Gen. 4.12). Hearing this and moved to compassion for him, Ida urged him to repent of his transgression and return to his monastery, lest he become like *the dog that went back to its vomit* (II Pet. 2.22). Let him *reach out*, rather, *to what lies ahead* (Philem. 3.13), and with the goodwill of a longsuffering heart, let him follow after Ezekiel's *living creatures, that went and did not turn back* (Ezek. 1.9–14).[64] This he promised he would do. Then he requested the suffrage of her prayers and withdrew.

16. Ida Reassures a Canon Regular about his Sins

(16a) A Premonstratensian canon, a man both religious and fond of doing good, was at one time worn weary in his conscience by a formidable scruple,[65] afraid he

---

[62] *Cum de monasterio fugere deberes:* Goswin often uses *debeo* (I ought to) in this sense of 'I am all lined up to', and the action is often something morally inferior, as here and in *Arn* II.19a and *Ab* 12c, 18d. See also *Niv* 1d; *Arn* II.8a, 19a.

[63] Walter Simons informs me that this is the Premonstratensian monastery of Ninove, located in what is today the rather large Flemish town of the same name, twenty-four kilometres west of Brussels. The secular canons there had adopted the Premonstratensian (or Norbertine) customs in 1138. The *Monasticon Belge* (VII.3, pp. 569–75) sheds no light on this episode of Ida's, and I presume the same is true of a short notice of Brigitte Meijns in *Aken of Jeruzalem? Het ontstaan en de hervorming van de kanonikale instellingen in Vlaanderen tot circa 1155* (Leuven: University Press, 2000), II, pp. 851–52.

[64] Sentence omitted by Henriquez. Same simile from Ezekiel in *Ab* 5a.

[65] *Nimia scrupulositate fatigatus [...] tam grandis turbasset scrupulositas, inspiratio omnipotentis dni [...] vulneravit cor ejus:* Henriquez, in whose day *scrupulositas* had a bad press, bowdlerizes here. He changes the first use of it to *curiositate*, and for the second use, he suppresses the *inspiratio omnipotentis Domini*, with the result that it is no longer the Holy Spirit who wounds the heart, but rather the stormy scruple itself. But for Goswin, this

had not confessed his sins sufficiently. This scruple had greatly ruffled his mind already for quite a time, when an inspiration came from the Lord almighty and wounded his heart with the vehemence of sharp arrow, and he seemed at the moment to hear a voice deep within his spirit telling him: 'Pay a visit, brother; a visit to Sister Ida of La Ramée! She will give you certitude about your sins.' But being tied down to his task at the monastery, he could not easily get permission to leave for a visit to her. Hence he grew somewhat gloomy and anxious while thinking of what to do.

(16b) But then too, outside in the world, he had his mother, who had been paying frequent visits to La Ramée and exchanging intimate words with Sister Ida. On one such visit, the Holy Spirit had informed Ida of the son's anxiety, and so she told the mother: 'Pay a visit, madam,[66] to your son, for he is quite anxious and has been desiring a word with myself.'

(16c) She went to her son as bidden and asked: 'Dear son, why have you kept it hidden from me, this *anguish of heart* that has worn you weary these many days?' (II Cor 2.4). But he, imagining no one knew what he had been suffering, apart from God, the inescapable *scrutinizer of hearts* (Wisd. 1.6), answered: 'What anguish, mother? What affliction of mine?' The mother replied: 'I know it, dear son; I know that you are much tormented in conscience, for I have heard it from Lady Ida, the nun at La Ramée.' At this he marvelled and avowed that God's marvellous handmaid had told the truth.

(16d) Eventually, with permission, the canon came to La Ramée and confided to Ida his discomfort of mind. She, with gracious liberality, *comforted him in the Lord and in the power of his strength* (Eph. 6.10). This she did by putting the sleeve of her cowl in his hand and saying: 'Notice and acknowledge this! Just as truly as you are hanging on to my cowl-sleeve in your hand, equally truly *have your sins been let go of* by the Lord' (Matt. 9.5).[67] This *reply, received* as if *from* God (Luke 2.26), cheered him greatly. He thanked Ida for consoling him, set aside the sadness clouding his heart and made his way back to his own monastery.

(16e) If any should ask why, both here and elsewhere, the names of persons included in our narrative are kept under seal of silence, let them know this has been done deliberately. For if the names were widely published in the ears of many, the persons, if still alive, might either be put to shame by the vituperation of their evil, or else unsuitably uplifted by the praises of their good.[68]

'scrupulosity' is not the indecision of a small-minded cleric; it is the unease of a dedicated soul on the threshold of a spiritual breakthrough. See the notes on *Niv* 4a; 29b–1; *Arn* I.7c and *Ab* 10b; as also Cawley, 'Ida of Nivelles, Cistercian Nun', pp. 311–313.

[66] *Perge, o mulier:* Arnulf similarly addresses a matron *(o mulier)* in *Arn* II.20d.

[67] *Sicut verum esse attendis [...] tenes in manu tua [...] sic verum esse agnoscas remissa tibi [...]:* I rephrase slightly to stress the pedagogy: Ida does not first offer verbal comfort and follow up with a gesture; but first a non-verbal gesture and then its exegesis. What counts is not the outer feel of the wool but the inner strain of clinging and the relief of letting go.

[68] On such anonymity, see *Niv* 2e, n. 18.

17. A Religious Woman's Three Defects

(17a) An abbess[69] and Ida once arrived at a place where a number of religious women were dwelling. One of these, who was outstanding for lofty contemplation of heavenly things and for being comforted with various revelations from the Lord, spoke to Ida in the secrecy of a whisper and asked: 'Please tell me, milady: has anything been revealed to you about me, anything needing rebuke?'[70] Ida replied: 'Yes, something that you know and that I know too, namely what a burden weighs on you with those three defects of yours! For the first defect, you will *sojourn away from the Lord* in this exile all the longer (II Cor. 5.6); for the second, you will be tormented with longer punishments in purgatory; for the third, you will have a lesser glory in heaven, unless you make all the effort you can to correct all three defects.'[71] Ida then brought the defects, one by one, into the open and added: 'These defects you have confessed only to the abbot,[72] though you have had each of them in you for such and such length of time.'

(17b) This prompted the woman to tacit thoughts and suspicions about the abbot she had confessed to, how he had perhaps revealed the confession to Ida. Instantly Ida *responded to that thought* (Luke 5.22), as if peering deep within her, eye to eye: 'Do not think such things, my dear, nor harbour such suspicions about that abbot. He is a man of religion and would never disclose that confession. No, it was the Lord's *good spirit, the all-powerful, the all-surveying* (Luke 11.13; Wisd. 7.23), who revealed inwardly to my own spirit the three topics I told you of. And he it is who has just now revealed to me the thoughts you were thinking.' At this, the woman was dumbfounded and could not but rest assured[73] that the Holy Spirit was speaking openly through Ida's mouth.

(17c) She then asked Ida's counsel about her three defects and got from her the same counsel she had already had from the abbot. And from then on, while making

---

[69] Presumably Ida's own abbess.

[70] Ida may seem haughty; but it is a whispered exchange, transmitted to us by the woman herself. It stresses the frankness to enhance the marvel. See *Niv* 33f, n. 189.

[71] Not a platitude, but a device for hushing up the woman's identity and her defects. Ida was doubtless frank and gave her fellow mystic a powerful call to renewal of effort. See again *Niv* 2e, n. 18.

[72] *Soli tantummodo abbati:* not just an abbot but the abbot, namely the 'Father Immediate', the Abbot of Villers. If we date this mission after Ida's profession (1218), the abbot could be Walter (1214–21), but more probably William (1221–27).

[73] *Nihilque aliud potuit cognoscere/scire/conjicere de his quae audierat nisi [...]:* the key verb, in the infinitive, is unsure. B (fol. 15va) has *cognoscere;* A (fol. 160^r) has *scire,* both of which are synonyms of 'knowing'. Henriquez caters to the context and uses the better-fitting term *conjicere* (p. 242: conjecture). The reality is surely close to that of John 4.39–42: a holy person gazes into a mind less holy, and so elicits strength to face a truth never to be doubted again.

efforts to correct herself, she magnified the Lord for enriching his bride with such a privileged grace for clearly discerning the status and thoughts of others. Accordingly, after lengthy colloquies *about the salvation of souls* and heavenly topics,[74] both the abbess and Ida bade farewell and returned to their monastery.

(17d) Who would not be dumbfounded at these things, so great, so worthy of remembrance? For the hidden mind to peer into the consciences of others and discern their sins and virtues, their progress and their slips! How rare today are those who receive such gifts! *Who, then, will tell the Lord's mighty deeds?* Let such a one *recount all the praises* of his handmaid, since her praises are *praises of God* (Ps. 105.2)! For, indeed, whatever measure of grace Ida drew up from the fountain of supreme goodness in the bucket of her good will, she poured it all back into the fountain from which she drew it. From her wondrous God came the wondrous visions she saw and unto him she lived her wondrous life. *Not so are* the hypocrites, *not so* (Ps. 1.4)! Seduced by the demons' illusions they *see vain things and they divine lying messages* (Ezek. 13.6), imagining all the while that what they are seeing are true visions and not illusory.

(17e)[75] But you, oh virgin of Christ, *blessed among* nuns (Luke 1.42), enact what you are enacting; perform what you are performing. *Let it not be of concern to you* if anyone mock and ridicule you (Luke 10.40), or reckon as feigned that sleep of love by which you are often led into an *estrangement of mind* (II Macc. 5.17),[76] or if anyone judge your visions to be mere fantasies. Run rather to your Christ *amid glory and ignobility, amid infamy and good fame* (II Cor. 6.8), since whatever adversity you suffer for your Beloved will all be imputed to you as deserving of glory.

18. The Book of Life, the Mountaintop, and Hell

(18a) One night as Ida lay in her bed, behold, *a great brightness shone about her* (Luke 2.9; Acts 22.6), and amid this brightness there was shown to her a great book, in which not a few painted images could be seen. She contemplated the book with lengthy gaze, and as she gazed she wondered. Then the Holy Spirit, with whom she was on such familiar terms, taught her by a revelation that the book she was seeing was *the book of life* (Apoc. 3.5). She began reading it and found the names of many

---

[74] Conversational topics approved by *GC* 1233.6, etc. See also *Niv* 23a; 27a; *Arn* I.7b; 12a.

[75] For an almost identical apology, see *Arn* I.10d; *Ab* 9d.

[76] *In mentis alienationem:* one of Goswin's phrases for expressing Ida's mystical life, as mentioned in *Niv* Prol. c. He uses several variants, but always with the basic root *alienat-*. To enable the reader to recognize this sameness of root behind the variety of my translations, I earmark it each time with a reference to its nearest biblical equivalent, II Macc. 5.17: *ita alienatus mente Antiochus,* even though this politico–military context is anything but mystical!

persons written, some already dead and others still alive in this world. A pleasant vision it was, *a divine consolation gladdening her soul* (Ps. 93.19), for in it she received reliable indications about the salvation of several who had risked being sucked into the whirlpool of sin and about whose outcome she had earlier been in doubt.

(18b) On the other hand, there were some she found inscribed in the book, whom she now approached to disclose to them what she had seen. Thundering with salutary reproof, she terrified them about their living in false security and she exhorted them to *put off the old man and put on the new* (Col. 3.9; Eph. 4.24; *EO* 102.41–43) and to offer to the Lord a service marked by purity. Those who took her warnings did indeed *throw off the works of darkness* (Rom. 13.12) and woke up from the sleep of death; and thereafter their *conversatio* was marked by adequate fidelity.[77]

(18c) Another time too, when Ida was intent on her heavenly contemplation and relishing its agreeable savours, *the hand of the Lord came upon her* (Ezek. 1.3) and she melted inwardly before the divine fire, *as wax melts before its fire* (Ps. 67.3). Estranged (II Macc. 5.17) from her bodily senses, she was raptured away in spirit. And behold, she was shown in a vision a great castle, strongly fortified and of wondrous construction, situated atop a lofty mountain. As she gazed in wonderment at the beauty and loftiness of that castle, it was revealed to her that this was the place of eternal bliss. Down at the bottom there began a road, a slender road, for climbing up to the castle's gate. And around about were many footpaths, converging as short cuts to the castle. Many people were heading along the footpaths, some climbing quickly, others more slowly, but all eventually getting into the delightful interior of that castle. It was amid great gladness and exultation that they entered, though with great labour too; and the persons making the ascent by those pathways seemed relatively few and visibly poor and ignoble.

(18d) And how shall I interpret these pathways, if not as the institutions under the rules of the holy fathers Benedict, Augustine, Basil, and certain others? In these, as on so many slender pathways, many are travelling. Some go quicker, namely those *fervent in the Spirit* (Acts 18.25; Rom. 12.11); while others go more tardily, namely those somewhat remiss in *regular discipline* (*RB* 60.5). Yet they all reach that fortified place of bliss supreme.

(18e) Ida looked again and, behold, to the left of the castle lay a valley vast and deep. Towards its entry ran a highway wide enough for two great armies of opposing peoples to encounter one another. And down this road went the descent to the very depths of that valley, so deep and horrible. Ida was informed that further down its course lay hell itself, where, after the bodily resurrection, the reprobate will be tormented for ever and ever. On this highway were lots of persons venerable in countenance and garb, wondrously handsome in outward adornment, playing to one another on timbrels, lutes and other such instruments and *making festivity* (Ps.

---

[77] On the anonymity and generalization, again see *Niv* 2e, n.18.

75.11), as if hastening along to a high banquet of dainties. Yes, down, down they went, into the depths of that valley; and *down, down they sank,* all of them, *into hell* (Antiphon: St Andrew; Isa. 14.13).

(18f) Ida gazed long upon these two throngs, and reviewed both the one climbing to the fortress and other heading down to the valley. Among them she recognized some persons still living. It seemed to her that those entering the fortress were few as compared with those being absorbed into the whirlpool of hell, since these latter were as many *as the sands of the seashore,* altogether *impossible to count* (Gen. 22.17).

(18g) What are you doing, you wretched lovers of the world? What are you doing? Why be so senseless as to run open-eyed into hell, hastening down to death, down to everlasting death? *Your laughter will be mingled with grief, and mourning will overtake the last stages of your joys* (Prov. 14.13). If only it were possible for you to see now what hell is like, you would not allow yourselves to be caught in the net *of the devil's snares* (I Tim. 3.7), snares of one who wants you as eternal companions in his torments. Do you want to know what hell is like? Hell is broad without measure, deep without bottom; it is full of intolerably scorching heat, full of stench beyond compare. There you have misery, darkness, sheer disorder; there you have everlasting horror. There good knows no hope; evil knows no despair. Such is hell, and a thousand times worse; such, indeed, that no one's thought or wording can adequately grasp it. *Return, therefore,* you wretched *prevaricators; return to the heart* (Isa. 46.8)! *Take fright at torments* so horrible (*RB* 4.45)! Acknowledge the God who is your Saviour, the one who redeemed you from these very torments, there *on the gibbet of the cross* (Antiphon: St Andrew), and who has promised instead to give you everlasting delights, if only you will *be converted to him with all your heart* (Joel 2.12) and keep *the law of his commandments* to the end (Eph. 2.15).

19. The Christ Child Seen at Pentecost Dinner

(19a) On that sacred day when the Church recalls with veneration the Holy Spirit's longed-for coming upon the apostles,[78] Ida reverently approached the altar and received the lifegiving body and blood of the Lord. Yes, it was *a bread she could eat with gladness and a wine she could drink with joy, since her deeds were pleasing to her God* (Eccles. 9.7)! From such abundance and such a sweetly agreeable savour, Ida's soul was inebriated, and so much so, in fact, that it became a great toil for her even to go to choir and attend the hours.

(19b) When high mass and sext were over and Ida had entered the refectory with the others and begun to eat, suddenly *an immense brightness shone around her*

---

[78] Pentecost: Goswin the cantor names the feast in phrases even more fulsome than mine. See also *Niv* 33b.

(Luke 2.9; Acts 22.6) and her eyes were dazzled by its radiance. She covered her face with the sleeve of her cowl to avoid its glare, but in vain, since even thus it had access to her eyes! The others kept eating but Ida could not eat. Then, all unexpectedly, before her there stood her Beloved, *dressed in white, but himself all ruddy*, whom she had *chosen from among thousands* (Cant. 5.10): namely, Christ the Lord, in the guise of a twelve-year boy (Luke 2.42). So gracious, so lovable was he in his comeliness that she never was able to put that gracious comeliness and good cheer into words.[79] The garment he wore seemed deep sea-blue in colour; his face, wondrously lightsome and venerable, *like a flame of fire; the hairs of his head*, curly and coloured to a medium hue (Dan. 7.9; Apoc. 1.14).

(19c)[80] In coming to visit his beloved bride, did this child have no concern for the other nuns? Was it Ida alone that he met with? Ida alone that he smiled upon? Ida alone that he let bask under his gracious gaze?[81] Indeed not! Rather did he, from time to time, do the rounds of the refectory, coming along now to this sister and now to that, presenting himself one short moment at a time to each, only the more often to come back to Ida herself and stand *face to face* before her (Gen. 32.30) more lingeringly than for the rest. And deservedly so, since her love was more ardent and her desire more vehement, and therefore she allured God more frequently than did the others.[82] In *clinging to God* (Ps. 72.28) she was drawing God to herself and at the same time her whole self was *being drawn* to God by God (John 6.44, 12.32). As for the sisters, they, in the material refectory, were being refreshed with bodily foodstuffs; but Ida, in the refectory of love, was being refreshed and pastured on spiritual fare.[83] It should be noted too that, throughout the whole meal Ida never lacked the sweet boy's joyous and luminous presence.

(19d) When the sister reader put an end to the reading, this vision too received its ending. For it then seemed to Ida that the roof of the refectory opened up and that, amid the same brightness as at his arrival, the sweet lad betook himself on high. She followed after him with the sweet gaze of her eyes but very shortly the heavens flung wide and received him, and so she could see him no longer. At that moment the

---

[79] *Tanta pulchritudine gratiosus et amabilis quod modum ejus pulchritudinis gratiosae et hilaritatis [...]:* Henriquez omits the note of 'hilarity', perhaps finding it unseemly in Christ.

[80] Henriquez mysteriously replaces this paragraph with a brief assertion of the opposite: 'His regard fell uniquely upon his beloved bride, whom he had come to visit, and thus it in no way took in the other nuns who happened to be in the refectory.' Goswin's original reflects a theme he also touches on in the selflessly cenobitic visions of Abundus. See notes on *Ab* 11d and 11e.

[81] *Assistens arridebat [...] aspectu refovebat:* regarding *refovere*. See *Niv* 7a, n. 36.

[82] *Eum prae caeteris frequentissime alliciebat:* the boy Abundus similarly 'allures the Redeemer's grace' upon himself (*Ab* 3a).

[83] Henriquez's text does include this sentence, though modified to his context. See *Ab* 7c, n. 38.

sisters were entering the church together to *give to the bounteous giver of all good things their thanks for all of his benefits* (Ritual: meal prayers), but Ida remained behind in the refectory, incapable of entering the church with them.

(19e) And little wonder, seeing how magnificently she had been comforted by the vision shown to her, and how vehemently inebriated she was with the *cup of spiced wine* (Cant. 8.2) received from her Beloved, and how sated she was inwardly *with such an abundance so agreeably savoured* (Ps. 144.7). With all this she could not cope, short of losing all bodily strength, just as it had been for that *man of desires*, the holy Daniel (Dan. 10.5–18). Yes, Daniel writes of how he beheld the Lord in the guise of a man of wondrous outward mien, and of how, trembling in a stupor, he declared to him: '*My Lord, at the sight of you my joints are all undone*, my courage fails *and nothing of strength is left in me at all; my very breathing is cut short* (ibid. 16).' There you have it: the prophet's own witness that in this vision no strength was left in him at all!

(19f) Let all pay attention to this and blush, all those rude and truly rustic persons, men as well as women, whose heart is too gross, if I may say so, ever to receive from heaven any such grace, so copious, so agreeable, so apt to lift them to a loftier mind and leave them destitute of bodily strength. Instead, they mock persons holier than themselves and worthier of God. Those who have such a grace, they ridicule and do not fear to detract. In their reckoning, this falling asleep is not through excess of contemplation, and this impotence is not a *withdrawal* from the body (II. Macc. 5.17). but it is all a weighing down under a lethargic, even a pretended, slumber! Still, *what business of mine is it to judge* others' consciences (I Cor. 5.12)? Rather, let the individuals judge themselves, as many as are aware of their own guilt on this score, and let them not be boldly finding fault with the Lord's omnipotence when he, in accord with the good pleasure of his will,[84] deigns to impart to some of his faithful a grace more privileged than to the rest.

20. The Eucharist during the Harvest

(20a) Harvest time was at hand and part of the community of La Ramée journeyed with its prioress to the grange of Kerkom[85] to harvest the crops; *and* Sister Ida *was with them* (Gen. 12.4). As they lingered there more than the eight days,[86] Ida became quite anxious and gloomy at being deferred longer than usual from receiving

---

[84] *Secundum beneplacitum voluntatis suae:* this expression, found also in *Arn* I.9c, is nowhere found as such in the Bible; but all its terms are found close together in a passage of Ephesians (1.5–11). For two similar re-splicings see *Niv* 21d and 27c *(misericordiae suae* and *beneplacitum gratiae suae).*

[85] Doubtless the same place as in *Niv* 2a, retained as a grange.

[86] For more such rich eucharistic themes, see the notes on *Niv* 29b–4.

the Lord's body and blood. This occasioned in her an intolerable *languishing of love and of desire* (Cant. 2.5; 5.8), forcing upon her little body such a faintness that she could not follow the others out to work. Moreover, as often as she heard the bells ringing in nearby churches, her heart's grief was stirred anew, as if stricken with *wound upon wound* (Job 16.15).[87]

(20b) The Lord, wishing to provide a suitable medicine for Ida's languor, permitted a little old woman residing in a nearby village to come down with an illness so grave that she lost the power of speech and was, in the reckoning of all present, already at death's door. Once when the nuns had to pass by the house where she lay ill, Ida was with them and her compassion went out to the ailing woman. So she told her sisters: 'In yonder house a neighbour woman[88] lies ill; please, do let's go and visit her.' Entering the house they found the woman deathly pale of face. By now the illness was so intense that it had deprived her of all use of her tongue. But they appealed to the Lord for her with many devout prayers, that, though she seemed to be drawing her very last breath, he would nevertheless give her back her lost power of speech. Their prayer penetrated the heavens and reached the ears of the Lord, and so *the dumb one spoke* (Matt. 9.33). Then Ida urged the woman to summon a priest to give her the Eucharist; which she accordingly did.

(20c) The priest came, bringing the pyx with the Lord's body in it. He communicated the woman with only a particle of a host, fearing she would be unable to swallow a whole one. As it was, the severe illness prevented her masticating or swallowing even the particle, and the priest had to withdraw it from her mouth, still intact. He was quite disappointed to find that the nourishment he had brought for the woman's soul at so late a stage had been brought in vain.[89] But when Ida saw this, she conceived the hope for herself to gain a taste of that saving food, then and there, with God *bringing a gladness to her own soul, commensurate with the anxiety in her heart* (Ps. 93.19). So she spoke up and asked the priest: 'Please, milord, do not be upset, since here am I, quite ready and only too willing to receive my Lord's body, and with no difficulty at all!' The priest approved the request and communicated her.

(20d) Receiving the sacrament and being visited by the Lord, Ida was not *defrauded of her desire* (Ps. 77.30) but was immediately imbued with heavenly

---

[87] How many bells could Ida hear? A modern map shows within a five kilometre radius of Kerkom: five functioning religious houses, three railroad stations and some twelve named settlements. If such hamlets had churches in her day, there would have been many bells.

[88] *In hac domo vicina mulier quaedam:* the anonymity probably stems from Goswin; the woman was perhaps an old friend of the nuns, whom it was appropriate for them to visit. On Ida's authoritative leadership, see *Niv* 11a, n. 49.

[89] *Tristis admodum factus [...] alimoniam [...] quam [...] sero [...] obtulit [...] frustra se attulissse perpendit:* had this priest been pastor to the nuns in their pre-Cistercian days? His 'sadness', in any case, is not motivated by the woman's deprivation but the nuns' having bothered him in vain. Is Goswin hushing up a backlog of other negative emotions in their regard?

grace. So thrilling was the flow of that grace down to her soul from the aqueduct of love that her bodily strength gave out and her *mind overflowed unto God* (II Cor. 5.13). Dropping headlong[90] to the floor, for a long time she could not be budged from the spot. One of the nuns, one who loved her a great deal in Christ and who took pride in her saintly strivings and virtues, now remained behind with her as her solicitous guardian. And when Ida finally *came back to herself* (Acts 12.11), she was soon over her earlier mysterious languor, that hunger after this most sacred of foods, this holy flesh of the Lord. And with her bodily strength thus restored, from then on she got back to work with her sisters.

(20e)[91] From the foregoing one can weigh up what great confounding shame the holy devotion of this virgin should inculcate to the many endowed with the priestly office, especially those in the garb of religion, who approach the altar day by day and present anew to God the Father the sacred and holy passion of his only begotten for the salvation of the Church, but who rush through those sweet words recited in the canon with a dry heart and without devotion, as they neglect to prepare and hallow that heart for the Lord with at least a little contrition, both before receiving the Lord's body and blood and afterwards too. Perhaps they will reply: 'We are poor folk and have no such copious supply of grace as had Christ's handmaid Ida.' This I do not deny to be true. Nevertheless, since there should be no approaching the table of the altar without bringing the sacrifice of a pious devotion, I justly reckon it should be deputed to their negligence and torpor that *they approach* so tepidly *to draw water* from the wellspring of tears, and that they *find no water there and so bring their jars away empty* (Jer. 14.3). Rather, let such persons petition the Lord for the grace of devotion, and what they have petitioned they will surely attain, if they but cry to the Lord wholeheartedly and with all insistence, and if their wills be at no point discordant with the will of God.

21. The Christ Child at the Christmas Masses

(21a) Once on that most sacred night when *the Lord of majesty* (Ps. 28.3) *deigned to be born of the Virgin* (Antiphon: Christmas), bodily illness confined Ida to the infirmary regime.[92] When vigils were over she sat out in the cloister, waiting

---

[90] *Soloque procumbens [...] moveri non posset:* this could mean either an ecstatic 'flopping headlong to the ground', as in *Niv* 26d, 29b–4, or else a wide-awake prostration as simple as kneeling, as in *Niv* 35biv, *Ab* 3b.

[91] Goswin's wordiness here reveals so much of his personality that my translation mimics it much closer than usual. Henriquez suppresses the whole passage.

[92] *In infirmitorio cogebat detineri:* for participation in the liturgy by those in the infirmary, see *EO* 91 and 92. Ida was attending the Christmas hours in church, seated behind the choir.

expectantly for the Lord to send her a grace-filled blessing.[93] Then, at the first mass, when the celebrant was elevating the host, she saw in his hand a little boy, newborn it seemed and truly fair beyond the beauty of little ones anywhere.

(21b) But on seeing him, *there came over her a fear and a trembling* (Ps. 54.6), because never had she had any longing to see him in that human guise. She was concerned lest her faith prove incomplete and fall short of believing in the wondrous mystery of this sacrament and thus lessen her merit with God, inasmuch as human reason, or rather human sight, would be providing experiential evidence. But the Lord knew full well the firmness of her faith and he did not let her be upset for long, for at that very moment he inwardly bade her rid her mind of all such scruples. Reassured thus by the Lord, her attention went to the priest who was singing the mass and to the status of his soul, as she watched his manner of dividing that little boy *into the three parts* (*EO* 53.100), and to his trembling reverence as he consumed that delightful and salutary banquet-fare. She lingered on in the cloister,[94] seated again at the same spot, until the end of lauds, inwardly relishing the sweetness of that wondrous vision, and ever jubilantly joyous of mind.

(21c) After lauds had been sung, Ida washed her hands and rinsed the inside of her mouth,[95] and so entered the church with the other infirm nuns (*EO* 4.10), and sat down in a corner to the rear of the choir. Then, while the second mass was being sung, she again beheld in the priest's hands that little boy, so refined and so gracious of countenance, whose inner joyousness showed outwardly like an overflow of honey.

(21d) When the other infirm sisters were going in procession up to the altar to communicate (*EO* 57 and 58), Ida was somewhat terrified and *withdrew her foot* (Gregory, *Dial* II Prol. 1), lest she be caught within the procession still unable to ingest that living babe.[96] Hence with ardent yearning she begged her Beloved to show the goodwill of his mercy by tempering these wondrous visions of his sacramental body and enabling her to partake of it unimpaired and to welcome his whole self into her entrails and into the very marrow of her soul.[97] She lingered at

---

[93] *Expectans a Domino sibi transmitti gratiae benedictionem:* another aspect of the 'send me God' theme, from which I draw my title for Goswin's works. See Introduction to the Lives, pp. 20–22 above.

[94] *In eodem autem loco claustri in quo residebat. [...] usque ad finem laudum permansit:* a chilly spot on Christmas night for someone sick, but the community as a whole was expected to sit there for the intervals between the Christmas offices and masses. Individually, however, they also had the option of warming up in the calefactory, though not that of going back to bed (*EO* 4).

[95] I do not find this personal oral ablution mentioned elsewhere.

[96] The nuns' embarrassment over this elaborate ritual is illustrated in *Lew* 19.

[97] *Et totum totis animae suae medullis inviscerare posset.* Literally: 'be able to inviscerate the whole him with the total marrows of her soul'. See *Arn* I.3b, n. 21.

the same spot until high mass. Even then, just as in the earlier masses, she again beheld the little boy, slightly taller this time in stature. He was coming down from the altar to offer her his embrace and his kiss, and in his sweet warm mercy he was delightfully surrendering himself to be embraced and kissed by her in return. And then in a gracious whisper he told her: 'Oh, sweet friend, I have been showing you my humanity such as it underlies the form of the bread. This I have done, not from any doubt about your faith or your readiness to believe, but from my own wish to let you know with what love, what concern, what zeal I regard yourself!' Hearing this, Ida answered in the silence of her thoughts: 'But oh, my sweetest one, what gratitude, what joyous exultation would fill my inmost heart if you would instead show me how praiseworthy, how love worthy you are in your divinity.' The sweet boy replied to her thought saying: 'Do not ask such things of me, daughter, since no mortal can, in this life, come to know what I am like in my divinity. For the present, peace to you, oh friend of peace; have peace in me; for when *I make all things new* and gather you to myself (Apoc. 21.5), then can you come to know the glory of my divinity *face to face* (Gen. 32.30).'

(21e) Then, lest her sisters be scandalized that on a day of such solemnity she not receive Christ's sacrament, she asked her beloved Jesus[98] to deign to allow her the possibility of receiving his body without difficulty. Accordingly, the vision came to an end and she approached the altar with the rest of her sisters and received with all peace the very author of peace. And the wondrously *abundant and agreeable savour* (Ps. 144.7) which divinely inebriated her that day, was to persevere in her soul up until Candlemas.

22. A Night of Story-telling at Liège

(22a) One day Ida and a certain nun were travelling together and stopped off at Liège on business. In that city, as in a garden rich with flowers and fruits, dwell numerous religious virgins, as so many *friends* of God *among the daughters of Babylon* (Zech. 2.7), so many *lilies there among the thorns* (Cant. 2.2). They arrived when *day was declining towards evening* (Luke 24.29), and so they *fulfilled their vesper liturgy* (*RB* 16.2; 17.7) and the Office of the Dead.[99] Then, as it was the

---

[98] *Rogavit dilectum suum Jesum:* for Goswin's rather rare uses of the name Jesus, see *Niv* 2e, n. 16; *Niv* 29b–3; *Arn* II.5b; *Ab* 11e. The less emotionally-charged name, 'Christ', can come without supportive terms of reverence or endearment, and can be written as a simple 'x', imitating the Greek monogram. The grammatical ending is then added as a superscript. But not so here, as Ida invokes Jesus in prayer, she embellishes the name with a term of affection (beloved). In B fol. 19[vb] *Jesus* is spelt out in full, and its Greek monogram worked in: *ihesum*. In A fol. 164[r] there is simply monogram *ihm* (the 'm' being for the grammatical case) but an extra term of affection is slipped in: the adjective *pium*, (her *loving, kind,* beloved, Jesus).

[99] Office of the Dead: on weekdays that were not feasts of saints, the major hours of the

Tuesday after the first Sunday of Lent and they had accordingly fasted, they now dined, using Lenten fare. After the meal, with the sun sinking and the day drawing to a close, they were advised by the residents of the house to go to bed and revive their weary bodies with slumber. Accordingly, *they climbed to the upstairs chamber* (Josh. 2.6; I Sam. 9.25) and sat down together by the beds made up for them. *A candle was lit* (*RB* 22.4), measuring a mere finger's length and was affixed to the wall. They were to say compline[100] and get straight into bed to take their rest, but instead, that nun made a request of her colleague, Ida:[101] would she, for edification, expand a little on some of *the good things of the Lord* with which Mother Grace[102] had enriched her (Ps. 26.23)? Ida could scarcely refuse her request, as they were on particularly familiar terms. So she *opened her mouth* (Matt. 5.2) and began to *bring wondrous things to light* (Ecclus. 24.31), in such words as the following:

(22b) 'I was once spending some days in the infirmary, incapacitated by a bodily weakness but also by the sheer strength of a love, of an insatiable longing, for the supreme divinity. *My heart grew hot within me and in my innermost core a fire burst forth* (Ps. 38.4), *not a consuming* fire *but an enlightening* and inflaming one (Antiphon: Pentecost). Suddenly there stood before me a man, venerable of mien and robed in a cloak of purest white. From his mouth issued a fluid, appetizing to look at, white in colour, seemingly comparable to *the manna* (Exod. 16.31). This man was gazing upon me with a gracious familiarity and, his eyes all starry,[103] he said: "My dearest, you have been longing vehemently to learn as much as is allowable of the unspeakable knowledge of my divinity and to relish its sweetness. I in turn shall most willingly fulfill that burning desire of your soul: I shall instil and let drip bountifully into your heart this tastiest of honeycombs, which is that of my divinity."[104] 'This said, he took some of the fluid issuing from his mouth and dripped it into my own. Immediately my soul was inwardly lit up with an awareness of the blessed Trinity, so great, so sweet, so divine, that the level of acquaintanceship granted me that day has remained in me ever since.'

(22c) 'An abundance of light then streamed from the inexhaustible fountain of

---

liturgy were followed by the recitation of extra psalms, readings and prayers as a suffrage for deceased benefactors.

[100] Compline is the last hour of the day, and after it there is strict silence *(RB* 42). The two sisters accordingly postpone their joint recitation of this hour in order to prolong their spiritual exchange. See *Arn* I.7b, n. 39.

[101] *Contubernalem suam Idam*: see Cawley, 'Mulieres Religiosae', p. 105.

[102] *Gratia mater ditaverat*: concerning grace as mother, see *Niv* 3b, n. 24.

[103] *Stellantibus oculis*: omitted by Henriquez. Goswin's rich vocabulary of light and sight deserves study.

[104] *Super omnia sapidissimum divinitatis meae favum cordi tuo ad cumulum instillabo*: Goswin's theme of grace as a fluid (see *Niv* 4a, n. 24). Goswin also makes frequent use of the expression *ad cumulum* (unto a heaping).

lightsomeness on high and came into my inward parts, filling them so wondrously full as to make me totally lightsome, outwardly as well as inwardly. From then on, whenever I have been in the pitch dark of night and have lacked illumination borrowed from other sources, I have been able to see with my own bodily eyes, always having adequate light, in fact, to read a book or to do any task, since my hands and my face glow for me with rays quite as serviceable for my eyesight as the sunbeams of *the great luminary* itself (Gen. 1.16).[105] Moreover, on the occasion of this grace and for a long time after it, I was given from heaven the ability to look into the status of many persons.'

(22d) All this, Ida recounted to that nun, along with many another charismatic grace of the kind she abounded in, and she kept it up even till the signal for matins.[106] Her face was aflame and her eyes radiant, as befitted a disciple of the Holy Spirit, while she freely proffered from the bookcase[107] of her inmost heart these wondrous pronouncements, these words of fire, words *sweeter than honey and its comb* (Ps. 18.11). The nun sitting beside her kept *gazing upon that countenance as upon the countenance of an angel* (Antiphon: St Stephen), and she greatly *marvelled at the things* she heard *from that mouth* (Luke 4.22), but she also feared that from so honey-laden a colloquy Ida's body might suffer a fainting spell.

(22e) At the signal for matins, Ida looked over at the candle, still alight. It had been so short when first set on the wall and had since provided light throughout that long night. So she smiled a little and remarked: 'The candle's light will soon be failing!'[108] The nun replied: 'How can you say such a thing? Myself, I trust in the Lord, and readily presume upon his loving-kindness, that this candle will amply provide us with its own little light however long we keep up this grace-filled colloquy about the joyous contemplation of the true light and the intimate relish and agreeable savour of *the good things of the land of the living* (Ps. 26.13).' With that, they said compline; and then they also recited vigils and lauds by the light of that same candle.

(22f) Let no one doubt that the candle's providing light so long a time without going out stemmed from the holiness of that colloquy and especially from the

---

[105] A similar luminosity is attributed to Abbot Conrad of Villers in *Chronica* 9 (Martène-Durand, 1276A; Waitz, p. 199.1) where it is cited from Thomas of Cantimpré, who in turn gives Abbot William of Villers as his oral source (Thomas, *BUA* 1.9.3). Similarly in Caesarius, *DM* 8.22, p. 100, a nun reads the psalms by the glow from the arm of a crucifix.

[106] *Donec ad matutinas pulsaretur:* Goswin normally refers to the night office as vigils, but when speaking of non-Cistercian churches, he calls the first hour available to early risers by its popular name, matins (*Niv* 1h, *Arn* I.1bc).

[107] *De intimo cordis armariolo:* this is a diminutive of the *armarium,* the cupboard in the cloister where the books were kept, and of which cantors, such as Goswin, had charge (*EO* 115.33). Henriquez omits the word.

[108] *Quia cito deficeret:* a gentle pun: in the Latin, Ida's fainting and the candle's failing are expressed by one and the same word, *defectum/deficeret.* The nun fears, but Ida smiles.

privileged merits of Ida. Nor let anyone doubt that this case is comparable to that of Joshua, when he prayed and *the sun stood still, motionless in the midst of the sky, not declining towards its setting until* Israel had gained victory *over its enemies* (Josh. 10.13).

(22g) If any find it incredible that Ida be even outwardly so lightsome that she saw clearly in the night, let them answer this question. Take the sun, whose light our bodies enjoy in this world alone: is its light greater than the light divine, by which souls are enlightened inwardly, or is it less? Suppose they say the sun's light is greater than the light divine (which it is altogether too absurd to believe or to say). Then they seem obviously opposed to God and his omnipotence. The same holds for the eye: the soul's eye, by which we see spiritual things, is readily proved far more lightsome than that of the body, by which we see bodily things. Suppose, on the contrary, that they claim the sun's light bears no comparison with the light divine, which penetrates and illuminates all things, lofty or lowly, intimate or wide open. In that case they will doubtless easily grasp, and not find incredible, that God, who is the supreme light of lights, should, by his own wondrous light, have rendered his beloved handmaid both inwardly and outwardly lightsome.

23. Mary Offers her Son to Ida

(23a) A Cistercian abbot, a man of religion and faithful friend of all the best,[109] came to La Ramée one day and began a devout and holy colloquy with Ida. They were speaking together *of the salvation of souls* (*GC* 1233.6) and the charismatic graces of the Almighty, when suddenly grace *rushed upon* Ida (Luke 1.35) and she was so *wounded with charity* (Cant. 4.9) as to be unable to bear the abundance. She instantly became *destitute* of her *bodily strength* (Dan. 10.8–17), and, *beside herself in mind* (Ps. 30.23), gently fell into her customary form of sleep, right in front of all who were sitting there. Some reached out to touch her and bring her back to herself, but there was no waking her at all; indeed, she remained in the same spot, enraptured, until compline, after which the sisters took her to the infirmary. In fact, she remained under the impact of that sweet experience all next day until vespers, ever celebrating in the inner joy of her soul *a Sabbath kept delicate* (Isa. 58.13) amid heavenly festivity with her God.

(23b) On the third day, this abbot was celebrating mass in a church near Liège, and during the canon, he prayed to his saving Lord for Ida with earnest, humble devotion of heart. His prayer took wings and came before the Lord God of hosts. On that same day Ida was inwardly enlightened with an immense brightness, and within the brightness there suddenly appeared she whom all mortals must venerate, the

---

[109] *Omnium bonorum amicus fidelis:* the *bonorum* could be either masculine or neuter, 'of all good persons' or 'of all good projects'. See *Niv* 1f, n. 8.

queen of mercy, the Virgin Mary. In her motherly arms she was carrying *the blessed fruit of her womb,* Jesus Christ. And she now bent *those eyes of her mercy* (Antiphon: *Salve Regina*) towards Ida and, with all sweet and tender warmth, proffered her son to her, and said: 'O sweet friend of my son, receive this son of mine from my hands, sent to you by your beloved abbot,[110] who spoke to you the day before yesterday. Receive him, I say, and set him on your lap and *make festivity* with him (Ps. 75.11), enjoying all the embraces and kisses you have longed for.' Ida receiving the child, embraced him *tightly* in her bosom and began *kissing* him (Gen. 33.4; *Niv* 2e) ceaselessly with insatiable desire. Meanwhile, the queen of glory sat back on the bedside chair and gazed for some time upon the delightful game they were playing together in their sweet and holy familiarity.

(23c) Finally, when the joyous kissing and embracing was over, the sweet theotokos[111] received her son back from Ida's hands and instantly disappeared. The great heavenly *abundance of agreeable savor* (Ps. 144.7), of which Ida partook that hour, was to remain in her soul as a lingering bounty for two more months to come.

24. The Christ Child Seen Catching Ida's Tears

(24a) *A certain religious and God-fearing man* (Acts 10.1–2) was once praying devoutly before a crucifix in a church, when, all unexpectedly, there appeared to him a boy. It was then revealed to him that this was *the fairest of the children of men* (Ps. 44.3), Christ Jesus. He forthwith prostrated himself on the ground and in all humility adored him and made this petition: that he be freed from an importunate temptation, which had been wearying him severely.

(24b) The boy turned to him and said: 'Not just now, son; as I first have to *make festivity* (Ps. 75.11) in the holy familiarity of love with my friend Ida of Nivelles, the nun at La Ramée.' When he had said this, Ida herself promptly appeared on the scene with the sweet boy and, casting upon him a regard of remarkable friendliness,[112] began shedding great streams of tears from her eyes. The boy wished to show how acceptable he found the shedding of such tears, welling up from the

---

[110] *Quem abbas dilectus tuus [...] mittit:* literally, 'an abbot, a beloved of yours [...]'; but I translate 'your beloved abbot', since it is hard to imagine any abbot other than the immediate higher superior of her house so singling her out. It is probably William (see *Niv* 17a, n. 72). Also notice the theme of 'send me God', both in the present episode and in *Niv* 21a, n. 93.

[111] *Dulcissima theotokos:* Henriquez replaces this Greek title with the simple Latin *virgo.*

[112] *Coepitque amicabili vultu quodam coram eo [...]:* I treat this strange *quodam* as equivalent to an indefinite article, based on the nearest Goswinian parallels: *eodem vultu; eodem animo laetabundus* (*Arn* II.3d), *quasi in quodam speculo lucidissimo redivivam* (*Niv* Prol. d), *sed quodam, ut ita dicam, sudario consolatoriae promissionis* (*Niv* 10e), *quasi jocosum quoddam verbum protulit* (*Niv* 27a). Also, *coram eo* is ambiguous: does it mean friendliness to Jesus or to the seer? I retain the ambiguity.

love of so warm a heart. And so there instantly appeared in his hands a golden basin, which he held to Ida's face to catch the tears she wept, and with them he bathed his own gracious face. Two angels likewise appeared instantly and rendered service to the boy, having in their hands a towel of the whitest linen with which to wipe his tear-dampened face.[113]

(24c) Oh what a sweet and joyous spectacle the Lord kindly granted that man to gaze upon! Little wonder if his *soul was then filled with fat and marrow* (Ps. 62.6) to behold himself thus *set within a paradise of delights* (Gen. 2.15). Deservedly could he cry out: 'I am *seeing the Lord face to face,* and I hope that, thanks to him, *my soul shall be saved!*' (Gen. 32.30). This delightful vision of the gracious familiarity Christ's beloved self showed to Ida[114] afforded the man such great progress and such magnificent encouragement that he was freed, from that moment on, of all the temptation that had wearied him.

(24d) When the vision was over, the man *desired with a very* great *desire* (Luke 22.15) to see this Ida, so beloved by the Lord. Indeed, *his soul refused to be consoled* (Ps. 76.3) short of *his heart's desire* being speedily fulfilled in this regard (Ps. 20.3). Now, just at that time a new altar had been set up for La Ramée's newly built basilica, and it had been arranged, with the pope's permission, for an indulgence of forty days to be granted anyone prayerfully visiting this altar. So this man thought to journey to La Ramée with this prayerful intent and also to see Ida and enjoy the privilege of a holy colloquy with her. At that moment the nuns were gathered and were standing beside that newly consecrated altar, *like an encampment in battle array* (Cant. 6.3, 9), with Sister Ida out in front in the lead, carrying the banner of religion and ranking in the central position of all.[115] The man surveyed them all diligently and spotted her as the one he was seeking. He had seen her in his vision, though never in the flesh, and *now he recognized her on sight* (Tob. 11.6).

---

[113] *Gratiosam faciem suam rigabat [...] faciem ejus madidam extergebant:* I read this as meaning that Jesus bathed Jesus's face; but the rules for use of *suus* and *ejus* would equally allow it to mean that Ida bathed Ida's face. Henriquez takes this latter sense, perhaps because Jesus already has his hands full holding the basin. In his interpretation, the adjective 'gracious', applies to Ida's face rather than Jesus's; to avoid this Henriquez simply suppressed the adjective (though he retains the equivalent adjective 'blessed' in *Niv* 24e below). The confusion could have arisen in the course of the story's oral transmission. In Goswin's written form Jesus does have his hands full with the basin, but why are there two angels involved? How do two angels simultaneously manipulate one towel? I suggest that in the story's earlier oral form one of the angels took over the basin at the moment Jesus wished to begin bathing himself. The story is retold in *Niv* 24e, where two participles (*suscipientem [...] rigantem*) are used to indicate that Jesus catches the tears and bathes his face. The tears were certainly Ida's and this time the rules for *suus/ejus* make the face that of Jesus, confirming my interpretation.

[114] *Gratiosa familiaritate dilecti ad dilectam.*

[115] *Primiceria [...] vexillum religionis [...]* : extending the military image of Canticles, Goswin makes Ida 'pacesetter' of the march as well as bearer of the processional cross.

(24e) Approaching one of the religious girls who had come along from outside, the man inquired if the particular sister was Ida of Nivelles. She replied: 'Yes, milord'. When at length the community retired inside the enclosure, this man of God approached the guest window and had the window sister summon Sister Ida for him. He then recounted to her how he had been praying in a church and had, to his great astonishment and wonder, beheld her and seen her weeping and seen the Lord Jesus, in the guise of a boy, catching her tears in a basin of gold, and bathing his own blessed face therein. Yes, and a pair of angels on hand, to dry his face with the whitest of towels. He went on to add: 'And when I saw all this, milady, I was filled with so agreeable a savour of heavenly grace that I was freed, utterly freed there and then, from a certain temptation that had been very burdensome to me.'

(24f) *The Lord is* indeed *good to those who hope in him, to the* soul *that seeks him* (Lam. 3.25). Yes, he graciously used this vision both to free his servant from that bothersome temptation and to afford him a clear idea of the holy religion found in Ida. And lest any should doubt that the foregoing is all true, the man himself manifested it all to a nun of La Ramée named Christina, who is still alive to this day. Anyone who wishes to learn the truth of the matter can do so from her.[116]

25. A Friend Familiar with Mary and with Ida

(25a) One day Ida was raptured away in spirit and had a divine revelation about a person familiar and very dear to herself.[117] She saw how this person was undergoing the same affective experience that she herself was used to, and was being drawn aloft into the sacred recesses of the divine majesty in the same way she herself was often plunged into the abyss of divine light. Likewise, the person in question had a similar revelation regarding Sister Ida, a revelation in which it was also seen that a love, greater or less, was stirring many holy souls and was drawing them up to the superlatively delightful mansion of the divine majesty on high. Some of these souls are still alive in the flesh, though others have been loosed from it.

(25b) This person was also sometimes allowed to sense within her spirit that wondrously ardent love which was the prerogative of the Virgin Mary in her

---

[116] Henriquez (p. 261) omits the whole of 24f. The MS A fol. 166ᵛ omits what follows after Christina's name; B fol. 22ᵛᵃ, copied earlier, and presumably locally, retains the invitation for the reader to meet Christina and confirm the story in person.

[117] This friend could well be Beatrice of Nazareth. Reypens prints a critical edition of this chapter (his Appendix 6, pp. 218–20). To help anyone wishing to explore that identity, I keep the translation very literal. One point is clear: the friend is a woman. Goswin tries to hide even her sex behind the ambivalent feminine word *persona*. As long as the pronouns, adjectives and participles take their form from *persona*, we have no clue as to the sex; but in several passages, all in direct speech, *persona* disappears and the pronouns take their femininity from the sex of the friend. See the notes on *Niv* 25d, below.

ineffable loving of the supreme and indivisible Trinity. After first receiving this sense of the surpassing fullness of love in the blessed Virgin's soul, this person's veneration for her knew no bounds, for she was at once the Lord's blessed mother, the Trinity's special lover and the same Trinity's especially beloved.

(25c) This venerable person is still alive to this day, and supposes she will remain on in this life for a long time yet. She is known to be a spiritual person of holy *conversatio*, and has been privileged to know many of her beloved Ida's secrets and revelations, some of which deserve to be told here. This person and Ida had a special mindfulness of each other, their hearts being linked together in Christ's love, and they gave ample proof of *having but one heart and one soul* in Christ (Acts 4.32). The Lord himself testifies how such familiar and holy love pleases God, for he says in the Gospel: *'Amen I say to you: if two of you reach consensus on earth over asking for anything, it will be done for them by my heavenly Father'* (Matt. 18.19).

(25d) One day this memorable person was sitting in a place somewhat apart and was as usual turning over in her heart the agreeable memory of her beloved Ida. Thereupon, the Virgin Mary appeared within her spirit, showing herself in a wondrous manner marked by most ardent charity. This most blessed Virgin, humblest of all virgins, addressed the person in a sweet whisper: 'I wish from now on to be as special to your heart as Ida of Nivelles has been. I wish you to take the same attitude towards me that you used to take[118] towards Ida. And that same attitude you took those many days towards Ida, I shall take towards yourself.[119] And thus shall we be covenanted together[120] by a perpetual bond of indissoluble charity. Me you shall love as the supremely loved [mother] of your own beloved [Groom], and I shall greatly love you as the beloved [bride][121] of my own beloved [Son]. And Ida too will be as one of us.' When she heard this, she did not become elated or attribute the revelation to her own merits; yet neither did she believe she was at all under illusion, knowing for certain that the spirit of her Beloved was steadying her on every side. So in wholehearted recourse to her Beloved, she broke out into these

---

[118] *Qualem te exhibere solebas Idae:* Henriquez changes the imperfect, *solebas*, to the present, *soles*, which is more consistent with the rest of the chapter. The imperfect could imply that Ida was already dead at the time of the vision; but it could equally envisage a past which had been interrupted by a geographical separation of the two friends, as would befit the case of Beatrice.

[119] *Ego quoque [me] talem [tibi] exhibebo:* for the confusion in the manuscripts regarding the pronouns; see the critical edition of this chapter in Reypens, p. 219, lines 35–41, with the footnotes. I take the sense from the context, as does he.

[120] *Erimusque [...] foederatae:* our Lady uses the feminine plural to qualify the implicit pronoun 'we'. Latin only allows that when none of the persons embraced by the pronoun are masculine.

[121] The nouns, 'mother, groom, bride', are not expressed in the Latin. I insert them simply to convey the gender of each Latin participle.

words: 'Thank you, my Beloved; thank you for choosing me to be your friend,[122] along with that most special friend of your heart: along with her, indeed, albeit in a manner and a measure far short of hers!'

(25e) That this vision was not a matter of fantasy is made clear by several pieces of evidence given by our Lady, the Virgin Mary, both to Sister Ida and to this person.[123]

(25f) Another time this person was pouring out her prayer to the Lord on behalf of her beloved Ida, and she fell to doing what is habitual with holy folk, namely, she started affectionately praising the Lord from her inmost heart for all the good things he so frequently did for Ida, his bride. The Lord replied thus: 'Why praise me for what I do for my beloved, or rather for my own very heart? Should any be praised for loving their own heart or soul, things they love so naturally that they cannot not love them? And is Ida not my own very heart and my soul?' On hearing this, the person was wondrously encouraged, but she missed the nuance of the reply received and so went ahead with the prayer she had begun: 'Please, Lord, in your *loving kindness, safeguard* this love *for all eternity* (I Chron. 29.18), which you so graciously show towards your dear Ida and which she so ardently reciprocates towards yourself.' Then the Lord replied: 'Why keep pushing me with these many pleas that I safeguard my own heart? Surely person and heart cannot be separated like that!'

(25g) When she heard this, defeated by the magnitude of the Lord's *abundantly agreeable savour* (Ps. 144.7), she was forced to interrupt her prayer and simply admire in blissful silence the wondrous holiness of the venerable Ida, unto the praise of her Bridegroom, our Lord Jesus Christ, *who is above all things God blessed unto all ages. Amen* (Rom. 9.5).

26. A Doubting Priest Comes to Belief in Ida

(26a) A certain priest, *a religious* enough *and God-loving man* (Acts 10.2), had been hearing the fame of Ida's wondrous *conversatio* from the many who made much of her, but he put no trust in their good, holy and praiseworthy testimonials. He was still lingering in this doubtfulness when a Cistercian abbess urged him to pay Ida a visit. He eventually did betake himself to her, but only to scrutinize if she were of such holiness as many claimed. Of all this Ida was aware, thanks to her ever-familiar spirit of the Lord, and so when she spoke to him at the window, she said but little and he went home with little or no inspiration from her holy exchange. He

---

[122] *Me [...] pariter in amicam eligere:* the femininity of *amicam* comes uniquely from the sex of *me.* Indeed, *persona* is completely absent from this paragraph, and all the feminines seem to stem from the seer's sex.

[123] Henriquez omits this paragraph.

returned a second and a third time, but remained ever with the same ambiguity within his scarcely-inspired heart.

(26b) Coming home, however, from the third visit, he was celebrating a mass in some church in the hope that this ambivalence might be removed from his heart. During the canon of this mass he had a vision of Ida's gracious face and heard the Lord's voice telling him: 'Behold, son: just as I now show you Ida's outward face, so shall I show you her inward state. Thus will you acknowledge that my beloved Ida is like a fountain issuing ceaselessly from the earth, so that anyone coming to it to draw water may draw abundantly and unimpeded. *Such is my beloved* Ida (Cant. 16): whoever come to her weighed down and confined by any kind of sorrow and trouble can draw from her and obtain for themselves whatever consoling relief they need. And all of this by no means diminishes the grace of devotion within her but rather increases it, and cumulatively so.' Thereupon it was divinely revealed to him with how great a compassion Ida drew upon herself everyone's every calamity, and with how appropriate a consolation she relieved all the needs of all who flocked to her, and how, making herself approachable for all, she proved to be most ardent in her charity towards God and towards all.

(26c) The priest was astounded at *the vision he had seen* (Antiphon: Second Sunday in Lent) and at *the word of grace* he had heard (Luke 4.22), and so he continued that mass to the end with all devotion and, for many a day thereafter, enjoyed a more abundant measure of grace than he had been used to. His *soul*, however, *refused to be consoled* (Ps. 76.3) unless he could shortly see again the face shown him at the altar. And so, as if impatient of delay, he returned to her. But upon arrival, he found her sick.[124]

(26d) When once more able to set eyes on her, he seemed to be seeing her glorified, glorified both in soul and in body. Instantly he dropped to the floor, *destitute of bodily strength, beside himself in mind* (Dan. 10.8–17; Acts 11.5; *Niv* 20d[87]) and raptured aloft to heaven. And Ida, on seeing this, likewise perceived him as if glorified in soul and body, and she too was instantly *estranged* from her bodily senses (II Macc. 5.17) and raptured aloft to heaven, where both now mutually beheld one another and celebrated *festivity together* (Ps. 75.11).

(e) He, after a space, returned from that sweet slumber into which he had dozed from the first taste of that heavenly sweetness, being absorbed, as it were, into God. But now, as he bade farewell to all present and said he was leaving, those seated around put the question why he had not spoken to Ida. He replied: 'I did speak to her and spoke to my heart's content, though only in the honey-laden whisper used in heaven by the souls of the saints.' Having thus experienced Ida's abundance of heavenly grace, in which he had earlier disbelieved, he now *set out on his way*

---

[124] *Invenitque eam aegrotantem. Cumque oculos defixisset in eam:* the verb *invenire* means literally 'to come upon', and is the ordinary Latin equivalent for 'to find'; hence, my double translation of it as 'arrival' and 'finding'. The verb *defigere* implies a penetrating gaze. See *Arn* II.18 c.

rejoicing (Acts 8.39). Shortly afterwards Ida too awoke from her most restful sleep of love, and she too was questioned by those sitting around why she had not spoken to the man of God, who had come simply out of a holy love for her. She gave the same reply: 'I did speak to him, quite as much as I pleased, up in heaven above!'

(26f) *Blessed*, therefore, *is God in his gifts, and holy in all his* revelations. He both removed this scruple and doubt from his servant's heart, for him to believe in Ida's holy and religious devotion, and he wondrously revealed to him the edifying wonders of the grace that was hers.

27. The Priests of Maagdendaal and Thuin

(27a) Another priest, quite religious and, in fact, *a most ardent lover of religion and of poverty* (*EC* II.6),[125] had acquired a holy familiarity with Ida and had long desired to experience in his soul some little comforting grace of devotion stemming from his relationship with her.[126] Thus it came about one day, at Maagdendaal, that he and the local abbess were speaking privately about *the good things of the Lord* (Ps. 26.13) and *about the salvation of souls* (*GC* 1233.6), when suddenly he swooned for a while, as if in ecstasy.

(27b) Waking from that slumber after a little, he came out jokingly in the hearing of the astonished abbess, and said: 'Had I bow and arrow at hand, I'd shoot her back for shooting me!' The abbess, dumbfounded at such a word, asked what he meant, and he replied: 'Lady Ida has received the Lord's body today and has, as usual, passed over into *estrangement* from the senses (II Macc. 5.17) and been caught up in ecstasy into heaven. And there she has poured out to the Lord on my behalf the sweet utterance of a devoted prayer.'

(27c) Having said that, he again became *beside himself in mind* (Acts 11.5) and was in turn caught up into heaven. There he found his beloved Ida standing in the presence of *the Lord of hosts and King of glory* (Ps. 23.10), the same Lord who says: *'I love those who love me, and those who watch for me each morning shall find me'* (Prov. 8.17). And now, in accord with the good pleasure of his grace, he was telling his bride Ida: 'My daughter, give this man a part of the grace I have allotted so abundantly and gratuitously and cumulatively to yourself.' When the priest heard this word, this *goodly, agreeable* word (Wisd. 12.1), this *word for the gladdening of his heart* (Jer. 15.16), he took his place on bended knee before the Lord and in full

---

[125] *Plurimum religiosus, religionisque ac paupertatis amator ardentissimus:* the epithet, taken from *EC*, suggests the priest was also a Cistercian monk. His awareness of Ida and his intimacy with this abbess would befit a chaplain at Maagdendaal. This was the convent of Beatrice of Nazareth throughout her friendship with Ida. It was located five kilometres north-east of Tienen (Tirlemont).

[126] *Diu ex parte ejusdem sentire desideravit in anima sua confortativam aliquantulae devotionis gratiam:* again the theme of 'send me God.' See *Niv* 21a, n. 23.

view of Ida herself, and bowed his head as for a blessing. Ida too had been cheered by the Lord's word of command and now readily approached the priest and *kissed* him *with the holy kiss* (Rom. 16.16). This kissing was a pressing of spirit to spirit, not of mouth to mouth, since the vision was spiritual, not corporeal. At that moment it seemed to the man of God that his own spirit became so inseparably joined to Ida's spirit as to become, through an *unfeigned charity, one single spirit in the Lord* (I Cor. 7.17; II Cor. 6.6). No sooner had he received that sweet kiss than he also received from the kindly Lord's abundance a new and larger measure of grace, a new and larger manner of thinking about God. The measure and manner were those that had long enriched Ida, and she had made use of them as her own capacity allowed.[127]

(27d) When he finally made his way back from *the region of the living* (Ps. 114.9), he openly confessed to the abbess that never in all his life had he received such abundance of divine awareness as he experienced on the occasion of that wondrous vision, in any writings,[128] any sermons, any masses he had celebrated or secret colloquies he had held with God. The abbess, for her part, later made an inquiry and learned that Ida had indeed been enraptured in spirit that day, just as she had heard the man of God declare.

(27e) It is worth relating what befell another priest who was loved by Ida and who loved her in return. Once on the joyous feast of Christmas, there in the village of Thuin, he was at the altar, vested and about to offer up to God the Father the sacrificial body and blood of the Lord for the salvation of the people. He had reached the canon and the words *qui pridie quam pateretur* and had elevated the host, when Sister Ida, albeit a day's journey away in body, was present with him by having a vision of him in spirit. In it she beheld *a pillar of fire* (Exod. 13.21) descending upon his head and hovering over him until the end of the mass. Simultaneously the Holy Spirit poured into the priest's own heart fiery sparks from on high. *His entrails grew warm within him* (Ps. 38.4) and he inwardly tasted an agreeably honeyed spiritual savor, *meted out to him* (II Cor. 10.13) by the distributor of heaven's gifts. Indeed, I would say, had he been allowed any longer taste of that savor he would have thought himself carried him off to some *paradise of delights* (Gen. 2.8).

(27f) Back in those days there was in this priest's heart somewhat of a disposition to maintain a fitting abundance in such temporal goods as were needful to him. This was not out of any cupidity *for having* (RB 59.3), as happens with many, but from simple, honest planning, such as good, discerning men frequently engage in with a view to a more liberal giving of gifts. But God now so disposed that this will was abolished from his heart, thanks to the grace that came over him in such abundance

---

[127] *Modum gratiae et cogitationis ad Deum quo ancilla Christi ditata et, secundum capacitatem suam, usa fuerat, copiosa Domini benignitate abundanter accepit:* Latin uses one word, *modus,* where English would use two: we speak of a 'measure' of grace and a 'manner' of thinking, but Goswin can speak more concisely of a *modus gratiae et cogitationis ad Deum.*

[128] *Neque in scripturis:* the comprehensive listing suggests we use a generic term embracing divine Scriptures and patristic writings.

and thanks also to Ida's merits.

(27g) When he later came along to La Ramée,[129] Ida confided to him the story of her vision, point by point, how in his celebrating mass he had experienced a consolation, and how she had seen a pillar of fire descending upon his head. He in turn attributed nothing of what he heard to any merits of his, but everything to the goodness and grace of the supreme and bountiful giver. Then, feeling most generously encouraged, he took his leave of her.

28. The Seven Gifts; The Trinity; Maagdendaal

(28a) Ida at one time *desired with* a very great *desire* (Luke 22.15) to be enlightened[130] inwardly on the seven gifts of the Holy Spirit. Accordingly at mass, once, on Saint Andrew's Day, which that year was also the first day of Advent,[131] she had a vision. She was sitting at a spot in the church, and when the priest at the altar elevated the Lord's most holy body, she saw that host wondrously changed to the colour the sun takes on at dawn, all reddish and warm, and from it there issued seven rays of light, all of which beamed down into the banquet-hall of her own pure heart.

(28b) This magnificent visitation by the Holy Spirit instantly filled Ida so full of enlightenment that, from that day on, she could rejoice in having received the seven gifts in unusual abundance. Nor was it only that day, but every day throughout Advent, whether at mass, at work, at conversation or wherever she might be, she was time and again divinely visited with these great charismatic graces. For half a year after this, the grace she had received gave her mind more capacity, her will more promptitude, her imagination more subtlety *in searching out the hidden things of God* (I Cor. 9.2) as she ruminated and contemplated spiritual topics. The same heavenly gift enabled her to recognize the status of soul in various persons, the good as well as the evil.

(28c) On another occasion, during the canon of the mass, she had a wondrous, unutterable vision of the three persons, one in substance, gathered together upon the

---

[129] *Igitur cum [...] postmodum venisset:* unlike the two previous stories, this one gives no hint that the priest's mystical experience had conscious reference to Ida or prompted his forthcoming visit to her. Thus the visit could have been a routine one, made partly for the purpose of offering the nuns an alms, especially inasmuch as almsgiving was touched upon in his Christmas experience.

[130] *Septem Sancti Spiritus donis illustrari:* Goswin always uses *illustrare* in the sense of 'floodlighting' a cognitive faculty, with emphasis on a dazzling clarity, rather than on any helpful, 'illustrative' exemplification, in the modern sense.

[131] In Ida's time at La Ramée St Andrew's Day coincided with the first Sunday of Advent only in 1225 and 1231. The latter year is ruled out, since her death came just eleven days after the feast, and that fact would surely be mentioned.

altar. This was not, of course, under the form of bread, since it was not the Trinity that became incarnate (a belief alien to the Catholic faith), but simply the three persons as they co-operated in the Lord's incarnation and now co-operate in the lifegiving sacrament of his body, it being established beyond doubt that the works of the Trinity are inseparable.

(28d) For many days thereafter, wherever she might be while a mass was being celebrated, she could glimpse the holy Trinity's presence on the altar just as she had that time. In this sweet vision, she received from God considerable consolation, though never was she able to put entirely into words what she had then intuited of that divine, inscrutable mystery. She used to say that, just as sealing wax pressed with a hot signet ring retains the image of the signet, so too with her soul: smeared with the sealing glue of love, her soul was so pressed upon by the holy Trinity that *her spirit became one spirit with the Lord* (I Cor. 6.17).[132]

(28e) On the feast of Saints Philip and James,[133] Ida was beside herself in rapture. This occurred in the presence of a certain nun and it lasted from the time of the mass until after sext, when the nuns took their dinner together. That nun, however, did not leave Ida but remained on, awaiting her return from on high.

(28f) When she awoke from her slumber she was asked by that nun where she had been, and she replied that she had been raptured into the pure divinity and had, in that rapture, tasted and sensed the blessed Trinity in a measure beyond that of any experience she had previously perceived. She also did her best to explain how it had been revealed to her that the essence of *the Father was in the Son, that of the Son in the Father* and that of the Holy Spirit in them both.[134] She added that the blessed Trinity had deigned to converse with her in the gentle whisperings of a bridegroom to his bride, and that she too had spoken to the blessed Trinity with all the sweet friendliness of a bride to her groom.[135]

(28g) After giving this account, she again became *beside herself in mind* (Acts. 11.5), and she remained in the same condition as before, up until none. Eventually returning and being asked by her guardian where she had been, she replied: 'I was at

---

[132] *Sicut cera impressa sigillo sigilli retinet imaginem, sic ejus anima Sanctae Trinitati glutino ardentissimi amoris impressa erat, ita ut spiritus ejus unus cum Domino spiritus efficeretur:* this analogy limps badly: the *cera impressa sigillo* (wax stamped by a seal) seems meant to parallel the *anima impressa glutino* (soul stamped by a [liquid] glue). One possible sense would be this: an ordinary seal, once it has made its impression, is removed from the wax. But, given Ida's strongly adhesive love, once the holy Trinity had made its impression, it could not be removed. Stamp and stamped stayed stuck together.

[133] Until recent years this feast was on 1 May.

[134] Echo of John 14.10, the Gospel passage read on St Philip's Day.

[135] *Tamquam dilectum cum dilecta [...] dilectam cum dilecto:* for my intrusion of bridal terms, see *Niv* 25d, n. 121.

Maagdendaal, where I saw the bishop blessing the newcomers.[136] The status of each of them was revealed to me; and in token of that, here are their names [...].' Thereupon she cited the names one by one, adding that, while they were being blessed, the savour of heavenly grace which they inwardly tasted had been so impressive that they were *deprived of their bodily strength* (Dan. 10.8–17) and collapsed to the floor. And though this, swooning had come upon each of them, it occurred to different individuals in different times and places, coming either during the ceremony or afterwards; and Ida was able to tell, in orderly fashion, the location of each one's swooning.

(28h) Not long afterwards, a certain lay brother of Maagdendaal[137] came to La Ramée and was met by the nun already mentioned. She inquired of him diligently about what she had heard of the nuns of Maagdendaal, and it proved that everything had happened just as she had heard.

29. Ida's Eight Topics of Contemplation[138]

(29a) Thus far I have presented but little of Ida's thinking, but few of the things she used to contemplate, but few of the virtues she practised. And so it seems fitting, before coming to her glorious passing, to give a brief description of her thoughtful, many-sided contemplation, her virtuous charity and compassion, her virtuous humility, obedience and patience. Let me offer these things to the readers and listeners for their souls' consolation, offer them in the manner of dainty dishes, of fragrant specialties, of tasty titbits, such as diners relish once the body has been basically nourished.

(29b–1)[139] Ida was still young when she took to gathering her thoughts together and dwelling lengthily, at times, on her sins, giving them diligent consideration and investigation. For in order to *flee from the adder's face* (Ecclus. 21.2), she ever

---

[136] *Quemdam episcopum novitias benedicentem:* in Cistercian parlance, 'blessing novices' usually means receiving their profession, a thing done by the abbot. The episcopal blessing of these virgins would be another ceremony, one usually performed at (or soon after) the age of twenty-five. This same ceremony at Maagdendaal is described in *Beat* I.7, 76–77. Goswin gives the impression that Ida's vision of the ceremony came on the same day as the Trinitarian experience described above, whereas *Beat* sets it one week later, on Ascension Day, 8 May 1225.

[137] This may have been Beatrice's own father, but her Life does not mention such a journey on his part.

[138] *De octo considerationibus, vel potius contemplationibus ejus:* note the plural form. Thematically, Goswin uses roughly the same sequence for the 'considerations' as he did for the anecdotes in the body of the Life. To highlight this, some of the following notes point to the series of chapters being echoed in each 'consideration'. Henriquez omits 29a.

[139] This paragraph echoes the self-critical themes in *Niv* 1c–4a.

avoided wantonness, steered away from unseemly talk, rose above worldly-mindedness, scrutinized her heart with all watchfulness[140] and was as cautious of occasions for sin as of a deadly poison. And since good minds fear blame *where there is no* blame (Ps. 13.5), Ida had a custom of *always reckoning herself accountable* (*RB* 7.64) for any sins she heard mentioned in sermons or other spoken exchanges, and she would, in the wondrous scrupulosity of her heart, confess them to Christ's vicar without delay.[141]

(29b–2)[142] The second thing she considered was the sins of others, for she desired their salvation with all her heart. Often she laboured for this even beyond her ability, adding prayer upon prayer and tears upon tears. And, by counsel and example, she called numbers of them back to the way of salvation.

(29b–3)[143] The third thing she considered, or rather contemplated, was the Lord's saving cross and passion. This she did in the bitterness of her heart and the exceeding anguish of her grief, and not only before receiving the habit of the Order but afterwards too,[144] often saying within her heart for only God and herself to hear: 'Sweetest Jesus, what have you done to have to endure so harsh a death on a cross? Surely you did not deserve such a death! Not at all, my Lord! Rather the cause of your death was my iniquity; your wounds were made by my sins. I, my wretched self, committed what you bore the lash for; what I *stole, you paid the price for* (Ps. 68.5).' Such words as these Ida daily repeated, in her mind as on her lips. Nor could she look upon the image of the cross, or listen to others speaking of Christ's passion, without feeling great bitterness. To rid her mind of this cloud of gloom in favour of clear-skied spiritual joy, she alternated such thoughts with remembrance of that most ardent love whose sheer immensity and spontaneous force drove the Lord of majesty to allow himself *to be given over into the hands of the hurtful and undergo the torment of the cross* (Collect: Triduum). In thus *thinking thoughts of peace and not*

---

[140] *Omni custodia cor suum scrutans:* I give a rather bland translation for this powerful Goswinian echo of Ps. 7.10, because while the reading is unmistakable in B fol. 26ᵛᵃ, the key word *scrutans* (searching) is replaced in A fol. 170ʳ by the more usual *servans* (maintaining). Henriquez skips straight from the 'adder's face' to 'was as cautious' (p. 272).

[141] For *scrupulositas* see *Niv* 16a, n. 65. For confessing to the *Christi vicarius*, see *Niv* 1h, n. 10.

[142] Echoes of themes of fraternal correction in *Niv* 4b–18g.

[143] Surprisingly, this item on the passion has no real echoes from earlier chapters, except vaguely in *Niv* 9b.

[144] *Antequam scilicet [...] quin etiam postea:* the *scilicet* and *quin etiam* make Passion-centred prayer sound normal early in life but surprising later on. Some nuns did, in fact, move from the humanity of Christ towards his divinity. See *Lew* 21. See also Cawley 'Our Lady and the Nuns and Monks of Thirteenth-Century Belgium', pp. 102–04. Nevertheless, I would presume that a nun as compassionate as Ida, and as responsive to seasons and sermons, would surely linger often on Christ's sufferings, and that it is purely by accident that Goswin has no anecdotes involving that theme.

of affliction (Jer. 29.11), Ida would be inwardly filled anew from the abundance of such sweetness and her heart would be so honeyed, so anointed with salvation's *oil of gladness* (Ps. 44.8), that she would exchange her previous grief for vehement joy.[145]

(29b–4)[146] The fourth thing Ida contemplated was the life-filled and honour-giving sacrament of the altar.[147] While still out in the world, she was so moved with desire for this sacrament that she would have desired to receive it frequently, but the sting of humility held her back and she dared not act. But if she knew of any of the religious girls languishing with the same kind of desire and being inwardly tormented by too prolonged a waiting, she could not stay still but would run hither and yon to inform some priest of the matter so that he could fulfill the girl's desire.[148] When finally permitted to be clothed in the venerable habit of the Order, this way-bread became Ida's whole hope and sweetest consolation; so much so that she often passed over from the refectory of the saving Eucharist to a spiritual dormitory, in which, estranged from her bodily senses, she dozed off into the happiest of repose, enwrapped in the arms of her groom. In the act of receiving, the thought of ingesting a Lord of such majesty would make her body swoon, as we have said, and straight after receiving she would drop to the ground, there in the choir of the priests or even at the very corner of the altar. And there she would remain a long time, unable to carry on with the ceremonial. Her friends would take her to task for giving her neighbours occasion for scandal, but she would meekly reply that she was at such times so lacking in control that even if it involved falling all the way to hell, she could not keep from falling. Again, as often as she passed in front of the altar where the Lord's body was reserved in the pyx, she would tremble and all her entrails would jostle inside her. And whenever the priest was celebrating mass, whether she was in choir or at work or lying in bed in the infirmary or elsewhere, during the canon she would sense the Lord's presence on the altar.[149]

---

[145] Her antidote to Good Friday's gloom lies in the love behind it, not explicitly in the Easter that follows.

[146] Echoes of eucharistic themes found first in *Niv* 3bc and then intermittently in *Niv* 19a through 28d; and briefly in 32d and 34b.

[147] *Vitale et honorificum:* Goswin uses *vitalis* in two notable texts (*Niv* 6a and *Ab* 17b), but nowhere else dies he use *honorificum*.

[148] *Aliquam ex religiosis puellis [...] negotium hoc nuntiabat alicui sacredoti:* Henriquez changes *nuntiabat* to *quaerebat*, thereby changing the meaning of the anonymity See *Niv* 2e, n. 18. Goswin surely intends his *alicui sacerdoti* to mean 'a certain priest', whereas Henriquez has Ida 'digging up any old priest'. Even as a child Ida had a gift for approaching reluctant persons.

[149] Such eucharistic 'radar' is frequent among Ida's contemporaries. Henriquez makes Ida aware not merely of the Lord's 'presence' on the altar (*adesse*) but of the moment of his 'descent' (*descendentem*).

(29b–5)[150] The fifth thing Ida contemplated was the sweet humanity of our Saviour , so deserving to be embraced with all devotion. She would recall how, though he was God almighty, sufficient unto himself and lacking in nothing, *he emptied himself and took the form of a servant* (Phil. 2.7) that he might set *the one-hundredth stray sheep upon his sacred shoulders and so bring it back to the flock* (*RB* 27.9; compare Luke 15.4–5). She was also moved by the sweet recalling of his holy members: feet, hands, eyes, lips, side, face, heart and so on. The frequent remembrance of these kept her well-watered, as might a clear stream, springing from the place of delight. Or again, she would of a sudden inwardly sense the full vigour of his love, and would melt inwardly away, *as wax does before a fire* (Ps. 67.3), and then her body would swoon. At times too she would *remember the Lord's works* (Ps. 76.12) and turn her gaze to the creatures God had made, namely: flowers or trees or water or other creatures, and she would scarcely be able to look at them without shedding tears. This was because, starting from the creature, she would conceive of the goodness and wisdom of its creator and so would most joyfully pour out unutterable acts of thanksgiving to its maker. Again at times she deliberately gave her attention to these outward things so as to temper her tendency to think only of God,[151] for it seemed to her that God was so jealous for her that if she gave him room to enter into her heart, his excessive tenderness and playful familiarity would utterly absorb her into the lightsome abyss of his divinity. No need to wonder that this was how she was remembered, since night and day she bore in her heart what I might call a 'sane insanity', so vehement that at times it left her talkative and twitching.[152]

(29b–6)[153] The sixth thing Ida contemplated was the wondrously inexhaustible goodness of God, not only in the benefits he had conferred on her and other mortals, nor just in his having created such wonderful creatures, but for the simple fact that

---

[150] Echoes of visions of the infant Jesus and his mother in *Niv* 19, 21 and 23–25. Ida's prayerful response to earthly creation is found in *Niv* 2c.

[151] *Ut sibi occasionem cogitandi de Deo temperaret:* such 'managing' of 'occasions' for change in moral orientation has parallels in *Niv* 29b–1 *(occasiones peccandi quasi poculum mortis verebatur),* in 29b–4 *(quare proximis occasionem scandali daret)* and *Ab* 9c *(dare volens occasionem quibusdam resipiscendi a peccatis).*

[152] *Eam interdum supra modum loqui et gestis corporis sui frequenter alterare cogebat:* Henriquez omits this paragraph. My 'talkative and twitching' are more homely than the Latin. Goswin's *supra modum* is very Pauline (Rom. 7.13; Gal. 1.13; etc.; see also *Ab* 16b). So too is his *alterare*, which he uses again in *Niv* 33g, perhaps echoing Paul's eschatological *immutabimur* (I Cor 15.52). Just as Goswin elsewhere responds to attacks on Ida's 'sleepy' ecstasies, so here he refutes complaints about fits of excess in speech and oddity in deportment. In English it is easy to echo the complainers, but hard to find concise terms to echo Paul.

[153] The *bonitas* of God comes (in passing) in *Niv* 4a, 17d, 27g, and 35biii; *Arn* II.4f, 15a; *Ab* 3c, 6j and 20d.

he was ineffably good in himself. And the more strongly and perfectly she loved him, the more perfectly did she experience his sweet goodness within her soul.

(29b–7)[154] The seventh thing Ida contemplated was the whole range of the heavenly orders, those of saints but also those of angels. She looked into the diverse glory of the saints, proportioned to their merits, and she yearned unceasingly after their blissful fellowship. Then she considered the choirs of angels and how with great purity those blessed spirits behold in God the objects of their contemplation, being both enlightened and made replete with that divine nourishment, and how they therefore are always praising God, always *desiring to gaze deep within him* (I Pet. 1.12) and always taking delight in fulfilling their *ministry* (Heb. 1.14). She also considered how the blessed souls of the elect on high are inebriated with *the plenty of the house of God and are watered at* his *torrent of pleasure* (Ps. 35.9), and how therein they gladden the angels too, by the very fullness of their joy. Nor should we wonder at that, since, if *there is joy for the angels of God even over one sinner doing penance* (Luke 15.10), what manner of magnificent joy should we not imagine them to have over the outstandingly brilliant fellowship of so many thousands of saints?

(29b–8)[155] The eighth thing Ida contemplated was the holy and undivided Trinity, of whose immense majesty she had already received as great a revelation as is permitted (*Niv* 22b, 28f). And so she found it a joy above all joys and above all delights to lapse into a holy quiet as she mused upon that Trinity.[156] Ever considering holy things in a holy manner, Ida considered the power of the Father and the wisdom of the Son and the benignity of the Holy Spirit, and in the perspective of these, as in an outstanding fountainhead, she considered both the supreme good and every other good, both in heaven and on earth. And so her whole yearning was the aspiration to

---

[154] Vague echoes in the 'throng of heavenly virgins' accompanying the recently deceased young nun in *Niv* 8ad. A more solitary eschatology is reflected in *Niv* 10b and in the whole of *Niv* 18. In fact *Niv* 18 shows more solidarity among the hell-bound merry-makers than among those on shortcuts to heaven. Even on her deathbed, Ida is devoid of heavenly companions, especially when compared with someone like Lutgard, who is ever haunted with them, singly or in pairs or throngs (*Lut* II 29, 34, 39, 42-43; III 13, 16; etc.). Alice, isolated as a leper, craved the company of the eleven thousand virgins of Cologne (*Al* xv). Caesarius's novice names that throng 'our own virgins', and longs to hear reports of their apparitions (*DM* 8.84, p. 151). For Ida's trend away from homely Marian themes and towards those of the lofty Trinity, see Cawley 'Our Lady and the Nuns and Monks of Thirteenth-Century Belgium', pp. 99–102.

[155] The themes of the Trinity, or 'pure divinity', come as high points of devotion in *Niv* 21d, 22b, 25b, 28cdf and even more significantly in 33bde. But in *Niv* 2d, 29b–5 and 34g their mention is more incidental.

[156] *In ejus sancta et superdelectabili speculatione quiescere:* Goswin is discreet with his superlatives, but he is also creative with the particle *super-: in superlativo gradu, Niv* 31b, *Ab* 19e; *superabunde, superuffluentem, Arn* I.4b; II.16b; *superglorioso, superluminosa, supermundanum, Ab* 7b, *Niv* 33h, *Arn* II.6a.

pass from the looking glass of faith to the vision of reality,[157] that is to say, to the longed-for presence of the blessed Trinity.

30. Her Charity and Compassion

(30a) Since charity *wins first place among all the virtues* (*Arn* II.1a), we should first say a few things about Ida's charity and afterwards proceed to discourse in proper order on her other virtues. Note should be taken of what we mentioned in describing her childhood years, how it was remembered that already in her girlhood charity had been conceived in her heart and was coming to birth. Already at that time she was beginning to love her God after the manner of *the vineyard of the Lord Sabaoth* (Isa. 5.7), *extending her branches* (Ps. 79.12) to her neighbours in works of pity and of mercy, expressing thereby the charity she had towards them in Christ. As the blessed father Saint Augustine[158] testifies: *for charity to be born in a soul, it first has to be conceived in that soul; then, once born, it has to be nourished; once nourished, it has to be strengthened; once strengthened, it has to be perfected; and once perfected, it casts out fear* (I John 4.18). Such a soul, asleep to things worldly and awake to things spiritual, enjoys a *Sabbath kept delicate* (Isa. 58.13) and finds it pleasant indeed to *taste* frequently *and see how sweet is the Lord* (Ps. 33.9) and to yearn ardently after a heaven affluent with delights. Yes, with the Apostle such a soul can say: *I long to be dissolved and to be with Christ* (Phil. 1.23), and again to say: *Daughters of Jerusalem, announce to the Beloved that I am languishing with love* (Cant. 5.8).

(30b) And the signs of perfect charity are these: in kindliness it stretches itself out to relieve a neighbour's needs; poverty is no burden for it; injuries it does not resent;[159] ill-treatment it scoffs at; wrongs it ignores; *death* it accounts a *gain* (Phil. 1.21). Indeed, it does not even think of itself as dying, being assured rather of *passing over from death to life* (I John 5.24). And were not all these traits, and more besides, realized in Ida? Were they not evidence of her wondrous charity? They were indeed, and deservedly could she say: *For me, to live is Christ and death is gain* (Phil. 1.21).

(30c) She aimed to adapt herself to everyone in accord with God's charity. Thus, if she saw others conscientious in God's law and given to religious living, she smiled grateful approval upon their good works.[160] And if she saw, or otherwise knew, some

---

[157] *De speculo fidei ad visionem speciei [...] toto desiderio suspirabat:* Compare I Cor 13.12; II Cor 5.7. On *speculum* as 'mirror' or as 'looking-glass', see *Ab* 8b, n. 44.

[158] I have not located this passage in Augustine.

[159] *Non sentit injurias:* normally Goswin uses *sentire* to mean 'sense perception', such as 'feeling' pain in *Niv* 33h and 35bx. Here it is more 'resenting' or 'opining', as in *Niv* 31b, 33f.

[160] *Cum gratiarum actione bonis eorum operibus ar-RID-e-bat* – the approving smile.

to be enmeshed in sins, she did not immediately condemn them, as many habitually do. Instead, she compassionated them affectionately from the heart, hoping soon to hear *better things* about them, *things nearer to their salvation* (Heb. 6.9), things very different from the Lord's sentencing them to death, let alone to death everlasting. Yet when all was said and done, she would come back to her own case to see how clearly the Lord had *enlarged his mercy with her* (Luke 1.58). She thanked him for that, well aware that she could have fallen into many perversities, had she ever, like other sinners, been abandoned by the Lord.

(30d) To the righteous she *used to appeal to have them progress to even better things* (*RB* 2.25). But to sinners she often *read the lesson of true salvation from the book of charity,*[161] bidding them *doff the old man with his deeds and don the new, who is created in accord with God in the righteousness and holiness of the truth* (*EO* 102.41–43; Eph. 4.24).

(30e) Hence many, both righteous and sinners, used to hasten to her for consolation, unashamed to lay open to her their temptations, either carnal or spiritual, and their troubles of every kind. For she was a painstaking consoler, ready to give all a hearing on every topic, to respond helpfully and to comfort *with a charity appropriate* to each one's troubles.[162]

(30f) One astounding fact was that, though hearing of so many carnal excesses and horrible perversities, she could not recall ever experiencing even the first stirrings of her own flesh, as she herself testified to one of her familiar friends. And little wonder, for as soon as anyone started speaking to her of their sinning and riotousness, a mighty fire of charity would set her ablaze inside and her whole *soul would melt* (Cant. 5.6) into compassion. And this compassion was her saving remedy, as she herself proclaimed, for it kept her from sensing even the slightest tickle within her own flesh.[163]

(30g) A chief concern of hers was to comfort the sinners she admonished and always to take care of them as if she had herself *mothered* them all (I Cor. 4.15). She used to say that, if God so pleased, she would willingly linger long in this life, so full of calamities, just, in all charity, to impart counsel and help to the desolate and the sinful. For she surely knew the truth of that bold saying: *it is a goodly sadness and, one might say, a blessed wretchedness to be troubled about vices not one's own, troubled but not entangled, grieved but not gripped, bowed in sorrow but not drawn to follow.*[164]

(30h) To her sisters she eagerly ministered out of charity, always willingly and

---

[161] Same image in *Ab* 7e and *Arn* II.1f.

[162] *Tamquam studiosae consolatrici [...] caritate debita:* the whole sentence is omitted by Henriquez. There is an allusion to Rom. 13.8, where our only 'debt' is charity.

[163] *Primum saltem motum se sensisse [...] saltem vel modicam sentire carnis titillationem.*

[164] *Pia est tristitia et, si dici potest, beata miseria: vitiis alienis tribulari, non implicari; moerere, non haerere; dolore contrahi, non amore attrahi:* Henriquez omits this passage.

devotedly. With those sick in the infirmary, she eagerly stayed up at night, even beyond her strength. She eagerly and perseveringly attended the wakes of those who died. At times too she would *leave God for God's sake* (*Arn* II.4b), to be of charitable service to her neighbours.

(30i) The sublimity of the divine revelations made to Ida was itself a manifest proof that the charity within her was of God. The Lord says as much to his disciples: *I no longer call you servants but friends, since all that I have heard from my Father I have made known to you* (Antiphon: Apostles; John 15.15). It should be common knowledge that the gauge for the revelations she received from on high depended on the magnitude of her charity. For when so frequently *introduced* by her Beloved *into the wine cellar* (Cant. 2.4) and receiving from him *the cup of spiced wine* (Cant. 8.2), Ida was promptly inebriated and carried off in a transport of mind, to imbibe with ease and enjoyment the drafts of divine revelation, the intimate savourings of whose truth she most ardently desired.[165] At such times *the capacity of her mind opened up wider* (Gregory, *Dial* II 35.6) than its natural limit, and her understanding was wafted along by divine inspiration and it expanded beyond the dimensions, not only of this person or that, but of human nature in general and of all human craft. For it was indeed beyond human nature for anyone to see what Ida saw: to see among things past what is no longer; among things future what is not yet; among things present what is afar; yes, and to see among secrets of another's heart what is subject to none of the senses; among things divine what is above every sense.

(30j) When Ida's occasional raptures and transports left her lying immobile for long stretches at a time, there were some who praised God and made much of his doing such wondrous deeds in her. These were persons of lofty religious outlook. But there were others, small-minded and *unsalted* (Mark 9.49), who had never tasted the banquet-fare of ardent charity, and these were scandalized. They could not bring themselves to cough up a single good word about it.[166] Bewildered, they each interpreted her slumber in any way they could. Now the Lord himself had *adjured* Ida's spiritual sisters *by the hinds and gazelles of the fields* (Cant. 2.7, 3.5) that they

---

[165] *Ex divinis revelationibus summa cum facilitate. [...] hauriebat quod [...] desiderabat:* this dense paragraph is helpfully clarified by Henriquez, who adds a label to identify the 'spiced wine': it is a draught of *amor divinus,* affording a taste of what it is to have a 'divine lover'. Thus Ida readily drinks in from her revelations all she wishes, and she enhances her charity accordingly.

[166] *Pusilli et insulsi, qui ardentis caritatis epulum quod non gustaverant ructare non poterant [...]:* this pejorative use of *pusillus* is unique in Goswin and contrasts sharply with the Gospel sense of 'childlike' (for example Mark 9.41, found also in *RB* 31.16). It is not the same as *pusillanimus* (*Niv* 33a, *Ab* 15d; *Arn* I.10d), but indicates a 'smallness' as blameworthy in a person's character as 'saltlessness' is blameworthy in food (Mark 9.49; Job 6.6). My expression, 'cough up a single good word', is a euphemism for the digestive metaphor of Ps. 44.2 and 144.7. Literally Goswin is saying that, not having ingested charity, these folk cannot regurgitate it.

not arouse her until she awaken of her own accord; yet some of them made light of this adjuration and attempted to stir her by various movements and outward signals. But she simply could not be moved, for it was into the arms of her groom that she had dozed, and her sleep was that of a spiritual drunkenness. She, in the meantime, ever gazed with the lightsome eye of her soul upon the things her groom deigned inwardly to reveal to her.

(30k) Charity first inwardly *melted* her, like *wax* (Ps. 21.15); then it upwardly released her, in a transport, to see *visions and revelations of the Lord* (II Cor 12.1); until finally back down again it shrank her, for her to strive to compassionate those in trouble and show them mercy. For *charity* was a *debt* she owed to all and sundry (Rom. 13.8), and she *paid* it with so generous a goodwill (*RB* 72.8) that, far from losing any of it, she retained it with a surplus all the greater, the more lavishly she spent it on the needs of anyone she found afflicted.[167]

31. Her Humility and Obedience

(31a) After describing Ida's charity, we should say something of her humility and obedience.[168] From earliest childhood Ida entered into discipleship under her Lord and master, Jesus Christ, to *learn from him how to be meek and humble of heart* (Matt. 11.29). It was by daily increments that humility grew in her heart, so that she gradually acquired a humility that was altogether true. For humility is not only *the greatest virtue of the saints* (*Arn* II.3c); it is also *the one in which, through truest self-knowledge, one sees oneself as of ever lesser account* (Bern, *De Grad.* I.2).[169]

(31b) Though Ida was reaching far above the level of her flesh in the spiritual life she led, a life flooded to overflowing with heavenly delights, and though people saw her as on a superlative level of holy religion, far above the others, she herself thought very well of those others and considered them all as saints, professing herself, both in her heart and in speech, *to be lower* (*RB* 7.51) and *less reputable* (*RB* 1.11) than any. It was habitual with her that if her outpourings of heavenly grace happened to come to the notice of others, she would so blush with inner bashfulness that her one wish would be to hide underground and go unnoticed on earth. A still greater bashfulness would drench[170] her whenever people showed more respect for her than

---

[167] Henriquez mysteriously omits this superb sentence.

[168] Henriquez adds the possessive *ipsius* (her humility, etc.). This matches the wording of the titles of Chapters 30, 31 and 32, and also the opening words of 30a and 32a, though both manuscripts have the synonymous *ejus* instead of Henriquez' *ipsius*.

[169] *Sibi ipsi vilescit:* 'vileness' also comes up in *Niv* 1h (*vilipenderetur*), in *Niv* 13a *(vile lutum)* and especially in *Arn* II.3a *(sibi vilis, ante Deum magnus)*. These passages have as common denominator the small account taken of one 'dressed in ragged clothes', of mud 'trodden in the street' and of a human set alongside God.

[170] *Majori etiam verecundia perfundebatur:* bashfulness too, like grace, is for Goswin a

for others, quite as if they were hurling outrages and contumely on her instead, and *provoking her with curses* (II Macc. 12.14). It was just as with blessed Father Bernard, when, astonished at the miracles the Lord was working through him, he said: *Much do I marvel at what these miracles mean. What is God looking for in performing such feats through such a fellow? (VP* 7.20; PL 185.314d). So too did Ida, out of humility, wonder at what the revelations with which her groom had dignified her could mean; and in her gracious playfulness,[171] she said she did not know. When asked by friends what came to mind when people hurled poisonous outrages and curses at her, or when others sang her praises, she answered that the evils alleged brought her no more disturbance of mind, and the praises no more elation, than if proffered in regard to some other person at random.

(31c) Her attitude to people, both in heart and in speech, was one of lowliness. She would not consent to take even an adequate share of food, drink, clothing or other bodily needs. This was her way of impoverishing herself, of becoming *the last of all (RB* 43.5), and the very lowliness of it afforded an example of poverty all could embrace.[172]

(31d) Then too, since true humility always has at its side as a companion the truest of obedience, it should be noted that, from her earliest entry into the monastery up to her happy death, Ida took care to carry out obedience beyond reproach. For obedience is the virtue *which inserts the other virtues into the mind, and, once inserted, guards them there* (Greg. *Mor* 35.14.28; *Arn* II.4a). Obedience, I say, *is the key of David, which opens and no one shuts* (Isa. 22.22). And for Ida it unlocked the secret things of God.[173]

---

drenching fluid. See *Niv* 4a, n. 24.

[171] *Joco suo gratioso:* Ida's attitude differs from Bernard's: she spontaneously blushes and cheerily jokes; he speculates in all seriousness. Bernard sees his healings as at the service, not of the sick but of sound doctrine; Ida sees her revelations as at the service of those she compassionates.

[172] *Humilitatem exhibens [...] omnibus per humilitatem amplectandae paupertatis praeberet exemplum:* Goswin's verbs, *exhibere* and *praebere*, do not imply exhibitionism or deliberate example-setting. The two verbs can be synonymous, as when one and the same thing (a kiss) is *exhibitum* in *Niv* 9c and *praebitum* in *Ab* 10a. But they also contrast. Thus, *exhibere* comes some eighteen times in *Niv* and mostly means 'showing an attitude', whereas *praebere* comes four times and has the less deliberate sense of 'affording of an opportunity'. For example in *Niv* 31b 'reverence' is 'exhibited', whereas in *Niv* 21b 'human reasoning' risks 'affording' a cheap substitute for faith.

[173] The term *obedientia* is also used of similar attitudes in *Arn* II.4 and *Ab* 5, though we today would call them simply 'fidelity to grace'. Goswin's rarely uses *obedientia* elsewhere, and it then comes close to the feudal term *obeisance*. Thus, in *Niv* 13d, *Arn* II.5c, and *Ab* 12c, devout *obeisance* is shown respectively by the demons to Ida, by the angels to our Lady and by the ideal nun to the Crucified. In *Arn* I.8c, Arnulf's body shows *obeisance* to his soul, and in II.2c, the very pigs show it to himself. As for 'obedience' in the modern sense of a co-

(31e) Obedience was what made Ida confident as she prayed and what enabled her to obtain from the Lord what she asked, since, as we must firmly believe, *the prayer of those who humble themselves penetrates the clouds* (Ecclus. 35.21) and *one prayer from the obedient is more acceptable to God than ten thousand from the contemptuous* (*Arn* II.4c: Gregory). So too we can deservedly believe that, since *God looks upon the prayer of the humble* (Ps. 101.18), and *gives the humble his grace* (Prov. 3.34), he must have accepted the *humility of his handmaid* Ida (Luke 1.48) and her humble obedience too, along with her humble praying, as a sacrifice offered by her *for a sweet-smelling odour* (Exod. 29.41).

32. Her Patience

(32a) The three virtues we have briefly described in Ida, namely her charity, humility and obedience, can be compared to three gems inserted in the diadem of her supreme King and Spouse.[174] To them a fourth[175] gem can be added, namely her most valiant patience, upon which something must also be briefly said.

(32b) Being a *prudent virgin* (Matt. 25.2), Ida reflected on how the pain of the present life is brief and how the depravity of evil folk 'does not kill but skills'.[176] Hence she was not afraid to endure for Christ whatever persecutions were hurled at her, nor did she shrink from the poisonous slander of mouths that bit. Her attitude to reproaches, outrages and other blackening of her reputation by calumniators was to smile at *the wrongs* thus flung *at her* (*RB* 58.3) and to embrace them as patiently as *the meekest lamb* (Jer. 11.19), knowing how much more glorious it is to flee from injurious words by keeping silence than to utter a reply that overcomes. Hence could she deservedly say with the prophet, and indeed with her Lord and Spouse, those words which the prophet presents him as saying to God the Father at the time of the

---

operative relationship with one's superiors, Goswin depicts the reality, though without using the term, as in *Niv* 15b, where Ida leans loyally on her abbess's bosom, and in 3b, where she is at ease with her chaplain. He never uses *obedientia* for compliance with humdrum orders. However, see *Arn* I.8c, II.8a.

[174] *Quae diademati summi regis et sponsi sui insererentur:* the crown is Christ's in that he bestows it, but, if we judge by *Niv* 8bc, it is Ida who wears it.

[175] *Descriptis breviter tribus [...] virtutibus [...] quarta superadditur:* the same 'four' appear in *Arn* II.1–3. The present list fails to include compassion (*Niv* 30), which would make a total of five virtues. The same basic list appears in *Arn* II. 4a. Other times it seems to be borrowed from Caesarius (*DM* 8.19, p. 97), who in turn ascribes it to Jerome. Originally each virtue was identified with one of metaphorical nails, pegging the monk to his metaphorical cross. I have not found the locus in pseudo-Jerome.

[176] *Considerans quia [...] et quia malorum pravitas non occidit sed erudit:* here, and twice in the next paragraphs, the tone is 'proverbial' and suggestive of a literary borrowing. I cannot identify a source, but I mimic the tone with puns.

passion: '*For your sake, O Lord, I have borne with reproach, and confusion has covered my face*' (Ps. 68.8). And again: '*In your sight are all who trouble me; my heart has anticipated upbraiding and misery*' (Ps. 68.21). Hence it was that, as often as her persecutors' opposition took the form of savage calumnies, her own inner mind grew in tranquillity, so that the greater the wrong her opponents sought to do her, the more effectively did her patience overcome them.[177] For she had heard from the Apostle that *all who wish to live devoutly in Christ do suffer persecution* (II Tim. 3.12).

(32c) Ida's Lord was sometimes minded to forewarn and forearm her by revealing in the spirit at what time and from which persons and in what manner or measure such *wrongs* would be *inflicted* for her to endure (*RB* 58.3). Thereupon, like a valiant *virago* (Gen. 2.23), she would go to some of her friends and urge them not to take at all amiss the trouble she would soon be suffering, as it would be for her growth in virtue and in heavenly merit. Any lies concocted against her she preferred to brush aside in silence rather than allow herself to be known to her adversaries for what she was.

(32d) Just as a fish cannot live without water, nor a bird without air, so neither could Ida live without persecution. It seemed to her, and altogether truly, that she was never as secure[178] in time of prosperity as in time of adversity. And so when she had less adversity to bear than usual, she would secretly enter the church and position herself on her knees before the cross and before the ciborium in which the Lord's body was reserved within the pyx, and there, amid tearful sighs and with a half-joking smile, she would whisper to the Lord:[179] '*Why, my sweetest Lord, are you sleeping* so long a slumber (Ps. 43.23), and permitting me, your handmaid, to lack any vexing troubles?'

(32e) *Not so with the* wretched children of Adam, *not so* (Ps. 1.4)! Theirs to seek prosperity, not adversity; but Ida's it was to glory hard-pressed by adversity, taking no rest in prosperity! Myself, I make bold to protest, convinced by my own wits, that, had princes and tyrants in our time brought persecution to bear upon Christians, as in the primitive Church, Ida would have spontaneously offered herself to the butchers, running headlong with all constancy towards martyrdom, to let her sufferings glorify her spouse, our king.[180] Indeed, to hold on to patience amid adversities: what else is this, even short of bloodshed, but a kind of martyrdom?

(32f) What Ida desired, frequently and vehemently, was more adversity! But how few the emulators she had in that (Compare *Arn* I.12e)! Indeed, in our times *iniquity*

---

[177] Concerning Ida's opponents, see my discussion of her authority in the Introduction to the Lives, p. 9, above ; see also, *Niv* 11a, n. 49.

[178] *Eam tam esse securam:* see *Niv* 10b, n. 46.

[179] Henriquez mysteriously omits the words: *et ciborium in quo Domini corpus intra pixidem erat reconditum/ repositum;* and after the 'sighs' he omits: *cum jocoso susurrio.*

[180] Henriquez omits virtually the rest of the chapter.

has abounded and the charity of many has grown cold (Matt. 24.12). Neither humility nor patience can maintain a dwelling within a frigid breast, let alone in a frigid behaviour.

(32g) This much, then, have I written about Ida to commend her holiness, and more could have been written if further information had reached me, but now I must try and put an end to my narrative, though not an end to her lofty praises, and so I propose to put my hand to describing her blessed passing.

33. Her Last Illness

(33a) The end of Ida's life was drawing near, and the Lord, who had enlightened her mind with the rays of heavenly grace and had guarded her body in his holy service, wished now to call her from the darkness of this mortality to the lightsome mansion of the city on high, and therefore he so flogged her with a bodily illness that she lay bedridden continually.[181] For fourteen months she was confined to the frying pan of feebleness.[182] This was burdensome enough for her tender frame, but it never prompted her to faintheartedness, or to *acedia*, or impatience. Rather, she always showed herself ready to endure even severer feebleness, should the Lord so please.

(33b) When about seven months had passed, there came that solemn day, that truly memorable day, on which *the Paraclete Spirit came gleaming upon the disciples* (Hymn: Pentecost). Thereupon, as on other major feasts, Ida's devotion was sated with the richest of heavenly fare,[183] and from then until her passing, her gaze was upon the Trinity, *as upon a looking-glass* (I Cor. 13.12), and in some wondrous, unutterable way she contemplated herself in the Trinity and the Trinity in herself.

(33c) When she had been ill a whole year, she asked the Lord in her usual prayerful familiarity, that if he wished her to languish much longer, he make the languor more severe from now on.[184] The prayer had the immediate result that she was stricken with a quite intense fever. She then told a spiritual friend of hers[185] that

---

[181] *Flagellavit infirmitate ita ut continue decumberet:* God's 'flogging' is part of Goswin's theology of 'suffering'. See *Niv* 5a, 6a, 8b; *Arn* II.11c. Henriquez changes *continue* (continually) to *continuo* (forthwith), as for a sudden taking to her bed, rather than a bedridden state.

[182] *Frigorio coarctaretur:* Henriquez spells it *frixorio*, a matter of orthography. The same term comes in *Niv* 9c and *Ab* 14a.

[183] *Abundantiori coelitus saginata est pinguedine devotionis:* rich biblical jargon, literally: 'by heaven's doing, she was made plump on a more overflowing fat of devotion.'

[184] *Si diutius vellet eam languere, languor ejus in posterum aggravaretur:* an 'aggravation' of the lingering illness, enough to preclude deceptive ameliorations, but not necessarily calling for constant escalation.

[185] *Cuidam amico suo spirituali:* masculine and of known (but concealed) identity.

the severity would keep increasing until her death. Events were to prove this true. But she also said that the more her body was pressed down by the weight of the illness, the more freely was her spirit lifted up and able to pass over to God.

(33d) On the Saturday evening before the first Sunday of Advent, Ida's blood-Sister Hersendis, a woman of reputable life,[186] was sitting at her side as she languished, and *they were conversing* about *the good things of the Lord* (IV Kings 2.11; Ps. 26.13). Ida was affirming her esteem and love for those hallowed days prior to Christmas and the awesome mystery of the Lord's incarnation, when she suddenly broke off and, with joy-filled mind and easy voice, told her sister: 'Behold, sister, behold, the blessed Trinity is thundering, ready to come down to earth!'[187]

(33e) What have you said, O blissful soul? What does it mean for the blessed Trinity to 'thunder'? What is their 'thunder'? The thunder of the holy Trinity, unless I am mistaken, is the incarnate Son. Like the thunder proffered when clouds converge and run together, so was he proffered to our notice when the ancient fathers' prophecies converged and came together in him. Yes, he appeared visibly among us, flashing like lightning in his miracles, thundering terribly against sinners in his salutary preaching, foretelling fire everlasting for them if they persevered in their transgressions and sins, but life everlasting if they ceased to sin and happily persevered in keeping his commandments. Hence even apostles, begotten by the grace of Christ, were called *boanerges*, that is, 'sons of thunder' (Mark 3.17). Thus was the son of man, Jesus Christ, both lightning in his miracles and thunder in his preaching. Thus too did he, at *the will of* the Father and by co-operation of the Holy Spirit, deign by *his* passion and *death to give life to the world* (Ordo Missae). And this is what Ida understood spiritually of that thunder, but her sister could not catch the meaning of the term, for it was obscure and figurative.

(33f) The illness went on increasing after that, and the less she took of outward nourishment, the feebler and more attenuated her body became, and the more speedily, in her estimation, did the day of her passing approach. On the fifth day before migrating, Ida sensed *the dissolution of her body to be imminent* (Antiphon: St Martin) and asked to be anointed with the oil of the sick. She immediately felt the action of this sacramental anointing at work within her, and her spirit quietened into a great peace, tranquillized by the tranquil God, who gives all things their tranquillity.[188] Ida then asked the abbess to have everyone dismissed from the building in which she lay sick. This was mainly because her spirit could not bear the impurity of the various spirits.[189] The abbess gave a nod and her wish was

---

[186] *Mulier honestae vitae:* presumably a secular. See *Niv* 33f, n. 189, below.

[187] *Mente jucunda [...] ore placido:* Goswin's only use of *placidus*, but *jucundus* is common enough in his rich vocabulary of 'joy'.

[188] *Spiritusque ejus magna pace quiescere coepit, tranquillatus a tranquillo Deo, qui tranquillat omnia:* the Latin is sonorous and climactic in Goswin's ear. See *Niv* 1e, n. 6.

[189] *Universos a domo in qua aegrotabat [...] diversorum spirituum impuritatem ferre non*

immediately carried out. When the sun had set at the close of that day and the first watch of the night was beginning, Ida became entirely estranged from her bodily senses and was raptured up into heaven, into the presence of the divine majesty. She rested quietly in this way for a rather long time *in the peace of God which surpasses every sense* (Phil. 4.7). Meanwhile, to those who were on hand her face seemed wondrously lightsome and, I might almost say, glorified. One nun was sitting at Ida's bedside and could *see* how great and wondrous was the *grace of God* at work in her (Acts 11.23). Thereupon the nun herself began reacting quite wondrously, for at that moment she perceived an abundance of grace, dripping like dew down from heaven into her soul. It was as if the nun could see Ida's Lord and Saviour present there. This gave the nun so magnificent an inner joyousness that she kept devoutly kissing Ida's hands and feet, and repeatedly gazing upon her countenance, scarcely able to slake the eagerness the Holy Spirit was kindling within her.[190]

(33g) When the greater part of the night had been spent, Ida returned from the heavenly halls[191] and opened her eyes. And, seeing the abbess and this nun sitting at her side, she said how glad she was to notice that none of the other women[192] were present. They asked her in sign language[193] where she had tarried so long a stretch of the night, and she answered in a hushed voice that she had been mercifully raptured to heaven by the Lord and had seemed to see herself there, glorified in soul and body, though with her body somehow altered. She also said the Lord had kindly shown her the glorious placement up there in heaven that he had *prepared for her* as her reward *from the beginning of the world* (Antiphon: Matt. 25.34). She was again asked in signs by one of the two sitting with her,[194] whether she knew the time she was due to migrate, and she asserted she did not know. The same companion then

---

poterat: the 'building' was not the regular 'infirmary', and the visitors, indicated in the masculine, must have included some men, as well as the (secular?) blood-sisters. For the apparent snobbishness, see *Niv* 31c, n. 172.

[190] *Manus et pedes ejus et frequenti oculorum impressione:* Goswin is vague as to who is who. Henriquez mistakenly adds *salvatoris,* as if 'the Saviour's presence were visible and his limbs available for kissing, whereas that presence is merely sensed *(tamquam praesentem videret).* Goswin says nothing of Christ's posture or limbs, and so the hands and feet kissed are those of Ida, and the repeated 'impressing of the eyes' is the nun's repeated gaze upon Ida. For *imprimere, impressio,* see *Niv* 27c, 28d.

[191] *De coelestibus regrediens officinis:* the *officina* are literally the 'workshops', as in *RB* 4.78; but in Cistercian usage they include the chapter, refectory, calefactory, and other halls (*EO* 15.6; 55.14, 15; 72.8; 120.8). The joyous 'heavenly halls' come again in *Ab* 6f and *Arn* II.6i.

[102] *Praeter eas nullam caeterarum:* all are feminine.

[193] *Aliquo signorum nutu:* the night silence still applies.

[194] *Ab una earum quae assidebant ei:* Goswin's effort at anonymity slips up here: if not the 'aforesaid nun' *(praedicta monialis),* the speaker must be the abbess herself. Henriquez suppresses the identifying phrase. See *Niv* 2e, n. 5.

told by signs how unhesitatingly she herself believed God could easily reveal the hour if Ida would but plead for it with insistent prayer. Ida replied that nothing belonging in God's disposition met with distrust from her and that she at times had such trust in the Lord's omnipotence that if some accident, or some person, were to fling her into the deepest of water, or the clouds were to shower on her the heaviest of downpours, she believed that even *amid such a downpour* she would feel *never a drop* (Conrad, *EM* iii.10), and amid such *churning waters* (Exod. 15.10) she would have never a thought of danger to her life.

(33h)[195] Ida went on to add: 'Oh how gladly would I share with you more of this pleasant whispering, but I dread my sisters' coming in again. My spirit could not hold up amid the impurity of their spirits;[196] not that I abhor their *conversatio*; my Lord God himself having once assured me that they are to be saved.' Her blood sisters, who had been getting some sleep in an adjoining nook of the building, had in fact been woken. So Ida again bade the abbess turn visitors away from the place where she lay, on the grounds of her testimony that this heightened the tranquillity she felt in her inward spirit and afforded an insensitivity to the pains and constraints of the illness. On the morrow, which was the Monday, Ida remained all day in the same tranquillity, and everybody who stepped in to gaze on her, marvelled with unswerving eye at the super luminous[197] beauty of her countenance.

34. Her Death

(34a) Ida was still thus resting in joyous anticipation when the longed-for day of her passing arrived, that truly festive day, that *day of the gladness of her heart* (Cant. 3.11). It was, in fact, the Thursday, the day before the eve of Saint Lucy. About the hour of none her illness took a turn for the worse, constraining her holy little frame and giving advance evidence that death was now almost at the doorposts. It was then that she is remembered to have said, among other things, this word well worth recording: 'Oh, how truly blessed is death, with its power to free from all ills!'[198]

(34b) Another thing she said was:[199] 'Please let them bring me the holy body of the Lord and Saviour, the body of my own Beloved! Although, constrained by

---

[195] Henriquez omits 33h except for the last sentence.

[196] *Quarum spiritus meus minime sustinere posset impuritatem spirituum earum:* on the seeming snobbery, see *Niv* 33f, n. 189.

[197] *Superluminosa pulchritudine:* Henriquez omits *super-.*; see *Niv* 29b–8, n. 156.

[197] *Mors, quae [...] potens est:* Henriquez changes to *potens es,* making it an apostrophe to death, as in Hos. 13.14, 1 Cor 15.55.

[198] *Et subinferens, 'Obsecro', inquit:* all Goswin's other uses of *subinferens* are modified by expressions of time, such as *deinde* or *ad haec: Niv* 8b, 33h; *Arn* I.9b, II.16b; *Ab* 12b. No such expression of immediacy is included here.

illness and failing in body, I cannot now receive him, let my soul at least conceive from mere sight of him the inward relief of some sweet consolation.' Then an abbot, who was on hand, donned an alb, took up stole and maniple and, bringing along the revered body of the Lord, presented it to Ida with all reverence. But by now she was on the verge of paying her dues to bodily death. Her deadly illness, taking on new violence, now robbed her of her eyesight and dissipated the effectiveness of her other senses, leaving her incapable of gazing upon the Lord's holy body. Seeing this, the abbot went straight back to church and without delay restored the saving host to its pyx within the ciborium.

(34c) At that very moment, before the abbot could unvest, Ida's holy soul was released from the body. Immediately, in accord with the custom of the Order, the death gong was sounded,[200] the sisters hastened together and the commendation was recited for her soul, that soul which she herself had commended so totally to God from childhood onwards. By the time her body was transferred to church, night was coming on, and the customary wake was kept up at the bier, with psalms recited by the sisters. Next day mass was solemnly celebrated for her soul's absolution and her venerable body was given over to burial.

(34d) At such an hour, who could forebear to weep, looking on as one so *beloved by God and by all* (Ecclus. 45.1) was snatched from everyone's sight and a treasure so rare and valuable was covered over with earth? *Oh, what* gloom then obsessed the bosom of every bystander! Oh, how right and just it was that copious tears flow from the eyes of those consecrated *nuns!* How *fitting that they weep for* Ida, now deceased, whose bodily presence they would no longer see; yet more *fitting* still *to have rejoiced* with Ida alive! (Antiphon: St Martin). Not much mourning was needed for earth returning to earth; but altogether fuller rejoicing was called for over *the spirit* departing and ascending aloft *to the God who* had made *it* (Eccles. 12.7).

(34e) On this her burial day, there was a girl suffering from intolerable toothache, who, with firm hope of recovering her wholeness, put one of Ida's teeth on her cheek;[201] after which all the aching pain was put to flight.

(34f)[202] Oh what a virgin, so worthy of panegyric praise! *Brought to consummation in so brief a time, yet filling her seasons so full* (Wisd. 4.13)! Her venerable and god worthy *conversatio* suffices to suggest *how precious in the sight of the Lord* must have been her *death* (Ps. 115.15). *To eyes unwise she seemed to be dying* (Wisd. 3.2), but to wiser eyes she was seen, far from dying, to be *passing from death to life* (John 5.24)! Oh how happy and truly blessed was she, who so lived as never to be ashamed of living among her sisters, and who did not fear to die, because

---

[200] *Tabula defunctoria:* see *Arn* I.11c, n. 64.

[201] *Maxillae suae apposuit, statimque [...]:* another such removal of a saint's teeth as relics is vividly described in Thomas, *Lut* III.19.

[202] Entire section omitted by Henriquez.

she held God to be so good.[203] And why did she hold God to be so good? Because she loved him so ardently; and if she loved God so ardently it was because, being equipped with an ardent charity, she by no means dreaded departure from the body, for she could take with her *a glory all her own, the testimony of her conscience* (II Cor 1.12).

(34g) Therefore, in the year of the Lord's incarnation 1231,[204] the venerable Ida, having completed in the Cistercian Order sixteen years and nine months, rich in merits and virtues, after many crowns of patience, in the thirty-second year and ninth month of her age, on the day before the eve of the ides of December,[205] doffed the mortal tunic and, taking flight to the gate of paradise, arrived at the heavenly fatherland, whose citizens are the angels, whose temple is God, whose splendour is the Son, whose charity is the Holy Spirit; and there she enjoys with the blessed virgins an unvarying security, a secure tranquillity, a tranquil joyousness, a felicity made eternal by endlessly contemplating the most brilliant and admirable looking-glass of all the saints, namely the most blessed Trinity, the one, the Almighty, the true God, whose kingdom and empire abide without end unto age upon age. Amen.

Here ends the Life of Ida, nun of La Ramée.

---

[203] *Quae non sic vixit ut puderet eam inter sorores ejus vivere, nec mori timuit, quia bonum Deum habebat:* this seems to be echoing a revered text, which I cannot identify, except for the echo of St Martin's antiphon: *[...] qui nec mori timuit, nec vivere recusavit.*

[204] This is the reading of A fol. 176[r-v] and of Henriquez (p. 292), whereas B fol. 33[va] clearly has '1232'. This latter is impossible, because the text counts down to her death in days both of the week and of the month, and only in 1231 do the figures coincide correctly. I suggest that the copyist's eye slipped back and forth between the Roman numerals for '31' in the year of the Lord, and for '32' that of in Ida's lifetime: $m^o cc^o xxxi^o$ and xxxii^o This would suggest that B, though belonging to La Ramée, was not the autograph text of Goswin himself. The text also tells us that Ida died three-quarters of the way through her 'thirty-second year'. Hence we can set her thirty-third birthday in March 1232, and her actual birth in March 1199. This is important for her dealings with Beatrice, and it prompted Father Roger DeGanck to tackle some bewildering details, which he published in English as 'Chronological Data in the Lives of Ida of Nivelles and Beatrice of Nazareth', *Ons Geestelijk Erf,* 57 (1983), 14–29. His article is summarized in French in *COCR* 47 (1985), *Bulletin* no. 953, p. 561, and in English by Rozanne Elder, *CSQ,* 19, (1984), *Bulletin* no. 263 [p. 638–639]. Father Roger agrees that Ida was born in 1199, and sets Beatrice's birth in 1200. Thus Ida was slightly senior to Beatrice in age, but slightly junior in monastic profession.

[205] 11 December, 1231.

35. Posthumous Miracles

(35a) Here begins the Prologue[206] to Ida's miracles, performed after her death. Having thus briefly described the holy *conversatio* of our virgin, I had intended to write no more. Her life was a lucid looking-glass, and any who carefully peer into it can focus upon any shortcomings or progress of their own. Spontaneously, however, some miracles have presented themselves for me to write up as well, some occurring at her tomb and others elsewhere.[207]

(35b) Ida's Life was admirable enough on its own to afford progress for all the faithful; but neither should we suffer her miracles to lie hidden under the fruitless cover of silence, since God may well have wrought them precisely as pointers to her holiness. It is one thing to proclaim this almighty God of ours *admirable in his* bride (Ps. 76.36) during her *conversatio* among mortals, but I shall go further and proclaim him admirable also in this display of her posthumous miracles. Here ends the Prologue.

(35bi) Here begin the miracles. A nun of La Ramée was once deprived of her faculty of hearing.[208] So she promised Ida a votive ear made of wax if, at her intercession, she was favoured with recovery of her lost hearing. The request, with its promise, promptly proved effective and the nun received back her hearing. This cheered her considerably and the other sisters made her a half-joking suggestion, to get from one of the monastery's priests a pilgrim pouch and staff. This she did, and taking along the waxen ear, made her way to Ida's tomb, and declared: 'Ida, milady: behold, I offer you what I promised. I thank God and I thank you that you have bestowed on me so prompt an aid!'

(35bii) A second nun of La Ramée was sick with catarrh, which left her with a fatiguing headache. It was Rogationtide,[209] and the jubilant feast of Ascension was at hand, so that the nun greatly desired relief from the indisposition and to have her voice fit for singing on the feast-day. For this sickness often impedes a singer by taking away the voice. And so, joking, chuckling and talking as if face to face, she even set Ida an hour, saying: 'Lady Ida, if between now and such and such an hour tomorrow you get God to get me over this,[210] I will not hesitate to visit your tomb in

---

[206] Henriquez omits this Prologue and many phrases of 35bi, iii, vi, and ix.

[207] *Quae vel ad sepulchrum.[...] vel alibi contigerunt:* stories i–vi and ix envisage the tomb and its votive offerings. Stories vii, viii and x involve portable relics.

[208] *Quodam tempore auditus officio privata est:* the ablative (*tempore*) implies a point in time, and so a sudden loss of hearing; had the deafness been chronic, *per* would have been used, with the accusative, as in *Niv* 16a, etc. *Officium* is similarly used for the functioning of a faculty in *Niv* 20b.

[209] The Monday, Tuesday and Wednesday before Ascension Thursday, when processions and masses were held to pray for good crops.

[210] *Impetrare sospitatem:* found only here and in *Arn* II.14b. It is hard to convey other than

thanksgiving and offer you a votive nose of wax.' But doubt was in her as she said it: distrust about Ida's intercession, distrust about her own cure. Indeed, from that moment until the morrow, the proposal slipped her mind. But on the day and at the very hour she had pre-set, she did gain the desired healing, thanks to Ida's merits and intercession. She revealed to her sisters the whole story of what had happened, and then made no delay in offering to her consoler what she had promised.

(35biii) Another nun, labouring with fever, came to Ida's tomb, so incredulous that she had no hope at all of regaining her health. Approaching the tomb, she said: 'Lady Ida, *if you can* (Mark 9.21–22), come to my aid with those prayers of yours to God!' And why, oh pauper, why proffer so ambivalent, so distrustful a word? Surely better to say: 'Lady Ida, greatly do you deserve of the Lord; and *great* too is *the faith* (Matt. 15.28) wherein I hope, by your suffrage and mediation, to be restored to health.'[211] And the outcome? She was healed from her illness, not for any faith or merits of her incredulous self, but for the Lord's goodness and the acceptable grace of that handmaid of his.[212]

(35biv) A lay brother of La Ramée had been labouring for three years under a serious illness and was in continual distress, unable to lie down at all or to sleep. But putting his hope of regaining his bodily health in the merits and prayers of Ida, he went one evening to her tomb and prostrated on the ground, praying with what devotion he could muster, that Christ's blessed friend not deny him the suffrage he longed for. His prayer rose up to the ears of the Lord God of armies and he came away healed; never again to experience that illness.

(35bv) A young man serving as a familiar at La Ramée had been in sore straits with a fever, suffering great bodily discomfort. One day at vesper time, pained by the fever and not yet having eaten that day, he fell to thinking of the many sick folk who came to Ida's tomb and were healed of their illnesses. So he rose from bed and went, barefoot, to the tomb. There, after making his prayer, he went to sleep on the spot, it being by then almost dusk. After resting a little, he awoke and found himself entirely cured. So he joyfully ran back to the guesthouse, where he was assigned as server. He had no further trace of pain.

---

by my colloquialism, 'get God to get me over this'. She, in fact, was speaking 'jokingly'.

[211] *Et quod nihilominus magna est fides tua:* Henriquez omits this (p. 294), and indeed everything from 'And why [...]' down to '[...]outcome?' Why does Goswin urge the nun to address to Ida these words of Jesus to the Canaanite woman (Matt. 15.28), as if the heavenly Ida were still walking by faith? The *tua* (thy) is clear in A fol. 177ʳ, but unfortunately its equivalent in B fol. 34ʳᵃ has had fire damage and is illegible. Possibly Goswin's *fides* means 'confident intercession', a 'faith' compatible with 'vision'. Or maybe he wrote *fides mea* (my faith), rather than 'yours'. I have translated to make sense and yet keep the ambiguities.

[212] *Propter Domini bonitatem et acceptabilem Domino ancillae ejus gratiam:* the *acceptabilem* is accusative: it is not Ida who is 'acceptable to the Lord', but the grace that is hers. See *Niv* 4a, n. 24.

(35bvi) A certain woman had a three- or four-year-old daughter labouring with fever. In motherly compassion for such grievous suffering she had been to many churches to beg suffrages of the saints, that they appeal to the merciful Lord for her daughter's ailment. But when she concluded that there was to be no remedy for her daughter from them, some folk persuaded her to hasten with her daughter to Ida's tomb. Agreeing to this salutary advice, she hastened thither. On reaching Ida's tomb, she held the daughter on her lap and bade her entreat Ida's help with whatever words she could. The little baby, as yet unable to speak properly, muttered some chopped-up syllables to say: 'Lady Ida, help me! Lady Ida, help me!' She repeated some such word, sighing over and over again, until, still on her mother's lap, she finally dozed off to sleep. After a while she awoke from sleep and began to laugh, saying: 'Mother, mother, I have recovered! I am well again!' The mother gave her thanks to God and to Ida, and so *made her way back to where she belonged* (Antiphon: St Benedict).

(35bvii) A friar of the Order of Preachers had for many days been afflicted with toothache. He could not eat and his eyes could get but little sleep. But a certain lay brother chanced to come to Liège, carrying with him one of Ida's teeth. Learning of it, the sick friar put the tooth into his mouth and was thus freed from the toothache, by Ida's merit and the power of the Lord. Indeed, when he took the tooth out again, a sweet taste ensued, which he experienced keenly. And from then on he felt no more of the aching at all.

(35bviii) There was a boy with a fistular ulcer on his eye, an ailment both burdensome and laborious. His parents took him to numerous physicians to be cured (Mark 5.26), but their efforts with his illness were in vain. But along came a lay brother with one of Ida's teeth, which he now applied to the boy's eye, touching the sore spot, so that, little by little, the severe ailment shrank to nothing. In this way, what could not be done by physicians of the body was brought to completion by the supreme physician, Christ, thanks to the merits of his handmaid Ida.

(35bix) A woman long labouring under a weighty illness promised that, if restored to health by Ida's prayers, she would visit the tomb and bring a candle. She came as she had promised, received her pristine health and *made her way back* safe and sound *to where she belonged* (Antiphon: St Benedict).[213] To confirm the truth of this matter, a certain Brother Walter, who was on hand, *has given his testimony* and there is no doubting that *his testimony is true* (John 19.35).

(35bx) A monk of Valdieu was one day eating a fish, a perch to be exact, and he carelessly swallowed a bone. The bone stuck in his throat passage and he could neither draw it in nor pull it out, though he could locate it within his throat by the pain. He had no idea what to do, but soon afterwards he and his abbot stopped off at

---

[213] The sequence of events in the promise differs from that in the fulfilment. The promise envisages first being cured, than paying a visit and offering a candle. In the fulfilment, there is first the visit, then the cure, but no mention of any candle.

Aywières[214], where he learned from a sister that there was on hand a white drape[215] said to have belonged to Ida. Applying this to his throat, he felt himself healed then and there. And from then on he experienced no such pain in his throat.

Here end the miracles.

---

[214] Aywières was a French-speaking convent, first founded in 1202 at Awirs, thirteen kilometres west-south-west of Liège, transferred by 1210 to Lillois, seven kilometres north-north-east of Nivelles, and finally moved between 1214 and 1217 to Couture-Saint-Germain, fourteen kilometres north-east of Nivelles. Lutgard entered Aywières in 1206. Its incorporation into the Order was under Aulne, rather than Villers. However the abbot thus visiting is from Valdieu, another key house of the area, first founded in 1180 at Hocht, eight kilometres north-east of Maastricht, but moved in 1215 to a site fourteen kilometres north-east of Liège.

[215] *Velum quoddam candidum, quod [...] Idae fuisse ferebatur.* A *velum* would normally be a nun's 'head veil', but would Ida's veil be white? If some other piece of cloth were meant, we would expect *pannus*, as in *Niv* 1h; *Arn* I.7c; and likewise in Matt. 9.16; Luke 2.7; *EO* 102.13; or else *mappula*, as in II Gregory, *Dial* 19.1; *RB* 55.19; *EO* 109.17. There could be a clue to Ida's use of the cloth in the shape and size implied when it was applied to the patient's throat, but here the manuscripts differ: B fol. 35ᵛ, at bottom, suggests a small piece, simply 'applied' to the neck (*imponens*), whereas A fol. 178ʳ and Henriquez (p. 197) suggest a long, perhaps narrow piece, 'wrapped around' it (*circumimponens).* My translation maintains the ambiguity.

Appendix I

The Verses

Here begin the verses concerning Ida.[216]

Ida novum claustri speculum, quae nonna fidelis
floruit eximio praefusa decore Rachelis.
Dulcis amica Dei, virtutum lampade clara,
se ferventer ei libavit amoris in ara.
5 *Omnibus ejus amor luxit cum mente serena*
tristibus et laetis infundens ubera plena.
Ejus amor flagrans ad Christum glorificatum
saepius hanc vexit ut amata videret amatum.
Desuper accepit etiam mirabile munus
10 *cui se concessit speculandum trinus et unus.*
Ejus amor prudens quae vitans omnia nociva
ad bona se vigilem dedit alto numine diva.
Ejus amor fortis quae rumpens vincula mortis,
Rebus in adversis patiens fuit absque querela.
15 *[Nec mirum: placuit Christi sibi namque sequela.]*

---

[216] The later manuscript (A) used by Henriquez, gives these verses a rubric (*incipiunt/ [...]* *expliciunt)* with the above title, and sets them immediately after *Niv* 34g with its description of Ida's death. This connection prompts Henriquez to change the title to 'Her Epitaph'. The earlier manuscript (B), the one from La Ramée, gives the verses no title, and simply appends them after the miracles. The poet laments Ida's death without alluding to a tomb on which the epitaph might be expected to appear. The style and the accurate echoing of themes from the Life suggest that Cantor Goswin is himself the author.

Carnis defectus, fletus, vomitusque cruoris
designant quanta fuerit, quam plena doloris.
Ejus miranda compassio qua tribulatis
jugiter occurrens implevit opus pietatis.
20 *Jam nunc flere libet quia nos mors impia caedit*
dum procul a nobis solatrix nostra recedit.
Aret solsequium, marcet rosa, lux tenebratur
falcastro mortis Idae dum vita putatur.
De tenebris raptam regnis coelestibus aptam
25 *Qui lucem donat Deus hanc sine fine coronat.(n)*
Jam canit inde la-sol et verum nunc habet esse
cujus multiplici cumulantur semina messe.
Ida, vale, nostrique memor per saecula vive,
quae non ulterius poteris lugere morive.

Ida, the cloister's new mirror,[217] the nun[218] ever-faithful,
she bloomed with a tinge,[219] the high decor of Rachel.[220]
Sweet friend of God, by the bright lamp[221] of virtue,
fervent self-libation on his altar of love.[222]
5 For all shone[223] her love from her mind so serene;
for the sad and the glad flowed[224] her full-breasted milk.
Her love, an outburst of flame to a glorified Christ,
oft whisking[225] her loved self to see her Beloved
From on high she received this wonderful gift,
10 that the triune bestow himself, a spectacle for her gaze.
Hers a prudent love, who shunned all hurtful things

---

[217] In prose passages I usually render this term as 'looking-glass', but see *Ab* 8b, n. 44.

[218] *nonna*, the feminine of *nonnus*, the reverential title for a senior monk (nun) in *RB* 63.12. From it comes the French term *nonne* and the English itself, nun.

[219] *Praefusa*, rare word, suggesting cosmetic smearing or, in this case of a mirror, a pleasing tint. Henriquez changes it to the more familiar *perfusa*, 'drenched'.

[220] Allusion to the more contemplative of the sisters in Gen. 29.17.

[221] Not the *lucerna* of Matt. 5.15 but the *lampas* of Matt. 25.1.

[222] 'Libation' is a lavish pouring, normally of a liquid; 'fervent' refers to a 'boiling'. The combination suggests a lavish vaporization and combustion of an oily fuel on the wick of the lamp.

[223] Here the reference swings from the *lampas* of Matt. 25.1 to the *lucerna* of Matt. 5.15

[224] Literally Ida 'pours' her breasts 'into' them.

[225] 'Carrying' envisaged by the verb *veho*, as in our English word 'vehicle'. The passive, 'vehor' is normally rendered in the more active sense of 'to ride'. See *Arn* II.20g, n. 179.

and kept watch for the good, with high God on her side.
Hers a strong love, who snapped the chain of death
In setbacks she was patient, without any complaining.
15 [And no wonder, since following Christ did so please her.][226]
Swooning of the flesh, weeping and vomiting of blood:
these show her measure, her fullness of grief.
Hers a compassion ever wondrous to all caught in trouble
how she hastened to meet, to fill their each pitied need.
20 Now weep for ourselves, whom death, ever loveless, is smiting
in smiting her, our consoler, who slips so far away.
Withers the sunflower, wilts the rose, dark goes the light,
when the scythe of death mows down the life of our Ida.
Snatched from dark shadows, as apter for heavenly realms,
25 her light-giving God there crowns her, crowns without end.
Now on a thrilling la-sol[227] she sings, has a truer existence:
seed sown and hundredfold-harvested time[228] and again!
Ida, farewell, and, mindful of us, live on for all ages,
where grieve you cannot, nor mourn more, nor die.

Here end the verses.

---

[226] The second line missing in both manuscripts (B fol. 34ra; A fol. 178^r), but what Henriquez supplies (p. 292) has a ring of authenticity.

[227] Both manuscripts read *canit in delasol* (B fol. 34rb; A fol. 178^r), which Henriquez transcribes as *canit inde la sol* (*sic*, with the period; p. 293). How well each understood the musical reference, I cannot say. Almost the same expression occurs in the epitaph given as the second appendix to the Life of Abundus, below: *Nunc canit in LA SOL qui quondam flevit in UT RE.* For further textual variants and for what is meant musically, see the introductory note to that appendix.

[228] Echoing the parable of Mark 4. 3–9.

Appendix II

Ida in the Dialogues of Caesarius[229]

Of a Virgin Abstaining from Gluttony,[230] to whom the Devil Offered a Goose·[231]

There was a certain virgin, born at Nivelles, who for the love of Christ abandoned her father's home and family[232] and joined the company of certain womenfolk of that province. Among them she gained her living by the work of her hands and so found leisure to engage in prayers and fasts. These virtues of hers became the envy of the devil, who thereupon seized a goose from her father's house and set it down upon the dinner table where she and those womenfolk were sitting. His comment was: 'Why, poor wretch? Why torment yourself with hunger. Take this and eat it!' She

---

[229] The anonymous heroine of this anecdote in Caesarius (*DM* 4.84, p. 251) is identified by Walter Simons, *City of Ladies*, p. 41 and p. 173, n. 29 as being Ida, despite doubts expressed by Alcantara Mens, *Oorsprong en betekenis van de nederlandse begijnen- en begarden-beweging. Vergelijkende studie: XIIde–XIIIde eeuw* (Leuven: Universiteitsbibliotheek, 1947), p. 367, n. 121. I agree with Simons, since it is entirely in character and in chronological harmony with our Ida. One wonders if the devil made use, not only of a local goose, but also of a local lad to carry it.

[230] *De virgine abstinente.* Not specifically abstinence from meat, but from inordinate eating. This whole section (Caesarius, *DM* 4.77–91), is about temptations to *gula* (gluttony), and in it Caesarius's two other uses of *abstinere* are either as a generic synonym for 'gluttony' (4.80, p. 248), or as specific abstinence from drinking (4.90, p. 256). In resisting the temptation, Ida cites no dietary rules, but only the commandment against theft.

[231] When the creature is named *anser*, the pronouns are masculine; and when it is named *avis*, they are feminine. What's sauce for the goose, is sauce for the gander.

[232] *Domum patris et parentes deserens:* according to *Niv* 1ef, the father died before she left home, and the mother soon afterwards. Perhaps Caesarius is using the plural, *parentes*, in a broader sense of a child's 'nuclear family', as in modern French.

replied: 'I am not allowed to eat of it, for it comes from theft.'[233] The devil retorted: 'Not at all, for it was from your father's house that I took it!' The virgin insisted: 'You are not going to be able to deny that it is stolen. Pick the goose up and off with you to restore it whence you stole it.' At that he could see he was getting nowhere and so, in full sight of the womenfolk, he lifted the bird and restored it to the shed from which he had stolen it. Indeed, it was thus attested by those of her father's household, for they had heard a great racket and outcry among the other geese both while the devil was removing this one and when he was putting it back. And so let me tell you[234] yet two more examples by which you will learn how the devil terrifies and confounds those whom he overcomes with a longing for dishes of meat.

---

[233] For Ida's concern for economic integrity, see *Niv* 4a, 10b, 15c, 27f. For a comparable episode in another Life, see *Lov* I–4b (and the whole third chapter that follows).

[234] Caesarius is here addressing the 'novice', the interlocutor of his 'dialogue' format. He regularly uses this device to announce the topic of upcoming chapters.

Appendix III

Ida in the Life of Beatrice of Nazareth

Just as Reypens, in his Latin edition of Beatrice's Life, offers as an appendix a critical edition of *Niv* 25a–g and 28e–h which involve Beatrice (*Bijlage* VI, pp. 218–220), so I here offer an annotated translation of passages in Beatrice's Life which involve Ida, namely *Beat* I.10–11, (numbers 49–60), I.14 (numbers 67–68) and part of III.1 (numbers 188–191). I do not include *Beat* I.17 (numbers 76–77, alluded to in my notes on *Niv* 28e–h), since it does not mention Ida and sheds no new light on her personality. It could, however, serve as an interesting example of 'sending God'. Readers with access to the CF edition of Beatrice will enjoy access to the Latin text on the facing page. My notes aim only to draw out what light the text throws upon the person and spirit of Ida.

The present selections are translated from the Latin Life, which faithfully reproduces a personal journal written by Beatrice herself, hence the extraordinary vividness of detail. The Christmas episode (nos 52–55) is surely the finest of all examples of 'sending God'. We need to remember that both its protagonists were still teenagers, and also that Walter, the pioneer of 'sending God', was still abbot of Villers.

There is also an excellent parallel to Arnulf's experience of tears and laughter (nos 55, 58). The description of the impact Ida's death had on Beatrice (nos 188–191) offers rich parallels to Ida's own 'campaigns' on behalf of recently deceased friends (*Niv* 5a; 8ab; 10ab; 14a–d), and her asking God to send her an illness as a suffrage (5a; 6a). It also echoes themes of intercession in *Arnulf*.

I 10. Her Profession and Assignment to La Ramée to Learn Penmanship

(49) After this year of probation as a novice, having done her best to keep the monastic Rule, Christ's virgin[1] is[2] accepted for profession and is fully initiated, body and mind, into Christ's band[3] of brides. Ah, it was something to see, fulfilled at last, so fervent and longstanding a desire of her heart, and one which she had been so afraid of desiring too strongly, lest it never come true in her lifetime. As the time for profession drew nearer, and she could see how soon she would be initiated into that band of Christ's handmaids, each time she recalled it, tears would well up from her tender eyes in such a flood that no exertion of hers could hold them back. On the profession day itself, she the poured tears from her eyes like streams flowing from a wellspring, as if the floodgates (Gen. 7.11) of her head had been set loose. It was her mind's unrestrained gratitude that made them flow on so ceaselessly, and the rampant gladness of her heart, which removed any obstacle to them which shame or sheer reasoning might raise. And so, in the following passages we shall explain, as best we can, what *conversatio* Christ's servant now began to adopt among her fellow nuns, once she was incorporated into their band; how integrally she carried out the observance of the Order's regime; how fervently she *bore the burdens of others* (Gal. 6.2) on her own shoulders; and above all how she presented herself to her Bridegroom, Christ the Lord.

(50) Thus it was that, when her year of probation was over and she had been united to the band of nuns, only a short time passed before her venerable abbess had the thought that she should be despatched to a monastery of the same Order named La Ramée, where she would learn the craft of penmanship, in which she would later

---

[1] In my translation of these selections, I often intrude the personal name 'Beatrice' where it is not found in the Latin. I do this simply to clarify who is who in the sentence. It is surprising in a Latin writer when the author himself five times uses that personal name without adding any qualifying noun or adjective. The epithet he does use most frequently (eight times) is *famula*, to which he joins a divine possessive or else a laudatory adjective. *Famula* is an adjective, whose abstract noun is *familia* (household); whence a *famula* is literally 'a female domestic servant'. The Latin New Testament avoids the word, except in Heb. 3.5, preferring the more radical terms *servus* (male slave) and *ancilla* (female slave). In monastic texts, however, *ancilla* becomes honorific, and so our author reserves it for the mature nuns of the community, presenting the young Beatrice as a *famula*. In the same way, alert to her youth, he twice calls her *juvencula* (damsel). He gives her the honorific title *virgo* (virgin) only in the ceremonial context of her profession. He once calls her God's *electa* (chosen one), for in that context she is singled out for a gift not shared by those around her.

[2] In exciting narrative passages, our author often lets his verbs slip thus into this historic present tense.

[3] Throughout these selections I use 'band' to translate *collegium*, and 'company' to render *societas*.

be engaged for copying books needed for her church. There she came upon a nun of that place, Ida of Nivelles. How privileged and deserving[4] this venerable[5] lady was with God, can be gauged from a book of her life, full of the wondrous deeds she accomplished by the favour of grace from above. These deeds are there for any to read for themselves, or to listen to when read in public.[6] To this blessed woman[7] the devoted damsel now linked herself with an inseparable bond of charity.[8] Daily she diligently came[9] to seek a *word of edification* (compare Eph. 4.26; *RB* 6.3) from

---

[4] *Magni meriti domina [...] qualis quantive meriti fueri [...].* In ecclesiastical usage, *mereri* has the twin meanings of 'deserving' and of 'being privileged'. I change the sequence a little to capture both senses.

[5] While the author usually names Beatrice a *famula* (servant), he habitually names Ida a *femina* (woman; see n. 7 below). But just as with Beatrice, so with Ida, he sometimes uses the personal name without adding any dignifying term in apposition, or at most adding *Nivellensis* (the Nivell-ite). This happens notably in rubrical passages introducing direct speech. When special honour is called for, the author will name her *domina* (lady), and Beatrice herself will address her as such.

[6] The author seems to foresee that his work will be used for public reading. In a nuns' house, with a limited library, the same work would be read again and again, especially before compline. The readers, if only semi-literate, would be more or less reciting the oft-heard text by heart. At Ida's La Ramée, we can take it that manuscript B of her Life was used in this way, probably for centuries. The author invites those able to follow the text to lend it an attentive ear.

[7] *Huic ergo beatae feminae:* As mentioned in n. 5 above, the author often calls Ida a *femina*. More precisely, eight times *he* calls her the *beata femina* (blessed woman), and once a *tanti meriti femina* (woman of such great merit). He also once calls her simply *beata* without the *femina*. He never calls her *mulier*, though that is the ordinary secular word for a grown woman. The word *femina* literally names only the person's female sex, and applies equally well to young and old, regardless of marital status or dignity. However, in hagiography it is honorific and is equivalent to the masculine *vir*, as in the expression, *vir Dei (man of God)*. The author thus honours Ida for her maturity, while treating Beatrice as a child. He seems unaware of their actual closeness in age.

[8] Beatrice is famous for her vernacular vocabulary of 'love'. In theses selections the author uses: [a] the verb *diligo* (the love of caring) three times; the adverb *diligenter four times*; the noun *diligentia* and *dilectio* once each [b] the noun *caritas* (the love of endearment) five times: the adjectival form, *carus*, is not used in this selection [c] the verb *amo*, (the love of attraction) only twice. In these selections it is used only of love between heavenly beings.

[9] *Ex ore suo quotidie diligenter expetiit:* The *Sitz im Leben* of these sessions is important. My word 'came' is not literally in the Latin, but is implicit in the intensive seeking *(ex-petiit)*. If Ida was barely literate, she would hardly be part of the writing class (though the other Ida, from Gorsleeuw, if already on hand, would surely be enlisted for it, either as fellow student or even as teacher. Hence Beatrice's sessions with Ida would take place later in the day, and probably in the nook of the novitiate where Ida habitually dealt with novice clients (see *Niv* 5a; 7ab). Though the author depicts a very vertical relationship between the two teenagers,

Ida's mouth, so as to seize upon it and *sow* it in the *fruitful soil* of her heart (Matt. 13.3, 8), And thus it was that, as they frequented each other's company, there grew up between them a covenant of spiritual caring, a covenant which was later to remain unbroken for as long as they both lived. This Ida, the one under discussion, who was from Nivelles,[10] had a revelation from the Holy Spirit to the effect that our Beatrice was, beyond a doubt, meant to be adopted by the Lord as a special bride of his, and that the fullness of his grace was to be poured *superabundantly* (Eph. 3.20) into the vessel of her soul. And for this reason Ida diligently made herself entirely available to Beatrice, and set herself totally at her service, putting all possible solicitude into shaping her for that role by means of salutary counselling. Our devoted virgin Beatrice, not ungrateful for benefits so generous, repaid them by putting herself at Ida's service in whatever way she could. In Ida she found and loved a mother, found and followed a leader, found and embraced a source of nourishment, even a wet-nurse, who daily suckled her with sweet conversation, and who assiduously trained her by word and example.

(51) For her part, Christ's devoted damsel was in wonderment over that blessed woman, just to think how diligent and how serviceful she daily showed herself. Beatrice, in fact, reckoned herself entirely unworthy to be admitted to such a treasury of intimacy, especially on the part of one who, she could not doubt, was of immense merit, of great authority and of high reputation *before God and mankind* (Wisd. 4.1) In contrast with Ida, she reckoned herself of no importance and of no merit, as being by no means worthy to be singled out like this and catered to with so sublime an intimacy. Wherefore, on *one of the days* (Luke 5.17) Beatrice made up her mind and approached the venerable Ida, to explore the truth of these dealings. She would converse with Ida humbly and familiarly until she found out the real meaning of so intimate an involvement, so sedulous a servicefulness, and so gracious a rapport,[11] shown to herself, who was so lowly and small, so different from her in merit, so unlike her in the way she lived. The venerable Ida replied: 'The reason I love you with so indissoluble an affection is less for any merits or virtues I presently see you adorned with, and more for those to which I know for certain that the Lord is going to raise you up later on. For I do not doubt that the loving-kind Lord of mercies is going to open the eyes of his pity upon you, and choose you as a most faithful bride for himself and drench you in a brimful outpouring of his grace. Your part, then, is earnestly to show those majestic eyes that you are not ungrateful for such generous

---

and a sacrosanct tone, I suggest there would also be a horizontal dimension, with Ida looking up to Beatrice as a tutor in Dutch.

[10] *Illa quippe quam prefatus sum Nivellensis Ida:* this strange expression would make good sense if the author intended it to distinguish between La Ramée's two Idas, but since he seems unaware even of Ida's age, I doubt that he knew of her namesake.

[11] Reypens's printer has interchanged lines 66 and 67. The error is repeated in the CF edition, both in Latin and in English.

benefits. If there lurks in the vessel of your heart anything superfluous, then take diligent care to rid yourself of it, and do your best to prepare in that heart a place apt for divine grace. For *he who has* already *begun* to show forth *in you* (Phil. 1.6) some indications of his liberality, will not in any way withdraw from you the hand of his wonted loving-kindness, and if in this world you take care to make good use of the honeyed gifts of his grace, he will correspondingly multiply your glory in the next.'

(52) On receiving this reply, Beatrice became wondrously exultant in the Lord, for she now had in hand a firm hope and a full trust in what was promised, perfectly sure as she was that so deserving a woman, begirt with such affluent graces, would never pronounce such things so emphatically unless she were proffering them as one enlightened from on high. For in making her promise, Ida had indeed used a tone of voice suggestive of such freedom, and without a trace of doubt. Thus began in Beatrice a desire of no mean intensity, and soon it was fanned into a flame to match many a torch. Accordingly, since Ida was the one who had received this assurance of a great perfection destined for herself, Beatrice now wish this blessed one graciously to offer a sacrifice of prayer to the Most High, in which she suppliantly commending herself to almighty God's clemency. This is why she again sought out the blessed woman's company and presented her request, humbly beseeching her and insistently begging that she fulfill this desire by assenting to her petitions.

And once more the most blessed Ida replied: 'What is it, my daughter, that you desire to receive this time, and what would you obtain through me? For you can be sure that I am ready to obey your good pleasure in all matters. No need ever to hesitate to tell me in full of any desire which grace from on high inspires in your heart.' Christ's humble servant then made answer: 'This I ask, milady, that you would take pains to pray to the merciful Lord and to obtain for me from him that he would refresh and strengthen me with a share and a taste of that singular grace, the experience of whose sweetness he gives only to his chosen ones and to those special friends whom he takes into his most intimate service even in this world.' To which Ida responded: 'Ready yourself for Christmas as the day on which the loving, kind Lord will without fail[12] deign to fulfill your heart's desire and to pour into it the grace for which you are asking.'

(53) On receiving this further reply from the blessed woman, Beatrice becomes glad beyond measure, and with the eagerness of one forewarned she begins looking forward to the appointed day and to await the grace of the Lord's visitation. To put it briefly, the holy day of Christmas arrives and each hour finds Beatrice longing for that grace to be poured in. However, though this was the day assigned in the promise, the divine clemency was now arranging the matter otherwise and letting its sequence unfold differently. The event she had been longing for did not now occur. Not once on that day she did not perceive the slightest taste, the slightest experience

---

[12] *Irrefragabiliter:* from *refrago*, meaning 'to resist, thwart, gainsay'. In the actual sequel, the grace does 'fail' to come on Christmas Day, but Ida will offer Beatrice a plausible liturgical alibi for that.

of the grace she had been hoping for. She was indeed *plunged into* considerable *grief* (Lam. 1.13), and yet she managed to take the brunt of the blow upon herself and to bear with it patiently, humbly interpreting her failure to obtain the enjoyment of a heavenly grace on this most holy day as something demanded by her sins.

Whereupon Beatrice approaches the venerable Ida with her lament and her humble request, insistently interrogating her to learn for what reason this had happened to her. And so the blessed woman once more replied: 'No, it was not as you suspect. And no, it was not your sins that imposed this and made it happen. Rather, you should make up your mind that what you are hoping for will indeed occur, and it will be within the Christmas octave. And it would not become you to think I was wrong in my earlier response, even though what I promised did not occur on Christmas day itself. The fact is that anyone wishing to give effective honour to the mystery of the intervention God carried out in this season, should with good reason count as one and the same Christmas, all the eight days that lead up to holy circumcision.' Once more Beatrice accepted the blessed woman's consoling reply, and so rose once more to a wonderful blooming of hope. She began anew her insistent pleas, begging day and night for the promised grace, and humbly awaiting, with great and deep-felt emotion, *the time of her visitation* (Luke 19.44).[13]

I 11. On her Rapture and the Heavenly Vision Shown to her in Spirit

(54) It was indeed during this Christmas octave that it pleased the loving, kind Lord of mercies to carry out in Beatrice, his devoted servant, this expression of that loving kindness of his. On *one of the days* (Luke 5.17) when, as the season demanded,[14] *daylight was already giving way to evening* (Luke 24.29) and compline was being sung in choir, it so happened that Beatrice was on hand with the nuns of the place. She was seated while they sang,[15] and as all outward noise quieted down and she was making one great effort to raise her heart to the Lord, just then there came to mind the tenor of an antiphon which holy Church customarily recites on those days in high commendation of God's charity. It runs thus: 'Because of that exceeding charity of his, by which God loved us, he sent his Son in the likeness of the flesh of sin, that he might save all' (fourth responsory for Christmas week). As she diligently examined the words of this antiphon and investigated the ample material they afforded for praising God, her very conceiving and recalling of the

---

[13] A perfect attitude for one to whom God is being 'sent'.

[14] *Secundum exigentiam tempori [...] advesperescente jam die [...]:* I take this to be a reference to the early sunset in winter in places like La Ramée, north of the fiftieth parallel and unable to observe literally the horarium guidelines of *RB* 41.8–9.

[15] Beatrice had been ill and was still attending Offices in the choir of the infirm.

words, together with some devout steps she took in her meditating, now allowed her to mount upwards, and so, amid meditative praise and humble thanks, she followed that same Son up to the very presence of the Father. And when in her meditating she had arrived and could mount no further, there came to mind a second text, namely the one that is sung as a responsory at Eastertide: 'And David, with the cantors, was plucking the harp in the house of the Lord.'[16]

(55) As she meditated upon these word, giving them fresh attention and ruminating sedulously upon them, her mind took one great leap and she was transported into rapture. And thus she began seeing, not with the bodily eyes of her flesh, but with the intellectual eyes of her mind. And what she saw was the lofty and deifying Trinity. Her manner of seeing surpassed all wonder, for there was the Trinity, all gleaming in its brilliant comeliness, almighty in its *eternal strength* (Rom. 1.20). And there was David too, and the cantors of the Jerusalem on high, all making harmony on lyre and harp, all praising the majesty of God's magnificent might. And there was rank upon rank of holy spirits, band upon orderly band of super-celestial powers, all of them gazing ceaselessly upon the presence of the supreme deity: gazing and fervently loving; loving and jubilantly chanting, though chanting in the tranquil silence of peace, tranquil and wondrously praising the supreme essence of the Trinity. Grateful to have been allowed to see these things, Beatrice now strove sedulously to raise her focus and her affections so as to join those throngs in magnifying the presence of their Creator.

At that moment, however, compline came to an end, and the community of nuns began climbing[17] to the dormitory to take their rest, each retiring to her bed. And as for Beatrice, not having adverted to any of what was going on outside her, she simply stayed put, motionless in the sweetness of her contemplation. When all had withdrawn, leaving her alone, there she was, all bent over on her stool, and seemingly asleep. One of her colleagues, imagining her overcome by ordinary sleep, approached and gently tugged on the hem of her outer garment, believing this would awaken her from that sleep. But she remained unaware of such outward happenings, and so the other kept tugging the harder on the garment and shaking her to jolt her out of her sleep, sure as she was that it was just a bodily slumber. And such was her importunity that Beatrice did eventually resume her outward human senses and come back to herself. Yes, this newly fledged contemplator of heaven's wonders finally came back to herself!

---

[16] The full text is found in the Westmalle Breviary as the ninth responsory for the third Sunday after Easter: 'The people of Israel was chanting, alleluia; and the whole multitude of Jacob was singing as prescribed: and David, with the cantors, was plucking the harp in the house of the Lord, and singing praises to God, alleluia, alleluia. And therefore the priests and Levites sanctified themselves and the whole of Israel brought along the ark of the covenant of the Lord in jubilation.' The responsory is based on I Chron. 15.27–28. Presumably Beatrice had been copying this text recently in her writing classes. See a parallel in *Lew* 18–19a, 52b.

[17] Typically a flight of steps led directly from the transept of the church to the dormitory.

(56) On coming back to herself, Beatrice took stock of what it meant thus to be recalled from the delights of heaven to the miseries of the human condition. There she was, planted solidly on the earth, she who moments before had mingled among the joys of the heavenly spirits. At such at though she sighed heavily and began to shed copious tears. Indeed, she so drenched her face with her crying that the one who had awoken her, and was still standing close by, became alarmed, convinced that some sudden attack was about to invade her body. So, as Beatrice wept and grieved, this fellow nun took a seat beside her and, taking hold of her wailing head, laid it in her bosom. After that, in the measure the night silence allowed, she wiped away those tears and nestled her as she wept, ministering to her grieving heart with all the good offices of a devout compassion.

A little later Beatrice was led to her bed, and there she began meditatively turning over what had happened to her, recalling where she had been and what she had seen. All of which moved her to a thankfulness so unspeakable, to a joyousness so unaccustomed, that no consciousness that has not experienced it could ever grasp the immense prodigality of it all. Indeed even one who has experienced it, could scarcely set it out in orderly words. Just then, however, something remarkable happens, prompted by that sheer overflow of tears. All this day Beatrice has been experiencing a persistent heaviness in her every member, such that she has the impression that she is being laid low with an immensely burning fever, or by the impact of some strange illness. But now, lo and behold, she recovered her bodily health, and so thoroughly that she could feels no further trace of the illness. No one could call into question the fact that this cure occurred outside the order of nature, since an outpouring of tears, when excessive like this, necessarily debilitates one, rather than relieving one from existing debility.

(57) The result of all this was a joyous gladness, which soon grew beyond bounds. Beatrice was lingering on the gladness when, a short time later, along came the venerable Ida and some other nuns of the same band. They were approaching simply to pay Ida a visit after hearing the news that something new and unusual had overtaken her, either in body or in mind, and that it happened because she had been pushing herself harder than usual.[18] Meanwhile there was just one person for whom the mystery behind the occurrence was no hidden secret, namely the one whose prayers had, so shortly before, obtained it as a grace from God. Seeing them advance towards her as a compact group, Beatrice suddenly burst into a great fit of laughter, stemming from her supreme gratitude. So vigorous was that laughter that her heart,

---

[18] *Ex eo quod plus solito se gerebat, insolentius accidisse:* the only other reflexive use of *gerere* I know of is in I Sam. 18.30, where David conducts himself 'more prudently than all'. Like that text, the present one also involves a comparison, *plus solito* (more than usual), and in the concrete situation Beatrice does sound as though she has been 'pushing herself too hard'. But to express that in good Latin, I would expect our author to add an adverb of intensity with the *plus*. Perhaps he did indeed supply such a word, but it somehow fell out in the copying. The EP edition translates as if *plus solito* were *modo insolito* (behaving in an unusual way).

for all its efforts, simply could not bear with their presence.[19] For it seemed to her that her heart would split apart under too great an onrush of gratitude if ever the venerable Ida moved even slightly closer.

(58) Undergoing this boundless madness of heart, and dreading that the new arrivals would notice if it went on any longer, Beatrice's one inner, wordless wish was to have her excessive, intemperate laughter escape their sight, precisely by having the lamp go out, which alone illuminated the entire dormitory. And that is just what happened, for the lamp forthwith fell down and went out, rendering the whole dormitory pitch dark. In obeying a divine command, it was catering also to a desire of God's servant Beatrice. But then, once again, even though she could not be seen, she feared she could at least be heard, and so she again turned to the Lord and poured out her pleas, begging him to turn away all those nuns who had come to her, and to free her once more from their presence, which was more than she could bear. And that too is just what happened. They had not yet come any closer to her when they received a divine instruction and withdrew forthwith. Going away like this, they left God's chosen one unmolested, her whose one wish now was to take leisure for God alone in the newness of the grace she had received. Divinely set at ease in this way, Christ's servant could now engage the more authentically in renewed enjoyment of the grace received, in that the dark and the silence of night left her so much the freer, with the others all asleep, and some of them even entirely ignorant of what had been happening. On the other hand, as time went on and she took prolonged and delightful pleasure in the sweetness of the new grace, she was still, willy-nilly, laughing that immoderate chuckle, and had still to keep begging the Lord, all night long, not to let the sound of her laughter be detected by the others. For the fact was that, until then, she had never experienced a joyousness of the kind she now had in the sweetness of this newly outpoured grace, and the effect of the novelty was to set her imagining, time and time again throughout the night, that she was floating in the air.

(59) And what wonder of it? She had been *introduced into the wine cellar* (Cant. 2.4), and so she could not but erupt into drunkenness, a drunkenness not of the outer senses, such as would alter them only outwardly, but a drunkenness that inwardly gladdened the mind with a sweetness full of unspeakable thankfulness and joy. Yes, dear reader, weigh it up for yourself. Think how great a bliss the spirits of the saints must have in the fatherland, as they cling perpetually to the supreme good itself, inasmuch as for this one moment Beatrice's own spirit could be exposed to it, and could bring back to this stranded and lingering life, so overflowing an abundance of delight. Nor did so copious a bliss suddenly vanish. Rather the sweetness of this heavenly grace perdured in her spirit for a full month and more.[20] From that time on

---

[19] Compare with other instances of the inability to 'bear a presence' in *Niv* 14c; 19e and especially 33f.

[20] For other such lingering consolations, see *Niv* 21e, 23c.

she was wondrously renewed in spirit and began pressing ever tighter in her loving embrace of the supreme good. For her eyes were now enlightened, and her affections thoroughly trained, and she was rid of all impeding torpor, with the result that she could henceforth renew herself daily in the service of almighty God and in the tolerance of all that came her way.

(60; I 12) A few days after these events, having now made enough progress in the art of penmanship, God's servant Beatrice bade farewell to La Ramée and made her way back to her own monastery of Florival. She was being recalled there by her venerable abbess, for it had been into that friendly band that she had earlier been incorporated by vow at her profession, and it was their company she would now rejoin.[21]

I 14. On the Subtlety of Spirit and the Fortitude which she Obtained from the Lord in Receiving the Sacrament

(67) That was also the time when Beatrice sent the above-mentioned venerable courier[22] to Ida of Nivelles, on whose patronage she relied with great and heartfelt trust. The courier explained to Ida all about Beatrice's recent disquiet, the form it had taken and the cause that lay behind it, and how, at a hint from the Lord, she had readily promised faithfully to make up for her earlier neglect . And, as a suppliant servant of Christ, Beatrice also suppliantly and earnestly asked Ida to propitiate the divine clemency in her regard by the suffrage of her prayers. That blessed woman immediately sent word back that Beatrice should take care to receive the communion of the saving mystery of our redemption, namely the life-giving sacrament of the Lord's body. With that, the loving, kind Lord would condone the negligence she feared, and his accustomed loving kindness would then pour into her mind the sweet draft of a yet newer grace, and she herself, on receiving this divine consolation, would by the new experience of the new grace, emend the status of her former life.

This reply from that blessed woman magnificently refreshed her, and she began forthwith to prepare the vessel of her body and to use every effort to focus her attention. Her thought was to follow the promptings of her conscience and so to use the hoe of confession to pluck out whatever there was in her of vice; and likewise to engage ceaselessly in earnest prayers (RB 4.56); and to keep a stricter watch than usual on the tenor of her regular observance and of the other works of the virtues. All this was to be the earnest and untiring preparation of her mind for receiving the divine grace. But in doing all this she was deceived by an excessive simplicity,

---

[21] *Ab olim incorporata fuerat, amico collegio denuo sociatur*: a rich vocabulary of community.

[22] Probably Bartholomew, the saintly father of Beatrice and her sisters, who had founded the monastery and now served it as a lay brother and a general exterior *factotum*.

imagining she could acquire the grace by this kind of exertion in outward toil. Grace, of course, is given gratis, but here she was, thinking to buy its incomparable gift by bargaining with bodily actions in exchange. She was, however, doing her best to renovate the house of her conscience, and so it was that, with an eye to the next Sunday, she arranged to be nourished with the food of life. Then, with humble heart, she duly received the life-giving sacrament of the Luke, just as she had been told to do.

(68) The promise thus received proved truthful and unmistaken. After receiving God's eucharistic pledge, Beatrice was immediately and wondrously reanimated in spirit, and felt herself inwardly strengthened by a new thrust[23] of spiritual fortitude and constancy, with the result that, willy-nilly, she had to follow that thrust whithersoever it led. At this time her spirit also received from the Lord's generosity an illumination for its understanding, such that the gaze of her discretion was now reinforced, and the energies of her reason were uplifted, and she could henceforth exercise her rational judgment without the need for words,[24] being enabled to recognize the pathway of truth on which she should walk, and she could perform the subtle and discreet examination needed for judging between things good and evil, things profane and serviceable.[25] This was also when, in a subtle insight of her spirit, she reverted to the plain evidence that she had been ill-advised in previously aspiring to bargain for a grace from heaven's liberality, for she now came to know and to grasp that heaven's gifts are distributed, as the etymology of the term implies, without any character of reward or recompense. Rather, *he who gives abundantly and ungrudgingly* (James 1.5), dispenses gratuitously to whom he wishes, in the

---

[23] *Nova quadam fortitudinis et constantiae spiritualis insolentia:* This last word, *insolentia*, though derived from the quite common term, *insolitus* (unaccustomed), is rather rare in the present sense of 'excess, insult, thrust, attack'. It seems, however, to be a favourite term of Beatrice's biographer, since it occurs repeatedly within our passage: twice in noun form, and once as an adverb. Like Goswin, our author is groping for vocabulary to express mystical experiences. Notice also his two uses of *vellet nollet*, from which comes the seemingly colloquial English, 'willy nilly'.

[24] A gift close to Ida's intuiting of the 'status' of anyone she met: Niv 4b; 9a; 10c; 11b; 17c; 18a; 21b; 22c; 18bg. Perhaps we today would describe it more in terms of a teenager's maturation, a transition from a starry-eyed awe of all adults to a greater confidence in her spontaneous assessment of them, purged, of course, of any distorting force, such as jealousy. I suggest that this was a major part of Ida's aim in her guiding of Beatrice. See also Goswin's use of *susurrium* in discussing such soul talk; see *Niv* 1eg, 4b, 9c, 12b, 17a, 21d, 25d, 26e, 28f, 32d, 33h; and also Cawley, 'Ida of Nivelles, Cistercian Nun', pp. 315–317).

[25] *Profanum et utile:* the biblical pair is rather *sanctum et profanum* (Lev. 10.10; Ezek. 22.26). Regarding *utile*, I cannot say if the author was thinking of that word's use in *RB*, but it may be worth comparing *RB* 3.2; 7.18; 32.2; 42.4; 72.7. See also the abstract noun, *utilitas*, which in the plural takes on a concrete meaning: *RB* 2.7; 3.2, etc. *Utilis* is rare in Goswin, but comes strikingly in *Ab* 12ce, precisely regarding Abundus's sister's vocation to La Ramée.

manner he wishes and when he wishes, without anything like venal calculation. As a result she now judged herself to blame for so great and excessive a presumption, and she resolved to make satisfaction to her almighty judge, and never again to rely on her own energies or to presume that she could attain to meriting a gift of divine grace. She obliged herself to this with a voluntary promise to the Lord. It was also from that time on that she resolved to bring a stronger desire to her pursuit and cultivation of the virtues, to try also to redirect the wayward wanderings of her thoughts, as well as all itching dissipation at work and in conversation. She would strive to turning these to good account within a well-mended life,[26] *lest she have received the grace of God in vain* (II Cor. 6.1). Thus with a firm resolve did she promise for the future to conform herself to the divine good pleasure.[27]

III 1. How Beatrice was Privileged to be Cleansed of all her Sins

[183b ... 187][28]

(188) For the next two weeks[29] Beatrice waited and waited in most fervent desire for the Lord to visit her, but the only significant thing to happen was the death of two very devout spiritual friends of hers. Both of them paid their share of the tribute imposed upon all flesh, and so took the common pathway and migrated to the state of immortality. One of these was the venerable Ida of Nivelles, whom we mentioned above. When talk of this reached God's servant Beatrice, she did indeed sustain great

---

[26] *Ad usum emendatioris vitae convertere studuit:* although each of these words has a strong background in *RB*, they do not seem to be deliberate borrowings. The nearest thing to this *emendatioris vitae* is where the abbot *efficitur a vitiis emendatus* (*RB* 2.40).

[27] *Divino beneplacito sese conformaturam:* this paragraph's talk of renewed human effort may seem to be in flat contradiction to what has just been said about the gratuity of grace. However, here all the talk is of moral reform in response to the 'divine good pleasure', whereas the talk of gratuity regarded the divine bestowal of mystical graces.

[28] In these opening paragraphs of the chapter, Beatrice asks the Lord to let her experience some intense suffering here on earth, in place of what would await her in purgatory. It is a kind of 'sending God' to oneself.

[29] From data given throughout the chapter (nos 83b–191), I suggest the following chronology in 1231 (a) 11 to 30 November: preliminary interlude: 'St Martin' (Tuesday) to 'first Sunday of Advent'; (b) 30 November to 14 December: the present *quindena* (fortnight): first-to-third Sundays of Advent; (c) 11 December: Ida dies: at sunset on the Thursday; (d) 12 December: Ida is buried and news of her death reaches Beatrice (Friday); (e) 14 December: Sunday:'fourth day' of Ida's death; beginning of Beatrice's 'five-day' illness; (f) 17 December: Beatrice, still in bed, sings Ember Wednesday's Marian liturgy (Missus est); (g) 18 December: 'seventh day' commemoration of Ida's death, and day of Beatrice's cure (Thursday) the fifth day since the illness began.

grief of heart from the temporal loss, but her patience soon regained its strength and allowed her to shake off the sting of grief and to rise to a great-hearted chorus of praise in honour of the clemency and loving-kindness of God.

(189) With these friends thus taken and gone, Beatrice began to meditate inwardly and to turn over in her mind the question of whether the very grief she had felt at their loss might not itself be the penalty the Lord was to have bestowed regarding her sins. To be sure, she reckoned such grief to be altogether too slight and trivial to suffice for the purpose, and so she was unwilling to settle for it, but began ceaselessly imploring the justice of God's majesty to let her receive some greater vindictive sentence, be it of body or of mind. Scarcely then has the fourth day dawned when, behold, Beatrice's whole body is invaded by a raging fever, of the kind they call acute.[30] At this, she is tormented with a raging bonfire, not only in her inner organs (as sometimes happens), but rather in every least particle of her body. Ah, but it was something to see! There she was from the first, with her spirit wondrously exultant and issuing devout praises of Almighty God, though her body lay in a painfulness so such excruciating that the whole local community reckoned that nothing else lay ahead for her but inevitable death. In fact, this very affliction of her body was itself the visitation her heart had been desiring from the Lord, and time and again she would break open her lips, groping for words of praise and of gratitude, and this is how she addressed him: 'O God, sweetness of my heart, smite me as much as you wish. I have brought myself to your justice as an object to be flogged.[31] Let not the rod of correction desist from its strokes and whipping, until everything I have ever done amiss has been filed flush.'[32]

(190) Secretly she drew added consolation from the words she thus repeated as she kept on invoking her God. This came from an ambiguity in her vernacular tongue, whereby the bystanders took her formula to be rather the outcry of a heart grown weak. Yet such was the vehement onslaught of the pain that in no part of her body could she get, even for the most fleeting moment, the slightest taste of respite. The one exception was when she would get a chance to bury her head in the pillow,[33] for then the noise of outward things would somehow quiet down and she could

---

[30] Meaning 'of brief duration'.

[31] *Tuae justitiae me flagellandum obtuli:* the *flegellandum* is not masculine, as if mistakenly used instead of the feminine, *flegellandam*, but neuter. We cannot but think of St Thérèse praying to become the plaything of baby Jesus. Compare also the prayer of Arnulf in *Arn* I 11b, etc.

[32] *Donec ad plenum elimata fuerint omnia quae deliqui:* mention of a 'file' makes perfect sense when we read it in the Epitaph of Arnulf, so familiar with blacksmiths, but one wonders how Beatrice brought the theme into her prayer.

[33] I suggest the relief came, not from the pillow but from the chance to warm her stomach against the mattress and so relax the adjacent muscles. Also, this posture signalled to visitors her need for silence.

meditate and turn over in her mind all the benefits God had bestowed on her. At those moments, as she faced down towards the bedding, those ministering to her would hush their chatter, as if to let her asleep. Freed in this way, her heart could express its devotion to the clemency of her Lord, who had seen fit to give her plea a hearing, and whom she could now honour with praise and thanksgiving. Just as water will wash away bodily smudges and stains, so she could sense the discomfort of this pain washing and inwardly cleaning her soul, and not letting anything remain in it by way of smudge, nor anything deserving of hurtful penalty, such as would call for cleansing later on in the bonfires of purgatory's flame.

(191) The more piercingly her little frame was pressed in upon from outside, so much the more joyous was the spiritual consolation refreshing her mind from within. And, wondrous to relate, neither could her body sense that inner sweetness, nor could her soul, so sated inwardly with those spiritual delights, get a taste of those outward molestations. Paradoxical as it is, the body's ailment was the soul's delight. For Beatrice's soul it was a time of renewal and recreation, of a sweetness beyond compare, a time for praise and exultation, and for resting quietly in the Lord. These were the Ember Days, with the liturgical Offices customary in the Church, and though Beatrice was still very sick in body, she was most healthy in mind. She was still bedridden, but throughout the time for mass she kept singing away out loud, associating herself to the band of singers there in the community, if not in body, certainly in heart and mind. And in this way she sang along with them for every piece prescribed for that Office. Five days passed between when the fever struck and when, by the clemency of providence she got well again. The outcome for her was like that of fire-tried gold, to which the blaze restores the natural sheen. And so it was when Beatrice's little frame passed through the scorching fires of that fever and came out more pure than gold refined in a cupel, more gleaming than any crystal. Yes, she had recovered an absolute purity of heart and had migrated into *the freedom of the children of God* (Rom. 8.21), as into some place of delightful refreshment.

Top: Arnulf's early patrons, Abbots Charles and Conrad of Villers.
Bottom: Arnulf of Brussels, lay brother of Villers.

The medallions here and on pp. 26 and 206 are from a large plate entitled *Soleil de Villers*, published by Anthony Sanderus, in his *Chronographia sacra Brabantiae*, Brussels, 1659. A copy is preserved at Westmalle Abbey, Belgium, whose librarian, Renaat Hus has kindly permitted this reproduction. This plate is studied by Jacques Pineault and Thomas Coomans: 'Le "Soleil de Villers", cycle iconographique cistercien du xviie siècle', *Cîteaux*, 45 (1994), 121–53. They argue convincingly that, although the plate survives only in the work of Sanderus, it was originally prepared for a work of Chrisostomo Henriquez, *Sol Cisterciensis in Belgio*, never printed. Henriquez, the great popularizer of Cistercian saints of this region, would have suggested to the anonymous engraver what traits to include in each medallion.

The Life of Arnulf

Lay Brother of Villers

Preface

(Pref. a; I.1)[1] The earth's vegetation, ranging from grasses to trees, is not all of a single species, nor of a single genus; rather, each and every plant germinates to the form of its own genus and to the characteristic of its own pedigree. Yet a plant's full adornment is bestowed on it, not all at once from the start, but in an orderly growth, carried ahead along predetermined steps of cumulative enlargement until a size is reached typical of maturity. So too for the seeding of the divine charisms and the sprouting of the virtues, as they move towards birth in the seed-ground of a human heart. Not straightway are they wholly what they are going to be, nor will you easily detect at their beginning what their ripening will show, nor at their outset how their finished look will be. By the same comparison, *no one becomes suddenly supreme* (Hugh, *Juet* Praef. 1), but different persons move ahead at differing paces, progressing *from virtue to virtue* (Ps. 83.8) according as God's grace has been smiling on each.[2] For his is the gift that enables *the unmeriting to move towards merit,* and from him we each acquire, *prior to any toil of our own,* the title to *earn a reward based on our eventual toil.*[3] *For there are diversities of graces* (I Cor. 12.4), as the blessed Apostle says, and *all have their own proper gift from God, one after this manner, another after that* (I Cor. 7.7). We can grant that our God Almighty

---

[1] The references follow Goswin's own division of this Life into a preface and two books, each of the latter having numbered chapters (12 and 21 respectively). To these chapter numbers, I append alphabetical letters in parentheses, to pinpoint the passage concerned more precisely. The other references (also in parentheses) are borrowed from the Bollandists, who replace Goswin's divisions with a system they apply widely in the AASS. I ignore the Bollandists' lengthy 'chapters', but offer their paragraph numbering within each book. In practice, I find Goswin's divisions more suitable and more helpful than those of the Bollandists, and all my cross-references are in his terms. I include the Bollandist paragraphs for the sake of readers wishing to check the Latin.

[2] *Secundum quod eis gratia Dei arriserit:* grace is often thus personified in Goswin. For example, he speaks of 'Mother Grace' in Pref. b and I.2f; also in *Ab* Prol. c and *Niv* 22a.

[3] Here and in the following paragraphs, I italicize several slogan-like phrases without knowing their source, perhaps taken from Augustine.

sometimes achieves in one or other servant of his, things singularly wonderful and wonderfully singular, things scarcely to be found in others. Nevertheless, such things do not set a precedent to make *the privileges of a few a norm for the many*.

(I.2) If such be the case; indeed, because such is the case, we deservedly treat as privileged the venerable *conversatio* our latter-day martyr,[4] Brother Arnulf. Indeed, you will scarcely find today in this mortal life anyone who would dare attempt an austerity of life like his, let alone keep it up in every detail.

(Pref. b) In the time that Arnulf was still conversant with this life, the private aspects of his *conversatio* were partly known and partly unknown. And so one Walter, a monk of Villers on very familiar terms with Arnulf, time and again asked him in private to share with him some of the edifying *good things of the Lord* (Ps. 26.13) with which Mother Grace had enriched him. Arnulf resisted every time, until Walter told him outright how greatly this saddened him and how he was not going to give up bothering him for it until he shared some such things. This insistence finally won out. Arnulf catered to Walter by disclosing many of his secrets. We in turn snatched these up[5] from Walter's mouth and commended them to memory with the intent of later putting them into writing. There have also been certain seculars, persons of proven religiosity, and certain brethren here at Villers, who have told us other secrets, which they had heard from Arnulf's own mouth. Their *testimony* seems *credible* to us (Ps. 92.5) and apt for throwing light on his *conversatio*.

(I.3) So, let the *lamp, once set on its candlestick, shed light for* the faithful *in* God's Church (Matt. 5.15)! Let us briefly throw light on Arnulf's wondrously righteous *conversatio*, as recounted to us by Walter and the other truthful witnesses. Let us call on the Holy Spirit to help us in this desire. Let his grace govern our heart and tongue and enable us to write what will benefit both our contemporaries and

[4] The theme of Arnulf as 'martyr' comes up also in Pref. c. In Book I it comes at 3d, 4b, 5e, 6cd, 11ac, 12be; and in Book II at 5c and 21aj.

[5] *Quae nos ab ejusdem monachi ore rapientes memoriae commendavimus, ut scripto postmodum traderemus:* the participle *rapientes* (snatching) suggests that Goswin heard from Walter, not in a private interview but in a public conference following Arnulf's death, in which Walter was a key speaker and Goswin an unofficial recorder. Walter is again named in II.7a, and is probably the unnamed witness in many other passages.

readers of the future.

(Pref. c) And in view of the many bodily afflictions the blessed man sustained, it seems fitting that Book I of his Life be confined to spelling out just the afflictions themselves and the instruments with which he inflicted them on his body.[6] From this all can learn how his prolonged martyrdom won him his crown. Then in Book II, with the Lord's help, we shall describe his virtues and revelations, along with the rest of his deeds.

---

[6] *Non solum corporales ejus afflictiones, sed etiam instrumenta afflictionum tantummodo annotare:* Book I is, in fact, built around such a list of instruments and austerities.

Book I

Arnulf and his Austerities

1. Early Life and Initial *Conversatio*

(I.1a; I.4) There lived in the diocese of Cambrai, in a leading Brabantine[7] town called Brussels, a youth by the name of Arnulf. They say he stemmed from middle-class parents. In the first flower of his youth, Arnulf paid no heed to Solomon's word about how *vain is youth and all its wanton revelry* (Eccles. 11.10); and he had no inkling of the good things the Lord was to do for him in the future. In his baptismal vows he had promised to *renounce the devil and all his pomps* (Liturgy of Baptism), but far from keeping such vows unsullied to the end, he had slipped into that levity of behaviour and of speech which is typical of a wandering wayfarer, bent on the twisting pathways to death and catering all he likes to the voluptuous whims of his flesh.

(I.1b) *The Lord, however, had set* Arnulf *apart since his mother's womb, and now it pleased the Lord graciously to call him* (Gal. 1.15) and to send him a spirit of saving counsel to enlighten the darkness of his heart and bring him back from his *wandering,* back to *the highway of truth* (Collect: third Sunday of Easter). The sweet whispering of this spirit awoke him from the sleep of death, and off he went to a priest, a vicar of Christ,[8] and vomited up in confession the harmful virus of his sins, *putting off the old Adam and his activities and putting on the new, created in accord with God in the justice and holiness of truth* (Eph. 4.22–4, Col. 3.9, *EO* 102.41–43).

---

[7] *Verae Brabantiae:* this is Goswin's only use of *verus* (true) with a place name. I would take Goswin to be vindicating the town's Brabantine character while admitting that it belonged to a generally non-Brabantine diocese, but Walter Simons tells me that Goswin means rather that Brussels is by now a town of note, already rivalling Leuven as the leading town of Brabant.

[8] Same expression in *Niv* 13c, 29b–1 and in *Ab* 16e.

(I.5) Thereupon he in turn *set himself* industriously *apart*, apart from the ill-disposed comradeship of worldly folk. Instead of them, he began frequenting the company of religious persons and exposing himself to familiar intercourse with the better of the menfolk. Their hortative influence and their holy prayers would make it easier for him to progress in his own betterment, as he ever more forcefully renounced all carnal enticement, all worldly vanity. He attended as many masses as he could, and on Sunday nights and the feasts of the saints, when the bells rang for early morning matins, he headed straight for church, anything but lazy!

(I.1c) If ever sleep oppressed him too lingeringly, so that he did not wake and rise at the sound of the bell but only later, he would nonetheless come to church, albeit tardy and with matins half over. But then, dejected and ashamed, ashamed before God, not before mere mortals, he would refuse to go inside to stand before his Lord; instead he *stood outside* (John 18.16) at a spot where *dripping raindrops dribbled* from the roof *to the ground* (Ps. 71.6). Yet only rarely did such tardiness befall him.

(I.1d; I.6) It is written that *the furnace proves the potter's ware, and troublesome temptation the chaste* (Ecclus. 27.6). Arnulf too was once tempted. The instigation was diabolic,[9] but Arnulf proved true. A woman, youthful in age, lewd in behaviour, worldly in her living, had seen how *handsome a lad he looked, and, caught in the trap of her own eyes she had blazed into a longing after him* (*VP*, I.iii.7; Ecclus. 9. 9). But, noticing how God-fearing he was, and how given to religious living, she blushed to lay bare the naked truth of her heart's love for him. And how rotten and stinking that love was! A mere drive towards lustful coition! Thus it was that she planned an artful way to lure him into sin. The opportunity she seized upon came at night time: he had settled down to rest on the bedding spread out for him and she, under cover of dark, sneaked into the chamber and up to the bed. Impudently she settled herself down beside him and launched into wanton words, words to egg him on to sin. But he, on hearing her, leapt from the bed and fled, leaving the poor frustrated wretch to grieve over her hopes thus confounded, and to slink away. But thereupon *a carnal temptation* seized upon Arnulf, and so forcefully (Gregory, *Dial* II 2.1)[10] that he would almost have slid into the whirlpool of sin, were it not for the Lord's proffering him the helping hand of his grace. For the Lord does not *suffer* his servants *to be tempted beyond what they are capable of; rather, he arranges an outlet from the temptation, so as to enable them to bear it* (I Cor. 10.13). Glad and thankful was Arnulf for the Lord's thus rescuing him, and he said: 'O Lord my God, in you I trust, hoping that, just as I have now been set free of this deadly fire, so henceforth, by your protection, no such *blaze* will ever master me' (Gregory, *Dial* II ibid.).

---

[9] *Instinctu diaboli tentatus est, sed probatus:* this is Goswin's only use of *instinctus*, but in Thomas, *Lut* I.22 we meet an *instinctus divinus*.

[10] Here the Life of Bernard is echoed more literally than that of Benedict, but thematically, Goswin clearly has both in mind.

(I.1e; I.7A)[11] For the rest, Arnulf fought on, a new athlete[12] manfully *preparing his soul for temptations* (Ecclus. 2.1). He passed another two years in this religious stance, ever building up his weaponry and keeping guard as best he could *against vices and sins* (*RB* 7.12). Yet he dreaded a relapse, which would make *his last state worse than his first* (Matt. 12.45), and so he resolved to pass over to the Cistercian regime. It was as if *he had received from the Holy Spirit an answer that he would not see death until* (Luke 2.26) he had become a lay brother under that regime and was living as admirable a life as any. To this end, without delay he enlisted two travelling companions: the fear of God and the hope of pardon.[13] His relatives and acquaintances, he now left behind (Luke 2.44), going his way and bidding the world farewell *forever and world without end* (Ps. 20.5).

2. Entering Villers; Three Penitential Ropes

(I. 2a; I.7B) And so Christ's new recruit stepped forth with Abraham, *out from his own land and kindred, to go to a land that God had shown him* (Gen. 12.1). He was in his twenty-second year,[14] and the monastery he came to was Villers. It was in the time of Abbot Charles that he applied and was received. And so, laying aside his secular garb and taking up that of the Order, he was granted fellowship within the lay brothers' community. Having become a novice, he looked forward with all goodwill and longsuffering to the appointed day, a year later, when his profession would come due. That day came around and as he made profession to his own abbot, the abbot supreme on high[15] was lavishing on him an abundant and quite singular blessing of heavenly grace, which we shall throw light upon as we proceed.

(I.2b; I.8) His year of probation was not yet far spent when he began to feel a *wholesome sadness* (II Cor. 7.10), for he had the impression of finding less than he had envisaged by way of toil and affliction. Inwardly, in his unspoken thoughts, he complained of himself and to himself: '*Why have I come* to this Order (*VP* I.iv.19)? Am I not wasting my days away in vain? Had I but stayed out in the world, I could have sustained far more affliction of body than I do here. And another thing inwardly tormenting me is how my body's every need is catered to, by way of food and clothing, all without any solicitude on my part, and far more abundantly than my body or stomach need. Look! I am but wasting my time! My days are flitting by, quite undeserving and fruitless!'

---

[11] The Bollandist numbering straddles the break between Chapters 1 and 2, and so I print their numeral (7) twice, here and at the head of Chapter 2, rendering them as '7A' and '7B'.

[12] The theme of 'athlete' comes also in *Arn* I.2g, 11a and II.8d.

[13] A comparable personification comes in *Ab* 15b; an even closer one in *Al* iv (4).

[14] From the figures in *Arn* II.21j, we know he entered Villers about the end of 1201.

[15] For a similar interplay between heaven and earth at a profession ceremony, see *Ab* 5c.

(I.2c; I. 9) Turning these matters over in his mind, and others like them, he used to wonder if the Order's penitential practices were not being somehow kept hidden from him. Thus, time and again he fell to thinking of something stiffer and more penitential to inflict on his flesh, something over and above the norm. And so he came up with one torment seemingly burdensome enough for his body. He stealthily made himself a pair of cords from fresh-spun horsehair, furnished him by the tail of a steed.[16] Oh how tightly he fastened those cords from knee to hip, wearing them many a day, till the hurt they did his flesh became vehement!

(I.2d) Then one day some bodily weakness made him swoon and he collapsed and slumped to the ground unconscious. A brother who saw it happen, feared that he must have imposed some unusual affliction on his body; and so, shortly after Arnulf's return to his senses he privately told him: 'Brother Arnulf, beware of overstepping the common practices of the Order and taking upon yourself without permission the singularity of a more rugged, more austere life. It could do great damage to your body!' The remark left him inwardly ashamed of himself and so he approached the monk who was his confessor and confessed to him having worn those cords without permission. The confessor upbraided him and enjoined a penance, forbidding him ever again to dare attempt the likes of it without permission.

(I.2e; I.10) His master's rebuke left him only the more constant, and so, with permission now, he made himself another cord, longer than before. Tying many a knot in it and winding it around his waist, he fastened it so tightly against his body that it served as a medicine all the more painful for its digging the more quickly through the skin, right into the flesh. It is remembered that he wore this cord for many a day, until after piercing the skin, it became so firmly embedded that the flesh began to rot and wriggle with worms. And what a stench all this belched forth!

(I.2f) Oh, the happiness of this newborn child, for whom Mother Grace is so solicitous that she not only nourishes him with the sweetness of her milk but also pours him a wine to drink, spiced with a stinging myrrh! There in his infant cradle, she swaddles him in the bands of these piercing cords, and with so sharp a flint knife, she circumcizes away any lewdness in his flesh.

(I.2g) Arnulf, the mighty athlete, was afraid the stench issuing from his rotting flesh might prove injurious to his neighbours, and so he took the step of withdrawing the rope from his flesh altogether. This was not from any lack of endurance but simply for the motive we have expressed.

---

[16] A more literal rendition would be grandiloquent: 'spun from the bristle which an equine tail ministered to him'. Notice that he already has access to horses, even if not yet officially a wagoner.

3. Rods and Broom Stems as Whips; Arnulf Explains his Intent

(I.3a; I.11) And so *the mighty warrior* (Jer. 20.11)[17] cast away those cords, and from then on planned an even fiercer plot against his body: yes, from then on, if any instrument of punishment came to mind with a new aptitude for hacking away at his flesh, it too he would be sure to mobilize into his warfare (ibid. 21.5). Accordingly, after pondering for some time the various rods and the kinds of blows each could impart,[18] he equipped his hand with a set of them. After that, he would strip to the waist, or at times disrobe entirely, and bring to bear on himself so severe a torment of beating that, wherever the smiting hand could reach, there the flesh would show many a furrowed stripe.

(I.3b) Offering the Lord such a sacrifice time and again, he endured the blows of those savage rods with such equanimity as to prove himself a true disciple of that Lord and master who had once yielded his own most holy flesh to a similar mangling and flogging. Progressing daily under the schooling of that master, the simple-hearted Arnulf *learned to be meek, to be humble of heart* (Matt. 11.29). He learned also that *art of arts, which is the art of loving.*[19] Of such love, the blessed Bernard asserts that it is *precipitous, vehement, flagrant, and impetuous, that it does not allow one to think of aught but loving, that it jumbles orderliness, dissimulates convention, ignores restriction, that it triumphs over, and reduces to captivity, everything that would seem to belong to propriety, to reasonableness, to respectability, to advisability or to mere judiciousness.*[20]

(I.12) Such then, was the love Arnulf longed to incorporate, with all the marrow of his heart, into his very viscera.[21] Thus he came to set less store by himself and somehow began to forget his body. Indeed, he came to despise earthly things and desired the heavenly instead, hovering aloft in love for the eternal.

(I.3c) This led him to see it as trivial to beat himself with mere rods, and so he took to gathering from the forests a woody and prickly-leafed evergreen called butchers' broom,[22] whose branches he bundled to beat himself with in private at any

---

[17] *Bellator fortis*: also used in *Arn* I.12b and, in the feminine, in *Niv* 13d, 14a.

[18] *Virgarum verbera consulens*: echoes of *RB*, the closest one being *plagarum virgae* in *RB* 28.3. Arnulf's equipment is again of the kind available to wagoners and stable hands.

[19] Opening words of William of St Thierry's *De natura et dignitate amoris*, ed. by M.-M. Davy, *Deux traités de l'amour de Dieu* (Paris: Vrin, 1953), p. 70; PL 184, 379c.

[20] From a treatise *De caritate*, chapter 6, edited by Mabillon and Migne (PL 184, 598c). It is a florilegium which those editors trace to St Bernard, in particular to his *Sermones in cantica* 79.1, ed. by J. Leclercq, *Sancti Bernardi opera* 1:272. In Mabillon/Migne the passage is in the second person singular, addressed to love; in Goswin, it is in the third person.

[21] *Totis medullis cordis inviscerare sibi*: same strong words in *Niv* 21d.

[22] *Roscum [...] lignum [...] virentibus semper foliis aculeatum*: literally, the *roscus* (or *ruscus*), a woody plant, prickly by reason of its evergreen leaves. Modern botanists, in fact,

time, summer or winter, with only Sundays and saints' days excepted. Let all give him credit for it: wherever his smiting hand found a free spot on his body, there in his relentless self-discipline he would strike until the blood flowed. The very branches of his prickly scourge he had to change repeatedly, taking up fresher ones in place of the many he shattered amid his persistent pounding. Not content to afflict his flesh with these beatings, he would think out new methods of affliction. Thus at times he would take those prickly leaves of the butchers' broom and tuck them into his bosom, next to the flesh. At other times he would take piles of the *thorny* twigs, spread them on the ground like a bed, and then *roll* in them, *entirely naked* (Gregory, *Dial* II 2.2).

(I.3d; I.13) One day a monk came to the grange where the man of the Lord was lodging. He inquired of the stable-keeper where Arnulf might be. The keeper, whose name was Nicholas, replied that he was 'in his purgatory'. This word puzzled the monk, who then asked what kind of purgatory was meant. So Nicholas told him Arnulf was engaged in afflicting his body with his customary purgatorial beatings. 'Oh', said the monk, 'gladly would I converse with him, were he to allow it; but I take it that, when he is engaged in such a matter, it is out of the question for him to come out to see me.' 'On the contrary', said the other, 'once informed of your arrival, he would be along without delay!' With this, Nicholas knocked on the cell door, announced the monk by name and told of his arrival and of his keen and friendly desire for a holy interview. Arnulf rapidly gathered his tunic around him, put his hooded cloak back on, and came straight out. The monk, noticing how muddied his tunic was with blood, and how the blood still trickled and ran from the freshly flogged body, was so pained at heart that he burst into tears, prompting Arnulf to ask why. The monk replied: 'I am pained and touched to the quick to behold such martyrdom! But why, dearest friend, why put yourself to such a death?' To which he offered only the joking reply that it was not himself he was putting to death, but his sins! Yet small wonder, given that the such frequent, sharp afflicting of the flesh so often exempts God's servants from a whole range of occasions for sin.

(I.3e; I.14) Another time he was in his cell for his customary whipping, unaware of a man standing at the wall outside and taking stock of his manner and measure of beating himself. This man tallied the number of strokes Arnulf gave himself: nineteen hundred of them, before ever he stopped![23]

---

call it *ruscus aculeatus*. The young shoots resemble asparagus, and are edible. By the time it flowers, it resembles holly, and is used in decoration. Dried and stripped of foliage, the straight, stiff stems are used for heavy-duty brooms around stables and barns. Hence the common name, butchers' broom. Arnulf would have gathered it in the forest primarily as material for brooms around the stable. It was likewise used penitentially by Ida the Eager of Leuven, along with clippings from her father's vines (*Lov* I.12b).

[23] This total, though rounded off to an even hundred, is not a mystical number. It rings true. At a rhythm of one stroke per second, it comes to thirty-one minutes and forty seconds. We can only guess how the eavesdropper tallied the total, but traditionally such episodes were

(I.3f) What a wonder! Who will not stand aghast at it! Oh, friend of God Almighty, what is it you are doing? Other folk seek only comfort, how to pamper their flesh! The world's military men do their battling, to be sure, but against their foes and never against themselves. But you, you do the opposite: you fight your own very flesh, declaring against it wars ever new, as might a crazed soldier in his fury. For Christ's sake, take pity on that poor, frail flesh, your own flesh, which you cannot live without! Or, if you really want to afflict it, at least talk it over with *Dame Discretion, that wet-nurse of the virtues* (*RB* 64.19), and allow her to teach you what measure of burden to load upon that beast which is your flesh. 'Not at all', he answers us, 'no such persuasion shall take effect! The foe for me is this flesh of mine, a foe the more formidable for being closer at hand! Beast of burden, indeed it is, needing to be jabbed with spikes and shoved, or it will laze in its lewdness and drag me to the whirlpool of death. And so I intend to keep stirring up against it wars ever new, wars ever fresh!'

4. A Cane to Beat himself; Nettles to Roll in

(I.4a; I.15) Arnulf, like a valiant soldier,[24] persevered in his holy resolve to battle against his flesh, until the torments already applied, or soon to be applied, to his body made him resemble a *lion, balking at the onslaught of none* (Prov. 30.30). Thus he came up with a kind of scourge whose blows would seem to many today quite unendurable. Indeed, many would be stunned and horrified even at the sight of it, a smiting-cane, which he fashioned from a wooden stick[25] and to which he gummed the pelt of a hedgehog, bristling with many a quill. This he would snatch up in *the power of the holy cross* (I Cor. 1.18) and then, like one *wisely unlearned* (Gregory, *Dial* II Prol. 1), he would flog himself wherever his flesh was thick enough and his smiting hand found access.

(I.4b) No, he would not spare himself at all. He would do more than even the martyrs of old, for they, in the wringing contortions they underwent, suffered always at the hands of others, whereas, for him, it was his own hands that did the striking, his own hands that heaped torment after torment upon him. Such merciless perforating of his body, such multiple jabbing, made each gash bleed enough to

---

measured by the number of repetitions they allowed of some common prayer formula, such as the *Pater noster* or the *Miserere* (Psalm 50).

[24] *Igitur miles fortissimus*: this military term, familiar from *RB*, is found also in *Arn* I.3f, 5e, 6ab, II.1d, 4e, 10a, 18d. The root *milit-* is also found in *Ab* Prol. a, 4b, 19a but never in *Niv*. However, see *bellatrix* (warrior dame) in *Niv* 13d, 14a.

[25] *Ferula*: Latin for the giant fennel, whose stalks were used as canes to discipline slaves and schoolboys. I take it that Goswin means to connect it the verb *ferire* (to smite), which he uses often; hence my translation, 'smiting cane'. For hedgehogs, see *Arn* I.6a, n. 32.

splash his entire hand and to coat it all blood-red. And yet, after each such furious whipping, whether with rods or with broom stems or with smiting-cane, when the next day came around, he would nonetheless find his body healed, divinely healed, with barely a few spots showing blackish on the flesh, where the stripes and puncturing had been.

(I.4c) Then again, fresh from a flogging, he would at times *roll naked amid nettles* (Gregory, *Dial* II 2.2), until, as he himself was to testify, the pains brought on by the biting nettles seemed sharper to him and more unbearable than any of the pain earlier endured.

(I.4d; I.16) Oh servant of the God on high, how can we tell of your grandeur? Not only did you think up, and make your own, those cords, those rods, those broom stems, but you added this smiting-cane; and what a smiter it was! Where, or when, did you ever hear of anyone daring to beat himself with a cane like that? Common enough among schoolboys is the wooden cane. It is used when they are practising their Latin dialogues. If one of them comes out with a grammatical blunder, and the classmate with the cane detects it, he smites the offender in the hollow of the hand and passes to him his role of minding the cane. Likewise perhaps, we could say that you too, when back in the world, somehow blundered over Christ's rule on how to live, and came out with some barbaric behaviour. But thereupon the *holy fear of God* (Ps. 18.10) drove you to use that special cane to smite, sharply and repeatedly, not just your hand but many another part of your body too! In the end you were offering the Lord of majesty your very blood, and fittingly so, since that same Lord had, at the time of his Passion, graciously offered God the Father his own blood on behalf of you! But what ever prompted you to conceive of something so daring as to hack at your flesh with the strokes of so horrible a cane, and, going further, to scorch it amid those nettles? Surely it was love: a love fervent to the point of presuming even the likes of this, a love welling up from the depths of your heart, a love frothing through the wounds of your flesh. To the attack, then, for all you are worth![26] Adopt whatever tools of torture you can lay your hands upon. Oh, the freedom the Lord has awarded you, a freedom to live by the spirit, a freedom great enough to make you invincible in face of anything mobilized against your body! From now on it would be unworthy of this *freedom of yours that it be judged by a conscience alien to your own* (I Cor. 10.29).

5. Garments of Sackcloth and a Triple Chain

(I.5a; I.17) Harrowed and bloodied by all this scourging, yet still undefeated, Arnulf took to wearing a hair shirt of sackcloth next to the skin. In this you could say he was doing no less than the other Arnulf, Bishop of Metz, whose *Gesta* mention a

---

[26] Similar encouragement is offered in *Arn* I.10d and *Niv* 17e.

hair shirt he used to wear.[27] But granted the blessed bishop wore a shirt of that kind, he is not described as wearing such gaiters on his legs, or such socks on his feet,[28] whereas this martyr of ours is reported as beyond doubt using gaiters and socks of just that kind. Even when choosing to travel on foot from his grange back to the monastery for the night office of Sundays and saints' days,[29] he did not fail to wear those socks, despite the chafing of his feet on so coarse a fabric (*RB* 55; *UC* 16.2).

(I.5b; I.18) The sackcloth he initially used, though itself quite coarse, had been woven of rather fine threads of mohair, and after a while he grew accustomed to it and began to regard its roughness as trivial. It seemed to him not sufficiently prickly, and actually quite smooth to wear. Moved, therefore, with great indignation against his flesh, he fell to thinking up more scathing discomforts with which to chafe it. Unwilling to drop such thoughts, lest the fervour of his heart cool ever so slightly, he procured some horsehair and stealthily spun it into stout pieces of cord, to twine around the shirt and gather it in, thus providing his body with a garment still harsher, still more horrible to behold. It was so stiff, one might even say so numbing, to the body, that when he stood up with it on, he could not turn from side to side, nor could he bend down at all.

(I.5c) This was all eventually discovered by the grange master Sygerus. This devout man, this friend of all good folk, was afraid that Arnulf would be burdening his beast of a body to a point where it would fail under the strain. So he used a tricky piece of seductive cunning to lure Arnulf away and deprive him of that insupportable torment. Grieved to be thus deprived of a shirt so congenial, Arnulf from that day on simply wore the sacking he was used to.

(I.5d) Those interested in the manner and frequency of Arnulf's use of the sackcloth shirt, gaiters and socks, may take it that he linked such garments to his flesh with so unbreakable a covenant that he wore them virtually all the time. Indeed, garments of sackcloth were ready at hand for him, woven by a devout man on familiar terms with him, who supplied him with them quite often.[30]

(I.5e; I.19) And so our soldier, ever undefeated, again gave thought to find something more to apply to his body and add to its torment. Getting hold of three iron chains, he honoured the Holy Trinity by associating a trinity of chains with the other trinity of shirt, gaiters and socks.

---

[27] Arnulf, Bishop of Metz (ca 614–630). See AASS for 16 August, and *New Catholic Encyclopedia* (New York: McGraw-Hill, 1967), I: 848. He was progenitor of the Carolingian dynasty, and also father-in-law to the sister of Gertrude of Nivelles. In its Chapter 4 we read: 'He wore a hair shirt, albeit secretly. Perpetual use of it wasted and emaciated his members; but he went further and added to it the twin torment of vigils and abstention from eating.'

[28] *Caligas cilicinas in cruribus et pedules cilicinos in pedibus.*

[29] As a wagoner transporting food supplies, Arnulf had the right to ride back to the abbey on weekends, rather than walking like the rest (*GC* 1221.17).

[30] A wagoner would naturally be in contact with a maker of mohair tarpaulins.

The first chain he wound between the shoulder blades and under the armpits, fastening it where it passed across the front of the chest. The second chain he used as something of a sash, passing around from behind to buckle at the top of his belly. The third did duty where he set it around the hips. All three chains he would tighten or loosen as he pleased.

(I.5f) John, in his Apocalypse, once saw a man *girt about the chest with a band of gold* (Apoc. 13; 15.6), but we, with trustworthy eyewitness,[31] have gazed on something yet greater: a wondrous man, tied tight around the chest with a chain of iron (meant to repress any noxious thoughts taking rise from the heart); girt also with a second chain around the belly (to repress the concupiscence of gluttony); and with a third about the loins (to bridle the movements of lust). This is that *triple cord* which is *difficult to break,* and all the more so in that it is not of linen (Eccles. 4.12) but of yet stronger iron. And it is recollected that it was most certainly for a long period of time that Arnulf girded himself with these chains and wore them.

6. His Vest of Hedgehog Pelts

(I.6a; I.20) Triumphant in all torments mentioned thus far, Christ's soldier was eager to add to his knightly deeds by a *renewal of signs and a transforming of wonders* (Ecclus. 36.6). And so he daringly undertook a great deed deserving of commendation above the rest. He collected pelts of the common hedgehog,[32] sometimes more of them and sometimes fewer, according as he could procure them. Of these he made wondrous use, not hesitating to apply their quills to prick his flesh with multiple perforations.

(I.6b) And lest he long cheat his flesh of its share of such prickling, he urged the sheepherders that, whenever they found a hedgehog in a thicket, or a thistle patch, or elsewhere, they would skin it and give him the pelt for a present. Indeed, one familiar friend at times even purchased such pelts for him.[33]

Although we cannot cite the exact number of the pelts, readers present and future may at least rest assured of eleven of them, which he had stitched together to be

---

[31] *Nos vero oculata fide majus aliquid inspeximus: hominem mirabilem [...].* We meet *oculata fide* also in *Arn* II.16d, on the lips of the Queen of Sheba. We also meet *inspicere* in *Niv* 17d, 22c, 28b, 35a; see *Arn* II.1d for this verb in the sense of gazing into consciences, as into a mirror or a book. We should not imagine that the refined cantor, Goswin, was on familiar terms with the hardy, but hysterical wagoner, Arnulf. Hence I minimize the reference to his being a direct eyewitness to Arnulf's practices.

[32] *Pelles ericiorum.* The old world hedgehog superficially resembles the new world porcupine, but is smaller, a mere twenty-five centimetres from snout to tiny tail, and its quills are shorter and not barbed. Again, it is the farmer's ally, for it feeds only on insect pests.

[33] Livestock pelts were part of a lay brothers' protection against inclement weather, but wild animals' pelts (feral cats, rabbits, etc.) were forbidden (*UC* 16.2,4; 22.2).

worn as a kind of vest: six of them in front and around the sides and five of them behind.[34] Over these he would don the hair shirt and fasten it around the body with the belt, lest the pelts loosen their contact with the body. He wore the same set of pelts for a long period, though freely doffing and donning them to suit the situation and the season.[35]

(I.6c; I.21) Some may be puzzled and think that the abbots concerned were very indiscreet, to say the least, in allowing this man to apply to his body these hedgehog pelts, so horrible to look at and to touch, and indiscreet in the first place to let him so afflict himself beyond measure with any of these instruments. To satisfy such inquirers, we would answer that Arnulf lived his courageous soldiering for the Lord under four abbots: Milords Charles, Conrad, Walter, and William. These abbots gave him leave to apply the bodily torments, but they also at times forbade him, fearing he might collapse under a martyrdom so multiple and extensive.[36] He, though, kept asserting he was strong enough for it all and, in season and out of season, he strove to twist out of them anew any permissions they had withdrawn. Indeed, they discerned in him a privileged grace of endurance and found they could neither rebuff him nor *contradict the assertions of one so righteous* (Job 6.10), one whom God had so clearly endowed with prowess *against the days of his battling* (Antiphon: Martyrs), one in whom collapse was out of the question.

(I.6d) If we were to run through the epochs of both the Old and the New Testaments, no one would we find martyrizing the body like this blessed man, with rods of butchers' broom or spikes of hedgehog pelts (I.22). True, Pope Gregory tells how Saint Benedict, the father of monks, when *discovered by shepherds as he lay hidden in a grotto,* was himself *dressed in animal pelts* (Gregory, *Dial* II 1.8).[37] Now we do not presume to compare this martyr of ours with that blessed father, but we do

---

[34] Detailed visualization would demand knowing the shape of a dried hedgehog pelt. The live animal is chubby and the quilled part of its skin hangs loosely, except when the defensive posture is adopted. My own image of them is as of twenty-five centimetres squares. The pelts in front have the even number of six, suggesting a front-opening waistcoat. Those in the rear, with the odd number of five, suggest a T-shaped arrangement across the shoulders. I shudder at the risk of piercing a blood vessel in the neck or armpit!

[35] *Easdem etiam pelles multo tempore tulit, quas tamen ad libitum suum pro loco et tempore vel deposuit vel resumpsit:* The verb *tulit* (perfect tense of *fero*) is also used for the 'wearing' of the vest in a posthumous miracle story (II.21-1). At the end of I.6e, Goswin implies that Arnulf wore all his penitential gear all day and all night, but here he is perhaps suggesting that the hedgehog vest served only for occasional sessions of particularly intense intercession.

[36] On these four superiors, and on the preponderant role of Conrad in Arnulf's penitential career, see Cawley, 'Four Abbots'.

[37] Goswin seems unaware how foreign 'self-martyrizing' is to both testaments. His inclusion of the Life of Benedict in the New Testament is, of course, only in a chronological sense.

say that their pelts were very dissimilar, and if people today were asked to choose between Benedict's pelts and Arnulf's, all, in our opinion, would certainly choose Benedict's and would spurn and anathematize those of Arnulf.

(I.6e) Why wonder over his bearing with equanimity those pelts, so terribly spiked, given that he was ever mindful of the Lord's sufferings and that he frequently held his sins up *before his eyes* (*RB* 4.47), as also the day of judgement and the torments of hell. Never, since entering the Order, had he *fulfilled his own will* (*RB* 7.31), as he himself testified. Rather, ever turning his affections back to God, ever determined to become consummately good, he had always given God *skin for skin* (Job 2.4). That is to say, he was giving the skin of this wretched flesh in exchange for the glorious skin of the Resurrection! It should also be noted that it was not his custom, even after spending all the daylight hours in good works and holy prayers, to betake himself to bed for repose without his hair shirt, gaiters, socks and vest.

7. His Bedding

(I.7a; I.23) With this mention of Arnulf's bed, it should be noted that the bed he rigged up for taking his rest was not florid (Cant. 1.15), but horrid, strewn not with straw but with stones, large and flat, on top of which he laid some tough wooden rods. Over the rods he stretched a woollen blanket (*RB* 55.15; *EO* 88), intended for concealing the torment done to his body. And lest his head be cheated of a share in the general discomfort, at the top of the bed he set one large stone. As for a pillow under his head, though the other brothers each had one (*EO* ibid.), he had none at all.

(I.7b) With this bed he made a pact, or covenant, so strong that he could scarcely endure to be separated from it for even a single night. We have nevertheless heard of one night when he did take his rest on another bed. The same monk who was mentioned above, as being familiar with him (*Arn* I. 3d), was to spend a night at the grange where brother was in residence. The two of them had spoken together, using a room built on to the dormitory. Their converse had been both familiar and intimate, as they exchanged remarks on *the good things of the Lord* (*Ps.* 26.13), *on the welfare of souls* (*GC* 1233.6) and on their own secrets. When they had spent a good part of the night thus speaking, Arnulf said he wished to go off to rest. At that, the monk spoke up: 'Dear Brother Arnulf, do please stay here with me tonight, for I am alone, and my loneliness would be more bearable if I had your company.' Arnulf went silent awhile, and then said: 'Agreed! I shall do as you ask; but I reckon I would not consent to many others on this score! Too long a time have I been at this grange, never lavishing on my body so friendly a pittance as the comfort I shall afford it tonight!' To this the monk replied: 'Dear brother, I am warmly touched and I gladly give you permission to do as you wish! I would not wish that on my account any soul suffer deprivation when in need of your help.'[38] Arnulf answered: 'Not at all! Any honour and consolation I show my body tonight at your request, I shall make up for later on, with torments even greater!'

(I.24) This said, and compline having been recited,[39] both turned to the beds for repose. The monk wanted to cover Arnulf with mantles[40] and other garments, afraid he might take harm from the severe wintry cold; but he, with a faint smile, rejected them altogether, and likewise pushed aside a cushion the monk tucked under his head. As for the monk, he covered himself with many garments in face of the severe cold, and even so he barely escaped the chill. Meanwhile Arnulf, unafraid *in face of the cold* (Ps. 47.17), wore only his tunic and hair shirt. He shrank his body into the shape of a ball, and in this posture wrapped himself in the scant cover of his cape,[41] and so sampled a trifle of restful sleep. After that he arose and engaged in his prayers, which he prolonged until time for *the brothers' vigils.*[42]

(I.7c) Let us reflect a moment on Arnulf's remarkably *scrupulous attention to detail* (RB 40.2).[43] All he did was to lie a short part of one night on a bed, a bed equipped with so scant a sheet and so little straw. And yet he called this 'an offering of honour and consolation' to his body! From this much, and from more like it, we gather that what was a consolation for others was a desolation for him: what others declared to be their desolation, he considered his consolation. He fled what most people found appetizing, and had an appetite for what most people fled.

---

[38] The monk takes it for granted that Arnulf's austerities are all intended as suffrages for individual clients. This is the first mention of that theme, but it is common hereafter

[39] *His dictis, dicto completorio [...].ambo [...]:* in *Niv* 22ae two friends similarly end an evening of sharing by reciting compline together. Both women being choir nuns, they pray the same text, but what text did the monk and lay brother pray together? Did both pray the five *Paters* of UC 1.12? Or did the monk recite the Latin psalms and Arnulf devoutly listen, as was the custom for the bedridden in the infirmary (*EO* 68.27)? Goswin does not say.

[40] *Mantellis [...]. pulvinar.* Spare garments of this kind would be kept in an annex to the dormitory of the grange.

[41] *Tunica [...] cappae:* the 'tunic' was an ankle-length robe, like that of the monks', and the 'cape' was a hooded shawl of similar length, corresponding to the *cuculla*, or 'cowl', of the monks, but without sleeves, and open all down the front.

[42] 'The brothers' vigils': in the course of the regular vigils in the choir, a bell was rung to awaken the lay brethren. The moment for this was carefully adjusted to the season, early enough for the brothers to get to church and recite their *Paters* as a pre-dawn prayer, and yet late enough to allow them adequate sleep (*UC* Chapter 2).

[43] *Mirabilem viri Dei scrupulositatem:* Goswin uses of this term in a slightly pejorative sense in *Niv* 26f and *Ab* 10b; but in *Niv* 4a, 16a, 21b and 29b–1 it denotes a praiseworthy delicacy of conscience.

8. His Food and Drink

(I.8a; I.25) At one period Arnulf dwelt with three or four brothers at a lodging bestowed on the abbot of Villers in freehold by a rich man named Uppo.[44] The solitude of the place delighted Arnulf, affording him greater privacy and freedom for afflicting himself. Here he daringly launched upon something beyond his custom, a diet of the very tough black biscuit, normally eaten by the dogs, and of the leftovers from regular portions (*RB* 39.1, 3), by then two or three days old. On the rare occasions when he could not get that bread, which he preferred, he made his meal of the coarse black bread which was the diet of familiars attached to the house.[45]

(I.8b Portions retained so long naturally stank and were less apt to nourish the stomach than to prompt the eater to vomiting, but Arnulf, marvellous man that he was, did himself violence, and addressed his stomach indignantly as follows: 'How comes it you disdain the foods I present you? *Hard for you to kick against the goad*, isn't it! (Acts 9.5) But, like it or not, you've got to swallow these distasteful foods, or I'll fight you into accepting them as a blessing straight from me!' (Compare Gen. 32.26; Gregory, *Dial* II 8.2; *RB* 56.1).[46] Yes indeed, by the grace of Christ, that was how he took care of his belly, tirelessly getting it accustomed to such a diet for three years and more. And what wonder that he should be so unrestrainedly aggressive against the belly of his body, seeing how lavishly, *by God's grace*,[47] he used to fill the belly of his soul with delicate banquet fare from paradise. And there was prudence in the plan he was acting on, since the insane demands of the belly are worse than all other evils. All the virtues of a soul can be destroyed by the vice of overeating.

(I.8c; I.26) At other times, however, and in every season, from the beginning of his *conversatio* onwards, Arnulf always ate the same foods as the community used, and he kept a measure in his eating, not to miss the claims of discretion. Moreover, there were occasions when for a while he would cater to his body and take certain foodstuffs, in greater or lesser quantities, aware that without such refreshing relief, the body could not go on. Yet in the years immediately prior to his death, he never consented to take anything by way of pittance, eating only the bread, the regular portions and the orchard fruits. And small wonder, seeing how he had that body so

---

[44] *Mansiuncula [...] libere contulerat:* I find no mention of Uppo in Moreau or in the *Monasticon Belge*, nor any light on the economic technicalities of his gift.

[45] On Cistercian bread, see index of *GC* under *panis*, where eight out of ten entries are in Goswin's time (1211–42). Prosperity usually showed itself in the use of bread made with a better kind of grain. Arnulf had contact with the bakery as its wagoner, but only in this time at Uppo's lodge did he have a kitchen role allowing him a choice among breads and access to left over portions.

[46] *Alioquin pugnabo adversum te, nisi benedictionem meam susceperis.*

[47] *Secundum datam sibi gratiam:* a twist echoing Rom. 12.6.

thoroughly broken in, so completely *subjected to servicefulness* (I Cor. 9.27). No longer did he *obey the body* (Rom 6.12; 8.12); the body obeyed him. Just as it is written: *not on bread alone does man live, but on every word issuing from the mouth of God* (Deut. 8.3; Matt. 4.4), so was it fitting that he who had given himself, soul and body, totally to God, be fed, soul and body, his ration of grace from on high. On one occasion, nevertheless, when a pittance was ordered for him by the abbot,[48] Arnulf interrupted his rigorous abstinence and ate the pittance *with thanksgiving* (Rom 14.6; I Cor. 10.30), quite ready to obey again as often as that might happen.

(I.8d; I.27) As for drinking, this he did rather sparingly in all seasons and always only at mealtime. Rarely, if ever, did he take the after mealtime drink.[49] On occasion, too, when very thirsty, he would bring to his mouth an earthenware jar filled with water, not intending to drink of it, but to tease the gluttonous desire. His very jaws sorely ached for dryness, but his concern remained prudent, for he patiently bore with this discomfort of thirst without compromising the freedom of will he had attained.[50] In this he matched the example of a hungry hermit who once hung a cucumber before his eyes so that the sight of it would coax him to a greedy desire to eat; but he also held to his resolve not to eat, and so was not deprived of the merit of his abstinence. All of which gives us matter for thought on how wondrously Arnulf opposed his own attractions: how violently he forced into his belly the foods he abhorred, and yet he disdained to minister to his lips the scantiest drink of water, even when vehemently thirsty!

9. His Work, his Vigils, his Sleep

(I.9a; I.28) Arnulf's measure of work, we understand, was as follows. In the early stage of his conversion he used to carry out with equanimity any work enjoined on him, *hurrying back and forth at* his master's *beck and call* (I Sam. 22.14). Note, however, that he was never bidden to engage persistently in heavy tasks; for while out in the world he had learned precious little of any craft at which, after joining the Order, he might ordinarily be officially employed. As time went by, however, and he *put out his hand to strong things* (Prov. 31.19), that is to say, when by the Lord's grace he became engaged in many things quite repugnant to human nature, his

---

[48] *Ab abbate missa [...] pitantia:* the abbot normally ate with the guests, apart from the monks, and completely apart from the lay brothers (*RB* 54.1; *EO* 76.17), so we presume this incident occurred during an abbot's visit to a grange, where Arnulf was eating.

[49] A drink of water served in the refectory just before compline reading and, in summer, also just after none. All had to come, but none was obliged to drink (*EO* 80; 83).

[50] *Satagebat [...] vir prudens [...] incommoditatem [...] tolerare, quam statum voluntariae libertatis immutare:* the text in AASS seems to lack a needed conjunction or adverb. Goswin's other two uses of *satago* are normal (*Niv* Prol. d, *Ab* 1a).

masters used to grant him a freedom broad enough to exempt him from virtually all duties and occupations, allowing him to give himself over to whole days of salutary leisure and divine contemplation,[51] restful for both mind and body, or else to pursue his devout prayers, or finally to beat and chastise his body.

(I.9b; I.29) His measure for keeping watch and for sleeping should also be briefly intimated. While still a novice and still taking his repose on a bed of his own within the brothers' dormitory, Arnulf would first drowse awhile and then wake up and ruminate some prayers. His untimely whispering of these occasionally interrupted the sleep of the brother in the next bed along. His name was Baldwin, and it was he who eventually took Arnulf aside and asked: 'Brother Arnulf, what do you have in view, that when others are asleep, you are not? Moreover, those *noisy prayers of yours* (*RB* 52.4) rob a fellow of the quiet he needs for sleep.' Arnulf's reply was playful, and rather pleasant: 'Dear brother, do not be alarmed at my wakefulness. You well know how busy the good God is, and how he is busier by day than by night. And so it is by night that I keep watch and spend time with him, that he *hearken to the voice of my prayer and graciously hear me* (Ps. 5.3).

(I.9c) In saying this, Arnulf's grounds were not really that the Lord was thronged with petitioners more by day than by night, all clamouring for him to attend to their pleas, tears, desires, needs and welfare of body and soul. God's dealing with such things is not a laborious or preoccupying task. Unlike us humans, God is in no way subject to change of mood or to fatigue. Rather, he abides forever at rest, his attention going out to all as easily as it goes to each, and to each as easily as to all. He protects and governs the whole sweep of *everything embraced by heaven* and earth (Esther 13.10) according to the good pleasure of his will,[52] without the need of anyone to help him, since he, all on his own, is everlastingly almighty.

(I.9d; I.30) Let us listen to his own account of the forethought and effort Arnulf put into his struggle to overcome sleep, as he tells us: 'When I feel a little sturdier than usual and more able to stay awake, it is then that I impart *some sleep to my eyes* (Ps. 131.4), and I slumber as long as I please. But when I feel a disquieting demand driving me towards sleep, then I turn the tables and violently shake the sleep from my eyes, *reducing it to captivity* as often as I wish' (II Cor. 10.5). Such was, indeed, the case: what he said, that he also did, spending the night hours to his utmost ability in prayer and in watching, short only of doing great harm to his body. To some it will probably seem strange that he could get any sleep for his eyes at all, what with the bed of stone he lay upon, clad in that vermin-ridden hair shirt and vehemently

---

[51] *Ut ab omnibus fere officiis et occupationibus absolutus aut salutaribus divinae contemplationis feriis deditus tam corpore quam mente requiesceret:* this is Goswin's unique use of *feria* in its classic sense of a 'day of leisure'. Elsewhere he reflects the Christian liturgical use of the term in the sense of 'weekday', usually followed by an ordinal numeral (*secunda* to *sexta*, for 'Monday' to 'Friday'). But notice his use of *diem festum agere* in *Niv* 9c, 18e, 23c, 24b, 26d (to keep a day festive), echoing Ps. 75.11.

[52] *Secundum beneplacitum voluntatis suae:* same beautiful expression in *Niv* 19f.

jabbed by that vest of hedgehog pelts (*Arn* I.5; I 6). The answer lies in the force of his bodily fatigue, which was such that, all day and every day, it was easy for him to relax into sleep. After all, if he had the grace to keep awake far beyond his body's capacity, and if, despite his discomforts, he also had the grace to get some little sleep, then we scarcely need be surprised at the ease with which he made that sleep deliberate.

(I.9e) As for taking the extra sleep on the Sunday nights spent at the monastery, and the other festive vigils there, he either avoided it altogether, or at most he kept it brief.[53] Instead, he kept up his vigil, sedulously directing to God the attention of his devout heart. For some years before his death, he spent the vigils hour standing some distance apart from the assembled brothers. There he fatigued his body by keeping in the standing posture from the beginning of vigils to the end, not sitting down at all, or at the most very briefly.[54]

10. His Regimes for Winter and for Summer

(I.10a; I.31) Wonder upon wonder, striking amazement into the hearers! Let us then hear the kind of medicine this new physician[55] applied to his body to counter it in winter time. When the others would be wearing a second and a third tunic to ward off the cold, and a sheepskin as well, Arnulf on the contrary would don just a single tunic, and it, I assure you, was his *most threadbare one* (*RB* 55.5; *UC* 16.2). And yet, it is not such a wonder, for he was warmed from within by the fire of the Holy Spirit and could count as nothing any cold coming from outside, however excruciating it might be. And if it chanced that the horrid winter chill grew sharper than usual, prompting others to fortify their limbs with layer upon layer of added clothing, he would refuse such a semblance of *standing at the coals* with Peter *to warm himself* (John 18.18), and would manfully *follow* the Lord Christ to his passion (ibid. 15). Nor did he ever let the proverbial *cold* of sloth prompt him to omit his resolve to *harrow* the earth of his body with the ploughshare of the discipline, lest later on he be forced to join with *the lazy in their begging* in the truly famished *summer time* of the judgement to come (Prov. 20.4).

---

[53] *Aut numquam aut modice dormitabat:* not a reprehensible dozing off (Matt. 25.5) but a generous foregoing of privilege. When grange brothers came home for Sundays or feasts, they rose for vigils with the monks; but, unlike the house brothers, they were permitted to go back to bed as soon as their *Paters* were finished (*UC* 2.10). Arnulf generously forewent this.

[54] Similar isolation at vigils in *Arn* II.7a. This stems not from aloofness, but from lack of room in the church, still under construction. On the makeshift seating for lay brothers in Arnulf's time, see B. K. de Meerendré's fourteen sketches of successive stages of building (Coomans, *L'Abbaye de Villers*, pp. 132–33). A number of contemporary Lives show their heroes favouring nooks in or around their church (for example, *Lut* III. 20; *Lew* 32c, 48a; etc.)

[55] Comparable medical images come also in *Arn* I.2d, *Ab* 18b, *Niv* 20b.

(I.10b) Yet the sharp winter cold did trouble him greatly, and it showed outwardly in the paleness of his blood-drained face. Nevertheless, he would not resort to the warming room to take advantage of its cozy fire to warm his body. Or, if ever he did chance to do so, it was for the sake of brethren coming to pay him a friendly visit. At times too, during winter, when the brothers' vigils were over (UC 2.2) and they were all sitting at the fire and peeling hemp fibre until daylight,[56] Arnulf would sit with them, not, indeed, to warm his chilly body but simply to do the same task as his fellows.

(I.10c; I.32) As for the summer time, when the sun would mount high in the heavens and shed its fiery heat upon the land, and when almost everyone would wear just a single tunic in face of that torrid hotness, then Arnulf, on the contrary, would clothe himself the more warmly so as to be the more afflicted by the heat. He bore these bodily discomforts, and many another too, without ever growing fainthearted or ever needing the rest and solace of the infirmary. In doing this, it was he who *was bearing* the Lord (I Cor. 6.20); yet the Lord, for his part, was bearing him along![57]

(I.10d)[58] Go ahead, manservant of Christ, go ahead! Do what you are doing, perform what you are performing. Take no notice if anyone sneers or ridicules you, or if any viper-mouthed critic tries to bite and tear you apart, or to cloud over your wondrous deeds by insinuating the vice of hypocritical simulation. Keep running towards your Christ, *amid glory and dishonour, amid ill repute and good* (II Cor. 6.8). Be not overcome by weariness; do not let go of your bodily afflictions, even the least of them, until you have taken hold of the perseverance that means bliss. *For the sufferings of this time are not worthy to be compared with the glory that is to come* (Rom. 8.18).

---

[56] *Canabum decorticantes:* hemp has three commercially useful parts, the stalk (for a fibre used in ropes, sacking, etc.), the foliage and flower (which yield the drug marijuana) and the seed (rich in oil). Distinct strains of hemp have long existed to meet each market, but Villers was clearly dealing with the fibre-making variety. This has long, straight stalks, taller than human stature. Its foliage, mainly confined to the top, was probably lopped off during harvest, to facilitate soaking the stalks. Once fully soaked, the pulpy component breaks loose from around the fibres and can easily be removed by hand. It is amusing to guess that at Villers some waste would get into the fire and produce fumes with pharmaceutical potency. But it would be a very weak drug if it lacked the top foliage, especially in a climate as temperate as at Villers.

[57] *Cum [...] sustineret incommoda [...] ipse portans Dominum a Domino portaretur:* echo of the Candlemas antiphon: *Senex puerum portaba [...],* where Simeon 'carries' the Child and is himself 'governed' or 'steered', (*regebat*) by that Child. The antiphon is cited and commented upon in *Ab* 11c. For Goswin, thinking in French, *portare* means both 'to wear' and 'to carry', a pun hard to capture in English.

[58] This whole paragraph is found also in *Niv* 17e, almost verbatim.

11. His Daily Regime in Lent

(I.11a; I.33) Let us hear yet more of the suffering this just man brought on himself and, within that suffering, what an *acceptable sacrifice* (Ordo Missae) he brought to God.[59] During the Lenten fast,[60] just as all the faithful afflict themselves beyond their ordinary penitential efforts and apply themselves more lengthily to prayer, so as those sacred days approached, this athlete of ours, far from doing less than his norm, strove even to double his accustomed torment of the body. Thus, *from the beginning of Lent until Easter*, on all ferial days, *from early morning until terce, he took leisure for* prayer (*RB* 48.14). After terce, he cast off his tunic, hair shirt and gaiters, and stayed behind locked doors until vespers, stark naked and beating himself all the time with butchers' broom.[61] He inflicted *wound upon wound* (Job 16.15), wherever the smiting hand could find room on the body. Nor would he cease from the blows until many a patch of his flesh had been pierced by the many spikes and stood all bloodied. On Saturdays, it was only *from early morning* until sext (*RB* 48.14) that he thus inflicted on his naked self this martyrdom of blows, since on Saturdays custom required him to return to the monastery for divine service. One severe winter, when the keenest of chills was piercing his limbs like sharp arrows, he kept motionless and let that wintry harshness set him so shivering all over that his teeth chattered as in a fever.

(I.11b; I.34) Arnulf had a hut in the orchard of the grange; here he liked to lock himself often and carry out this holy and praiseworthy task with all the alacrity of his spirit; and this, not only in Lent but at other seasons too. He tried to do it secretly but could not hide it entirely or keep the noise of the blows from often being overheard by the brothers or other personnel attached to the grange. It should be noted that, when beating himself with a scourge, Arnulf had in mind particular brethren or familiar friends, and he could be heard muttering away to himself:[62] 'Got to be

---

[59] *Passionem intulerit [...] et in hac passione [...] sacrificium obtulerit*: both 'suffering' and 'offering' are frequent themes in Goswin, but the actual term 'sacrifice' comes only here and in *Arn* I.3b, II.1e and in *Niv* 1h, 5a, 9a, 20e and 31e.

[60] Some expressions of time in this chapter are ambiguous. Is it a question of Lent itself, or the approach of that season? Of just one particularly cold Lent, or of every Lent? Is the 'evening hour' just an early sunset? At least in I.11c it is clearly the liturgical hour of vespers.

[61] *Post tertiam [...], usque ad horam vespertinam [...] nudus omnino remanebat in conclavi [...]. In sabbatis autem, a mane usque ad horam sextam nudus permanens [...]*. Literally, this paragraph has Arnulf flogging himself non-stop from terce until vespers. I suggest that Goswin's source meant simply that, in Lent, Arnulf repaired to his penitential cell after each of the little hours, donned his penitential garb and whipped himself for a half-hour session like that of *Arn* I.3f.

[62] The Latin is robust, though scarcely rustic; forceful, though scarcely rhythmic. Goswin would be working from an original, in Arnulf's vernacular, in which the text presumably matched the rhythm of the flogging. '*Agendum est mihi fortiter, agendum viriliter, viriliter*

braver; got to be manly; *manly I've got to be* (Ps. 26.14); friends need it badly; this stroke for this one; that stroke for that one; take *that* in the name of God.' As the flogging went on and on, he kept remembering and naming now this particular brother, now those various friends, and now these devout women, much beloved to him in Christ. Flogging hard and begging hard[63] that the Lord transmit to each a gracious forgiving of some sin of theirs, or a lightening of some trouble. There were times when the flogging went on too long and his arms grew tired and he simply had to pause for a while; but as soon as his strength was back he resumed the task begun, never growing faint at it and never failing.

(I.11c; I.35) 'Oh, blessed martyr of the Lord, how long will you suffer yourself to be chilled in so freezing a cold? Why so tire yourself with beatings so prolonged? Already the wooden gong has sounded for none![64] Please now! *Arise quickly and put on your clothes!* (Acts 12.7–8) Do not afflict yourself beyond discretion with this cold and these beatings, or you will contract an illness more bothersome than you can stand. You need to realize that the Lord of majesty himself, when hanging on the wood of the cross, marked the hour of none as the consummating triumph of his Passion, the time for *bowing his head, for sending forth his Spirit'* (John 19.30). 'True enough,' he answers, 'true enough is what I am hearing; yet it was till vespers that he kept hanging upon that wood; only then was he taken down; only then buried in the tomb. Therefore neither shall I let myself be put down from this cross till once more the gong sounds for vespers.' Notice how holy, how brave is his obstinacy; how the good man combats his body's comfort! Though excruciatingly tormented, almost to the breathing out of his soul, he is not going to give up in the combat once begun. Thus it was ever when the gong sounded for daily vespers that he resumed his clothing, *paid his debt of service to the Lord* (*RB* 50.4) in accord with the Order's custom, and came to table with his brethren to refresh his lacerated body.

12. His Coat of Mail

(I.12a; I.36) Why, dearest brethren, should we wonder at this just man's penitence, wonderful though it be and unheard of? From the outset of conversion onwards, it was one and the same penitence, ever growing and growing, with wonder

---

inquam agendum quia valde necessarium est amicis meis; [...] ictus istos et istos pro illis et pro illis [...] infero mihi in nomine Domini.'

[63] *Flagellando [...] flagitabat:* to render the Latin pun I echo the Irish Catholic idiom: 'Please, do pray hard for so and so.'

[64] *Tabula jam pulsata est:* within the monastery the gong-board was used only to alert brethren at close range that it was time for work, or for prayers in the infirmary; but in the close quarters of the granges it apparently replaced the bells even to announce the hours.

upon wonder.[65] Thus, the year before his blissful parting, worn out by his excruciating treatment of himself and with no intention yet of sparing himself, he thought up a supreme instrument of punishment to apply to his flesh, an agenda for fatiguing it yet more. This was a coat of mail, borrowed from a friend. It was dense with scaly links of steel, which he would wear next to the flesh. The moist skin would rust and roughen it and make it dig in deeper and more sensitively. Then he took hedgehog pelts and applied them to the mail for the quills to poke through the gaps to the flesh and prick it severely. If he twisted to right or left, any quills jammed between the links were driven yet more savagely into his flesh, providing him with a torment more painful than ever. Finally, by pulling the hair shirt over the pelts and buckling up the girdle of chain, he could vary the intensity of chafing at intervals as he saw fit.

(I.12b; I. 37) Oh, what a blissful warrior, so illustrious, so victorious! Not enough for his body, tamed though it had been for so long, just to be clad in mail, just to feel that hard, cold steel. No, over and above he must add pelts, horrible to look at, horrible to touch! A shirt too of sackcloth must he add, to triple his martyrdom, matching the stiff, heavy mail with the jabbing, smarting quills, and the tight fit of the shirt. Thus did he pass his days and nights, with discomfort indeed of body, but with, oh, what well-wishing, what cheeriness of heart![66]

(I.12c) Arnulf wore this coat of mail long enough, it is claimed, to blacken his flesh and to let him make his own the word of the bride in the love song: '*I am black but lovely, oh daughters of Jerusalem* (Cant. 1.4): *black*, from the chafing pressures I freely and willingly bear with; *lovely*, from the radiant comeliness of such virtues as come to me from the Lord's enriching grace.' And again: '*Do not think of me as one too swarthy, for it is the sun that has discoloured me* (ibid. 1.5), the true sun, namely, the *bright white and ruddy red* sun, which is Christ, my Lord and *my Beloved* (ibid. 5.10). Yes, it is the ardent love-beams from him that discolour me in my scourged, afflicted body. Even so, still other love-beams, equally from him, colour me afresh in my inward mind.' Yes, indeed: Arnulf was coloured inwardly by the heavenly grace that floodlit his soul; discoloured too, by the manifold torments that afflicted his flesh; yet he will be coloured anew, and oh, how gloriously, at the universal and ever-blessed rising again of our bodies, when all assemblies of all saints, rank upon rank, order by order, *will shine out like the sun in their Father's kingdom* (Matt.

---

[65] *Dum mirandis plus miranda succedunt. Et quid [...] tam admirabilem [...] poenitentiam [...] miramur, cum [...]semper ejus creverit poenitentia, dum mirandis plus miranda succedunt?* To appreciate Goswin's elusive logic in both bidding and forbidding wonder, we should note how frequently he introduces his appostrophes with *Et quid [...]*: three times in *Niv*, six times in *Ab*, and six times in *Arn*. The precise formula *Et quid mirum [...] ?* comes in *Arn* I.6e, 8b; II.6f, 7a; *Ab* 6f, 11d, and plays between *miranda* and *mirandis*, or its equivalent in *Arn* I.10a, 12a and II.7a.

[66] *Dies et noctes cum molestia corporis, sed cum omni benevolentia et hilaritate cordis transigeret.*

13.43), *when all will become God's people, and God with them will forever be their God* (Apoc. 21.3).

(I.12d; I.38) Arnulf's afflictions, as described thus far, offer many persons a challenge, so that they in their turn should bear with their bodily afflictions. On our reckoning, however, actual imitators of Arnulf will be few, for too fondly does Adam's brood seeks its own convenience! Attention, therefore, all and sundry! Take a look at all the bodily sufferings this blessed man endured, from his earliest conversion right up to his passing. Perceive in his holy *conversatio*, as in the clearest of looking-glasses, how trivial in comparison is what you yourselves ever suffer for Christ! From Arnulf's own mouth we have heard it, and based on his own assertion we believe it:[67] scarcely could even seven men together have borne the afflictions over which, with God's grace for helpmate,[68] he triumphed in his body. Yes, he always stayed sound in body, never needing the infirmary for solace or for rest, but having recourse instead to a refectory, that of the Holy Spirit[69], where in all seasons he could relish a diet of heavenly grace. Little wonder that Arnulf spared not his own body but handed it over instead to the ever-present cross,[70] for he was mindful how God the Father had *spared not his own Son, but had handed him over* to redeem even his Arnulf (Rom. 8.32).

(I.12e) Let me use even greater emphasis to declare to the world Arnulf's multiple victories. We already have given his probity and holiness a superlative ranking among recruits to religion in these our times. But now let us offer all religious, of whatever order, the instruments, all the instruments, with which he afflicted himself. Let all experience how agreeable, how wholesome it is to be afflicted with martyrdoms so extensive and lingering. But see how they all shrink away, as, shall we say, from some deadly pit! Instruments as horrible to look at as a hacking saw, as horrible to handle as a pecking beak! They all abhor them, eschew them, flee them, as frantically as they would a snake met face to face. Since, therefore, none dare accept these instruments, we hand them back safe and sound to our martyr, convinced that all others find them unbearable.

(I.12f) Having thus described, in simple style and as best the Lord enabled us, this blessed man's bodily afflictions, along with the instruments he used for them, we can now magnify the Lord in him, magnify the Saviour whose privileged grace equipped him for so novel a warfare and crowned him with so blissful a perseverance. Our material, being thus all unfolded, prompts us to put an end to this

---

[67] *Ab ejus enim ore audivimus, et verum esse credimus, ipso asserente [...]:* not to be understood as a private word of Arnulf to Goswin, but as a cantor's overhearing of a deathbed exchange with a superior.

[68] *Adjutrice Domini gratia triumphavit:* another of Goswin's personifications of grace.

[69] For other metaphorical refectories, see *Niv* 19c, 29b–4, *Ab* 7c.

[70] *Sed cruci continuae* (fem. adj. dat. sing: to the continuous cross) *tradidit illud.* I suspect the orthography should rather be *continue* (adverb: continuously).

first book of ours. But before we move on to treat of Arnulf's virtues, his revelations and the rest of his deeds, let us allow ourselves a little breathing space.

Book II

His Virtues and his Deeds

1. Arnulf's Charity

(II.1a; II.1) Having, as it were, piloted this mariner of ours unscathed through many a heavy sea and many a long cruise, and having brought him almost to the calm anchorage of the home port, all that remains for us is to present any further facts provided by the material available on him. Accordingly, we make our starting point that *which holds first place among all virtues, namely, charity* (*Niv* 30a), and we go on to tell what fervent charity Arnulf possessed in his heart.

(II.1b) Whenever, for instance, anyone requested the help of Arnulf's suffrages and prayers for God's clemency, he would, from the overflowing *viscera of his mercy* (Phil. 2.1; Col. 3.12), show himself most ready to meet their need, and would say: 'Right willingly shall I pray for you!' And, as we ourselves have heard with our own ears, at times he would not only pledge his prayers but would add this further word, quite deserving of remembrance: 'I'll give more than I'm promising.'[71] And such was, indeed, the case; for he never repulsed anyone, but came promptly to their aid with his far-reaching liberality. Thus would he *tuck the alms* of his prayers *into the bosom of any afflicted* (Ecclus. 29.15) who needed his spiritual suffrage, and he would engage his mind and body totally in their concerns in the course of his tear-filled prayers and under the self-afflicting sting of the lash.

(II.1c) Again, so great was his innocence of mind and sincerity of behaviour, that he lived among his brothers like a child, never detracting anyone at all, nor affording

---

[71] *Sicut ipsi auribus nostris audivimus [...]. Libenter orabo pro vobis![...]. Ego majora dabo quam promittam.* My version is colloquial to suggest a vernacular wording overheard by Cantor Goswin, presumably during some liturgical act at Arnulf's sickbed. But, judging from comparable scenes in other Lives, and allowing for Arnulf's problematic laughter, the responses may well have been in sign language (*Niv* 33g; *Lew* 32a, 52a).

any an occasion for scandal. Rather with all his associates, he maintained a blameless peace, even with those who ridiculed him. In this way he showed charity to all, aware that the broader a soul's love for neighbour, the deeper will be its acquaintance with God. He was also aware that no one arrives whither he is heading without first taking the road, and that likewise without charity, which the Apostle aptly terms *a road* (I Cor. 12.31), no one can walk free from straying. Charity is a link, a congenial, wholesome link, of mind to mind: without it, the wealthy are paupers; with it, paupers are wealthy; and through it, Arnulf abounded in all good things.

(II.1d; II.2) His renown for holiness and ardent charity spread in all directions, until quite a number were coming from various places just to see him and commend themselves to his prayers. This included persons of knightly rank from the vicinity of the grange. To some such visitors he foretold events that were to happen to them and which subsequently they did experience. He also at times interrupted his congenial colloquies with God for the sake of the guests who flocked to him. Then too, just as Saint Benedict lays down in his Rule that *the divine law should be read out for the guest's edification* (*RB* 53.9), so this scholar of ours used at times to read out for guests, friend and stranger alike, the lesson of true salvation from the book of charity.[72] There were also the books of people's consciences, all scrawled and smudged with the hideous lettering of the devil's quill: these too Arnulf would sometimes peruse with the lightsome eye of his mind. Then the charity *which does not seek its own* (I Cor. 13.5) *would urge him on* (II Cor. 5.15), and he would make utmost use of the scalpel of holy exhortation, and of devout prayer, to erase the deadly script.

(II.1e) Adorned though he was with many a virtue and many a wondrous deed, Arnulf had so stamped out all trace of vainglory, and had so let charity occupy his heart, that no room was left for vanity to enter in. And as for charity itself, is it not a fire, a most ardent fire? Yes, and so ardently was Arnulf's heart aflame with it that drops of fiery red blood often broke from his body like sparks.

(II.3) Again, what trait was it in him that his many admirers embraced most of all? Surely his most endearing rarity was precisely his rare endearment[73], his charity towards God and neighbour. And deservedly his charity, rather than his afflicting of the body, for the afflicting stemmed from the charity, and not vice versa. And it readily makes sense that, had he endured bodily torments far greater even than those he bore, they, without the charity, would have availed him for salvation nothing at all. As the Apostle says: *If I hand my body over to ardent burning, but do not have*

---

[72] Such metaphorical 'books' are found also in *Niv* 30d and *Ab* 7e. See also the metaphorical 'refectory', in *Arn* I.12d, n. 69, above.

[73] *Nisi caram raritatem, raram scilicet caritatem:* amid the barrage of logic, I paraphrase a little to bring out what seems to be Goswin's point: what impressed Arnulf's admirers was less the obvious austerities and more the underlying charity. The Latin noun *caritas* is the abstract of the adjective *carus*, 'dear'; hence 'dearness, endearment'.

charity, it avails me nothing (I Cor. 13.3). For a vivid idea of how vast his charity was, let us recall the wondrously horrible sufferings of his body, particularly those he so charitably undertook daily in Lent. These were always on behalf of brethren and friends, men or women of devotion, for all of whose welfare he thus offered himself to the Lord in total sacrifice (compare I.11b). As for relieving the needs of the poor, he was so moved with compassion for their calamities that he would have proved another Martin, had the Order's laws not restrained him.[74] Likewise, the loving-kindness with which he joined in grief over the straying of sinners was such that never without heartache could he hear tell of anyone's slipping into the eddies of vice. He used to speak of wishing to be dragged off and handed over for sale into the power of the Saracens, or even to have his members torn apart piecemeal, if only that would bring fuller aid to the needs of the poor and bring sinners to abandon the darkness of ignorance and infidelity and to be converted to the true light, which is Christ the Lord.

(II.1f; II.4a)[75] Some may choose to find fault with words Arnulf at times proffered, as seeming almost boastful, almost apt to dim the radiance of his luminous *conversatio* with a fog of hypocrisy. We would reply by taking for granted the single-mindedness of his heart's intent. We would excuse him as being a simple, innocent man of God. The next chapter will likewise deal with something remarkable regarding his charity.

2. Pigs Forbidden to Grunt, and then Given Away

(II.2a; II.4b) One time, while in residence at the grange of Sart, the duty was laid upon Arnulf that, as often as needed, he should enlist a domestic, load harvest grain into sacks and cart it over to the monastery. Then, on the return trip, he should bring back in the same sacks enough bread to supply the grange brothers for the next several days of that week.[76]

(II.2b) One day he loaded his cart with grain, came to the monastery, unloaded the cart, emptied the sacks at the front of the mill, and then set out with the cart for some business at the nearby grange of La Neuve Cour.[77] After completing his business

---

[74] Reference to St Martin's sharing his cloak with a beggar, identified as Christ (Sulp. *VM* 3.2). For Villers's restraints on individual almsgiving see *Arn* II.2 and 3; see also Moreau, pp. 261–66, and Cawley, 'Four Abbots', pp. 321–23.

[75] For the Bollandist numbering here, see *Arn* I.1e, n. 11, above.

[76] *In eisdem saccis panes qui fratribus grangiae certis per hebdomadam diebus sufficere possent.* From available maps Sart (also known as Sart-Risbart) seems about thirteen kilometres east-north-east of Villers, and so I suggest a Saturday afternoon trip in and Sunday afternoon trip back, with a full round trip occupying all of Wednesday, but bearing in mind the exceptions noted in I.5a.

[77] La Neuve Cour was only half as far (out westward) from Villers as Sart, and so, a round

there, he took a pair of pigs and stuffed them into two sacks, for he was intending, with his prelate's permission, to give the pigs to the poor. Tying the openings of the sacks, he laid them on the cart and headed back to the monastery.

(II.2c; II.5) As he neared the monastery gate, the pigs, ever such unquiet animals were grunting away so importunately that Arnulf feared they would arouse suspicions. And so he addressed those brute animals, just as if they had the use of reason: 'Listen, oh pigs; listen to my words! If it is displeasing in the eyes of the Lord that I dispose of you, as I have been meaning to do, for the benefit of the poor, then permission is yours to grunt away just as you have been doing; but if it is a thing favourable and acceptable to my God that at my hand your flesh should gratify the craving hunger of the poor, then *I command you in the name of Jesus Christ* our God (Acts 16.18; Gregory, *Dial* II 8.3) to desist completely from this importunate grunting.' Wondrous thing! Forthwith, those pigs, long clamouring away loudly in their sacks, now obeyed. Adjured by this commanding order, they dropped all their grunting. Thereupon, with the pigs fully silenced, Arnulf entered the monastery and headed for the bakery,[78] where he would fill his sacks with bread. This done, the sacks of bread were duly tossed on top of the pigs, who were still stuffed away in their own two sacks. Then, wondrous to tell, it was as if the pigs were dead, since none of this coaxed from them the slightest grunt! All because our God Almighty, in response to Arnulf's plea, had somehow *rendered them dumb* (Mark 4.39), and was not going to restore their natural grunting except by his servant's permission.[79] After loading the cart with the loaves and setting out on the road and having already gone quite a distance from the monastery wall, Arnulf turned to the pigs and, with one word, restored their permission to grunt. Thereupon they let out a clamour and with their habitual disquiet grunted away ceaselessly, carrying on their insane uproar until the grange was reached. And there, as planned, Arnulf gave them away to the poor.

3. His Humility and Patience

(II.3a; II.6) Now let us turn our pen to his humility and patience, to inform

---

trip, with time for changing loads, would take only a day The same grange figures in the beautiful story of *Arn* II.19.

[78] *Pistrinum*: 'bakery', distinct from the 'mill' (*molendinum*), where he had unloaded the grain. In classical Latin, the term, *pistrinum* covered both mill and bakery, but in *RB* 46.1, 66.6, and *GC* (passim) *molendinum* is the mill proper, where the grain is ground, and *pistrinum* the place where the bread is made. At Villers the two were distinct parts of a single building, predecessor of the modern hotel-restaurant (See Select Bibliography: *Autour de Villers-la-Ville*, pp. 45, 67; Coomans, p. 502).

[79] One wonders if Arnulf helped grace along by feeding the pigs some hemp leaves! See *Arn* I.10b, n. 56, above.

everyone how humble and how patient this blessed one was.[80] Outwardly he was graced with an *uprightness of behaviour* (*RB* 73.1) that was *single-minded and all of a piece*), with an *approachability* worthy of a free man (Ecclus. 4.7), a loving-kindness all steeped in honey, an *eagerness* entirely spiritual (III Kings 8.66), ever adapting himself to the manner, the measure, of the individual (*RB* 2.32), yet for everyone he was ever his same *gracious, lovable* self (Esther 2.15). Small enough in his own eyes to be great in the Lord's, he well knew how a paltry rating of self makes one great before God, and how displeasure over self keeps one pleasing to God. Thus he became the more precious to God, the more despicably he viewed himself. And deservedly so, since *humility is the virtue in which truest self-knowledge lowers the price the mortal sets upon self* (Bern, *De Grad.* I. 2).

(II.3b) Anyone confronting Arnulf with a word of reproof found that he could not be ruffled, thanks to his maintaining humility within the secret chamber of his mind, ever unjolted and unsullied. Yes, humility, that greatest of the virtues of the saints: how well Arnulf exemplified it in the outward bearing of his body, a bearing at once reserved and modest, patiently humble and humbly patient!

(II.3c; II.7) Wonder as we might, our wonderment will never match the measure of this man's grip on humility, his grip on patience, or his ability to exemplify these virtues to the world, especially from the midst of those bodily afflictions of his, ever as numerous and as severe as if he lay plunged in some sort of hell. Contrast with him the many to be seen today losing all their humility, all their patience, not over some intense bodily affliction, but upon just a slight provocation amid a trivial occupation. But in Arnulf's case, Almighty God took a hand, privileging him with a grace that lifted the early stages of his *conversatio* to sublime heights, and later powerfully reinforced that grace, enabling his humility and patience, inward and outward, to keep on growing, until many could bear witness to his holy *conversatio* and could assert that no one had ever seen him angry or upset. And, indeed, how could he be moved to ready resentment, or provoked to easy wrath, when all along he was welcoming *the God of peace and of love* (II Cor. 13.11) to come and dwell within the *flowery cell* of his heart? (Cant. 1.15) To give everyone a clearer idea of how humble Arnulf was, and how patient, we append a brief illustration of both his patience and his humility.

(II 3d; II 8) When Villers was under Abbot N.,[81] that friend of all good folk, Arnulf secretly asked his abbatial permission to give some bread to the needy, forty-two

---

[80] In this paragraph I italicize several classic literary echoes, but I rather suspect Goswin is borrowing in bulk from a ready-made florilegium. See I.3b, n. 20, above.

[81] This would be Abbot William, the only one of Arnulf's abbots alive and in need of anonymity at the time of writing. The episode is also entirely in character for William, see Cawley 'Four Abbots', pp. 319–26. Moreover, William's reign and Arnulf's last years correspond to the General Chapter's action against 'thieves' (*GC* 1221.10; 1222.2; 1226.4; 1226.22).

loaves of it.[82] Now this abbot was a merciful man, compassionating from his inmost marrow the straitened condition of the poor; and so he gave the request a favourable hearing, full of benevolence. Arnulf distributed the loaves to the needy as secretly as he could, but since *there is nothing hidden that shall not,* at some time or other, *be revealed* (Matt. 10.26; Luke 8.17), he was soon reported to the abbot as giving numerous loaves away to the poor. The abbot took him to task in front of the brethren about doing such a thing,[83] but for a twofold motive Arnulf chose not to make public the fact of having permission: both to avoid scandal among the brethren and not to jeopardize future use of the broad permission of his kindly abbot. Hence he now acted as if guilty of transgressing the Order's regime and *promised the abbot full emendation* (*RB* 29.1). The abbot, in turn, to avoid the scandal many might take if such an episode went unpunished, ordered that Arnulf be put at the monastery gate as an outcast. Cast out like this, Arnulf lodged in a cell between the two gates, where he willingly bore his embarrassment in the view of all, persevering there in thanksgiving for eleven days,[84] with ever the same gladsome countenance and disposition. This gladness of his heart he expressed in one of his gracious jokes: 'Oh how well off I am and lucky! Now I'm even a gatekeeper, just like Saint Peter!'

(II.3e; II 9) Throughout his sojourn in this cell, he suffered great discomfort from the chill, but also frequently enjoyed great consolation from the Lord. Thus, one night when alone and directing his heart to the Lord, he suddenly received from on high what I might call a heaping measure of the Lord's grace. There stood the Virgin Mary, right in front of him, carrying her Son in her arms and offering him for Arnulf to embrace. At this, Arnulf's inner *soul so melted away* (Cant. 5.6) that he could barely stand the inrush of the grace that he felt drenching him, and he started leaping and clapping his hands like a drunkard. With newfound familiarity, his devout, filial

---

[82] 'Forty-two': presumably weighing the regular one-pound apiece (*RB* 39.4) and neatly filling one sack, enough to feed six persons for a week. Gilles tells us the oven had a capacity for two hundred and fifty loaves at a time (Gilles, *The Abbey of Our Lady*, p. 67) almost exactly six such sackfuls.

[83] Unauthorized almsgiving could jeopardize fairness in official aid to the poor, and pilfered goods could be bartered for unworthy purposes, such as the harlots of *Arn* II.8c or the apostasy of *Niv* 15c. See *Arn* II.1e, n. 73, above.

[84] *Cellam quae est inter duas portas pro domicilio habuit:* the modern guidebooks show three gates: that 'of Brussels' on the south-west, that 'of the farm' on the south, and that 'of Namur' on the south-east. That of Brussels, equipped with a pharmacy, looks the busiest and most apt for penal use, but Coomans (*L'Abbaye de Villers,* p. 480) describes in detail a pair of prison cells, more or less preserved, in what was later to become the 'court of honour' giving access to the abbot's palace. I cannot say if one of these was Arnulf's. The 'eleven days' would begin on the Sunday morning, straight after his denunciation at chapter, and would last until his release on the Wednesday of the second week, nine full days and two partial days. This would enable Arnulf to drive the cart back to the grange on its midweek run, presuming that he was being reinstated in this job, at least temporarily.

heart cried out to the blessed Virgin Mother: 'Take your Son away from me, I beg you, oh Lady, take him away! *Enough for me to have have his grace* (II Cor. 12.9), which as of now, I have!' Then, with great jubilee of heart, he shouted: 'Come, all you who love God! If you want to have God, come here!'[85] Over and over again he shouted: 'God is here! God is here! Come, come, come! Everyone, come here and find your God!' This was heard by the domestic assigned to help the monk porter, and by some others too. They had not yet gone to bed, though it was already after dusk. They put this bellowing and jubilee of Arnulf's down to some gloominess of heart or to a draining of his head. But to Arnulf, such human judgements were of little concern, for he had his heart firmly set in heaven and his foot, the foot, as it were of humility, had trampled to the dust any such sense of embarrassment. So when the eleven days were finally over and he was restored to his brethren in community,[86] Arnulf was as gladsome and exultant as ever.

(II.3f) The admirable heavenly grace, whose savour he sipped that night, had so thoroughly permeated the marrow of his soul that for forty days or so thereafter the flavour of any food he ate, or of any beverage he drank, was insipid to his palate.[87] Nor can we doubt that he experienced the same thing many times on other occasions too.

4. His Obedience and Prayer

(II.4a; II.10) So much for Arnulf's charity, humility and patience, and now to add something briefly about his obedience.[88] Saint Gregory says it is *obedience alone that implants the rest of the virtues in the mind and watches over them once implanted* (Gregory, *Mor* 35.14.28; *Niv* 31d). To such obedience Arnulf clung so manfully that, from the first stages of his *conversatio* to the day of his blissful falling asleep in Christ, he lived among his brothers a life beyond reproach, ever most ready *to pay obedience* in everything (*RB* 72.6), both to masters and to peers.

(II.4b) If at times he chanced to be disengaged from all outward affairs and to be taking leisure for himself and God, praying steadily within the enclosed chamber of

---

[85] A cry very consonant with the theme, 'send me God'.

[86] *Fratrum conventui restitutus est:* this could mean a definitive recall to the abbey, with removal from his position of trust on the grange and on the wagon run, but in that case I would expect Goswin to say so explicitly.

[87] Mention of 'forty days' may echo a forty-day period of satisfaction in the refectory (*GC* 1211.6).

[88] The same trio, humility–patience–obedience, comes also in *Niv* 31–32, though in the sequence humility–obedience–patience. It comes also in Caesarius (*DM* 8.1), in the sequence obedience–patience–humility. Caesarius attributes it to 'Jerome', for whom these three virtues are the three 'nails' that hold a monk, or a martyr, to his cross.

contemplation, and if suddenly some brother would summon him for some task or other, he would give ear to that summoning voice as if to the Lord's own call. He would immediately leap out and *take leave of God for the sake*, as it were, *of God* (*Niv* 30.5), choosing to break off his prayer and fulfill the bidding of obedience rather than cater to satisfying his own will. Indeed, if a man is obedient, his prayer will be cheerful and confident, or, to use Saint Augustine's phrase, better one prayer from the obedient than ten thousand from the disdainful.

(II.4c) Who is she that mothers all virtues? Obedience! Who is she that discovers the kingdom of heaven? Obedience! Who is she that opens heaven, that lifts up mortals from the earth? Obedience! Who is house-mate to the angels? Obedience! Who is food to all saints? Obedience! Yes, obedience is what the saints were fed from their weaning until they reached full stature. It was also obedience that guided Arnulf's prayer heavenward.[89] Without obedience, this prayer would no more have arrived there than a stone tossed upwards would ever hit the sky.

(II.4d; II.11) Mention of Arnulf's prayer prompts us to explain briefly the measure and manner of his praying. For a number of years in the early period of his conversion he was not allowed as much leisure for contemplative quiet and prayer as he might have wished. Later on, however, during his many years of residence at the grange of Chênoit (so named of old for its grove of oaks),[90] his grange masters cast a favourable smile on his holy endeavours and allowed him almost complete freedom from outward cares, so that he could *dwell with himself* Gregory, *Dial* II 3.5) and keep both a bodily Sabbath and a *Sabbath of delight* (Isa. 58.13; compare *Niv* 23a, 30b), for the mind *to taste and see how congenial is the Lord* (Ps. 33.9).

(II.4e) Thus in all seasons, summer as well as winter, Arnulf took leisure for prayer *from early morning until the hour of terce* (*RB* 48.14),[91] and so great a grace

---

[89] In relating 'prayer' to 'obedience', Goswin's point seems to be that, just as austerity without charity is worthless, so is worship if it lacks the teamwork we moderns think of when we use the word 'obedience', something like the 'two or three agreeing' of Matt. 18.19–20 In Arnulf's time a lay brother's 'obedience' seems to have been mainly a question of productivity at work, if we can judge by a General Chapter decree just four years before his death. There seems to have been a widespread discontent with recent recruits to the brotherhood, in that they were less productive than the hired workers. Grange masters were to 'stir up and compel' them to work (*GC* 1224.1). Interestingly, the next year the decree was revoked as unviable (*GC* 1225.3).

[90] Chênoit was one of the earliest granges, located only eight kilometres north of the abbey, at the confluence of the sources of the Dyle, near modern Cour St Étienne, some twenty-eight kilometres south of Leuven and thirteen kilometres east of Nivelles, at the heart of the Villers holdings. These latter which stretched mainly from Nivelles on the west to Sart-Mellemont on the east. Chênoit is again mentioned, along with Nivelles, in *Arn* II.12e. Moreau remains the handiest treatment of Chênoit (*L'Abbaye de Villers* III.1, 202–03). The whole of Book III (135–266) throws light upon Arnulf's milieu.

[91] On the length of Arnulf's devotions and whipping sessions, see the notes on I.3e and I.11a.

had he acquired for praying that he could remain at great length *intent* upon heavenly things, *his unconquerable spirit never relaxing from its prayer* (Antiphon: St Martin). He had rid himself of sluggishness and *acedia* (*RB* 48.18), two great impediments to the grace of assiduity in prayer, and he kept in mind how his Lord and Saviour had engaged in no task as often or as persistently as he did in prayer, repeatedly *spending* even *whole nights in prayer* (Luke 6.12). Yes, and when his Passion was at hand, *being in an agony, he prayed the longer* (Luke 22.43). Again, just as the soldiers of this world will not go out to battle without their weapons, so this soldier of ours would not march to spiritual combat without his prayer.

(II.4f; II.12) When at the grange, prayer strengthened him. En route to the abbey, or elsewhere, prayer accompanied him. Heading back again, prayer followed him still. Through prayer, at its purest, all things profitable were supplied to him by the Lord; and, no doubt, anything harmful was warded off as well. Nothing else was as congenial to him as this *clinging to God and putting his hope in the Lord his God* (Ps. 72.28). When attentively praying to the Lord for anyone hard pressed by sins or by weighty temptation, or anyone in sore straits over some tribulation, Arnulf could not restrain himself from melting wholly into tears. Sometimes too, when engaged in prayer and *pouring out his heart like water before the face of the Lord* his God (Lam. 2.19), he would, in his burning desire, be lifted to the heights, and from the treasuries of goodness on high, his heart would garner its fill of gladness, a devotion exuberant in tears. We believe his prayers were effective and profitable, not only for the living but also for the deceased, inasmuch as various brethren, both choir and lay, after migrating from this world, came back from death and appeared to him, asking to be helped before the merciful Lord by the suffrage of his prayers, his tears and his bodily afflictions.

(II.4g; II.13) Each day then, at terce,[92] to bring his prayers to a close, Arnulf would lower his whole body to the ground and then rise and make a profound bow to the Lord, as though taking leave of him to retire. After that, as described in Book I, concerning his penances (*Arn* I.3), he would equip his right hand with the scourge of butchers' broom brambles and make sport of his body, beating it atrociously till the blood flowed free. Now, if the day was *a day of early dining* (*RB* 39.4; 41.4; 42.2; 42.3), this would last from terce until sext, and amid all the beating he would devoutly recite the fifty *Paters* prescribed as an office for mass time, though, of course, on weekdays he was not obliged to recite these at all.[93] If it was *a day of*

---

[92] Goswin does not mention the *mixt*, but this modest breakfast was prescribed for grange brothers in all but the very earliest redactions of *UC* 15.4.

[93] *Officium missae*: for each liturgical hour the brothers recited *Paters* and *glorias*, ranging in number from five for a little hour to forty for vigils on feast days (*UC* 1.6, 11–13). There was no written requirement of *Paters* for the mass, even for the grange brothers, who had no daily mass to attend. But, as a Bollandist note suggests (AASS p. 620, n. b), there was apparently an unwritten understanding encouraging them to make up for the mass with these extra fifty *Paters*.

fasting (*RB* 42.2,5), then it was from terce until none that he sedulously fulfilled the same office. And in Lent, he kept it up until the hour for vespers. Yet what we have undertaken to describe is not the afflicting of his body, already sufficiently explained above, but rather the measure and manner, of his prayer. And of this we can suitably assert that in the eyes of the Lord his entire *conversatio* counted as all one great and holy prayer.

5. Our Lady Reveals to Arnulf her Seven Heavenly Joys

(II.5a; II.14) Already in his first years of conversion, when this *man of venerable life* (Gregory, *Dial* II Prol. 1) was beginning to meditate intently on things heavenly and was steering his heart towards God, he was also becoming a devout lover of blessed Mary the Virgin, attentively venerating her for her loving-kindness, and frequently saluting her as worthy of all praise. The fuller the favour he obtained with the mother, the more easily could he, through her, reach out and make his own the mercy of the Son.

(II.5b) Each day Arnulf made a point of going over in sedulous meditation the seven joys[94] that the blessed Virgin most rejoiced in while still tied down in this world. First, her joy when the angel greeted her and she could reply: *'Be it done to me according to your word'* (Luke 1.38); for it was then that, by the Holy Spirit, she conceived the Son of God. Second, her joy at *the words of grace* (Luke 4.22) that Elizabeth spoke in response to her own greeting (Luke 1.42–45). Third, her joy when *bringing forth without pain the Saviour of the ages, she, a virgin before childbirth, a virgin in childbirth and a virgin after childbirth* (Antiphon: Christmastide). Fourth, her joy when the three Magi[95] ventured forth from eastern parts *with a star for guide* (Collect: Epiphany), and entered the house where she and Joseph were staying; for it was then that she saw them humbly fall down before Jesus and *offer him their mystical gifts* (Antiphon: Epiphany). Fifth, her joy on the day of her son's oblation at the temple, when she saw Simeon the just hasten gladly to gather him in his arms, to give thanks for one so long desired and to take pleasure in the newborn child, whom he pronounced *the light* to enlighten *the Gentiles* (Luke 2.32). Then too the Virgin heard Anna the widow confessing the Lord's praises and *speaking of the child to all who awaited the redeeming of Israel* (ibid. 38). Sixth, her joy when she saw her son risen from the dead, whom shortly beforehand she had tearfully seen buffeted with

---

[94] *Septem gaudia:* The sacred number seven also comes up in the devotional life of non-literate Cistercians in *Niv* 8c, 28a, etc. The number seven had the advantage of matching the seven day hours of the Divine Office, each with its need for a topic of pious meditation if one did not understand the Latin words. See also the Trappist *Directoire spirituel* (1869), p. 367.

[95] *Cum videret tres magos:* note the influence of popular piety in numbering the Magi as 'three' and in making Luke's 'redemption' of the firstborn into an 'oblation', as in I Sam 1.24. The sixth and seventh joys draw us still deeper into popular piety.

many injuries and hanging on the gibbet of the cross. Seventh, her joy on the fortieth day after his resurrection, when, with a blissful gaze of her eyes and unutterable yearning of her charity, she followed him as he was wafted on the clouds to penetrate by his heavenly power into the heavenly heights. [II.15] These seven joys Arnulf daily brought back to memory, both to venerate the glorious Virgin and to delight himself in so congenial a recollection.[96]

(II.5c) The blessed Virgin, however, wished to enhance her servant's devotion by extending it to her ever more sublime, more blissful joys, and so one day during a sojourn of his in the infirmary,[97] she appeared to him and said: 'Why, my beloved, do you daily meditate only on the joys that were my gladness and bliss while still in this world? Add to them those other joys beyond compare, in which I rejoice everlastingly in heaven.' And then she gave him this lesson: 'Firstly, I rejoice that, on being assumed into heaven, I found a glory prepared for me greater than I had hoped for or known of, greater, indeed, than can be put into words or reckoned with; so much so that this glory of mine, taken alone and at its full, surpasses in excellence the manifold glory of all the saints and all the angels. Secondly, I rejoice that, just as the daytime is lit up by the sun, so the whole heavenly court is lit the more abundantly, the more gladsomely, by the bliss that is mine. Thirdly, I rejoice that when all the citizens of that court obey me, they are treating me as mother of their king. Fourthly, I rejoice that the will of the Supreme Majesty and my own will are together but one will, and that what pleases my will in anything meets benign and ready favour and consent from the supreme, undivided Trinity. Fifthly, I rejoice that those who serve me in this world are rewarded in the next, in the measure my will chooses for them. Sixthly, I rejoice that, being exalted above the choirs of the angels, I am allotted a privileged closeness to the holy Trinity, a joyous association with all the saints. Seventhly, I rejoice that I am completely assured that my glory will never decrease, never falter.'

(II.16) These things the Virgin most clement graciously disclosed to her servant, and then bade him farewell and vanished from his eyes. He in turn drew strength from these holy admonitions of his ady, his consoler, and grew the more devout in serving her thereafter.

(II.5d) It should be further noted that the *mother of mercy* (Antiphon: *Salve*) quite frequently appeared thus visibly to her faithful servant. And so warm and loving-

---

[96] See the Introduction to the Lives, pp 15–16, where I ask if meditation on these joys was not linked with Arnulf's efforts to control his compulsive laughter

[97] *In infirmitorio consistenti*: what role has a sickroom in this story? Ida, for one, is at home with the sick (*Niv* 13b, 21a, 22b, 23a), and Abundus at least contacts them (*Ab* 20eg; cf. *Niv* 30h); but Arnulf scarcely goes near the place (I.10–d, 12–e). I suggest that the story early became a conversation piece for those who visited the infirmary with the aim of cheering the patients. Their story would be all the more moving if they were to locate it precisely in that hall of suffering.

kind was the familiarity she showed him that, as often as he had something to negotiate, it was she who carried his message of it to her son. Meanwhile, Arnulf would wait, his heart's mouth open wide for morsels, as it were, of heavenly grace that she would bring to him, along with the happy outcome of his request to her son.

6. Jesus Offers Arnulf ever Loftier Visions

(II 6a; II.17) Once when Arnulf was at prayer, the present life, so full of manifold calamities, took on for him a heartfelt loathsomeness. Growing oblivious to outward things, he ardently yearned to take a place in the choir of the saints on high,[98] and, if it were but possible, to begin enjoying already the blissful face-to-face vision of his Maker. In the meantime, deep within him, the Lord's grace[99] was more fully enlightening him, and suddenly his soul was caught up in suspense and admiration of the beauty that exists on high. Thereupon, so great a fire of love enkindled his soul and so vehement a stupor struck upon it, that, shaken to his very foundations, he was lifted out of his normal state and wafted aloft, in one leap of the mind, into the world on high.

(II.6b Already drenched in a copious dew of heavenly grace, Arnulf now had an apparition of Jesus Christ, his Lord, serenely gazing upon him and asking: 'What do you seek from me? *What do you wish me to do for you, my son?*' (Mark 10.51) Arnulf, recognizing him for his Lord and Saviour made reply: *'You, my Lord, you know what!'* (Ezek. 37.3; Apoc. 7.14) So the Lord asked: 'Is it enough for you that for your sake I saw fit to cloth myself in flesh? That *for your sake, I suffered reproach* (Ps. 68.8), suffered spittle, blows, scourges, a thorny crown and nails? Enough that, bearing even greater confusion, I hung naked on the gibbet of the cross? Enough that, in overcoming death on that gibbet, I let death overcome me and let myself *be reputed with the wicked* (Isa. 53.12) and be myself sentenced innocently to die? Are all these things enough for you?' And Arnulf replied: *'No, my Lord, not at all!'* (I Sam. 1.15; Acts 11.8). In saying this, his grounds for saying it were not, of course,[100] that the Lord's Passion was insufficient for himself, and for the whole world, as far as redemption was concerned; rather he meant that what his heart was ardently yearning for was the blissful vision of the holy Trinity. And so he immediately went on to add: *'You, Lord, you know what I desire!'* (Jer. 15.15)

(II.6c; II.18) Then the Lord beamed yet more wondrously upon Arnulf's heart with

---

[98] *Choris coelestium interesse sanctorum:* heavenly choirs come again in *Arn* II.6cd. This vision occurred when Arnulf was 'at prayer' *(cum esset aliquando orans vir Dei)*. Was it in the abbey church, with the (earthly) choir singing, as in *Ab* 8ab, 11abd?

[99] *Copioso gratiae coelestis rore perfunderetur:* this chapter is rich in Goswin's metaphors for grace as light, fire, loftiness, dew.

[100] *Non ideo utique dixit:* typical of Goswin's scholastic side.

the lightsome rays of his grace, and said: 'Look upwards and contemplate what wonders *I show you!*' (Ezek. 40.4) So he lifted his eyes and *saw the heavens open wide* (Ezek. 1.1); and then, in such measure as mortals are allowed it, he saw the choirs of all the saints: the patriarchs, prophets, apostles, martyrs, confessors, virgins and monks; yes, and the choirs of angels besides. Lucid and distinct was his gaze as he took in their several orders and saw how refulgent they were, how incalculably bright! He marvelled at the glory that was theirs; but even amid all this still his spirit could *find no rest* (Matt. 11.29; 12.43). So their common Lord then asked him: 'Are all these things enough for you, my son? or is your desire for things more sublime still?' He replied they were not at all enough.

(II.6d) So the Lord again told him: '*Lift up your eyes and contemplate* (Gen. 13.14) my glorious mother, whom I shall now show you.' Arnulf immediately aimed his eyes higher, and there he beheld Mary, that looking-glass into which all the heavenly court gazes; Mary, that one and only queen, venerable in name, venerable in merit; Mary, loftier than the angels' choirs; Mary, the grandeur of whose comeliness, the fullness of whose glory, nobody's thought, nobody's insight, will ever be adequate to touch upon. Hers, therefore, was the glory he was now to consider, at a loss in his wonderment, in his *astonishment* (Ezek. 26.16). Yet even in all this admirable glory of hers he seemed not yet to find the all-embracing repose his spirit needed.

(II.19) *Again the Lord spoke to him, saying* (Gen. 18.29): 'Are all these things you have seen enough for you yet? Or do you want things more sublime still by far to gaze upon?' Arnulf answered that in all he had been shown he had by no means found what he desired. And this holy obstinacy, this vehement desire of his heart, his Lord once more understood.

(II.6e) And so that Lord bade him: 'Wing your way up, my son, far higher still; take full advantage of the grace I see fit to measure out to you; yes, contemplate for yourself the lofty wonders of the majesty, the ineffable delights of the glory, that are forever my own.' Thereupon it seemed to Arnulf that he was plunged into an unsearchable abyss of divine light and was, in some measure, initiated by the master of the universe, so that he saw wondrously, wondrously, I say, he saw[101], inasmuch as seeing was allowed, *the triune in persons, the substantially one*. Yes, Arnulf saw him and saw the unutterable treasures of his glory, treasures such that to linger among and enjoy them, to be sated with contemplating them and to possess them lastingly is, in itself, *the life everlasting* (John 17.3). Therein our contemplative attained to and found the stable consolation, the true repose, the everlasting joy he had desired, and deservedly could he now say: '*My Beloved to me and I to him*' (Cant. 2.16), or again: '*I have found the one my soul so loves; I shall hold him fast and not let him go*' (ibid. 3.4).

(II.6f) What wonder that this new scholar should learn all this? Such a simple

---

[101] See the almost identical vision in *Ab* 6c, and close parallels in *Niv* 22b, 28f, 33b.

man, but educated by grace in the school of supreme divinity, where he learned what many of the wise of this world, for all their wisdom, never have discovered! (I Cor. 1.19–21). Indeed, some time later a master of theology put to him some questions about the blessed Trinity, and he, being one of those *simple folk* with whom *God's wisdom had held converse* (Prov. 3.32), readily disentangled his questions and did so with a nicety to which that master bears witness.[102] But now to return to our topic.

(II.6g; II.20) After Arnulf had seen such great wonders, *the Lord of glory spoke to him* again and said (Acts 7. 2–3) 'Behold, my son, *you have seen my glory; you have seen it and rejoiced* (John 1.14; 8.56; 12.41). So let me tell you this: if all the leaves on all the trees, or if all the drops of all the waters in the sea, became human and were destined for my kingdom, along with all those saints of mine already destined to reign with me there; even then, let me tell you, even then there would be enough, enough for them and enough for you, in this same wondrous abundance of my glory, glimpsed by you just now!' When the Lord Jesus had said this, he disappeared from his servant's eyes, and that blessed vision was over.

(II.6h) And so this keen lover of the heavenly life wound his way back from those heights, *like one awaking from a heavy sleep* (Gen. 45.26), and with him he brought a joy of mind worthy of those workshops of joy. From that day on he often surrendered himself to congenial reminiscence on these lofty encounters with the holy ones and on the delight he had taken in the glory of his God. Certain persons, in fact, have considered that these revelations were the source from which he drew the topic for the jubilant laughter that was to become characteristic of him, but on this point we have no certainly one way or the other.[103]

7. His Laughter

(II.7a; II.21) Once when Arnulf had come home to the monastery for a major feast, he happened to be standing during vigils apart from the stalls and adjacent to the monks engaged in the psalmody.[104] Heavenly grace then flowed into his heart, and

---

[102] *Eodem magistro testimonio perhibente:* was this a visiting master, who bore witness just once? or a resident who bore it repeatedly? The ablative absolute conceals any clue.

[103] *Ex praecedentium occasione revelationum:* the vision is so similar to that of *Ab* 6c that one might suppose it to be a literary creation of Goswin's. This impression is strengthened by its detachment from any particular time or place, and from any friend of Arnulf as witness. But the present remark presupposes some sort of historical basis.

[104] The abbey church was under construction throughout Arnulf's time. Coomans reproduces an excellent drawing of Charles Licot suggesting its shape at the time of this incident, with only the first four bays of the nave in use (p. 131). Lay brothers, who would normally have stalls in bays further back, had to find room in the side aisles. Those coming in from granges fitted themselves in for vigils as best they could. Lighting was dim, but enough for distinguishing faces on the opposite side. See *Arn* I.9e, n. 54, above.

he conceived a devotion he could not conceal, nor keep from showing up in some bodily gesture. Facing him stood one of the brethren, Walter by name,[105] who now looked up and noticed Arnulf softly laughing, bobbing his head and rhythmically tapping his foot on the ground. It was then (as we have it from Walter's own mouth) that this habit of jubilant laughter began its growth in him; since previously little or no trace of such laughter and tapping had ever been detected in him.[106] Here a prime consideration for our hearers should be wonderment at Arnulf's wondrous *conversatio*, for while enduring such pain from his bodily affliction, he could yet nourish an inward joy and keep it up so heartily as to break out into full-throated laughter. But again, what wonder of it that such novel and wonderful things be told of a wondrous man doing wondrous deeds, thanks to a wondrous God?[107]

(II.7b; II.22) Sometimes while lacerating his flesh, as mentioned above, and beating it with those thorny scourges (*Arn* I.3, 4, 6), Arnulf would conceive in his inner heart a joy great enough to force him into outbursts of rollicking laughter, a laughter at once spiritual and yet seemingly wanton. He would fling away his scourge, clap his hands and tap-dance with his feet. We could then deservedly adapt to him what the bride says in the canticle of love: *'Daughters of Jerusalem, tell the beloved how I languish with love'* (Cant. 5.8). Whenever this overflow of inward joy made him dissolve into this outward laughter, his face turned fiery red all over, as if the face itself did the laughing. Yet the vigour of the laughter had its impact on his whole body, jolting it and fatiguing it until he seemed to feel his inward viscera torn to shreds.

(II.7c) When he attended the sermons of those[108] preaching in chapter, if mention were made of the Lord's Passion, or of sin, or of how things can be so transitory, or of the torments of hell, or other such topics, then his heart would become depressed with so massive a gloom that from the depths of his lungs he would heave long-drawn sighs. But if the preacher waxed eloquent and dwelt on the canticle of love or jubilation of the heart, on the vision of the blessed Trinity or the glory of the saints, on the cherubim and seraphim or topics like these, then the force of the words and their sheer congeniality acted upon his soul until it was *sated with marrow, sated with fatness* (Ps. 62.6). He was then compelled to bring forth the inward joy, thus conceived, in the form of outward laughter. At times too, this jubilant laughter would

---

[105] Presumably the same Walter as in *Arn* Pref. b, key witness to Arnulf's intimate life. Not to be confused with Abbot Walter, who died seven years before Arnulf's own death.

[106] *Leniter ridentem, caput agitantem et etiam solo pede saepius tripudiantem:* Walter saw grace at work in this behaviour, but for a pejorative view, see *Arn* I.10d, II.1c, etc.

[107] *Et quid mirum si de mirabili viro per mirabilem Deum mirabilia faciente, nova quodammodo et miranda dicantur.* Goswinianism at its purest.

[108] *Et quando sermonibus intererat sermocinantium in capitulo:* the preachers are named in the plural. All mentions of festive sermons in *EO* are too impersonal to reveal who preaches, but at the daily chapter, *EO* 70.28–37 envisages a variety of speakers.

grew so strong in him that it forced him to dart out of chapter like an exile, whether it was the chapter of the monks or that of the brothers,[109] and so get into church and tap out his jubilant festive dance until the wine of his drunkenness was gradually digested.

(II.23) Note also that wherever he was, whether with brethren at the grange or among religious persons outside, if he chanced to hear anything provoking enjoyment on a considerable scale, he could not hold back this vigorous laughter— so involuntary and surprising that it became at times an embarrassment for him, especially among seculars, who had no idea what such strong laughter could mean.

(II.7d) Some there were who lacked the spirit that governed Arnulf. These interpreted his jubilant laughter in an evil light; but just let them see for themselves whether they can justify their own conscience or not. Oh, would that those who laughed to scorn his laughter, and who held his innocence in contempt, themselves had a few tears, enough tears in the peacetime of their heart to match the laughter, the ample spiritual laughter, in the horrible wartime of Arnulf's afflicting of his body! Nevertheless, let this much suffice on his jubilation and on his laughter. It is said that these were the diet on which, *the Lord pastured him seven years and more* (Dan. 4.20),[110] and so let us now pursue what else remains to be told.

8. Four Encounters with Demons

(II.8a; II.24) On Sundays and saints' days in summer time the grange brothers, conforming to the schedule of the monks, *used to take some rest after dinner on their beds* (*RB* 48.5; *UC* 2.12).[111] But Arnulf refused to indulge in outward bodily slumber. He used to seek instead a secluded spot, where he could pour out his prayers more privately to the Lord and relax into an inward sleep of the spirit amid the delights of holy love. However, one of the brethren reproached him for this before the master of lay brothers, who enjoined him to go and sleep at that time, just

---

[109] *Ab utroque capitulo, monachorum videlicet et conversorum:* on Sundays, the brothers had their own chapter *(capitulum suum proprium)*, but Goswin means the major holidays, with the brothers attending the monks' chapter *(sermo in capitulo monachorum)* (*UC* Chapter 11). There, senior lay brothers, such as Arnulf, sat inside, while the overflow of juniors sat outside, adjacent to the door and its flanking windows. When laughter came on, Arnulf had a double gauntlet to run in his escape to the privacy of the church, first to get out the door as inconspicuously as possible, and then to dash past his juniors in the cloister. Compare *Ab* 19c.

[110] *Quibus, ut aiunt, per septem annos et amplius a Domino quodammodo pastus est:* these are the final years of Arnulf's life. The expression echoes Nebuchadnezzar's seven years of insanity *(et cum feris sit pabulum ejus donec septem tempora mutentur super eum:* Dan. 4.20), but whereas that king recovered, Arnulf was prone to laughter to the end.

[111] On summer weekdays, the brothers made up for the short nights by rising later for vigils. See *Arn* I.9e, n. 53.

as the others did, since, if he kept awake like that, his brothers might be distressed out of pity for his body, which was fatigued from his excruciating torments. He obeyed this command of his master, prepared as always to be obedient in everything. When dinner was over,[112] however, and he had entered the dormitory and taken off his shoes to get into bed, there suddenly appeared to him a demon, laughing and making fun of him. It broke out into the words: 'Hey, brother, what are you up to? Where's all that holy religiosity of yours? What's become of those vigils you keep at this hour? Your fervour can't amount to much if you let your limbs get as listless as this and if you fail to go through with what you've begun. Up with you! Hurry up and get on with those vigils and prayers as you've always done in the past!' But Arnulf could tell it was a demon confronting him, and so he despised the seductive words that would coax him to stay awake against his master's command. This is the indignant reply he made: '*Depart from me*, wretched one; *depart from me!* (Luke 4.13) Whether you like it or not, I'm off to sleep, just to shame and irk you by my repose!' This said, the ancient foe turned and fled.

(II.8b; II.25) Another day, Arnulf was alone in his cell[113] and was, as usual, wearing himself thin with a scourge. Then there appeared to him a demon, seemingly human in form, but diminutive. This demon, to show how the penitential discipline saddened and irked him, now took one impetuous swipe and knocked the scourge out of Arnulf's hand. Recognizing him as a demon, Arnulf armed himself with a sign of the cross and, with one thrust of his arms, seized hold of him and wrestled with him. Yes, with help from the a*ngel of great counsel* (Isa. 9.6), Arnulf wrestled with that angel of evil counsel until, finally getting him prostrate on the ground, he could pummel him with his fist. The malicious demon then blurted out some insane mutterings: 'Alas, alas, brother; oh, how that hurts!' To which the ever-constant man of God replied: 'And why,[114] oh most wicked one, why should I forgo a chance to hurt you, when such a chance is granted me?' After that word, the malicious foe, unable to withstand his constancy any longer and already thrashed with many a blow, narrowly escaped at last from his hand, all gloomy and ashamed.

(II.8c; II.26) Another day, Arnulf was returning from the abbey and was bringing bread for the brothers at the grange. He had let the domestic go along ahead of him with the cart, while he followed along quite a way behind and all alone. Suddenly, at a spot where the road emerged from a wooded area, out from the woods stepped

---

[112] The reproach would come at the brothers' chapter on a Sunday, and the first application would come the same day, after dinner.

[113] *Dum intra cellam suam vir Dei solus erat:* Cistercians did not have private cells. Goswin is thinking of the 'purgatory' closet in *Arn* I.3e, which may have been the same as the orchard hut in *Arn* I.11c.

[114] *Quare [...] abstinerem, si [...] concederetur:* the impersonal passive implies a divine permission, even a divine urge. In this, Arnulf is hardly meek: he snubs an inner voice, trounces a smaller man, refuses women alms, chases a child away. The urge to such action each time seems to him divine, and the opposite seems correspondingly diabolic.

three women, all heading towards him and blocking the road where he was to pass. They gradually approached until he came to a halt; at this, one of them spoke up, while the others remained silent. She said to him: 'Come on, brother; come along now! Choose among the three of us the one most pleasing in your eyes and involve yourself with her as your fancy takes!' Upon hearing this, and thanks to the Holy Spirit, Arnulf recognized that under the appearance of these three women three demons were trying to seduce him. So he had recourse to that well known bodyguard, the sign of the cross, and put his trust in the Lord. He did not *tremble with fear* (Ps. 13.5), though many another might have trembled, might even have consented to the diabolic persuasion. Instead, he simply swung back to the woods and skirted around the three, leaving the roadway to them, and himself hurrying after the domestic on the cart. As for those trifling women (*GC* 1231.5),[115] they were mere masks worn by wiliness itself, and now they simply skipped back into the cover of the woods and *disappeared* (Gen. 44.28).

(II.8d; II.27) Another time, during vigils at the monastery, Arnulf was standing in the stalls[116] with the rest of his brothers, when once again a demon impudently presented itself to him, this time under the shape of a small boy, blacker than soot. As soon as our man of vision,[117] spotted him, a refulgent heavenly grace lit up his inner eyes, enabling him to sum up the boy as naught but a demon. Thereupon he sealed his forehead with the sign of the cross, breathed a puff into the demon's face and so forced him to flee from his presence. The same foe at other times used other tactics too, ever making a nuisance of himself for the servant of God. In response, the mighty athlete, never gave way; he gave walloping blows instead,[118] striking him with the Lord's cross[119] as with a crook, using the power of prayer to put that turncoat to flight and to set at naught his every ambush and snare.

---

[115] *Mulierculae [...] quas exterius diabolica assimilaverat versutia:* this time it is a vituperative term, used also in *GC* 1231.5, where grange masters and others are bidden to drive *mulierculae notam ferentes prostitutionis* (hags with a harlot look) as far from the gate as possible. But see *Niv* 6a, n. 29.

[116] His finding room among the lay brethren suggests that the episode occurred on an uncrowded weekday, and therefore after his recall to spend his final years at the abbey.

[117] *Vir speculativus:* this term is used also in *Arn* II.21h, *Ab* 13b, 16g and (with feminine, *sponsa Christi*) in *Niv* 6b, 11a. The Bible lacks this adjectival form, but has the noun form, *speculator* (watchman), some twenty times.

[118] *Non cedens ei sed caedens eum:* literally 'not yielding to him but smiting him'; but the pun is important, and so I render it as 'gave way, gave walloping [...].'

[119] In all but the first encounter (II.8a), Arnulf's weapon is the sign of the cross. In II.8a itself, the weapon is a curse borrowed from Scripture.

9. A Monk Freed from Rupture; 'Send me God'

(II.9a; II.28) A Cistercian monk, who was a lover of religion and was lovingly and faithfully disposed towards all good people, was once living at Villers as a guest. He chanced to fall into the serious debility known as rupture.[120] This handicap put him in sore straits, and we[121] noticed that he was confined to the infirmary for many days as a result. Having no idea what kind of cure could benefit his ailment, he asked for the prayers of Brother Arnulf, with whom he had won great familiarity in Christ. Arnulf, always wholehearted about meeting such a need in any neighbour, prayed all the more intently for this monk, whom he had come to love so much. The Lord gave Arnulf a gracious hearing, enabling him even to hint at the day and hour when the cure should be expected. Indeed, the cure came, quite in accord with his promise.

(II.9b; II.29) Subsequently this monk once asked Arnulf to send him God, using the phrase some are accustomed to when asking for prayers: 'send me God.'[122] Arnulf, full as ever of liberality and goodwill, bade him name what day he wished his request arranged. He answered: 'On the feast of Saint Lucy the virgin', and Arnulf promised to arrange for that, just as he requested. On that virgin's feast-day, the monk was out on horseback with another monk, who was visiting him and who had once been his abbot.[123] It was then that God's grace caused a *rupture of the floodgates* (Gen. 7.11) within the monk's head, and from his eyes there erupted a deluge of tears, such that, even had he wished it, he could not have held back their impetus.[124] So he fell behind his companion and with a spiritual avidity let himself relish the sweet pittance the Lord had sent him. The other monk, who had forged ahead, hailed him by name and bade him hurry along and catch up. But the monk's ears, as the saying goes, were deaf to the call. Not until an hour later when *the impetus of that flood-tide* had passed which had so *gladdened* his soul (Ps. 45.5), did he catch up with the first rider. Asked why he had dallied, he laid matters bare just as they had occurred: 'Brother Arnulf promised I would be getting a grace from the

---

[120] *Gravem infirmitatem quae ruptura vocatur:* presumably an inguinal hernia.

[121] *Detineri vidimus:* there is no pronoun to make the 'we' of the verb emphatic, as if Goswin had himself seen the guest while visiting the infirmary, but as cantor he would indeed be sensitive to such an absence of a guest-monk from choir.

[122] *Postmodum autem idem ille monachus semel rogavit eum quatenus sibi mitteret Deum, sicut consuetudinis est quibusdam dicere cum orationes aliorum expetunt: 'Mitte mihi Deum.':* this is the passage that prompted our title for Goswin's whole trilogy.

[123] *[Quondam ejus abbate]:* in the original manuscript this is the first occurrence of the square brackets which the Bollandists use to distinguish the longer text of one surviving manuscript from the shorter text of the other. See Select Bibliography, pp. xx–xxii, above.

[124] *Ruptae sunt cataractae capitis ejus [...] inundatio erupit:* a monk cured of rupture has the floodgates ruptured for an eruption of tears. The word *impetus* here echoes the 'impetus of the floodwaters' in Ps. 45. 5.

Lord today, and that is just what happened.' Arnulf likewise foretold that the Lord's grace would come to some nuns of Robertmont,[125] and we know from reliable information that this did happen, and it happened just as he had foretold.

10. The Convent of Argensolles Founded on Arnulf's Advice

(II.10a; II.30) Let us briefly explain how Arnulf's advice led to the construction of a monastery for nuns.[126] A powerful noble, Lord Eraldus of Rammery, had been violently oppressing the venerable Countess Blanche of Champagne, warring against her, besieging her castles and laying waste her land with loot and torch. For he claimed the county of all Champagne as his own by hereditary right, based on his marriage, while overseas, to the daughter of Henry of Champagne, who was also reigning as king in Jerusalem. The nobles of Champagne were rallying to him and abandoning the countess, some only secretly but others doing so quite openly, moved by their blood ties with that knight, or by family connections with his wife. Accordingly, the good matron, noble indeed by birth and nobler still for her dignified *conversatio morum*,[127] was by now practically destitute both of human aid and human counsel, and was left in great anxiety of mind. Thus she resorted to a heartfelt imploring of support from him who well knows how to rescue his own in their troubles. She also took care to commend herself to the holy prayers of good persons.

(II.10b) It was thus that she had a monk summoned from Larrivour,[128] one Gerard,

---

[125] Robertmont was located a mere five kilometres to the east of Liège, and had been founded for Augustinian nuns some decades previously. Ursmer Berlière, in the 1928 fascicule of the *Monasticon Belge* (II, pp. 179–186) tells us that the nuns took the Cistercian habit in 1216, but that local wars soon demanded their transfer to a safer location west of Liège. It was Arnulf's friend Conrad, by now a cardinal, who consecrated their new church in 1224.

[126] *Quo modo [...] paucis explicandum est:* although this solemn rubric for the Argensolles story contrasts with the simple one for the Robertmont story *(certa relatione cognovimus),* I nevertheless suggest Goswin had both stories from the same informant, Gerard of Larrivour (II.10b). He had recently gone to Argensolles as an envoy and then visited Liège on business, presumably with at least a stopover over at Robertmont.

[127] *Sed nobilior longe honesta morum conversatione:* We usually take *morum conversatio* as an echo of the formula of monastic profession in *RB* 58.17, and so as a synonym for monastic life, but Goswin did not make that connection, since his text of *RB* 58.17 had not *conversatio* but *conversio morum.*

[128] *Monachum quemdam de Ripatorio familarem sibi, Gerardum nomine:* Gerard is introduced as one unknown to the reader, but Larrivour is taken for granted. Yet in *Arn* II.20e, Larrivour itself is introduced as if unfamiliar *(quoddam Burgundiae monasterium, quod Ripatorium dicitur).* This suggests that the present story was honed near Larrivour,

with whom she was on familiar terms, and she put to him this question: 'Dear friend, do you know of any holy man able to come prayerfully to my aid in these troubles of mine?' He answered: 'Yes, milady, I know of a lay brother of venerable *conversatio* at Villers in Brabant. His name is Arnulf,[129] and I believe him well able to provide you with the kind of suffrage and prayers to the Lord that you need.' Hearing this, the countess rejoiced indeed and dispatched Brother Gerard to Arnulf for this purpose, permission having first been asked and received from the abbot of Larrivour.

(II.10c; II.31) Upon reaching his beloved Arnulf, the brother greeted him on behalf of the countess of Champagne, intimated his purpose in coming and then added: 'Dear brother, I need to go off to Liège, but would you please apply yourself to prayer, so that when I get back I can hear from you what I should report on all this to the lady countess.' Upon Gerard's departure, Arnulf gave himself over to wholehearted prayer for the intention enjoined on him, and amid this earnest prayer, he beheld a wondrous vision: a hen, bright white and with chicks of the same colour, all following her as a mother who afforded them the warmth of her wings.[130] This he saw, but he had no idea what it meant, and so he asked the Lord to reveal to him its significance. Thereupon a heavenly revelation informed him that the countess should construct a *coenobium* [131] for nuns, for he now understood the hen with her chicks to represent an abbess with her nuns. Some days later, Brother Gerard returned to get his answer on the matter, and Arnulf put a message into his mouth, based on the revelation: 'Return in peace, dear friend, to the lady countess who sent you; greet her in my name and explain to her on my behalf that, if she would found a monastery for Cistercian nuns, then, even as soon as she but conceives in her heart the will to do it, all that dispute going on between her and her detractor will be put to rest, and concord will ensue.'

---

presumably at Argensolles. If so, it is all the more striking how Argensolles treasures a bond with Arnulf in faraway Villers.

[129] *Nosti [...] aliquem virum sanctum [...]? Scio [...] fratrem [...] qui [...] ut credo [...]:* Blanche's *nosti,* suggests personal acquaintance, 'knowing someone', while Gerard's *scio* suggests factual information, 'knowing that this and that is thus and so'. But Gerard's answer lacks such a factual complement and the only object of his *scio* is the person of Arnulf. He does not just 'know of' Arnulf; he outright 'knows' him. In *Arn* II.10c Arnulf is Gerard's 'beloved Arnulf', whom he addresses as 'dear brother'. Presumably then, Gerard has met Arnulf in person on earlier trips through Brabant, and well knows the power of his prayers.

[130] *Gallinam candidam cum pullis ejusdem coloris:* we would expect the white colour to point to the heroine's name, 'Blanche' (French for white). Instead, attention goes to the first abbess and the white robes of her flock. Her name was Agnes of Liège.

[131] A Greek word current among Western monks, meaning 'a place of living in common'; compare *RB* 1.2,13; 5.12. Goswin uses a few other Greek words, for example *cenodoxia* (vainglory) at *Arn* II.1e and *charismata* at *Arn* I.1a and *Niv* 22d, 23a, 27e, 28b.

(II.10d; II.32) The monk was gladdened to hear this message, and bidding his dear Arnulf farewell, he made his way back to the venerable countess and reported to her all he had heard from him. She, on hearing it, *rejoiced with great joy* (Matt. 2.10) and, though she had never entertained any notion of constructing a monastery,[132] she now took action on it as on a plan received straight from God. Immediately, that very day, she set about arranging for what kind of new monastery she could found and for its location. And so, *in order that the saying* of the man of God *be fulfilled* (John 18.9), not long after this, that powerful and contumacious man who had so tumultuously opposed the countess, was won back to peace and concord. When at length the monastery and its workshops were all constructed, it was named Argensolles. There the noble matron assembled a community of virgins, taken from the diocese of Liège and from elsewhere, all to be trained as regulated by the Cistercian Order. She also copiously endowed and expanded the place with the revenues and possessions in which it currently abounds, so that to this day, it is flourishing in religious fervour.

11. Chiding a Recluse for Neglecting her Protégé

(II.11a; II.33) Not far from Villers dwelt a recluse, herself very devout and correspondingly gracious and lovable to many persons. To Arnulf she was a friend in Christ, so cherished that she addressed him as her own dearest father.[133] Now there was a cleric, a well-gifted student, who used frequently to come to her and take a seat outside the window of her *reclusorium*, and there she made a point of often giving him sound words of advice on *keeping away from sins and the vices* (*RB* 7.12), shunning the companionship of the worldly and striving to serve the Lord God in sincerity of life. He, being a well-disposed lad, one inwardly visited by grace, soon took to complying with the guidance the recluse was giving him, until it was even daily that he had recourse to her to hear from her mouth those words of holy consolation.

---

[132] *Quae numquam voluntatem construendi monasterii habuerat:* Blanche's idea of building Argensolles may well have thus come out of the blue; but she was soon to become a major friend of the whole Order, as shown in the General Chapters: *GC* 1221.48, 1224.20, 1228.7, 1229.11, 1231.14. Born in 1195 as daughter of the saintly King of Navarre, she married Theobald of Champagne, and died 1229.

[133] *Non longe a monasterio Villariensi degens:* we have three clues to the location of her cell: firstly, as a recluse, she would be attached to a church with full liturgical life; secondly, as guide to a clerical student, she would be near a church school; and thirdly, as calling Arnulf her 'dearest father', she would be on his route for distributing gifts of bread. This would point to a major church in Nivelles, fourteen kilometres west of the abbey, but only nine kilometres from the major grange of La Neuve Cour. It was not until 1235, seven years after Arnulf's death, that abbeys and granges were forbidden to bake for such women (*GC* 1235.12).

(II.11b) The recluse, however, could see that this new son of hers in Christ was losing whole days this way and neglecting to join his companions at study. So she admonished him to come more rarely in future and to get back to his classes more frequently than he had been doing. But his love for her in Christ was so tender that he refused his consent and kept up his very frequent recourse to her, for he accounted time spent at her school far from lost, since it was from her that he was learning *the pathway to life* (*RB* Prol. 20). Seeing this, the recluse became angry and indignant with him and vowed to the Lord, quite indiscreetly, that she would not speak to him for a month. Realizing this, the cleric was greatly alarmed and fell almost into despair. Indeed, he almost disowned the goodly doctrine he had been receiving from her as his teacher and mother. Still, rather than behave like *a dog returning to its vomit* (II Pet. 2.22), he did violence to himself, grabbed the bit between his teeth, as the saying goes, and plodded ahead along *the pathway to life,* which he had begun. But he lodged a complaint with the all-governing Lord about this teacher and mother of his, and about how she had more or less abandoned him and left him with no consolation at all, as if he were someone to be despaired of. Yet so as not to give occasion for her to overstep her vow, he never made bold to open any conversation with her, no matter how often during that month he was at her *reclusorium.*[134]

(II.11c[135]; II.34) Meanwhile the recluse was stricken with a fever, so severe that her teeth could be heard chattering from a long way off. Moreover, the Spirit revealed to Arnulf everything that had taken place between her and the cleric. Shortly after this, Arnulf came to her, but, though he found her struggling with the fever, he worded his greeting as if ignorant of it all, and asked: 'How is your health, dear friend?' 'Fever!' she said, 'I'm all in straits with fever!' 'And deservedly so!' he replied. 'Deservedly in straits with fever, after so senselessly rebuffing, and treating as a stranger, one whom you *had mothered in Christ* (I Cor. 4.15), a newborn infant you should still be cradling, still nursing with the milk *of consolation!* (Isa. 66.11).[136] Be sure then of this: for such an offence, our just and

---

[134] *Ante reclusorium ejus venit [...] loqui ei non praesumpsit:* I suspect a misprint. I would guess it should be *non* venit *[...] non praesumpsit.* Thus I translate to allow both senses.

[135] In this paragraph, the reader may be surprised by the bold tone assumed by Arnulf, and by his sophisticated and biblical diction. Presumably the narrative was shaped by storytellers different from those for the intramural episodes, it being not unusual for one regarded inside the cloister as a good-for-nothing, to be regarded outside as one whose prayers are powerful, and whose words come straight from God. One aspect of the style here is the fully Goswinian way of naming divine intervention, for instance, *per spiritum revelata* (as in *Arn* II.8c, 17 title; *Niv* 16b; *Ab* 13d); *coelitus* as in no fewer than eleven other passages of Arnulf alone; and *Deus meus* in *Arn* I.1c, II.2c, 21c; *Niv* 7b, 22h.

[136] Metaphor for a parental role rather than one of friendship; akin to the white hen and chicks of II.10c. I suggest the cleric was in his early-to-middle teens (*scholaris, adolescens*), the same age as Abundus had been when dealing with Yvette (Juetta) of Huy (*Ab* 4b), and as

merciful God was initially planning to punish you with a scourge exceedingly harsh; yes, he was even going to withdraw from you his grace. I, however, was informed of this from on high, and, unable to remain calm while seeing you sustain such a setback, I pleaded with the Lord my God to be propitious and to purge you of this offence, but not, oh not, with that spiritual scourge! Rather with some bodily scourge instead. And my God has done what I asked of him! He has sent you this fever, a fever so severe that probably none more severe could ever exist! But myself, by this time I was ill at ease over your lacking any allowance of heavenly nourishment, and so I turned once more to *the bounteous giver of all good things* (Ritual: Meals) and pleaded that he look on you with his eye of clemency and, far from *sending you away unfed* in face of this illness (Matt. 15.32; Mark 8.3), he graciously send you instead an affluence of heavenly grace as great as any you have ever had in your entire life. Tell me, then, in the name of the Lord, is this how it happened, or not?' That handmaid of Christ was astounded to hear all this, with these *words of grace coming forth from his mouth* (Luke 4.22). She answered that indeed everything had happened just as the blessed man had declared. So he offered her his comfort, as his beloved friend in Christ. And then he bade her farewell and headed back to the grange. *By the Lord was this thing done,* through his servant, *and it is wondrous in our eyes* (Ps. 117.23).

12. Foretelling the Death of a Priest's Mother

(II.12a; II.35) There was a devout priest, named Gerard, who used to live in Nivelles, at St Sixtus's church, functioning as chaplain. With him dwelt his mother, Cecilia by name. She, after a time, was stricken with an illness and took to her bed. Her son Gerard had been on quite familiar terms with Arnulf, and now came to see him and, in filial affection and compassion over his mother's illness, commended her to his prayers.

(II.12b) Upon his arrival, the two chatted on many topics, and then the priest asked Arnulf: 'Please, dearest brother in Christ, please do pray hard to God for my mother, for she is having a hard time with this illness.'[137] And he added: 'Could I also ask you to foretell for me the date when she is going to die?' Arnulf gave a joking reply: 'What's the point in asking me the likes of that? It's just idle curiosity to ask such things!' The priest answered: 'Not so by any means! And *if I have found any grace in your eyes* (Gen. 18.3, etc.), please give my plea a hearing, because I intend to twist it out of you anyway!' And so, to avoid saddening so dear a friend, the merciful Arnulf prayed to the Lord for the mother and won a hearing. Then,

---

Ida had been when dealing with Heylonbineth of Nivelles (*Niv* 1h).

[137] *Quae infirmitate laborat, Deum attentius exoretis:* favourite expressions of Goswin's, rendered colloquially to match the conversational context.

returning from his prayer, he told the priest his mother's death would occur within the twenty days of Christmas. The prediction itself was dated around the feast of Saint Remigius.[138]

(II.12c; II.36) With that, the priest bade Arnulf farewell, returned to his mother and ministered to her in her illness as solicitously and as well as he could. Then on the seventeenth day after Christmas the good woman's disease grew more serious and she became weaker than usual. So her son Gerard invited Master Guido of Nivelles, of pious memory,[139] and nine other priests to be present for his mother's anointing. In this way she was duly anointed, with all those priests standing by and praying for her. Before the actual anointing, however, one of the priests who had come called Gerard aside and spoke slanderously to him about Brother Arnulf, saying: 'Milord Gerard, why do you so readily trust this talkative Brother Arnulf when he foretells your mother's death within these twenty days?' Gerard thought ill of such talk and scolded the priest, asserting that Brother Arnulf was a man of virtue, a man *acceptable to God* in his deeds (Acts 10.35). Even so, far from hushing his slander, the priest clutched the cape he was wearing and said: 'Look, I'll let this cape be burned in the fire if ever your mother actually dies the way Brother Arnulf says she will.'

(II.12d) How wrong he was! For the woman died the very next day, which was the eighteenth day, and was indeed prior to the twentieth. She was buried on the nineteenth day. Gerard returned to Arnulf and, informing him of his mother's death, suppliantly urged him to make suffrage for her soul. Arnulf promptly replied: 'So my prediction about your mother came true! That priest's cape, though, has not yet been burned! He's holding onto it still!'

(II.37) Gerard was so amazed at this statement that he bade his beloved Arnulf farewell and headed straight back to Nivelles to tell the priest of Brother Arnulf's rebuke for not yet burning the cape. The priest blushed intensely to find himself wrong on both scores and he never again presumed to slander Arnulf. Indeed, he was so touched to the quick with regret for having detracted such a man, that he spoke up

---

[138] *Infra viginti dies post natale Domini:* although I have not met this expression elsewhere, I am sure 'the twenty days' would be jargon for the season running from Christmas through the Octave of Epiphany (25 December to 13 January). The feast of St Remigius (1 October) stood out at Villers as something a calendar landmark, firstly because that saint converted King Clovis (496–498 AD.), and this made him for Reims and its region something of what St Patrick was for Ireland. By Goswin's time the Order was honouring him liturgically, as also Thomas of Canterbury and Denis of Paris, to the rank of a 'feast on which we work' (*EO* 49.2, 19, 20). The selection of texts for his feast would serve as model for newer additions to the calendar (*GC* 1268.9, 1278.42).

[139] This Guido is presumably the same as the 'Master Guido of Nivelles often mentioned in the Life of Mary of Oignies and described there (*Oig* II.55) as 'a priest, a man humble and devoted, and a spiritual father to her'. This last title he shares (*Oig* II.57) with Master John of Nivelle, who is also mentioned in *Arn* II.13b and in *Ab* 15b.

and said: 'Milord Gerard, let us go to that man of God, for I want to speak with him and have sight of him too!'

(II.12e) Gerard agreed and *both set out together* (IV Kings 2.6) and arrived at the grange where he was staying, which, as we said above, was called Chênoit.[140] There they spoke with him to their heart's content, and as long as Arnulf was speaking for both to hear together, the topic was simply of *God or the welfare of souls* (*GC* 1233.6). Even this moved the priest to *compunction*, and almost to *tears* (*RB* 20.3), no matter how frozen his heart may have been on first arrival. And so it was that he finally took Brother Arnulf aside and spoke with him one-to-one. Arnulf's consoling words now so emboldened the priest in Christ that he made a formal request for pardon for the injurious slander he had flung out with a tongue all too prone to speak ill. Indeed, Arnulf's words emboldened him into protesting that it was here that he had discovered the grace of the Lord.[141] And so, with his companion Gerard, *he made his way back rejoicing to where he belonged* (Acts 8.39; Antiphon: St Benedict).

13. Reproving a Priest's Pretence of Religiosity

(II.13a; II.38) There was a secular priest of fairly respectable conduct, who outwardly seemed to be trying to live up to good people's standards. However, he always set store by *human glory* (John 12.43), human gloss,[142] while at the same time plunging himself into such a cesspool of carnal wantonness that in the eyes of an all-beholding God he counted for a hypocrite. Therefore, a certain devout woman persuaded him to go and see Brother Arnulf, both to make friends with him and to get the benefit of his prayers, seeing what a wide reputation the brother had for religious devotedness. The priest did as she had said. He made his way to Arnulf and was warmly received by him, who, to be sure, was warm to everyone.[143]

---

[140] From this point to the end of the chapter is one long sentence in Latin. The shorter text omits five phrases and I myself paraphrase slightly.

[141] *Gratiam Domini se in eo invenisse testatus est:* is 'finding grace' the priest's discernment of the presence of grace in Arnulf, or rather his personal recuperation of grace, occasioned by Arnulf? I leave it ambiguous, but Goswin's four other uses of *invenire gratiam* all echo of the biblical phrase, strongly in the second sense (*Niv* 4b, 10f, *Arn* II.12b, *Ab* 19c). Synonymous phrases are also in the second sense: *Niv* 28b *(consecuta est)*, *Arn* II.4e *(adeptus)*, II.5b *(obtineret)*, II.17c *(in te experta)*, *Ab* 3a *(sibi allicere, mereretur accipere)*, *Ab* 12b *(assequi posset)*.

[142] *Gloriam, vel gloriolam, hominum affectans:* only the longer text gives this very Goswinian pun.

[143] *Qui benignus erat omnibus:* a Goswinian generalization, found only in the longer text. See also *Arn* II.29b, *Ab* 2b, 5b, etc.

(II.13b) When he explained that his purpose in coming was to meet him and to ask his prayers, Arnulf replied: 'But how could a prayer of mine, or anyone else's, profit you so long as you go unashamed of the state you are living in?'[144] This word upset the priest a little and he answered: 'On what score is my life and its state judged blameworthy?' Arnulf responded: 'Why try cloaking over your behaviour and your counterfeit living? You have deceived many by such means, but from me you cannot conceal any of your wretched *conversatio!*' Then, taking a nod from the priest to mean assent, Arnulf let him hear an explicit account of his detestable doings, his unmentionable carryings on and the whole state of his conscience, with all its malicious and impure thinking. And to prove the truth of what he was saying, he gave him this sign: 'Whenever you have had a chance to confess to Master John of Nivelle,[145] or any other man as devoutly upright in Christ as he is, a chance, I say, to let out[146] how wretched your life has become, you have hushed up the very things I have been exposing one by one, hushed them up out of fear that by letting them out to such men, their opinion of you would be tarnished and your entire reputation as well. Instead, you have whispered in their ears a few peccadilloes, the better to cloak over your real behaviour.'

(II.39) The priest listened to this and his conscience joined in accusing him. No alibi could he find with which to face up to the man of God. Inwardly he was touched to the quick with grief; outwardly he was flushed to the face with shame. And so he avowed the certitude of all the servant of Christ had alleged against him.

(II.13c) Arnulf in turn *comforted him* in the Lord (Luke 22.43) and urged him for the future to rein in those excesses of his by using every kind of caution, and also to withdraw his bodily presence from the village where he currently dwelt. Thereupon the priest bade Arnulf farewell and went his way confounded. He did indeed move from his dwelling place and went elsewhere, but his shame was too great for him ever to return to Arnulf again.

(II.13d) Let all bluffing and lustful priests now blush for their simulation, who, under *their sheep-like garb, are ravening wolves* (Matt. 7.15). Contaminated with the filth of lust, they dare *to set the idol* (Jer. 32.34) of Venus alongside the Virgin's Son, since in celebrating the mass and proffering the sacred words, their unclean mouths are spitting into the Saviour's face; and in putting his holy flesh into those unclean mouths, they equivalently toss him to *the mud of the streets* (Ps. 17.43). Wretched they certainly are, and to be pitied, *for they have established a covenant with death, made a pact with hell itself* (Isa. 28.15). Let those who are this way now

---

[144] *In eo statu in quo nunc estis:* concern for the individual's 'state', which is a central theme in *Niv*, comes up three times here in *Arn* II.13. Unfortunately the Bollandists' printer failed to close one of the parentheses indicating the longer text, but certainly two, if not all three, of these allusions to 'state' are only in the longer text. See also *Arn* I.1g, I.8d, II.6a, etc.

[145] On John of Nivelle, see *Arn* II.12c, n. 139, above.

[146] *Ut miseram vestram vitam publicetis.*

come back to their senses and return to the Lord Jesus, their Saviour, to him *who dissimulates their sins for the sake of repentance* (Wisd. 11.24). Let them have recourse to him, to his merciful self, while yet they may! Yes, let them attain to such mercy while still the opportunity lasts!

14. Helping a Novice and Two Monks in Need

(II.14a; II.40) There was a novice at Villers, who was having to spend his year of probation *in the furnace of tribulation* (Ecclus. 2.5), and who could say with the psalmist: *'Tribulation have I found, and grief'* (Ps. 114.3). He was much afflicted with two unbearable illnesses, the first being an almost continuous headache, such that he could scarcely keep the silence or maintain decorum until mealtime,[147] and the second an illness we judge too unseemly and unrespectable to publish, and which we here cloak over out of decency. These twin sufferings *hacked away at him,* as it were, *gash upon gash* (Job 16.15), until the poor novice all but despaired of ever regaining his health, since there was no remedy he could find applicable to these illnesses. Thus in the end, with due permission, he privately confided his impasse to Arnulf.

(II.14b) Being a man of much loving-kindness, Arnulf took compassion from his inmost marrow on the novice's straits, praying for him and replying to him thus: *'Go in peace, take courage in the Lord* (Mark 5.34; Eph. 6.10), and know for certain that from this day on you will no more be troubled by the twin illnesses of which you complain and which have obsessed you until now.' And sure enough, the novice recovered from both illnesses and gave his thanks to Almighty God and to Arnulf his servant. Then, having rallied so promptly and unexpectedly to a renewed health, he waited out the twelvemonth with joy until the day of his profession.

(II.14c; II.41) Another monk of Villers was hard pressed by a severe temptation and likewise betook himself to Arnulf to reveal this molesting trial and to ask the help of his prayers. The answer he received was that he would shortly be entirely freed from the temptation. In fact, that very day Arnulf, like a second Moses, *lifted his hand* on high to pray and to put to flight the spiritual Amalech that had been attacking this Israel of ours (Exod. 17.11–12),[148] affording him a stable peace, no longer to be wearied by the temptation he had till then endured from the foe.

(II.14d) Another monk of Villers wished to consult Arnulf and to complain about

---

[147] *Silentii vix posset tenere censuram et usque ad horam vescendi decorum sustinere.*

[148] We glimpse here how, at Villers, faith ennobled even trivial things. The client is an anonymous monk, his temptation vague and his cure featureless. On the other hand, he is a *local* monk, *lonely* in his temptation, yet willing *trustfully to depend* on the *daring promise* of an equally local confrère. Goswin sees this small-scale act of faith as raising the sufferer to the dignity of a new Israel, and Arnulf to that of a new Moses. Even the demon behind the temptation takes on the dignity of an Amalech worth hating!

a fainthearted impoverishment of his soul, for he had been feeling a hardness of heart, especially on Sundays. Arnulf replied: 'Why make an issue, brother, about having hardness of heart on Sundays, when three days each week[149] you are nourished, albeit in small enough measure, with the honeyed victuals of heavenly grace?' The monk tried to deny this, but Arnulf pushed home his point: 'Stop trying to hide it! The facts are just as I say.' The monk thought over repeatedly whether this might be so, and whether, out of some low-heartedness, he were not, perhaps, overlooking a grace from the Lord, reaching him as often as three times a week. And indeed he came to realize that there was truth in what he had heard from the mouth of the servant of God.

15. Vision of a Monk Carried up to Heaven

(II.15a; II.42) We now offer something *for the edification of our hearers* (*RB* 38.12, 42.3, 47.3), which occurred at Villers and is worth the telling. On the Assumption of the blessed Virgin Mary, *at the beginning of vigils* (Lam. 2.19), when the monks were solemnly singing that jubilant song, the invitatory antiphon *Ave Maria*, along with its psalm, *Venite exultemus* (Ps. 94), one of them,[150] while singing along with the rest, began directing upward his heart's affection. So emphatically was he drawn aloft by grace, that he felt he was putting himself almost bodily into the presence of our glorious Lord and Saviour and of his most blessed mother. Upon being afforded this heavenly comfort for his inner soul, he felt called to entrust himself to the Lord's mercy, and so he experienced the hope that he too would yet be crowned by the Lord in heaven, crowned, not for any merits of his own, but in accord with the Lord's unspeakable goodness. Each time the invitatory antiphon was repeated, he sang along right joyfully, humbly sharing the sublime company of the king and queen on high, and feeling his holy devotion stir anew and grow greater yet.

(II.15b) Meanwhile Arnulf was also in church, and he too saw the saving Lord and his venerable mother. There they were, standing beside the monk, and as he sang along with a smile, they girded him about with a very beautiful belt, picked him up by the arms, right and left, and lifted him to sublime heights, far above the earth. And Arnulf, still at his prayers and letting his gaze follow as the monk went his way, now cried out: 'My brother, my brother, yet again and for sure, I shall see you!' (compare IV Kings 2.12) But the monk, still in those blessed hands of the king and

---

[149] The context gives no clue as to the occasion of these graces, but it could be a question of the Eucharist, especially if the monk was a priest celebrating thrice each week.

[150] The monk is kept anonymous because of the honour involved. I suggest it was one who often chatted with Arnulf on festive afternoons, perhaps even Walter himself (*Arn* Pref. c; II.7a).

queen, was wafted up to the constellations and could be seen by him no longer.

(II.15c; II.43) On that same Assumption Day, the monk obtained permission to speak with Arnulf, though quite unaware of the latter's having had this vision of himself the previous night. While they were thus *conversing together* (IV Kings ibid.), Arnulf dissolved, as he so often did, into laughter, and the monk was left wondering why there should be such laughter for no apparent cause. Then Arnulf told him how, during vigils the previous night, he had seen one of the monks visited in choir by the Virgin Mother and her Son and taken up to heaven in their holy hands. Hearing this, the other asked him to tell the monk's name and the moment that he was thus taken aloft. Arnulf was at first unwilling to answer that question but eventually yielded to his importunate queries and declared that he was himself the monk and that the invitatory was the moment when it happened.

(II.15d) The monk had, of course, had no grounds for ever supposing any such thing would happen to him, and so, far from being elated over such a heavenly benefit, he humbled himself in spirit before the eyes of the Lord. Accordingly, this vision was such that our contemplator saw it spiritually, and yet it was manifested to him with an almost corporeal vividness, just as if it had been a corporeal vision.[151]

(II.44) We, therefore, who *profess holy service* to the Lord (*RB* 5.3), should strive to follow the example of this monk, and, when *standing at the psalmody* (*RB* 19.7) we should strive *to understand* the psalms we are uttering (Ps. 31 title) and to sing in a human manner and not as with the voice of birds. For blackbirds and parrots and crows and other winged fowl are often taught by people to utter sounds they are ignorant of; whereas to sing knowingly is a gift the divine will grants to human nature, the same gift that the psalmist is commending when he says: *I shall sing and I shall understand* (Ps. 100.1–2). How can we imagine psalmody is going to please God when the voice, for its part, parades a semblance of someone at prayer but *the mind remains without fruit?* (I Cor. 14.14) The point is that those who handed down to us the form for our psalmody alerted us that we *should serve the Lord in fear* (Ps. 2.11; *RB* 19.3), should *sing psalms wisely* (Ps. 46.8; *RB* 19.4), *should so stand at the psalmody that our mind be in harmony with our voice* (*RB* 19.7). So let us keep our heart well guarded while applying ourselves to divine praise, and when we are bodily in choir, let our mind not be wandering abroad. Indeed, as the philosopher says: *Anyone who is everywhere, is really nowhere.* The first proof of a recollected mind is the ability to sit down and stay put; for it belongs to a sickly mind to be tossing about, running hither and yon, restless for variety of scenery. Yes, even while we linger bodily on earth, let us dwell mentally with the Lord in heaven, so that *where our treasure is, there may our heart be too* (Matt. 6.21).

---

[151] *Haec itaque visio, quam contemplator noster spiritualiter vidit acsi corporaliter accidisset, ei corporaliter manifestata est.* For Goswin's frequent discussion of 'spiritual' and 'corporeal' manifestations, see *Niv* 22g, 24d, 27ce, 30j, 33e, 34b; *Arn* I.2b; II.7b, 18c; *Ab* 12c. Interestingly, so typical an aside is found only in the longer text.

16. 'Sending God' to a Matron in Paris

(II.16a; II.45) A devout woman, having heard the fame of Arnulf's wondrous *conversatio*, wished to see his face and to have a chance to speak with him. This was Theophania, hostess at the hostel in Paris, the one facing the cathedral of Notre Dame.[152] But the long distance posed an obstacle and this heartfelt desire of hers went unmet. Unable to see the holy man face to face, or speak with him by word of mouth, she summoned a cleric who was studying there, a Brabantine by nationality, and made him her emissary to this servant of Christ, to act as a vicar for her conscience, so that by his mouth she could graciously greet Arnulf and ask him to implore the Lord to bestow on her a copious share of heavenly grace.

(II.16b) When the great-hearted Arnulf heard this from the messenger's mouth, he was pleased with the devoted and faithful matron's request and, in the gracious, eager style he used with everyone, he is said to have laughed for joy. This is the kind of reply he gave the messenger: 'Return, my friend, to the devout lady who sent you. First pass on from my lips the heartfelt wish for her fullest eternal welfare and then, as my message for her, inform her that on such and such a day she will have from the heavenly Lord such an overflow of grace as she has never had in her whole life.' Arnulf went on to designate for her the day this would be done, and he added: 'Unless some neglect on her part blocks the aqueduct through which the stream of grace should flow into her heart, the measure of grace will in no way be impeded from filling her heart to overflowing as abundantly as I have foretold for her.'

(II.16c; II.46) After hearing this, the cleric returned to Paris and greeted the devout woman with Arnulf's spoken message and gave her an orderly account of all he had heard from his lips. *She rejoiced in the things that were said to her* (Ps. 121.1) and began looking forward with great desire, and with no hesitation at all, to receiving the promised bountiful, grace-filled blessing from on high. When, a short while later, that festive *day was to dawn* (Antiphon: Epiphany), *the day of the gladness of her heart* (Cant. 3.11), and she herself was at prayer, it came to pass, suddenly and without warning, that *the spirit of the Lord rushed upon her* (Num. 24.2), *a spirit mighty* and strong (Acts 2.2), by whose powerful virtue all her entrails were jolted, and, *just as wax melts before the fire* (Ps. 67.3) so was *her soul* totally *liquefied* (Cant. 5.6) and poured out into the embraces of her Beloved, being at once nourished inwardly with the honeyed taste of a divine sweetness and also wondrously transported into a *paradise of delights* (Gen. 2.15).

---

[152] A footnote in AASS cites Jacques du Breul, *Les Antiquitez de la ville de Paris* (Paris, 1640), IV: 950–1005, where much is said on such hostels, and on how each catered to students of a particular nationality, but nothing is said specifically on this one for Brabantine students. The landladies would be important retailers of edifying news from 'back home'. It was, for instance, as a student in Paris that James of Vitry first heard of Mary of Oignies (*Oig* Suppl.1). Theophania had apparently heard stories of Arnulf's 'sending God' (*Arn.* II.9, 11) and now she eagerly requests the same gift for herself.

(II.16d) After being beside herself in this drunkenness, and then coming back to herself, *ever so gladsome* still, *ever so laudatory* (Isa. 35.2), she, like another Queen of Sheba, broke out into the praises of our Solomon and said: *'How true it was, that word I was hearing, here in this land, all about the virtues of that* holy man! And I was disbelieving those who told me of him: but that was only until I experienced for myself the force of his merits! And so, with the faith of an eyewitness I have now *seen and proved that not even half* his admirable life and virtues *had been reported to me! For his* holy devotion *is even greater than was rumoured to me!'* (III Kings 10. 6–7)

(II.16e) Thereafter, over and over again, this handmaid of Christ, sent Arnulf greetings in the Lord, by means both of the cleric already mentioned or of many others too,[153] sending him at the same time her thanks for his suffrages and prayers. She also publicized and commended his merits and virtues to all and sundry, praising and magnifying in him the Lord his Saviour, who had enriched him with the privilege of so copious a grace. If any are in ambiguity as to the truth of the foregoing let them, if at a distance, send the venerable woman a messenger,[154] or, if on the spot, let them interrogate her for themselves. She is still alive and is in the city of Paris to this day, and from her they can l for themselves the truth of this matter.

17. Awareness of a Grace Sent to a Devout Woman

(II.17a; II.47) There was another devout woman, linked to Arnulf with so indissoluble a bond of holy love that the pair of them had but *one heart and one soul* (Acts 4.32). To this handmaid of Christ, the Lord once granted a wondrous grace. This heavenly gift came on a Good Friday and lasted almost the whole of that day, the day when the Church universal recalls the sacred memory of her Lord's Passion. Arnulf too had a revelation, and by it he came to know the manner and sequence of the woman's grace. Accordingly he summoned one of the monks, a faithful sharer of the secrets of his heart, and indicated to him the kind and measure of good things the Lord had done for the woman that day. And he added: 'Behold, I am sending you to her;[155] go and give in her hearing an orderly account of all you have heard from me.'

---

[153] *Tam per clericum illum [...] quam per alios multos:* the three hundred mile distance and the plurality of bearers suggest many years of such shuttling, with Theophania ever a significant feminine influence at the university. The first such messenger is left anonymous. This is because he has since joined Villers? Could it even be Goswin himself? For another contact of Villers with Paris, see *Ab* 13e.

[154] Goswin here supposes a Parisian readership. Theophania had perhaps requested a copy of this Life for student use.

[155] Although the style here is biblical, *Ecce, mitto te [...]. Haec dicit tibi vir Dei [...],* it is nor really traceable to particular passages. As in so many of these extramural episodes, we marvel at Arnulf's authority to send envoys and to interpret visions.

(II.17b) The monk set out and came to her, and speaking on Arnulf's behalf, he broke forth with these words: 'This is what the man of God Arnulf has to say to you, and this is his message for me to pass on to you. On Good Friday this year, that day just before Easter, characterized by the adoration of the cross, you were in church, listening to the Passion of Christ recited by the priest. Your heart, as you well know, could muster no softening, no compassion at all; but then the hour came at which the Lord hung limp on the cross, and that hour[156] became for you the object of a heavenly manifestation. After that you could in no way withhold yourself or resist your entire heart's dissolving into streams swollen with tears.

(II.48) Within that hour you seemed to be seeing the Lord's side pierced by the lance, and the lance itself penetrating his heart; to be seeing also how blood flowed from his hands and feet, and how the crown of thorns was set upon his head. And while your attention was going to so bitter a grief of your Lord and Saviour it seemed to you that, like Saint Andrew,[157] you too would have to *undergo the torment of the cross* (Collect: Triduum) and die with your Lord. Then the loving-kind, Lord's own attention went out to you and he saw how you, his faithful friend, wished to die with him, and so he said to you in the warm tones of his loving-kindness: '*Come, sweet daughter, come after me!*' (Mark 1.17) Forthwith, looking upwards, you saw *the heavens opened* (John 1.51) and you gazed into them with the lightsome eyes of your mind, gazed upon the majesty most high. And behold, suddenly it seemed to you that you were in attendance upon the majesty supreme, as upon a king, a crowned king, and you heard him blissfully voicing such words as these: 'Peace, my daughter; have peace within you, and do away with this grieving of yours, for I am cured now, cured of the cross, cured of all its suffering!' On hearing this, you conceived such jubilee of laughter and exultation that there and then you entirely forgot the Lord's Passion, so forcefully, so perfectly, had the grace and glory of that supreme majesty absorbed your heart into itself. Yes, it seemed to you the Lord was turning himself into a looking-glass for you, now that you had smashed underfoot the your earlier looking glass, the world.[158] That is why the next sweet whisper you heard was of words such as these: 'Behold, sweet daughter, I am showing you my face, my blissful face! My wish is for you to go to sleep now, to sleep in my heart, and to let your own heart rest assured that in these delights of my glory you will live on eternally!' And while you were thus uplifted in your mental

---

[156] *Sed cum facta esset hora qua Dominus in cruce pependit, eadem hora coelitus tibi manifestata est:* I make both uses of *hora* nominative, and so does the editor of AASS, who, in the following sentence, prints a third use of the word with a circumflex accent (*horâ*), to stress that this time it is not nominative but ablative.

[157] The liturgy for St Andrew is lyrical about his love of the cross and his desire to share Christ's crucifixion.

[158] *Ut tibi videretur quod Dominus de seipso faceret tibi quoddam speculum, pro eo quod speculum mundi contriveras sub pedibus tuis:* for Goswin's idea of *speculum*, see *Arn* I.12s; II.6d; *Niv* Pref. d, 2e, 29b–8, 34bg, 35a, line 1; *Ab* 8b, 16a.

ecstasy, the Lord Christ seemed, with uplifted hand, to be blessing you and saying: 'Hold fast, my daughter, to this peace of mine, and steadily observe it, for it is *in peace that my dwelling place has been established* (Ps. 75.3).

(II.17c) 'Behold, my sister', continued the monk, 'behold the report I give you on behalf of your beloved Arnulf, his report of the kind and measure of the grace you experienced from the Lord that day. And now, to confirm the truth of my narrative, please accept one fact as a sign, the fact that the heavenly grace you so abundantly conceived that sacred day remained in your soul from that hour, when the Lord of majesty first hung on the gibbet of the cross, and up until the dusk of nightfall.' When the devout woman had heard all this, she *was filled with amazement and wonderment* (Acts 3.10), and blessed the Lord and Saviour for deigning to lavish so copious a gift of grace on his servant Arnulf.[159]

18. Arnulf Consulted by Two Clerics

(II.18a; II.49) Two youthful clerics came to Arnulf and asked him to tell them of any matter of conscience he judged worthy of reproach in them. He replied: 'For the moment I shall not answer, but go on to the neighbouring village and speak to the recluse who dwells there,[160] and rest assured that on your return I shall answer you.' They immediately went along, taking his remarks as a sign. He in the meanwhile prayed hard for God to reveal to him something of their status. And his prayer was graciously heard.

(II.18b) Upon their return that evening, one of them spoke with Arnulf separately and put the question: 'Good brother, which of my sins am I to be judged the most reproachable for?' Arnulf replied: 'I will tell you. The sin you are asking about is of the kind you vomited out at confession this very week.[161] And as a confirming sign, I mention that you have not yet begun to perform the penance enjoined for that sin.'

---

[159] Does the woman's wonderment confirm the accuracy of the recital? For similar ambiguities, see, for example, *Niv* 24e, 26de. Such recitals are meant to help clients take possession of a recent experience, be it a glorious one (as here), or a shameful one (as in *Niv* 7b, 12cd).

[160] I suggest it was just a stroll, comparable to the feast-day recreations in *Ab* 3a. The visit to Arnulf was perhaps just a stop-off en route to the recluse (compare, *Arn* II.11a). For such a stop-off on a strictly business trip, see *Arn* II.10c. Both times Arnulf is more helpful at the second visit, when his guests are homeward bound. Just as the process of 'sending God' calls for a 'countdown', so the answering of a spiritual question demands time for a 'build-up' to clarity of perspective.

[161] The first cleric apparently had only a minor peccadillo to worry about, but the second was involved in serious sinfulness. Which of them gave Goswin the story? Inasmuch as both went on to become Cistercians (II.18d), either could be his source, but I would say more probably the second, since it was on him that the exchange had the greater impact.

On hearing this and seeing himself caught, the cleric was amazed and openly asserted how right he was.

(II.18c; II.50) Next came the other cleric, likewise wishing to hear what testimony this man of wonders would bear in his regard. *It was, in fact, night time* (John 13.30). So Arnulf told him: 'Dear brother, inasmuch as it is your good pleasure that I express verbally how your life now stands, let me just say what your conscience is already aware of:[162] you have to some extent been managing an outward show of religion, keeping your behaviour respectable enough, but your heart is restless and vagabond and is often sullied by vain and wanton thoughts. Sometimes too, you put in a personal appearance at minor gatherings of devout women,[163] not for any advice they might give you on how to avoid your pitfalls and sins, or how to imitate the lives of better people, but rather you go there to show off, by carrying on with fancy gestures and the familiarities of laughter and joking, aimed at coaxing one or other of them into sin, or, at the least, at allowing yourself to experience glances and attentions such as could bring detriment to your soul. Accordingly, you can be sure of this, and you need to be aware of it in advance: if you linger on in the outside world, you are going to be like an unrestrained stallion, stumbling headlong into the deep pit of sin. So off you go and confess those sins of yours, something you badly need to do!'[164]

(II.51) The cleric could not deny what he heard Arnulf saying. Already perplexed in mind, he was outwardly ashamed, and would have been far more so had the darkness of night not provided a buffer, since the man of God had his eyes fixed right upon him.

(II.18d) But, being a merciful man, Arnulf now comforted them, and, with salutary words, he encouraged them to emulate the lives of better men. Then he dismissed them peace and they bade him their own farewell and went their way. As it turned out, both of them together transferred to the Cistercian Order, to devote themselves to monastic soldiering.

(II.18e) If any should wonder why, both here and elsewhere, we pass over in silence the names of persons whom we have included in our narrative, they may rest perfectly assured that the reason for this has been that, were they published now, while some are still alive, the persons might perhaps be elated over their praises or else, as the case may be, covered with shame at the blame imputed.[165]

---

[162] *Ut statum vitae tuae aliquo verborum modo exprimam, dico tibi secundum quod tua conscientia novit:* good definition of the mystic's role in Goswin.

[163] *Religiosarum conventiculis mulierum tuam corporaliter exhibes praesentiam:* echoing the language of *Arn* II.13; *Niv* 6, and exemplifying the behaviour of *Niv* 12.

[164] While this perceptive account of attitudes to women may owe more to Goswin than to Arnulf, the apt comparison with a 'stallion' surely stems from the wagoner. Compare Caesarius, *DM* 7.38; p. 53. Perhaps also the day's visit to the recluse had prepared the young cleric thus to come to grips with his sexuality.

[165] This apology is almost identical with that in *Niv* 16e.

19. Foretelling a Possessed Girl's Liberation

(II.19a; II.52) Near Villers's grange of La Neuve Cour[166] lived a woman named Alice. She had a daughter named Clemence, who was plagued, especially at night, by a malicious spirit. The spirit deprived her of all sleep and bodily rest, since she imagined it as a tomcat under her clothing, crawling up her flesh and scrambling towards her neck, scratching with its claws, biting with its mouth and all but choking her. The mother, upset about her daughter's wretched affliction, took her in hand and set out for the grange, since she had heard that Arnulf had shown up there. She had him summoned to the gate, along with Gumbert, the grange master, from whose mouth we have learned all this.[167] To both men she gave an account of her daughter's distress and then earnestly implored Arnulf to come graciously to her daughter's help with his meritorious prayers.

(II.19b) Arnulf then called Brother Gumbert aside, whispered in his ear and through him enjoined on the girl all that should be done to obtain her cure: first she should, with all purity of heart, confess her sins; then she should keep a good, simple watch over herself[168] until Candlemas, the day of our Lady's purification, when she should, at mass, receive the Eucharist from the hand of the priest, as *the hope for her salvation* (Acts 27.20; I Thess. 5.8). He also went on to assert that after taking this lifegiving sacrament she would never again experience that devil's plaguing vexation.(II.53) It was around the Lord's Epiphany that all this was done and said.[169]

(II.19c) Gumbert gave the girl an orderly account of everything he had heard from

---

[166] *Nova curia:* see the notes on *Arn* II.2b and 11a.

[167] Gumbert was still master there in 1234 (Moreau, p. 277). He obviously has excellent communication with Arnulf, and is at ease with his laughter. Also notice the courtesy between all parties: mother and daughter, local mother and local master, local daughter and local master, local master and revered saint, revered saint and local clergy, peer and peer in the Villers lay brotherhood, lay brother master and learned cantor-biographer, our Lady and the Eucharist, the Eucharist and the demon.

[168] *In omni puritate cordis [...] in bona simplicitate custodiret:* Goswin is fond of 'good simplicity': for simplicity of any kind, see *Arn* I.3b, 12f; II.1j (bis), 3a, 6g; *Ab* 2b, 3e, 4c, 8c; but for explicitly 'good' simplicity, see *Ab* Pref. e, 7f, 17a.

[169] Epiphany was on 6 January. The 'Purification of the Blessed Virgin' is traditionally called 'Candlemas' in English, and since Vatican II it has been known as the 'Presentation of the Lord'. It comes forty days after Christmas, on 2 February. Its ritual of candles, comes up in *Ab* 11e. For the lay brethren Candlemas was one of only seven communion days each year (*UC* 5.4). This is surprising, since Candlemas was not honoured with an obligatory sermon in chapter, whereas several major feasts with sermons were bypassed on the brothers' communion list: Epiphany, Ascension, Annunciation, Assumption, St John the Baptist, Saints Peter and Paul, St Benedict and the dedication of the local church (*EO* 77.3). There is little show of Marian devotion in Arnulf's Life, and even less of eucharistic fervour, but in this countdown to Candlemas we glimpse quite a store of both.

Arnulf, and she was very glad to hear it. Carrying out all she had been commanded to do, Clemence awaited the promise *in gladness and exultation* of heart (Ps. 44.16). When the day of Candlemas dawned, she went to church to attend the solemn mass. The Gospel was read and the candles offered as usual; the priest went through the canon; the *Agnus Dei* was said and the *pax* shared. Then at last, from the priest's hand she received the body of the Lord and was *strengthened in that Lord* (Eph. 6.10) *to the measure of her faith* (Matt. 9.29; Rom. 12.6). From that day on she was perfectly freed from being the plaything of the devil. Her mother returned to Brother Gumbert and, *ever so gladsome, ever so laudatory*, she said to him (Isa. 35.2): 'Dear brother master, please thank Almighty God; please thank his faithful servant, who, by his merits and prayers, has obtained from heaven my daughter's integral cure.'

20. Six Prophetic Predictions Verified

(II.20a; II.54) A knight with abundant revenues and riches was thinking of founding a monastery for women, who would *be formed* to the Cistercian regime (I Tim. 1.16).[170] He often went over in his mind the question of where and how to carry out this idea, but other persons, with other viewpoints, had been progressively dissuading him, until, lo and behold, a doubt now surfaced in mind, an impediment to his heart's plan. He now doubted whether he would be able to carry into effect the good deed conceived in his heart.[171] While the matter was still in suspense like this, he, without a word to anyone, came to Villers to ask Abbot William's advice,[172] and after speaking with him on it, he came over to the grange to speak with Arnulf and consult him as well.

(II.20b) Arnulf received him warmly and, though neither had ever seen the other before, the brother immediately turned to him and said: 'You are Sir Giles Berthold[173] and you have come to discuss the building of a new monastery. Why

---

[170] *Feminarum quae secundum Ordinem Cisterciensem informarentur:* the phrase *Ordinem Cisterciensem* is here close to its primitive sense of 'regime, style of observance', though by metonymy it also means 'the affiliation of monasteries' dependent on Cîteaux. For *informarentur* see n. 185 on *Arn* II.20j, below. I render it in modern jargon with term 'formed', since, like that word, it seems to indicate the training to be given to the recruits.

[171] *Quod dum saepius mente tractare [...] coepit repente ex obliqua dissuasione quorumdam propositum cordis ejus impedire quasi quaedam dubietas ne [...]:* I have had recourse to more modern diction than usual in order to capture the force of the *repente* (all of a sudden) in a context of a slowly changing resolve.

[172] On William see the notes on *Arn* I.6c; II.3d; 20e. See also Cawley, 'Four Abbots', pp. 319–26.

[173] *D(ominus) Aegidius Bertoldus:* founder of Roosendaal, the convent of Ida the Eager of Leuven. In *Lov* II.23 (number 39) he is described as *illustris vir descendens de nobili prosapia Mechlinensium dominorum*, and seems to have been Mechelen's highest civic officer at the

have you treated this task as unimportant, when it is so worthy of heavenly blessing and so deserving of such outspoken praise and remembrance? *Take courage* rather *in the Lord and in the strength of his power* (Eph. 6.10), and take action on this monastery for nuns! Carry it through now to fulfilment in outward deed, just as you originally conceived of it in your inward heart and will. And let me tell you this: it is something pleasing to the blessed Virgin Mother, and it is her will that you should have the new monastery built, just as you had proposed.'[174]

(II.20c) Hearing this, and noticing how Arnulf had detected his thinking, the knight was astonished and could allege nothing to the contrary. In the end, thanks to Arnulf, he felt considerably encouraged in Christ as he headed back home. He also felt strengthened in heart by heavenly grace in face of any who, on learning of his project, might *mock him and say: 'This* knight was planning in his heart *to build* a monastery, *but lacked the will to bring it to completion'* (Luke 14.29–30). So he founded the new monastery, which is Cistercian and is named Roosendaal.[175] He had nuns gathered for it from another monastery to offer devout service to the Lord day and night.

(II.20d; II.55) Two young laymen came to Arnulf, one named Lambert and the other Godfrey. They told him they had conceived a wish to renounce the world and enter Villers, becoming members of its lay brotherhood; and for this they asked him to strengthen them with his suffrages and prayers. Arnulf replied: 'As for you, Lambert, no, you will not be attaining this desire of yours to be numbered among the lay brothers of Villers. But you, Godfrey, yes, despite the need to plead and plead, despite the fatigue of prolonged persistence, prolonged *waiting and waiting again* (Isa. 28.10, 13), you will eventually be received as a lay brother of Villers.'

(II.20e) And events proved him right. Lambert, in fact, had two brothers, who were setting out for a Burgundian monastery named Larrivour,[176] and he wished to set out with them, hoping that his arriving and being received with them would lead to his being clothed with them in the garb of the Order.[177] He was, however,

---

time. Although the Berthold family is well documented, I do not find a section on Roosendaal in the *Monasticon Belge*.

[174] The same Marian note clinches a discussion in *Ab* 12–cd.

[175] *Vallis Rosarum:* Roosendaal (Val des Roses), on the south bank of the Nethe, near Waalhem, five kilometres north of Mechelen, founded in 1227, the year before Arnulf's death.

[176] *Ripatorium:* Larrivour was really in Champagne; not in Burgundy, but both provinces were in the same general direction from Villers. Clairvaux, in Champagne, was en route to the yearly chapter at Cîteaux, which was in Burgundy. See also *Arn* II.10a.

[177] *Ut quia cum ipsis receptus erat, cum eis ibidem vestibus ordinis indueretur:* nowadays we speak of the reception of a novice as a 'clothing', and even in Goswin's time novices wore uniform garments supplied by the monastery, but only at profession did they receive the essential garb of the Order, whether choir or lay. Lambert was made a novice along with his brothers, but unlike them, he died before profession.

forestalled by death and frustrated of his hope, so that neither at Larrivour nor at Villers, did he ever make profession as a lay brother. Godfrey, in turn, never lost his trust in Arnulf's promise and prayers, along with the prayers of others. Thus he kept casting himself time and time again at the knees of Abbot William, until he eventually won assent to his petition and was received into the house of his choice. To this day he is one of the blacksmiths, lodging with the brothers of that craft in the smithy adjacent to the monastery.

(II.20f; II.56) There was a woman sick with a chronic feebleness, who had a daughter noted for devout living and conduct and for looking after her ailing mother with all possible diligence. There was also a monk, who took compassion on the girl's anxiety and fatigue and who would have liked to see an early end to the laborious solicitude long shown to the mother. So he came and asked Arnulf to name the date when the woman would die. Arnulf first made a prayer and then answered: 'Do not feel it a duty, dear brother, to involve me in such a matter, since this feebleness is a purgatorial one, something the woman badly needs, for she was, in fact, brought up on funds illicitly acquired.'[178] When making this statement, Arnulf did not yet know who the girl might be, nor who her mother. The information he thus disclosed had come to him by revelation, and on hearing it the monk was astounded. After leaving Arnulf, he began a careful inquiry into what he had heard from him and he learned that the woman had indeed been brought up from her infant years in a wanton luxury, based on riches stemming from sordid gain.

(II.20g; II.57) One day Arnulf stopped off[179] at the house of a God-fearing, faithful woman named Elizabeth, who had a daughter who was religious. It was for the daughter's sake that Arnulf stopped by. While he and the daughter *were conversing together* (IV Kings 2.11), the mother, who was quite on in years, kept questioning him[180] on whether or not she could be cured of an eye ailment currently bothering her. A whiteness had largely clouded the pupil of the eye. He replied: 'You will be cured eventually, madam, but only with difficulty. Then, knowing he was a man of virtue and of holy *conversatio*, she went further and asked how many more years she yet had to live. On this the answer he now offered was less than the full truth; but on driving past again next day, on the way back from a nearby grange, he predicted she

---

[178] *De opibus illicite acquisitis [...] educatam:* frequent theme, especially in *Niv* and *Lov*.

[179] *Contigit [...] devenire [...] diverterat [...] in crastino revectus:* terms characteristic of driving a wagon. *Devenire* is frequent in Acts, and means coming abreast of a landmark. *Divertere*, corresponds to *diversorium* (an 'inn'), and means stopping off unexpectedly, as Jesus did at Zachaeus's house (Luke 19.7). *Revectus* is from *vehere*, which in the active voice means 'to carry' (as a 'vehicle' carries), but in the passive it becomes deponent, not so much 'being carried' as 'riding', or, for a wagoner 'driving'. The compound, *re-vectus*, refers to the 'driving back again' or 'the return journey'.

[180] Goswin's grammar is ambiguous as to who is speaking to whom. But since it was the girl's religious status that put the house on Arnulf's itinerary, I take the basic conversation to have been with the daughter, the elderly mother more or less interrupting.

would live another two full years, reaching the end of this mortal life within the half-year that would then follow. And we know this is how it turned out, as her own daughter's account informs us.

(II.20h; II.58) There was a devout girl named Gertrude, who had made herself an inward *reclusorium* for the mind, within which, so to say, she had enclosed her heart in God; but she desired also an outward *reclusorium* for her body too. However, being poor, she could not afford to have one constructed. So, with a wholesome sadness, she spoke to Arnulf. She intimated the wish conceived in her mind, but also asserted how destitute she was of help for carrying it out Arnulf *soothed and consoled her* (Gregory, *Dial* II 1.2), and bade her entertain no worry on the matter. He then asserted and foretold that, in the course of time a *reclusorium* would surely be fashioned for her, and at no cost to herself. This word gladdened her and for many a day she kept on the watch for the promise to come true. In her long waiting she endured quite a weariness of mind, yet she always sedulously came back, on the one hand, to Arnulf's trustworthy word of promise or, on the other, to the help of the Lord himself.

(II.20i) When at length many, many a day had passed like this, the poor girl's desire became known to a man of great charity and loving-kindness, who now relayed her predicament to certain persons of great wealth and launched an appeal among them, requesting and obtaining from them quite a sum of money, and from this he had a *reclusorium* fashioned for her, and so brought to fulfilment the word Arnulf had spoken. In this way the girl obtained her wish, and to this day she dwells there, over in the diocese of Cambrai,[181] hidden now from the world's tumults by a twin *reclusorium* of heart and of body. There she gets her foretaste of the delights of an unspeakable paradise and rests in the congenial quiet of the arms of holy love. There she looks forward in joy and exultation to her blissful Passover day.

(II.20j; II.59) It would be wrong to bypass in silence what the holy man foretold of conditions in time to come. Back in the year of the Lord 1226, no mention was as yet being made[182] of the horrible schism that was to arise in the Church, and indeed against the Church, under Emperor Frederick. But already Arnulf was beginning to make open, unhesitant pronouncements to certain persons that, within the coming decade, numerous wars and many tribulations would be stirred up within the Church. The following year, the one immediately prior to his death, sinister rumours began to be heard from overseas[183] to the effect that Frederick was trying to rise up against the

---

[181] The diocesan boundary ran a bare ten kilometres north-west of Villers.

[182] The relations of Frederick II with the papacy deteriorated from soon after his coronation in 1220 until his first excommunication in 1227, and again from soon after his reconciliation in 1230 until his renewed excommunication in 1239; see K. Pennington, *New Catholic Encyclopedia* (2nd edn 2002), V: 926–28. Goswin's remarks should be understood to mean that Arnulf took alarm at the situation well in advance of his associates.

[183] *Coeperunt sinistri rumores de partibus transmarinis audiri:* Goswin has confused the chronology a little. Only in the month of Arnulf's death, June 1228, did Frederick sail for the

Holy Father[184] and against the Church of the Lord. What evil could be more fierce than this? And who could, without heartfelt grief, compute or register how many evils this detestable schism has since caused? Let prudent readers accordingly pay heed, and let any farsighted interpreters think over how great and how many have been the horrendous evils occurring since Arnulf's utterance of that prophetic word. And let them think again how great and how many are, perhaps, still to occur within the decade he named, especially seeing how sudden, how unimaginable, has been the tribulation already befalling the Church from her very protector and his henchmen.

(II.20k; II.60) Other things, many other things there are which some consider worth narrating about this blessed man, but which have not yet come to our acquaintance. Certain other things have indeed come to our acquaintance, but we are passing them over for brevity's sake and *out of consideration for the readers,* declining to include them in our narrative *lest the abundance become crammed and give birth to nausea* (Sulp, *VM* 1). Any for whom a few things do not suffice for the forming of their lives will probably find many more just as insufficient.[185] Hence we turn to those who have loved this blessed man with a more special familiarity than the rest have enjoyed, and we beg that they not take it ill that we thus pass over in silence certain things that could still have been written of him. *After all,* as Sulpicius Severus says of his Martin, *we believe* that to provide an example for the hearers *it suffices if the more excellent things are noted* (ibid.). Up to this point, accordingly, we have traced as best we could the virtues of the holy man Arnulf, and his revelations and the rest of his praiseworthy deeds and sayings; and so now we propose to set our hand to describing his felicitous passing-over.

21. His Illness and Death

(II.21a; II.61) When the time was approaching for Arnulf's *precious death* (Ps. 115.5), or rather for his falling asleep in Christ, he slipped into a sickness of the kind physicians call a fever. The name refers to a certain hotness which spreads

---

Holy Land. He had been excommunicated since September 1227. The overseas rumour most likely to alarm Brabant would be that of Frederick's crowning of himself king in Jerusalem (March 1229). Incidentally, in the midst of all this turmoil, just seventeen days after Arnulf's death, the pope canonized St Francis of Assisi.

[184] 'Holy Father'. Goswin uses *Dominum papam,* the standard papal title in the Middle Ages, and I use what is standard today.

[185] *Cui enim ad informationem vitae suae pauca non sufficiunt:* this is the noun form of *informarentur,* used above (*Arn* II.20a). It comes also in I Tim. 1.16: *ad informationem eorum qui credituri sunt.* Interestingly, the Greek term there is *hypotyposis,* the term later chosen by Gregory of Nyssa as title for the work he wrote when retiring as bishop to become once more a simple monk, exhorting himself to make unremitting progress in virtue.

throughout the limbs and members of the patient.[186] Having the fever, he immediately cast aside the instruments of his self-martyrdom, since the goading sting of the ailment itself pressed him too sorely to allow of applying any other torments to his body. Never in his whole life, nor yet in these days of his final illness, did he entertain any wish to appeal to his God for a gracious revelation of the day or the season of his own *passing-over* (Exod. 12.11). Such a revelation was made, however, to a certain highly-regarded recluse: she foretold, even prior to his being stricken with the illness, that he would be leaving this world around the feast of the blessed John the Baptist.

(II.21b) In the course of this illness, the dewdrops of heavenly grace streamed into his heart so copiously, and the wine of divine love inebriated his soul so vehemently, that he was outwardly quite oblivious of his illness. Meanwhile, within his mind and his whole desire, he was yearning towards the God, whom all his life long he had so ardently loved and, although in the fervour of this divine love he protested that he felt no pain at all, be it in the heart, in the head or in the members, nevertheless, as his state of health grew daily more pressing and urgent, his bodily vigour dwindled and waned. Prolonged lack of food and the sheer weight of the illness weakened him greatly, and yet to the brothers assigned to his assistance,[187] and to such monks as were his familiar friends and now came on occasion to visit him, he spoke with such alacrity as if he had been far sounder of body. And this he continued to do even to the day of his parting. Arnulf sometimes had the Lord's lifegiving body brought to him and, receiving it from the priest's hand, his soul would experience a period of comfort from the saving power of the sacrament.

(II.21c; II.62) One day a monk came to the infirmary to visit Arnulf, and told how a recluse on familiar terms with him, whose name he gave, was grief-stricken and

---

[186] *Quidam calor per omnes artus diffundatur aegrotantis:* a generic diagnosis, suggesting that Arnulf's final ailment, if ever diagnosed, had been forgotten by the time of writing. On the other hand, several concrete symptoms are mentioned in what follows: incapacity for self-flagellation, painlessness and good cheer; weakness and lack of appetite; high rate of pulse; need of help to stand on his feet; a duration of several weeks. These symptoms come in the context of Arnulf's lifelong habits of inadequate intake of moisture, unhygienic treatment of minor wounds and illogical management of his body's warmth. Incidentally, Goswin's definition of 'fever' differs from Isidore's (Isidore, *Etym* IV.6.2).

[187] *Fratribus sibi ad solatium deputatis; monachis familiaribus suis:* key terms of Cistercian jargon. *Solatium* is a neuter noun, which in classical Latin means simply 'solace'. This is also its meaning in *RB* 1.4, which St Benedict borrows from the *Regula magistri*. But in passages peculiar to *RB* it takes on the technical meaning of a monk assigned to an officer as his regular helper (*RB* 31.17; 35.3–4; 53.18; 66.5). This latter sense carries over to the Cistercian Usages (*EO* 15.3; 17.4; 47.5; etc.), though oddly it is never specifically used for brethren thus doing chores for the infirmarian. Goswin's two phrases are, therefore, in contrast: brothers rendering practical aid, as against personal friends paying purely casual and spiritual visits. Interestingly, these are identified as 'monks', whereas the former would include 'lay brethren'.

anxiously afraid that this illness would bring him to *enter upon the way of all flesh* (III Kings 2.2).[188] Arnulf answered almost indignantly: 'God forbid such grief! God forbid! What wish have I to linger here? No, my desire is to go to my God!' And why should he not desire to go to his God, he who had served that God so fervently, had so kept that God's commandments, had so despised himself and all things earthly for love of that God, had so persistently sighed over any postponement of paradise and its eternal delights? In fact, the more he became acquainted with things eternal, the more bitterly did he grieve over this wretched exile of his!

(II.21d; II.63) Another day, a different monk, one trained in the skills of the medical art, was sitting beside him and *they were conversing* together (IV Kings 2.11), when Arnulf raised the question, often posed by the sick: was it possible, or was it not, for him to recover from the illness that had him in its grip? If the monk were not to intimate the nature of the illness as requested, he could later on be found guilty of hushing up the truth. And so he made a prediction of what he could best foresee from the pulse of the veins and the symptoms of the disease, declaring that Arnulf would not escape but would die. At this reply Arnulf, in heartfelt joy, promptly threw his arms around his neck and so hugged the poor monk as to cover him with embarrassment in front of the other sick brethren sitting round about, none of whom had any idea of what that embrace might mean. But Arnulf just smiled and said: 'Amen I say to you,[189] beloved friend, that never in all my life has my heart opened out so wide to you in loving affection as it has today. With this word, you have *gladdened my soul* (Ps. 93.19), a word not of desolation but very much *a word of consolation!'* (Zech. 1.13)

(II.21e; II.64) Day by day Arnulf's passing-over drew nearer, until one day, when he had risen from bed and was standing on his feet, with a brother named Radulfus at his side to support him by the arms, Arnulf was suddenly bereft of all bodily strength. Behold him there, so magnificent a man at that hour: there, in the hands of the brother, knees bent to the ground, *head bowed down,* and then, in three *gentle* puffs, each spaced with a delay, *sending forth* the last of his *spirit* (John 19.30; Gen. 2.7).[190] Such was his felicitous migration from the body.

(II.21f) The sackcloth sheet was now spread on the ground and the venerable body laid upon it. The death gong[191] was promptly sounded for him, and the monks

---

[188] One of the many popular euphemisms for death.

[189] We can usually presume that biblical echoes in quotations from Arnulf stem from Goswin or from his clerical witnesses, but recent local experience shows some of our least-educated brothers spontaneously making monastic jargon their own, even though their speech as a whole retains a rustic grammar. Such Latinisms as *Deo gratias,* or *mea culpa* are commonplace on their lips, to say nothing of such anglicized French terms as 'secular', 'cellarer', 'tierce' (for terce), etc.

[190] *Inclinato capite tribus trinarum morarum intervallis leniter emisso spiraculo feliciter migravit de corpore.*

[191] A wooden gong for time signals at close range. See *Arn* 11c n. 64 and also Cawley,

hurriedly assembled to see him off on this parting journey, commending him in solemn suffrage to God and to his saints. His body, duly washed, was arranged on the bier and carried to church, where the monks chanted psalmody around it, even as night crept in. In the course of the brethren's usual night watch around the deceased, certain goodly thieves seized some hair from his head and some teeth from his mouth, exactly seven of them, all to be kept for themselves as tokens of his saintliness. When the morrow dawned, the octave day of holy John the Baptist,[192] the customary mass was celebrated for him, and his holy body was reverently handed over to burial. And how loftily rang the monks' voices in chanting the antiphon, *Clementissime Deus,* with many a bystander moved to compunction and tears!

(II.21g; II.65) After his glorious departure, the blessed man came in apparition to a certain handmaid of Christ. He took the form of a child dressed in a robe, partly snow white, partly purple. She asked who he might be and he answered: 'I am Brother Arnulf, a servant of Christ.' She went on: 'Why is it in the form of a child that you are appearing to me, and in a robe of two colours?' He said: 'My showing a childlike face means that I wish you to understand that during my *conversatio* among mortals I was as humble as a child. The white colour of my robe lets you recognize that I led a clean life and loved cleanness; and the purple colour shows you my prolonged afflicting of the body and the shedding of blood that went with it.' Having said this much he disappeared from her sight. It was she herself who manifested *this vision which she had seen* (Antiphon: Transfiguration) to a certain monk of Villers.

(II.21h; II.66) Arnulf also appeared to one John, who, though unlettered, has been schooled inwardly by the pedagogy of the Paraclete Spirit and is very much a man of vision,[193] and even to this day, many revelations are made to him by the Lord. To John, therefore, Arnulf intimated how copious and wondrous a glorification his soul had received as its heavenly reward from the Lord. Then he added: 'Off you go to James the priest, that beloved and familiar friend of mine in Christ, and give him this message from me: tell him how, just as I promised, I shall never cease daily to implore the Lord of majesty for his welfare so as to obtain for him of the mercy that brings salvation.' So John went and told the priest how greatly and wondrously the blessed man's soul had been glorified, and also told him the other things revealed to him.

(II.21i) A short account is in order about what happened thanks to a quill-covered pelt Arnulf had worn in his life.

(II.67) One day Mother Lucy, Prioress of Épinlieu,[194] had arrived in the company

---

Ancient Usages, especially *EO* 94.2, etc.

[192] 1 July 1228.

[193] *Viro mire speculativo.* See *Arn* II.9a, n. 117, above.

[194] *Spineti locus:* a pun between the name of the monastery 'place thick with spiny thorn-bushes' and that of the relic, *particulam spinosae pellis ericii* (particle of a pelt of a spiny

of two other nuns at the gatehouse of Villers. Finishing the business they had come for, they moved along to the nearby village, also named Villers, and spent the night there in a house with two devout women. While they were there, it came to pass that a domestic of the house, a girl named Mary, began to writhe with abdominal pains. These were so severe that she was forced to howl like a woman in labour. Seeing this, the nuns had compassion and said to one another: 'Look, we have with us that particle of the spiny hedgehog pelt worn by the man of the Lord, Arnulf: let us apply that to the sore spot and see if the girl's bitter pangs will cease!' They applied it and, behold, even as they looked on in wonder, forthwith and against all likelihood, the girl's excruciating pains began shrinking to nothing, thanks to the grace of the Lord. But what need to wait for the Lord to do further miracles through this servant of his, inasmuch as his whole life in this world was one long miracle and his *death*, we believe, was correspondingly *precious in the Lord's sight?* (Ps. 115.15)

(II.21j; I.68) Thus it was in the twelve hundred and twenty-eighth year of the incarnation of the Word that the man of the Lord, Arnulf, migrated from this life, or rather, from this death and into life, from this exile to the fatherland. Well does he deserve title of modern martyr for the extraordinary martyrdom of manifold penances inflicted upon his body. He is deserving of other titles too, for the virtues and merits that adorn him. He migrated, to wit, on the last day of June, the commemoration of the apostle Paul, the day being Friday and the hour that of sext,[195] the very hour at which the Lord of majesty hung upon the cross. He had

---

hedgehog). Such a gift would normally come only from the abbot, who alone would be the appropriate host for a visiting prioress, so we have one more glimpse of Abbot William's esteem for Arnulf, an esteem with room for the fun of a pun. Épinlieu was near Mons, some forty kilometres west-south-west of Villers. It is treated by Ursmer Berlière in *Monasticon Belge*, I, pp. 364–71. He makes it clear that this Lucy was prioress in the sense of a second superior (p. 365, n. 3). The abbess at the time was one Raimburge, who had been prioress in 1218 and who figures as abbess in documents dating from 1220 to 1234.

[195] Cawley, *Ancient Usages* (*EO* 95) regulated the hour of burial in terms of the hour of death. Whichever way that should have applied, Arnulf's body was buried only on the morrow; see II.21f and II.21i, above.

spent twenty-six years and some six months in the Cistercian Order. Now he has migrated to where there is that true *peace which surpasses all understanding* (Phil. 4.7), a peace loftier than peace, an unfailing exultation, to which the Lord led his servant in an exercise of his mercy, and to which may he also some day lead us too, *forestalling us with the blessings of his sweetness* (Ps. 20.4), he, Jesus Christ our Lord, *who came into this world that we might have life and have it more abundantly* (John 10.10), to whom, with the Father and the Holy Spirit, be glory, honour and kingship for all ages upon ages. Amen .

Appendix I

Verses about Arnulf's *Conversatio* and his Passing

Translator's Note

The Bollandists offer two poems at the end of Arnulf's Life. This first one,[196] which is anonymous, presents itself as addressed to monks who had known Arnulf in the flesh. It shows awareness of Book I of the Life, and of Goswin's theme of the inimitability of Arnulf's austerities, but it shows virtually no awareness of Book II, or even of Book I's stress on the primacy of Arnulf's charity. There are a few superficial similarities to Ida's Epitaph, which I consider indeed the work of Goswin, but I find it hard to attribute this far less personal piece to him. Also, I find the biblical allusions far too few and too trite for Goswin. Technically, however, both pieces have the same erratic syllable count, from thirteen to seventeen syllables per line. Both also have erratic patterns of rhyming, from four identical end-rhymes in a row, to unpredictable sequences of internal rhyme. Nevertheless, whoever the author might be, there can be little doubt that he belonged at Villers, and as such he deserves to have his piece translated here.

> *Nobilis egrediens hospes de corpore mortis,*
> *In patriam rediit, ad primae gaudia sortis;*
> *Qui fervens animo, dum pertulit aspera fortis,*
> *Fraternae meruit labarum portare cohortis.*
> 5 *Ejus vita fuit meritorum lampade clara;[197]*
> *Quae sibi mellita, plerisque videtur amara:*
> *Qui vir devotus, Domino fuit hostia cara,*
> *Dum Christo totus crucis est oblatus in ara.*

---

[196] This first poem is found in AASS (Antwerp 1709, June V, p. 631cd).

[197] Exactly the same ending as the third line of Ida's epitaph.

Laus tibi, summe Deus, quia martyr nester agones
10 *pertulit insolitos, ut ei nova praemia dones.*
Instrumenta crucis, quam pertulit ille, stupenda
Mentibus humanis, nulli reor est ferenda.
Et merito: quoniam terret nova passio cunctos,
quos oleo, rex Christe, tuo non invenit unctos.[198]
15 *Multi divino sunt uncti chrismate, verum*
Quemlibet ad tanta video miracula serum.
Sunt et agonistae fortes, sed fortior iste
Perstitit in Christo: quia gratia major in isto
Martyris huic ergo debetur jure corona,
20 *Cujus ad eudochiam*[199] *cum mente fuit caro prona.*
Eja sublatam   nobis plangamus, amatam
Mundo, personam;   non quod sine fine coronam
Sumat sublimis   a Christo, sed quod in imis
Post se nos miseros   liquit fortissimus heros
25 *Vosque qui memorem sancto debetis amorem,*
Vobis praepropere subductum   plangite justum;
Plangite devotum,   vobis per singula notum;
Plangite post cursum   cursorem, plangite rursum,
Plangite cum lacryma, Quod mortis ferrea lima
30 *Hunc elimavit,   Limatum terra voravit*
Sed qui carne ruit, hanc mortis falce secante,
Vivit nunc anima melius, quam vixerat ante.

The noble guest has stepped forth from the body of this death,[200]
and has returned to the fatherland, to the joys of its primeval lot.
Fervent he was in mind, and brave, in carrying his rugged load,
Privileged to bear the standard of the brotherly cohort.[201]
5 His life, lit up bright with the lamp of his merits,
was to him sweet as honey, but to most, ever so bitter.
A devout man he was, a victim dear to the Lord,
offered whole and entire to Christ on the altar of the cross.
Praise to you, O God supreme, because our martyr has borne
10 unwonted struggles, to have you grant him prizes all new.

---

[198] Possible allusion to I John 2.20, 27. But I do not find that theme in Goswin's Lives, and since the context is athletic, the poet could simply be using the term as an athletic metaphor.

[199] I find no *eudochia* in any Latin or Greek dictionary, but *eudokia* is a frequent New Testament term for 'good will, good pleasure', etc., along with its verbal from.

[200] Rom. 7.24.

[201] Possible echo of the *fraterna acies* (brotherly battle-line) of *RB* 1.5.

Stupendous beyond human reckoning, beyond human endurance,
I would say, were the instruments of the cross that he bore.
And rightly say I, since sufferings so unheard of would terrify all
but those, king Christ, whom your unction touches and smears.
15 And though there be many anointed with that divine chrism,
I see every one of them loath to attempt such wonders.
Wrestlers there are, valiant enough, but he is more valiant still,
ever standing his ground in Christ, with a greater grace within.
Whence by right he deserves a martyr's crown,
20 For his flesh was as eager as his mind for martyrdom's grace.
Alas, let us mourn his beloved person, withdrawn from us,
not mourning that aloft he should receive an everlasting crown
from Christ, but that here below
so valiant a hero is abandoning us to our misery.
25 And you, my brethren, owe this saint a loving remembrance.
Hasten to be first to mourn for the withdrawal of this just one.
Mourn for the devout one, so well known to you throughout.
Mourn again for the athlete who has run his course.
Mourn with tears that death's file of steel has filed him away,
30 and that earth has devoured what little the file had left.
His flesh may collapse before the reaping sickle of death,
but in soul he lives on with a goodlier life than before.

Appendix II

Laudatory Epitaph for the Blessed Arnulf by Franciscus Moschus

Translator's Note

The second poem, entitled *Epitaphium Encomiasticon Beati Arnulphi*, was authored by Franciscus Moschus and appended to his edition of the Lives of both Arnulf of Villers and Simon of Aulne, published at Arras in 1600.[202] The poem fictitiously presents itself as engraved on a marble tombstone, but it keeps to a regular syllable count of twelve (with allowance for elisions). What I like about this poem is that it first presents the Arnulf of Book II, and then organically incorporates the ascetic of Book I. Though the style is classic, rather than rhyming, it is perfectly free from all affectation, and is as simple as Goswin's prose. The Bollandists print the thirty-six lines without any gaps, and there is no regularity in the number of lines per stanza. The sentences, however, are clear cut. I follow the translation policy outlined in the Introduction to the Lives, pp. 22–24, above.

---

[202] This second poem is found in AASS (Antwerp, 1709, June, V, p. 631ef). Moschus is not listed in the *Dictionnaire des auteurs cisterciens*, nor in any other source available to me. The Berkeley on-line catalogue informs me that, in 1597 at Douai, he published the main historical work of James of Vitry. It is from Roisin that I first learned of his edition of Arnulf and Simon (Roisin, *L'Hagiographie cistercienne*, p. 32, n. 6).

Arnulphus hoc sub expolito marmore
Somnum capit, securus expectans diem,
Qua buccinae clangore suscitabitur,
Sumpturus aeternae coronam gloriae.
5 Asceta clarus exstitit virtutibus
Christi gerens inusta carni stigmata;
Mores probi, juges preces, vox lenior;
Fulsit fides plane orthodoxa, certa spes,
Deique fervens caritas et proximi
10 Cunctis serenus, comis, ac affabilis;
Sibi severus, corpori indulgens nihil.
Non ulla commotum dies, nec asperis
Verbis locutum vidit aut minacibus:
Nam Christus illi mellea dulcedine
15 Et unctione spiritum repleverat.
Virgis sibi carne frequens dirissimis
Domabat, ad cruoris usque copiam
Quin lectulum e rusco horrido constraverat
Somnum fugans, corpus regens, Deo canens.
20 Ecquid tuo (collega dixit quispiam)
Amice, mortem infers misello corpori?
Peccatum, ait, non corpus exstinguo flagris.
Dum sic voluptates severus abdicat,
Victa est caro cum daemone atque seculo.
25 Gaudet trophaeo victor athletes suo.
Ditat Deus summo clientem munere
Prophetico mentem beatque spiritu,
Arcana donans consequi coelestia.
Ac nunc beatae et aeviternae munere
30 Vitae frui datum²⁰³ probato militi;
Ubi aureae pacis potitur fructibus,
Et luce pura, quae tenebras nesciat.
Arnulfe, nos ab arce languidos juva,
Qui criminum mole obruti demergimur;
35 Ut a malorum vindicati nexibus,
Uno Deo et trino fruamur perpetim.

---

²⁰³ This stanza has no main verb, but the meaning is clear enough. I suspect *datum* (given) is a misprint for *datur* (is given).

It is Arnulf, here beneath this polished marble slab,
who takes his sleep and in security awaits the day
when the trumpet blare will waken him
to accept his crown of eternal glory.
5   An ascetic he was, brilliantly virtuous,
sporting the stigmata of Christ scorch-branded into his flesh,
shining with proven behaviour, ceaseless prayers, mild speech,
resplendent with straightforward orthodox faith and sure hope,
boiling over with charity for God and neighbour.
10   To all he was serene, courteous, approachable;
but to himself severe, indulging the body not at all.
Never a day spied him in commotion,
nor coming out with harsh or threatening words,
for Christ had filled his spirit full
15   of honeyed sweetness and of unction.
Rods of the toughest he regularly used on his flesh,
taming it till the blood flowed free.
Yes, and the bed he rigged for himself was of horrid broom:
sleep he fled, flesh he mastered, God he ever sang.
20   'And why', asks some colleague of his,
'why, dear friend, inflict such death on your poor old body?'
'It's sin', he replies, 'not the body, that my scourges quench!'
Wanton pleasures his severity disowns.
Victorious over the flesh, the demon, the world,
25   his is the athlete's joy in the trophy finally won.
God now enriches his client with the supreme gift,
gladdens his mind with the spirit of prophecy,
grants him to reach into the hidden secrets of heaven.
And now it is given to the well-proven soldier
30   to enjoy the gift of blessed and everlasting life,
where he makes his own the fruits of a golden peace
and of a pure light that knows no fall of night.
Arnulf, look down from your citadel and help our languid selves,
for we are drowning, dragged under by the weight of our crimes.
35   Win us freedom from our involvement in all these evils,
so that we may forever enjoy the God who is one and three.

Top: Gobert of Aspremont (see *Ab* Appendix III, p. 251), and Godfrey the Sacristan. The latter died shortly before Abundus entered Villers, but his Life and Abundus's have similarities (AASS, Antwerp, 1765), October, I, pp. 531–37.

Centre: Abundus of Huy, monk of Villers.

Bottom: Rainer and Godfrey Pachomius, mentioned in the letter of their blood brother, Thomas the Cantor, in *Ab* Appendix IV, p. 253.

For illustration credit, see p. 122, above.

The Life of Abundus

Monk of Villers

Prologue

Here begins the Prologue to the Life of Brother Abundus, monk of Villers.

(Prol. a) To all those *soldiering* for the Lord *under a rule and an abbot* after the Cistercian manner (*RB* 1.2),[1] my wish is that in the present life they be steeped in abundant dewfalls of heavenly grace, and that in the life to come, they be made blissful in the fullness of everlasting salvation, for I am a brother of theirs, here at Villers in Brabant, a monk indeed in garb, though all too lukewarm in *conversatio*.

(Prol. b) *Idleness is inimical to the soul* (*RB* 48.1). *Plough land once neglected, and not harrowed again and again, produces only fern-weed fit for the fire.*[2] Hence, with the Lord's grace and in the measure possible, I have sought to cast out from the field of my heart anything idle or weed-like,[3] cultivating it instead with the ploughshare of silence, and sowing it with the best of meditations for seed. To achieve this the more easily and effectively, my idea has been to get my lord abbot's permission and briefly set down in writing the life of Brother Abundus, a monk of ours.

(Prol. c) So I approached Abundus and asked him to share with me such good things as the Lord had done for him and was still doing. He initially refused consent. But, as he and I were on quite familiar terms in Christ Jesus, there was nothing my coaxing could not twist from him, however reluctant he might be. Hence he eventually took up the tale. beginning from his childhood and disclosing to me many things great and wonderful. things Mother Grace[4] had enriched him with, things I shall bring to light in the pages that follow.

---

[1] *Omnibus in Ordine Cisterciensi [...] militantibus:* on Goswin's use of 'Cistercian Order', see *Arn* II 20a, n. 170.

[2] Horace. *Satirae* 1.3.37.

[3] *Otiosas et noxias a me repellere:* feminine plural adjectives, which, as printed, lack a noun to qualify.

[4] *Quibus eum gratia mater ditaverat:* on Mother Grace, see *Niv* 4a, n. 24.

(Prol. d) I ventured the remark: 'Dear brother, be wary of these *visions you have been seeing*.[5] They could be mere fantasies, trumped up for your misguidance by him who *transfigures himself into an angel of light'* (II Cor. 11.14). 'Ah no', said he, 'it is not that way, too benign is he who teaches me. He unmasks the craftiness of the malignant one and *teaches man knowledge* (Ps. 93.10). Inwardly he teaches me what I should choose and what I should shun.' And so, let those willing to accept what I write of him accept it in the Lord's name and in good faith. As for those unwilling, let them rest assured that no one will be forced to accept my contribution.[6]

(Prol. e) All this being so, for the praise, then, and the glory of the blessed Trinity, and for the honour of the queen of virgins, herself both virgin and mother, I have, dearest brethren, deemed it worthwhile to write down the venerable life of the man of God, so that in you, and in all who in future become aware of it, his glowing, splendid, grace-filled *conversatio* may bring to birth a praiseworthy *respectability of behaviour* (*RB* 73.1), a salutary urge to emulate his *beautiful caring* (Ecclus. 24.24), his holy love,[7] his praiseworthy simplicity!

Here ends the Prologue.

1. Abundus's Background; Etymology of his Name

(1a) The man of God Abundus, *whose memory is in benediction,* (Ecclus. 45.1) came to birth in the year of the Lord's incarnation 1189, or thereabouts, in a town on the Meuse named Huy, of a father likewise named Abundus and a mother named Mary. The father was quite shrewd in temporal affairs but less given to religion; though the mother was a woman *of promise* (Gregory, *Dial* II 4.14), eager to train her sons and daughters more for God than for the secular world.

(1b) Two sons of hers, James and John, like the disciples of the same names, went on to submit themselves to the schooling of Christ and the discipleship of Saint

---

[5] An echo of the eleventh responsory, and of the communion antiphon, for the Feast of the Transfiguration. See Matt. 17.9.

[6] *Qui [...] recipere voluerit [...]; qui vero noluerit [...] , cogetur nemo munus habere meum:* the person of the verbs is indefinite singular, echoing Goswin's awareness of factions that had already belittled Arnulf and Ida. Their resentment regards, not Goswin's style, nor even precisely his heroes, but rather his own *munus,* which I translate as 'contribution'. In the Bible, *munus* means 'gift', but usually with traces of the classical meaning: 'office, function, service'. See Deut. 2.29, Ecclus. 50.21, Dan. 16–17. Goswin senses that the complainers have 'had enough' of his stories.

[7] *Pulchrae dilectionis sanctique amoris:* the phrase *sanctus amor* comes also in other Goswinian contexts of contemplative embrace and sleep: *Ab* 7b, 12c; *Arn* II.8a, 20e; *Niv* 4b, 18e, 26f.

Benedict, by taking the monastic habit at Val-Saint-Lambert.[8] This they did against their father's will. Similarly, two daughters of hers became nuns: one named Gela entering at Val-Notre-Dame and a second, named Mary, entering at La Ramée.[9] She had a third daughter, Walburgis by name,[10] prior in birth to Abundus. This daughter's mind was inwardly so enlightened by the Holy Spirit that she eventually won her father's reluctant consent and stayed on in the parental home, living a life of religious austerity as a virgin. *Made perfect in a short time,* Walburgis *filled out a lengthy span* (Wisd. 4.13), and from this Egyptian exile she was welcomed back by Christ, welcomed by him in his soothing gentleness, and installed aloft amid undying glory.

(1c) After Walburgis's birth came Abundus, *the boy-servant of the Lord* (Matt. 12.18). And deservedly was he christened 'Abundus', for in him the Lord foresaw a *vessel of election* (Acts 9.15), one to whom he would *give an abundant share of the fatness* of heavenly grace (Gen. 27.28). In this present life Abundus would *ruminate remembrance of the abundance* of the Lord's *agreeable savour* (Ps. 144.7), *meditating upon his law* day and night (Ps. 1.2). As for the future, what he would then enjoy would be the good things perennial in unspeakable abundance!

2. His Schooling

(2a) When Abundus had reached the end of his infant years, he *was entrusted by his father* to be instructed in letters (Antiphon: St Benedict; compare Gregory, *Dial* II Prol. 1) at the main church of the town, the one that stands under the cliff. The aim was simply for him to learn how to tabulate his father's debts and transactions, lest they slip from memory.

(2b) From these first years of boyhood, as he grew into a youth, his conduct likewise grew to be ever more commendable, especially his meekness, his sensitivity to shame and his *dovelike simplicity* (Matt. 10.16). Gracious to behold and lovable to all, he was endowed with an inborn mildness of disposition and a spontaneous poise in his behaviour,[11] which made his countenance seem almost angelic.

---

[8] *Magisterio Christi ac disciplinae beati patris Benedicti se subjicientes.* For *magisterio,* see *Arn* I.3b; II.21h. The monastery of Val-Saint-Lambert was founded in 1188, just before Abundus's birth. Then in 1212, when he was about twenty-three, it moved to a new site, about nineteen kilometres east of Huy and eight kilometres south west of Liège.

[9] Val-Notre-Dame *(Vallis beatae Mariae),* situated about five kilometres due north of Huy, was founded around 1202, when Abundus was about thirteen. On Mary's call to La Ramée, see *Ab* 12.

[10] In *Ab* 4a, she is named Wiburgis.

[11] Virtues often mentioned in this Life: *mansuetudo* comes two times; *verecundia,* four; *simplicitas,* seven; *lenitas,* three; *gravitas,* three. The most frequent of these, *simplicitas,* is in Abundus what *compassio* is in Ida.

(2c) When a few years had passed and Abundus had become quite adept at keeping his father's books,[12] the father was minded to withdraw him from literary studies. This was not to the mother's liking, for she loved him tenderly and was nurturing in her mind a future for him full of promise and progress. So she entrusted him to another schoolman, out at the canons' church of Newminster, beyond the town walls, there to be trained day by day, along with the other pupils. The father, on becoming aware of this, was greatly angered to see his will unfulfilled; but the mother, making light of her husband's mood, even tailored the son a linen surplice, this being the garment that pupils wear, especially at churches of canons. On feast-days and at certain hours, they would not think of entering choir without donning this garment over their other clothing. Our little scholar[13] used to carry this garment with him to church, tucked secretly under his clothes, and bring it home with equal secrecy, lest the father learn of it and, not sharing the good disposition it symbolized, be moved to one of his angry moods.[14]

3. Early Devotional Life

(3a) Ever regular in frequenting the classroom, *once* Abundus *had turned twelve years old* (Luke 2.42) he was prompted by an inward whisper of the Holy Spirit to frequent the church as well. Thus, on those feast-days which the other pupils generally spent in *leisurely chatter* or games (*RB* 43.8, 48.18), Abundus began spending instead in the main church,[15] doing the rounds of the altars, kneeling before the crucifix, gazing with fondly loving eyes on the nails driven through the hands

---

[12] The Latin here is: *rerum paternarum intitulator jam satis promptulus.* On the next line *studio [...] litteram* is an obvious misprint for *studio [...] litterarum.*

[13] *Scholaris noster:* Goswin uses such epithets with *noster* (our) as follows: *Arnulfus noster* (our Arnulf, *Arn* I.5a); *athleta* (athlete, *Arn* I.11a); *bellatrix,* (warrior lady, *Niv* 13d); *contemplator* (*Arn* II.6e, 15d; *Ab* 6d, 11e, 13d); *Israel* (*Arn* II.14c); *martyr* (*Arn* Pref. a; I.5a. 6d, 12e); *miles* (knight, *Arn* II.4e); *monachus* (monk, *Ab* Prol. b); *nauta* (mariner, *Arn* II.1a); *scholasticus, scholaris* (*Arn* II.1d; *Ab* 2c); *solatrix* (consoler lady, *Niv* verses, line 21); *Salomon* (*Arn* II.16d). Only twice is Ida called 'ours'; compare Arnulf (twelve times) and Abundus (five times). The most frequent such epithet is *contemplator noster,* shared by *Ab* (three times) and *Arn* (two times, both in *Arn* II). Only in *Arn* I do such ascetic-military epithets as *martyr noster* abound.

[14] *Patris animum potius ad iracundiam quam ad exemplum boni provocaret.*

[15] *Majoris ecclesiae frequentare limina:* the church of his first school, which I presume was the predecessor of the present collegiate church, nestled under the ancient cliff-top fort. These feast-day devotions belong, therefore, between his twelfth birthday and his entry into the canons' school, where his feast-days would be pre-empted by choir duties. But there were also ferial devotions, mentioned below, and these could fit either period. In 1906 an old crypt was discovered in the collegiate church, with a crucifix dating from Abundus's time.

and feet and on the scar of the wound in the side. And there in devout soliloquy he drew upon himself the loving-kind grace of his Redeemer. He also became a devoted lover of his Lord's blessed mother, venerating her for her loving-kindness, saluting her frequently for her worthiness of all praise. The more devotedly he thus applied himself to familiar service of the mother, the more deservedly would he receive the heaped up[16] grace of the son.

(3b) On ferial weekdays his resorting to church on his way home from school came at the approach of night. In winter, this meant after sunset, and he would not be leaving church until the bell rang for compline, well into the night. But in summer the bell for compline would ring while there was still enough daylight, and he would linger on in church long after the end of that hour. If anyone chanced by and noticed him there, prostrate on the ground or kneeling, he would be drenched with great embarrassment. And for this reason he often hid himself behind the pillars, if I may adapt the French term for those main supports of the building. Given the tenderness of his little frame, he was not able, nor would he have been allowed, to impose on it any major afflictions, but at times he would draw up the hem of his robe and lie with his bare side applied to the chilly stones.

(3c) The Lord noticed his little servant's frequent recourse to *the house of prayer* (Matt. 21.13), and how pure was his *heart's intent* (*RB* 52.4), how *insistent* his importunate *prayers* (*RB* Prol. 4), how wide open, so to say, were the jaws of his heart, gaping upward and panting for the Lord to pour into them mouthfuls of divine grace, fragrantly honeyed and so intimately drenching[17] as at times to force an overflow of sweet tears from his eyes. Had not the Lord himself promised his disciples in the Gospel: *Ask and it will be given to you; seek and you will find; knock and it will be opened unto you?* (Matt. 7.7) What wonder, then, that he thus heard the devout lad as he asked, sought and knocked! Indeed, just as dripping water, constantly striking a stone slab, digs in and pierces it through, so also the divine grace frequently petitioned from the Lord by this lad became like a trickle, nay a stream, from a living spring, penetrating his eager heart and sweetening all his affections, until his *thoughts about the Lord were of the goodliest.* For it was *in simplicity of heart* that he had *sought Him* (Wisd. 1.1), sought until he could *taste and see* how truly *agreeable was the Lord* (Ps. 33.9).

---

[16] *Cumulatiorem gratiam:* Goswin is fond of the word *cumulus* (heap) and its derivatives: six times in *Niv*, five in *Arn* and three in Ab. Compare *Niv* 22b, n. 104.

[17] *Mellitas gratiae suae bucellas coepit infundere, tanta intimae suavitatis flagrantia illum imbuens [...] cogeretur effundere:* one of Goswin's many images of grace as a heavenly fluid. I read *flagrantia* as *fragantia.* Compare J. F Niermeyer, *Mediae Latinitatis lexicon minus* (Leiden: Brill, 1997), p. 437, where the two spellings are interchangeable.

4. His Vocation: Walburgis, Yvette, Conrad

(4a) Ever a religious and affectionate lad,[18] Abundus was being invigorated by that grace which forestalls and follows up. He was also being coaxed on to ever better things by the example and exhortation of his virgin sister Wiburgis, whose fervent love for Christ we have already mentioned (*Ab* 1b). And so he pondered attentively *how passing the world is, and how passing its concupiscence* (I John 2.17), as also how burdensome for any Israelites is a *conversatio* set among Egyptians.[19]

(4b) Thus, with an eye to his future, Abundus resolved to renounce this world and to gird himself for spiritual soldiering in the monastery of Villers. But he first approached a certain Yvette,[20] a recluse of outstanding religious practice, for a colloquy with her *on the good things of the Lord and the salvation of his soul* (*GC* 1233.6). This virtuous woman perceived in him a wish to pass over to the sure hiding place which is the Cistercian Order,[21] and so she told him: 'My son, if you wish to be a monk, I propose to you two monasteries: the first Trois Fontaines and the other Orval.[22] Choose either of the two and I promise you *in charity unfeigned* (II Cor. 6.6) to arrange your case successfully with one whose goodwill I can rely upon, the abbot of Trois Fontaines. And then there are my own sons, one of them a monk at Trois Fontaines and the other at Orval: these too ought surely to add their support

---

[18] *Religiosus itaque et pius puer:* Goswin uses the root *pi-* some thirty-seven times, almost half of them in *Ab*, applying it to his eyes, his heart and his *viscera*, or else to our Lady's person. In *Niv*, it is used more for 'the Lord Jesus' and for such dispositions as Ida's own *conversatio* or *devotio*. In general, the root *pi-* names a tender surrender between those who mutually belong.

[19] *Et quia onerosum est Israelitis cum Aegyptiis conversari:* the same non-biblical text is applied to Ida in *Niv* 2a.

[20] The Life of Yvette, also known as Ivetta, Jutta, Juttha, or Juette is particularly well-written, authored by a local Premonstratensian canon and available in AASS, Jan 1, pp. 863–87. An English translation is available from Peregrina. She was born in 1158 to a wealthy manager of diocesan temporalities. Widowed at eighteen, she later settled her sons in Trois Fontaines and Orval. As a recluse, she was accessible to the schoolboys for edifying conversations. See *Arn* II.11a, n. 133.

[21] *Transire ad tutum ordinis Cisterciensis latibulum:* Goswin's unique use of *tutus* and of *latibulum*. His other derivatives of *lateo* are pejorative (*Niv* 7a, 12c, *Arn* I.1e, II.8c), except for a citation of Gregory, *Dial* II 1.6 in *Arn* I.6e (St Benedict 'hiding away in his cave', *in specu latitantem*). Here I translate *Ordinis Cisterciensis* to include its modern sense, but see Prol. a, n. 1, above.

[22] *Trium Fontium [...] Aureae Vallis:* Trois Fontaines was the first foundation ever made by Clairvaux, and was located eight kilometres north of St Dizier. It was mother-house to Orval, which in turn was located thirty-two kilometres west of Arlon, where a modern abbey of the same name now stands.

to mine on your behalf.' To this he replied: 'No, milady; that is not how it shall be done. Rather am I resolved to make my monastic profession at Villers, and there to consummate my life.'

(4c) Now it happened during those days[23] that Dom Conrad,[24] the prior of Villers, stopped off in the city of Liège, along with some monks who were to receive sacred orders. It also happened that Abundus, the beloved of the Lord, was on hand. By now he had passed from boyhood to adolescence and was about seventeen years old. Here, in the presence of Dom Conrad and the monks, he divulged the holy resolve he had in mind, and the venerable prior, impressed by his simplicity and modesty, encouraged him and cheerfully told him: 'Go ahead, son; go to our abbot, Dom Charles, and explain your wish to him. On arrival home, I myself and these monks of ours, will help your case along, standing on the sidelines, as it were.' Abundus gratefully agreed and returned home gladly confident that the promise thus made would find sure fulfilment and that he would eventually be received.

5. His Novitiate at Villers

(5a) Not long after this, Abundus bade farewell to his parents and friends, and also bade a wholehearted farewell to the world and its seductive promises. Off he went to the monastery of Villers, as festive and gladsome as if entering a *garden of delights* (Gen. 2.8), following the lead of those *living creatures, that went their way and never turned back* (Ezek. 1.9–14, 17).[25] And so Abundus came before Dom Charles, *the father of the monastery* (*RB* 33.5), and made his petition to be received as a novice. Certain monks, including the prior, made intercession for him. *And so it came to pass* (Gen. 1.5, etc.).

(5b) On entering the novices' probationary cell, Abundus maintained the same poised *behaviour* that had marked his conduct in the world outside, the same mildness of heart, affability of speech, readiness to conform to all and be a burden to none, the same lovable goodwill for everyone. The year ran its cycle and around came the longed-for day, the day for him to *promise stability, conversion of manners and obedience* (*RB* 58.17), a threefold promise to restrain himself, as by a *threefold cord, difficult to snap* (Eccles. 4.12).

---

[23] *In diebus illis:* an echo of the opening phrase for narrative lessons in the lectionary. See also at *Niv* 27f and *Arn* II.11a; but not as in *Ab* 18d, for in this case it is literally the opening of a relative clause.

[24] On Conrad, and on Charles (mentioned below), see Cawley, 'Four Abbots', pp. 307–14 and pp. 302–07.

[25] The same imagery come up in *Niv* 15c. This chapter of *Ab* has almost no anecdotic elements. Couched in traditional jargon, it could apply to any good novice. The opening chapters of Alice the Leper are similarly non-anecdotic. But also see *Ab* 6a, n. 28, below.

(5c) Outwardly he was being vested with a cowl ritually blessed, but what he experienced inwardly was a gracious visitation of the Holy Spirit. Small wonder, inasmuch as we read how one of the fathers claims to have seen the same Spirit hovering over the blessing of a cowl as John saw hovering over the baptizing of the Lord (John 1.32). And, to tell the truth, the blessed cowl that a novice receives is itself the *light which shines in the shadows*, shines, that is to say, even where the worldlings fix their gaze. *It shines, but the shadows grasp it not* (John 1.5). Admire it they may, and even at times praise the austerity, praise the entire *conversatio* of the cloister-dwellers; but being worldlings and pseudo-Christians, they shy away from it, shy away and show how little they have grasped of the mystery behind the cowl and its blessing.[26] Thus cowled, Christ's new recruit strove *to make more and more progress* (*RB* 62.4), for he well knew that unwillingness to progress is itself a retrogression.

(5d) *Jacob once saw a ladder* and on the ladder he saw *angels*, none of them just perching there, or slouching, but all *climbing* either *up or down* (Gen. 28.12), as much as to say that in this mortal life there is no state intermediate between advancing and slipping back. Just as surely as this body of ours is always either growing or shrinking, so too our spirit is necessarily always either advancing or slipping back. And so the young Abundus, like a strenuous runner, wished to set his goal where Christ set his, of whom it is said: *he became obedient even unto death* (Phil. 2.8). However far Abundus might run, only by reaching all the way to death could he *lay hold of the prize* (I Cor. 9.24), which itself was Christ (Phil. 3.14).

(5e) Then too it is written that *all who wish to live piously* will suffer persecution (II Tim 3.12). Thus, when the ancient foe saw Abundus's innocent and strenuous *conversatio*, he repeatedly tapped him on the heart with enticing suggestions, but to no avail. At times too he appeared to him visibly in the guise of a comely naked woman, using wanton words to coax him into sin. But he, as one of those who *approach the service of God* on a footing of justice and reverence and who *prepare their soul for temptations* (Ecclus. 2.1), simply signed himself with the cross and thereby powerfully put that turncoat[27] to flight!

6. Seven Years Later: His First Mystical Experience

(6a) Having brought to naught these temptations of the devil, and having completed his seventh year in the Order,[28] Abundus felt only disdain for life here

---

[26] *Cuculla*: the ample, ankle-length outer garment, with long, broad sleeves and a warm hood, given at solemn profession.

[27] *Signo crucis edito potenter a se versipellem fugavit:* almost identical with *Niv* 13d and *Arn* II.8d. This incident is the nearest thing to an actual anecdote in this chapter.

[28] *Cum jam septimum complesset annum in ordine:* given the non-anecdotal character of the last chapter and the schematic nature of the vision in this one, it is tempting to dismiss this

below, *full* as it is *of* manifold *wretchedness* (Job 14.1). He was ill at ease in bearing with it, as with some heavy yoke laid upon him. Meantime he steered his heart's every yearning upwards towards heaven, day and night intently giving himself over to assiduous prayer and divine contemplation. It was then that he resolved to beg something from the Almighty Lord, to beg it *in season and out of season* (II Tim 4.2), to beg with every fibre of his heart, begging for it in the fullest measure ever granted to mortals to experience while on sojourn in this frail flesh. Namely, he begged that the Lord deign in his unspeakable mercy to reveal to him those things that *eye has not seen, nor ear heard,* things that *have not arisen in the heart of man,* the things that *God has prepared for such as love him* (I Cor. 2.9).

In petitioning such things from the Lord, we should not imagine him acting out of presumptuous curiosity, since, as already stressed, his heart's whole longing was for his total transition, if possible, over to God, to be plunged into the lightsome, unfathomable abyss of the supreme divinity, there to *rest* in supreme jubilation, *in peace in the selfsame* (Ps. 4.9), in a *peace to surpass all imagining* (Phil. 4.7).

(6b) This prayer of his he protracted day after day, *wrestling,* like another *Jacob* (Gen. 32. 24), with the *angel of great counsel* (Isa. 9.6: LXX), valiantly holding his ground in that combat and, ever in the hope of a hearing, crying out with a cry more of the affections than of the tongue: *'I shall not let you go, Lord, until you have blessed me'* (Gen. 32.26). Finally, when fourteen days had passed and he was at prayer in church around the hour of terce, then, no mere *angel of the Lord,* but the very Lord of all angels *blessed him in the same place* (ibid. 29). For *there indeed the hand of the Lord was set upon him* (Ezek. 1.3; 3.22) and there came down on him so great and so sudden an outpouring of grace that he became verily drunk with it, drunk as with *spiced wine* (Cant. 8.2), and he passed over into a totally *other frame of mind* (II Macc. 5.17).[29]

(6c) Forthwith he beheld the *heavens open* before him (Acts 7.55), and he was raptured in spirit up into that admirable sanctuary of the supreme majesty. Upon entering, he beheld a vision, loftier than his soul's eye could grasp, loftier than his

---

date as an editorial 'round number'. However, see *Arn* II.6C where we find an equally schematic vision tied down to a well-established episode. Indeed, the end of Abundus's seventh year at Villers, 1213/14, was marked by a transition most significant to his career, the replacement of the 'stiff' Abbot Conrad by the 'merry' Abbot Walter. Again, see Cawley 'Four Abbots', p. 317. The added factor of a precise liturgical dating confirms the historicity of the event, around the time of terce, one day in Christmastide, after two weeks of praying for such a gift. This was Walter's first Christmas as abbot, and we might guess that some word of his, in Advent or at Christmas, prompted Abundus to pray for such a 'sending of God'. Just a couple of Christmases later, the young Ida and Beatrice would experience something very similar (*Beat* I.10–11, 52–59; and, as pointed out in the Introduction to the Lives, p. 21. *Niv* Appendix III, pp. 110–116, Walter was himself a leading advocate of the whole matter of 'sending God'.

[29] *Ut totus transiret in mentis alienationem:* see *Niv* 17e, n. 76.

entire mind. For he was beholding the unchangeable light of the Lord, wondrously beholding the wondrous Lord himself. Wondrously, I say, for he beheld him in a manner only the distributor of graces could allow him; beheld him, him who is triple in persons, single in substance: him whom to behold, whom to cling to, to rejoice in, to reign with, to possess without fail, is itself *life everlasting* (John 17.3). Nothing we could ever think up could be more joyous than such a beholding, nothing more lovable than such a bliss, nothing more delightful than such a glory!

(6d) This contemplative of ours (compare *Ab* 2c) beheld also the God-man, Christ the Lord, beheld him glorified at the right hand of the Father, with a glory beyond that of all angels and saints. And heard the invitation: *'Draw near to me, my son'* (Gen. 27.26), and he felt himself drawing nearer, and then he seemed to hear the words: 'Aha! you have beheld what you were yearning to behold: you have beheld Father, Son and Holy Spirit, one single Lord! You *have beheld and have been glad* (John 8.56)! Let me assure you, my son, that to behold this vision is nothing other than to behold those things that *eye has not seen nor ear heard,* those things that *have not arisen in the heart of man,* those things that I myself *have prepared for those who love me'* (I Cor. 2.9).

(6e) After beholding and hearkening to things so great and wondrous, Abundus made his way back from those studios of bliss to this vale of lament.[30] But he could still recall to memory *what he had hearkened to and beheld* (Matt. 11.4), and in his doing so, *the floodgates* of his head *burst open* (Gen. 7.11) and his eyes were drenched in a tidal wave of tears, a wave so great that for many a day thereafter he could scarce forbear to weep.[31] Thus, in his *thinking, his ever avid thinking* (Antiphon: St Benedict), he hurried back again and again to that lofty festivity, and drew from it no small consolation for himself. It should be noted that Abundus said it was between Christmas and Epiphany that he saw this vision, and also that for many a day after receiving such abundant refreshment at the sumptuous table of so sublime a host, all earthly food was insipid to his bodily palate. And small wonder, since divine nourishment is so potent, so effective, that the more abundantly a faithful, love-wounded soul is filled and fattened on it, the more thoroughly tasteless do all transitory consolations and bodily foods become for it. Hence, such a soul finds it joyous and sweet to have its *conversatio in heaven* (Phil. 3.20) and to *savour the things that are above* (Col. 3.2).

(6f) Along the same lines, there was, in our own time and region, a nun of holy *conversatio,*[32] the ardour of whose love and yearning was often so intense that she

---

[30] *De officinis gaudiorum ad vallem plorationis:* for the *studios* or 'workshops', see *Niv* 33g, n. 191.

[31] *Ruptae sunt cataractae:* see *Niv* 1i, and *Arn* II.9b, n. 124.

[32] Is this nun Ida the Compassionate of Nivelles? Five clues mildly suggest, or at least allow of an affirmative answer: (i) she is a *monialis,* and therefore presumably Cistercian; (ii) the verb tenses show her dead at the time of writing (mid-1230s), and Ida is the only local female Cistercian ecstatic known to have died before then; (iii) the theme of *anxietas amoris*

would fall into what outwardly seemed a bodily drowsing. She would become *beside herself in mind* (Acts 11.5) and be spiritually raptured aloft into heaven, where she would linger a long, long time, being deliciously pastured on the lifegiving nourishment of sublime contemplation, the very nourishment the angelic spirits are pastured upon. And subsequently she could take no bodily food or drink for as many as five to eight days, when at last *she would come back to herself* (Acts 12.11) and be once more restored to the common life and the comradeship of her sisters. And what wonder of it if this holy woman, on return from on high, found all bodily foods were insipid? She had been *forestalled* by her Bridegroom, *forestalled with the blessings of his sweetness* (Ps. 20.4). She had been stirred up, so to say, to a holy gluttony, stirred to fill the belly of her soul with a divine nourishment so abundant that, willingly or even against her will, she had to belch out her revelations,[33] those wondrous, marvellous revelations which the divine goodness used to show her. Nevertheless, such things must now be set aside while we return to the narrative proposed.

7. Experience on John the Baptist's Day

(7a) One time Abundus was on kitchen duty, along with another monk, both having been assigned on the Saturday. Their week was the one in which the birthday of the Lord's precursor was to fall. Throughout that week they were to take turns on alternate days fulfilling the allotted duties.[34] When the feast-day had dawned and high mass begun, Abundus donned his scapular[35] and went to the kitchen to afford

---

ac desiderii is germane to Ida (*Niv* 3c, 20ac, 29b–3). But there is also a pejorative 'anxiety' in *Niv* 16ab; (iv) though a duration of specifically five or eight days is not mentioned anywhere in Ida's anecdotes, it fits well with the gossip about her reflected in such apologies as *Niv* 17e; (v) the *contubernium* of cenobitic sisters, to which the ecstatic returns, is important to Ida. See *Niv* 12d, 22a.

[33] *Eructare oporteret eam miras et mirabiles revelationes:* the 'belching' echoes mainly Ps. 44. 2, *eructavit cor meum verbum bonum,* but also Pss 18.3; 118.171; 143.13; 144.7.

[34] Weekly duties were assigned by the cantor (Goswin) and announced on Saturday mornings (*EO* 70.21–24). The Cistercians revised the kitchen service envisaged by *RB* 35, since they had lay brothers available for the main tasks (*EO* 108; also 76 and 77). This left the monks doing little more than waiting at table and fulfilling such menial chores as hauling fuel and foodstuffs or scouring vessels. Another divergence from *RB* lay in *EO*'s calling for a pair of monks each week, who would serve on alternate days and be mutually on call in need. Large communities could assign two such pairs each week (*EO* 108.23), but Villers was apparently not yet doing that.

[35] This scapular is the apron of *RB* 55.6. Nowadays it is worn as an ornament for the tunic, and the cowl, when used, is donned over it, but in Goswin's time the scapular was still functional and went on outside the cowl, which, at least in theory, was worn at all times. Use

help to the lay brothers' cooking the portions. Then, towards the end of mass, he came out and was strolling in the cloister, when he heard the monks in choir singing the communion verse: *You, my child, shall be called prophet of the most high* (Luke 1. 76).

(7b) He reflected on the force of these words, and on the sweet-sounding modulation of the voices, so assiduously and intently that *his heart grew warm within him and in his meditation there sprang up that fire* (Ps. 38.4) which the Lord Jesus had *kindled upon the earth, vehemently wishing to see it blaze up* (Luke 12. 49). He forthwith turned aside into the chapter room and laid himself down on the flagstones, with his arms sweetly embracing, as it were, the guest of his soul in holy love. When mass was over, he did himself violence and hurried to the dormitory, lest any of the monks notice him. The signal was given for mixt, but given so unobtrusively that, with his mind intent on heavenly things, he forgot to take it (*RB* 35.12 and 38.10).[36] After sext he again donned the scapular, and at the dinner gong he entered the refectory to check that no brother lacked a portion. He then hurried away, leaving his partner, who was of lay estate, to replace him in the kitchen for the washing of the serving bowls.[37] Thus he returned to the chapter room, longing to regain the interrupted repose of his leisurely contemplation. And once there, he was of a sudden inebriated with such an abundance of grace that, *mentally beside himself* (Acts 11.5), he flew aloft to the fatherland and delightedly fixed his soul's eye on the more-than-glorious spectacle of that supreme city.

(7c) Meanwhile the brethren were in their material refectory, consuming their bodily meal and perhaps hearing the weekly reader recite some passage about the Lord's precursor as the *burning and glowing lamp* (John 5. 35). But Abundus was in this spiritual refectory, being fattened on the marrow of supreme sweetness and reading from the Book of Life a lesson containing the fullest and the best.[38] He spent

---

of the scapular was normally forbidden except for work, but it could be donned for warmth, on condition that one was already wearing all three tunics and both cowls (*EO* 74.19). For certain jobs one could go without the scapular, and even doff the cowl, wearing simply the tunic and belt (*EO* 72.20–22; *Arn* I.7b, 10ac). There was a strong tradition that one should be dressed in the cowl at the moment of death, and, of course, buried in it. This concern is beautifully explained in Caesarius, *DM* 11.36, p. 298.

[36] *Oblitus est mixtum accipere:* the mixt was the snack of bread and wine envisaged by *RB* 38.10 for servers and the reader before dinner. It was extended in *EO* to others with special needs. See *EO* 73, etc., and also *Arn* II.4g, n. 92.

[37] *Vicarium suum, fratrem laicum, relinquens [...] paropsides [...]:* this *laicus* (layman) is not a *conversus* (lay brother) but a fellow choir monk of lay status. Status as cleric or lay was a factor in choosing which days and which roles each server should take, especially in ceremonies (*EO* 77.2–6, 108.7–13). The word *paropsis* is not used in *EO*, where dishes to be washed are called *scutellae*. Goswin's term comes in Matt. 23. 25–6, 26. 23, and I suggest that the echo is intended.

[38] For another such metaphorical refectory, see *Niv* 19c, 29b–4. For a metaphorical book,

there the whole length of the meal in sabbatical leisure[39] and only afterwards awoke from his slumber of grace.

(7d) I imagine the *Father of mercies* (II Cor. 1.3) readily condoned his omission of any mealtime duties in kitchen or refectory. As for myself, so hardhearted, so lukewarm: woe is me! What can one so wretched say or do? I have no trace of spiritual fervour to bring before Christ my judge, whereas this blessed man has *kept up his innocence* (Ps. 36.37) and his goodly simplicity, fervently spending his days in holy meditations and divine contemplations.[40] The only thing for the likes of me to do is to turn to that *Father of mercies* who, in decreeing that his only-begotten Son become incarnate, *showed us his mercy* (Ps. 84.8), a mercy clad in our misery, a mercy operating in a manner wholly new, a mercy effecting a remedy by means of this very misery of our miserable selves![41] Let us therefore speak to him prayerfully and say: *Lord and Father, Lord of our life* (Ecclus. 23.1, 4), you have *redeemed us by the precious blood* of your Son (I Pet. 1.18–19); so please keep in mind now the suffering and the cross of that Son; *deal with us now, not in accord with our sins; repay us now, not in accord with our* torpor, our negligence; but *let your mercies swiftly forestall us, us who have become so poor, so very poor indeed* (Pss 102.10 and 78, as worded in the Lenten ferial tract).

8. The Virgin Seen Chanting with the Monks

(8a) Another time Abundus was assigned the duty of invitatory (*EO* 104, etc.). This was between Circumcision and Epiphany, when we sing the set of antiphons beginning with the *O admirabile commercium* and all dealing with the Lord's incarnation. On one of those days he was standing in choir at the beginning of terce and it was just as if he had said to the blessed Virgin Mother: '*Show me*, o sweetest

---

see *Niv* 22c, 30d; *Arn* II.1d. As cantor, Goswin was the one to assign refectory reading suitable to the liturgy of the day (*EO* 106.2, 115.32) and on this occasion there was indeed a strong possibility that the assignment was St Bernard's one extant sermon for the Baptist's birth, based precisely on John 5.35.

[39] *Sabbatizans*: unique participial use in Goswin, but see the plays on *sabbatum* in *Niv* 23a, 30b; *Arn* II.4d.

[40] *In sanctis meditationibus et divinis contemplationibus:* both these mental activities are in the plural, as in *Niv* 29.

[41] *Ut ego et mei similes rogemus Patrem misericordiarum, qui dum unigenitum suum incarnari constituit ostendit nobis misericordiam suam nostra indutam miseria et novo miserendi genere de ipsa miseria miserorum operantem remedia,* a word play hard to capture in English, since for us most of the key terms would be too closely related, or not related at all, or would have a twist alien to the Latin. In Latin, all four terms are cognate, and the play is the more pleasing in that first use of *misericordia,* in the plural, echoes Paul and the last, in the singular, echoes the psalms. See also *Arn* II.7a, n. 107.

one, *show me your face; and let your voice sound in my ears!'* (Cant. 2.14). For he suddenly beheld her standing at his side, the *most blessed among women* (Luke 1.28, 42), mother of the King of glory, dressed in a most beautiful cowl, with her head veiled like a nun's. But the veil was finely woven and was spotless in its cleanliness; also it was so arranged that it hung down a little in front of the face. And he heard her singing along with the monks, chanting that hymn composed to honour her and her most blessed Son: *A solis ortus cardine.*[42]

(8b). From this vision Abundus's spirit took so great an inward consolation that he marvelled at having the strength left to stand on his feet and not swoon away. So sweet was the blessed Virgin's voice as she sang, and her face so agreeable, so gracious, so resplendent that, had certain other monks chanced to see that face or hear that singing voice, they could scarcely have withheld tears in sheer jubilee of heart.[43] The holy Virgin, as we were saying, stood and sang with the singers; smiling a sweet smile as she joined the singers in their joy, in the yearning of their hearts, in the rise and fall of their voices, as they leapt up Godward, like David at play, *dancing and leaping with all his might before the Lord* (II Sam. 6.14–16). Yes, at that hour they were indeed magnifying and praising the Son in the mother and the mother in the Son. And at the last stanza of that hymn, the *Gloria tibi, Domine, qui natus es de virgine,* that same Virgin who, second only to her Son, is the mirror of all humility,[44] herself now bowed in all devout reverence along with the bowing choir. Afterwards, as invitator for the week, Abundus intoned the antiphon *Rubum quem viderat Moyses* (The Bush which Moses Saw) and she whose untinged virginity is symbolized by that *unsinged burning bush,* herself followed suit and intoned the psalm: *Ad Dominum cum tribularer clamavi* (To the Lord in the Hour of my Distress, I called, Ps. 119.1).[45] And from then until the end of the hour, she stayed on

---

[42] *A solis ortus cardine.* This hymn, in later times sung at lauds, was in Goswin's time sung at terce.

[43] *Ut si forte aliqui ex monachis ejus faciem vidissent:* as in *Niv* 29b-4, n. 148. I suggest, behind the anonymity, Goswin has particular monks in mind. See also *Niv* 2e.

[44] *Speculum totius humilitatis:* Goswin presents various 'looking-glasses': *Niv* Prol. d, 2e, 29b–8, 33b, 34g, 35a, 35: line 1; *Arn* I.12d; II.6d, 17b (bis); *Ab* 7b, 8b. He uses the verb form, *speculare,* in *Niv* verses, line 10; *Ab* 12b; the abstract noun, *speculatio,* in *Niv* 29b–8; the concrete noun, *spectaculum,* in *Niv* 2c, 29b–7; and, most significantly, the adjective, *speculativus,* in *Niv* 6b, 11a; *Arn* II.8d, 21h; *Ab* 13e, 16g. Goswin's three heroes are 'persons of the looking-glass': *vir speculativus* (masculine) or *speculativa Christi sponsa* (feminine). The 'looking-glass' can be conceived of as a crystal ball, or a lens, or a mirror. A looking-glass is often extolled for its lightsomeness, with such superlatives as *lucidissimum* or *supergloriosum.* In the present text, since superlatives hardly befit humility, Goswin uses *totius* instead: for anyone gazing on Mary she becomes a lens focusing the whole of humility.

[45] The monks stood in choir in order of seniority, and when one member intoned an antiphon, the corresponding psalm was intoned by the one immediately junior to him at his side (*EO* 104.14).

in choir, conforming to the choir in everything, chanting with it, pausing with it in the middle of the verses, and likewise bowing down with it for the *Gloria* at the end of each psalm, until at last she withdrew from her servant's eyes and *became invisible* (III Kings 20.40; II Macc. 3.34).

(8c) Should anyone refuse this vision credence, as seeming fictitious in his estimation, I for my part shall presume on the man of God's simplicity and the sincere intention of his heart. Moreover, *in order to bear witness to its truth* (John 5. 3, 18.37) I shall bring forward what I have heard from his own mouth.

9. Abundus as Trusted Courier for the Virgin

(9a) For he told me[46] that, not only on this occasion did the blessed Virgin appear to him, but frequently indeed, as I shall explain below. Yet I was puzzled at his statement, and so I went on to ask whether or not, when the blessed Virgin appears to him, he recognizes the truth of the vision beyond any doubt. He answered: 'Indeed and very well! In a true vision my clue is always the blessed Virgin's face. She is not one to let me be led astray by him *who transfigures himself into an angel of* light' (II Cor. 11.14). He went on to say that, just as a drop of water added to a large quantity of wine is immediately and entirely absorbed by the wine, so was it with his own faculties of sense: at times while these were intent on things divine, he would pass over into *another frame of mind* (II Macc. 5.17), and then these sense faculties would be absorbed by the abundant onrush of grace. And when he was in such a state, and the blessed Virgin then made her presence felt, she and he would forthwith speak to one another, exchanging words back and forth.[47]

(9b) Hence, some who knew of his familiarity with the blessed Virgin would at times ask him to commend them to her in his holy prayers. Some likewise were concerned for the souls of recently deceased relatives and would at times ask him to request the blessed Virgin to reveal whether the souls had been assigned to purgatorial places (compare *Niv* 5a, 9a, 10b). He did as they bade him, and did it adroitly;[48] but, as he himself puts it, he sometimes hears promptly from the blessed Virgin, and sometimes only with delay.

---

[46] *Quod ab ejus ore audivi. Dixit enim mihi [...]*: the *dixit* begins a new chapter, but the *enim* links it so intimately with *audivi* as almost to make it part of the same sentence. This would suggest that the division of the Life into chapters was an afterthought.

[47] *Ita ut conserto ad invicem sermone loquerentur*: Goswin's only use of *conserere*. Elsewhere he uses instead the biblical *sermocinari* (chatting), or his favourite onomatopoetic noun *susurrium* (whisper): see *Ab* 17b, n. 100. The tone used for Abundus's exchanges with our Lady squares admirably with that in the Letter of Thomas the Cantor (Appendix IV, below). These experiences are not just passive upliftings in the course of liturgical euphoria, but also sublimations of intense altruistic intercession, as requested by third parties.

[48] Unique use of *sollerter*: by Goswin, occurring only once in the Bible, at Ecclus. 19.22.

(9c) Occasionally too, the blessed Virgin, wishing to give individuals a chance to outgrow a sinful habit,[49] would *put a word on the lips* of her servant, saying (II Sam 14.3): 'Go, my son, to such and such persons; speak to them of this and that; give them my word about these and those signs, so that they turn aside from such and such sins.' The persons to whom he was thus sent would then acknowledge themselves as the ones in question,[50] seeing they could not deny the many signs the mother of mercy had set up for them through her servant. They would then strive to live more correctly. Well impressed, they would go on to magnify the Lord who thus privileged his servant Abundus with this wondrous grace of recognizing by revelation what was on the consciences of others.

(9d) There should be no doubting these visions, or rather these revelations, made to Abundus, since so many of the things he said to such persons, or about them, have indeed come true. And if any should ask why I do not give the personal names of individuals I include here and elsewhere in my narrative, but cover them under a seal of silence, they may rest assured that this is lest any publishing of the names in the hearing of many make the persons either run the risk of elation over possible human applause, or else suffer embarrassment and scandal over vituperation from third parties.[51]

10. Exchange of Kisses with the Virgin

(10a) Another time when the blessed Virgin presented herself to him he spoke up, not out of the boldness characteristic of presumption but out of the affection characteristic of great love, and he said: 'O most kindly Lady, the Lord knows with what yearning, if you would allow it, I yearn for your, yes, your hand, yes, to kiss it!' [52] And how would the mother of loving-kindness reply, if not in words of loving-

---

[49] *Resipiscendi a peccatis:* this compact verb (growing wise anew) is widespread in monastic literature and also comes in *Niv* 11b; *Arn* II.14b, but occurs only once in Bible, at II Tim. 2.26.

[50] *Reatum suum agnoscentes:* the word *reatus* is the abstract noun for the adjective *reus, rea.* See *Arn* I.3d and *Niv* 29b–1, where it accurately echoes *RB* 7.64. *Reus* itself comes from the concrete noun *res* (thing, affair), and means 'the person involved in the affair', and since the context typically implies moral responsibility, the typical translation is 'the guilty one, the culprit'. Hence, the abstract *reatus* is often translated as 'guilt', as if it were synonymous with *culpa* (culpability). It would, however, be alien to Goswin's thought to use 'guilt' here, since in our day many use that term for something quite different, namely the perplexities of an ill-formed conscience. A similar problem attaches to translating Goswin's term *scrupulositas* in *Niv* 16a, n. 65.

[51] There is an almost identical apology in *Niv* 16e and in *Arn* 18b.

[52] *O, inquit, benignissima domina, Dominus novit quanto desiderio vestram, si id mihi a vobis concedatur, desidero manum osculari:* my English attempts to render Goswin's

kindness? Lifting her right hand to her loved one's face she said: 'Draw near, dear son; be it done for you as you request!' Trustingly he drew near, and reverently and sincerely and humbly. And then he was indeed privileged to kiss that venerable hand! But that *mother of fair love* (Ecclus. 24.24) wished to show even more aptly what holy love she had for her servant and so, wonderful to say, she in turn drew near to him, she in turn kissed him and said: 'Be not surprised, dearly beloved, that I have bestowed on you this kiss, for it does but show afresh the bond I have shown time and again, the unbreakable bond of holy charity that glues my heart to yours. And this, all the more so in that I know how purely, how unfeignedly, the love you show me is rooted in your heart!'

(10b) Should some murmur on hearing this, and declare my statements false and unheard of, let them read again that chapter in *The Miracles of the Blessed Virgin*,[53] where it is said how she once graciously offered a cleric whom she loved, and who loved her, her very breast to suck. That should make them remove any such incredulity in their heart! Nor indeed should they marvel that this kiss was given mouth-to-mouth, since it is a lesser thing by far for mouth to unite with mouth than a human mouth with the Holy Spirit.[54]

(10c) Note, however, that such nourishment on heaven's grace was coming to Abundus frequently and that on major feast-days he was repeatedly[55] and divinely comforted with a heaping fill of loving devotion and of holy revelations.

11. The Candlemas Vision

(11a) One Candlemas the Lord showed Abundus a delightfully joyous vision. Terce was over and the cantor[56] had begun the antiphon *Ave gratia plena, Dei*

---

[53] exquisite word order: Abundus begins with what is safest to mention, standard names for Mary and for God, and leaves for last what is most daring, the kiss.

[53] On lactation stories, see L. Dewez and A. van Iterson, 'La Lactation de Saint Bernard–Légende et iconographie', *Cîteaux*, 7 (1956), 165–89. See also Brian Patrick McGuire, 'Bernard and Mary's Milk: A Northern Contribution', in *The Difficult Saint: Bernard of Clairvaux and his Tradition*, CS, 126 (Kalamazoo: CP, 1991), pp. 189–225.

[54] *Cum multo minus sit conjungi os ori quam si conjungatur Sancto Spiritui:* I take the subject of *conjungatur* to be *os*, arguing from the Holy Spirit's union with the mouth of any prophet (Acts 1.16). In *Niv* 27c, 'mouth-to-mouth' kissing is contrasted with 'spirit-to-spirit'. In *EO* 53.101 it seems ambiguous whether the pax at a Cistercian mass is given mouth-to-mouth or cheek-to-cheek, but such narrative texts as Caesarius, *DM* 4.98 (p. 267) make it clear that it was mouth-to-mouth.

[55] The verbs are in the imperfect tense, not the perfect, hence my use of 'repeatedly'.

[56] *Cum post decantationem horae tertiae inchoasset antiphonam:* no subject is expressed for *inchoasset*. I supply 'the cantor', as is given in *Ab* 11e and as called for in *EO* 47.8. It was presumably Cantor Goswin himself.

genitrix virgo, and the monks, with lighted candles in hand, were moving out of choir for the procession through the cloisters. Meanwhile Abundus was thinking over the *fullness of grace* with which that *most blessed among women* (Luke 1.28, 42) was privileged beyond the rest of womankind: how she, while ever a virgin, was also a mother, and as such, brought forth Christ the Lord, the true light, or indeed, the *true sun, the very sun of justice,* as the same antiphon goes on to say: *for out of you has risen the sun of justice, which lights up everything that exists amid the darkness.* Thinking ever upon this, Abundus suddenly burst inwardly aflame with a divine fire vehement enough to melt him away, just *as wax melts away before the fire* (Ps. 67.3). Ah, how it cheered him, this meditation on the words of that antiphon and the sweet modulation of its chant!

(11b) Then, just when the first halt was being made, there in the first stretch of the cloister, by the chapter room, Abundus all of a sudden beheld his Lord and Saviour, himself seemingly on the march in the procession, heading for the universal judgment of the world, with the *chosen* glimpsed on *his right* and the reprobate on *his left;* these latter to be damned, while the former would pass over to reign with their Lord in life everlasting (Matt. 25.33).[57]

(11c) Small wonder that such a vision came at such a moment, for the same antiphon, in another clause, goes on to make of *the just man Simeon* a fit representative of all the chosen; *You too rejoice, oh righteous elder, for you are receiving into your arms the liberator of our souls, receiving the one who bestows on us all this and the resurrection too!*[58] Indeed, even in this life, the chosen *receive the liberator of their souls,* receiving him into the *arms,* as it were, of a *charity unfeigned* (II Cor. 6.6). This occurs for them when, thanks to that liberator, they rise up from sin. But in the universal resurrection, which he is yet to *bestow* on them, it is they who will be received, received by him. To him they will be bound by the indissoluble bond of his own eternal love;[59] with him also they shall glory, glory even as the bride does in the canticle of love, and they shall say: *'Let his right hand embrace me'* (Cant. 2.6; 8.3).

---

[57] *Cum autem prima statio fieret [...] vidit subito [...] procedentem, electis existentibus a dextris [...].* For a description of the Candlemas procession, see *EO* 47; and for the similar procession on Palm Sunday, see *EO* 17. The word *subito* is important: the vision was but an instantaneous glimpse, at the moment of coming to a halt. Christ, being in motion and at the head of the procession, initially had his back to Abundus, but in the process of halting, Christ, like the cross-bearer, would have wheeled around to face the long lines of monks, who themselves were halting and turning inwards, to face one another as opposite choirs. In this manoeuvre, the choir that had been on Christ's right suddenly is on his left, as in the judgement scene of Matt. 25.33, 34. Within this flash, it dawns on Abundus how important it is to be on Christ's right.

[58] *Donantem nobis et resurrectionem.*

[59] *In cantico amoris:* Goswin uses this epithet for the Song of Songs also in *Arn* II.7c; but in *Arn* I.12.d he calls it the *amatorium carmen.*

(11d) The aforesaid vision once ended, Abundus again beheld his Lord and Saviour, this time standing still and at the head of the procession, face-to-face with the abbot.[60] With serene countenance and loving-kind eyes, He gazed ceaselessly upon him, warming also to the monks as they sang their songs in praise of himself and of his blessed mother. Nor was it strange that he thus show himself present to them,[61] since in the Gospel he had promised as much to all his faithful: *where two or three are gathered in his name, there is he in the midst of them* (Matt. 18.20). If that be so; indeed, because it is so,[62] no one should doubt that the Lord is on hand wherever a community convenes, be it many or few in number. Throughout the second halt, and the third, the Lord thus graciously accompanied the community, until at length all re-entered the church to songs of praise.

(11e) When the cantor had begun the introit of the mass, *Suscepimus, Deus, misericordiam tuam* (Ps. 47.10; *RB* 53.14), our contemplative yet again *had his eyes opened* (Num. 24.16), and he beheld her of whom he was so fond, her whom he had so yearned for, her after whom he had so often sighed, that beloved lover of his,[63] none other than the Virgin Mary. Yes, there he saw her, nestling in her arms the *blessed fruit of her womb* (Luke 1.42) and walking the circuit of both choirs, presenting her infant son to each monk in turn, lingering a shorter time with some and longer with others.[64] I would imagine that those to whom, in her sweet

---

[60] *Finita visione praedicta, vidit iterum [...] stantem in capite processionis secus abbatem [...] ipsum intuentem:* they are halted, but this time the left/right positions of Matt. 25 are ignored. Christ, at the head of the procession, gazes down the ranks towards the abbot, who is halted between the choirs and facing forward. Christ's face beams approval of both abbot and monks. The preposition, *secus*, is important: when governing a linear object, such as a road or a river, *secus* means 'alongside'; but when governing a non-linear object, its English equivalent has to be tailored to context, with use of 'facing' or 'at', ' or 'beside', and so on. Here the object is a person, as also in *Niv* 13b; *Arn* II.7a, and the only acceptable translation is 'facing'. Accordingly, the phrase *ipsum intuentem* sets Christ's gaze upon the abbot, not upon Abundus. See also the next note.

[61] *Et quid mirum si eis suam exhibuit praesentiam?* Does this imply that the other monks also saw Christ? The phrase could mean this when used of the Marian apparitions (*Ab* 9a, 10a), or of worldly 'showing off' (*Arn* II.18c), though in the latter case, Goswin assures us that the 'presence' the cleric 'shows' to the groups of women is explicitly a 'corporal presence' (as in *Niv* 34d). From other viewpoints, in *Niv* 14c, a nun 'cannot stand the presence' of her kinswoman's ghost, and, in *Niv* 29b–8, Ida aspires to the Holy Trinity's 'presence'. Admittedly, therefore, in the present context, the words themselves could mean that all saw Jesus, but what the context suggests is rather the invisible presence cited from the Gospel. The dignity of seer is conferred on Abundus alone; but on the abbot and monks is conferred another dignity, that of being transfigured in his eyes. See *Ab* 20b and *Niv* 19c, n. 80.

[62] *Si ita est, immo quia ita est:* the same expression comes in *Ab* 13e and in *Arn* Pref. b. See also *Arn* II.6b.

[63] *Contemplator noster [...] dilectam dilectricem suam:* see *Ab* 2c, n. 13.

[64] The apparition gives no special attention to Abundus: see notes on *Ab* 11d, 14b, 20b.

kindliness, she thus more especially and more lingeringly offered her company, were ones she knew to have given greater proof of charity and service within her household, which is that also of her Son. After the chanting of the Apostles' Creed, the *Credo in unum Deum*,[65] the monks were each offering their candles into the abbot's hand, but Abundus, still stunned from the vision, dallied behind, until the Virgin tapped him with her hand to prompt him forward in procession with the others. After everyone else, she too offered her candle, namely the great *light for enlightening the gentiles* (Luke 2.32), the light the *Father had sent into the world* (John 10.36), none other than the child Jesus himself, whom the abbot now received with devout reverence. The holy Virgin assisted at this mass from beginning to end, all through the canon and up until the deacon said the *ite missa est* and the community responded *Deo gratias*. Only then did this *finder of grace* (Luke 1.30) end her gracious intervention[66] and suddenly disappear from her servant's sight.

12. Winning his Sister to La Ramée

(12a) One day, as Abundus raised his heart aloft to gaze upon the lightsome *mansions* (John 14.2)[67] of the heavenly city, he entertained a notable solicitude for his kindred and their welfare. Thereupon a revelation came to him from God informing him that a sister of his, Mary by name, a girl *of comely build* (II Sam 14.27), was being proposed by her father for entanglement in the bond of wedlock.[68]

(12b) This proposal left Abundus quite ill at ease, for he well knew how those under the covenant and law of wedlock are often wrapped up in sundry cares and

---

[65] Today we call it the 'Nicene Creed'.

[66] *Repente inter-ventrix gratiae [...] disparuit:* Goswin's only other use of *inter-venio* is at *Arn* II.10e *(inter-veniente concordia,* compare Wisd. 14.16). But he is fond of this prefix *inter*, and I suspect he adds it here to reinforce the more usual term, *in-ventrix* (as in *Arn* II.4c), and so to coin a Marian title echoing the *in-venisti gratiam* (thou has found grace) of Luke 1.30. Literally, *in-venio* itself means 'I come upon', but in practice it means 'I find', and by extension, 'I invent'. In itself, therefore, *in-ventrix gratiae* means 'she who found/invented grace', but when reinforced as *inter-ventrix gratiae,* it takes on an overtone of the verb *intervenio,* and becomes an 'intervening intercession'. Compare *Ab* 5a, 16b, *Ab* 17d, and notes on *Arn* II.12.3 and *Niv* 4a.

[67] *Lucidas mansiones:* compare *Niv* 9d and 33a.

[68] *Puella* elegantis formae, *a patre sue proponebatur conjugali vinculo innodari:* the same term is used for the beauty of Absalom's sister, Thamar (II Sam. 14.27). More spiritual epithets for women come in *Ab* 1a *(mulier bonae spei); Niv* 12d *(puellas religiosae vitae),* 33d *(mulier honestae vitae).* The verb *innodari* (get knotted up in) is pejorative, and so I translate it as 'entangled', which also fits into the context. Goswin's other uses of *nod-* are not pejorative, but are either literal (knot in *Arn* I.2d), or literary *(e-nodare:* unravel, in *Arn* I.12f, II.6f).

have little chance to spend leisure on the Lord. So he thought up something he could do, and he carried it through to a happy conclusion. Getting his abbot's permission, he set out for the monastery of La Ramée to try and win the good graces of the sisters there, and of *the mother of the monastery* (*RB* 33.5). With this, by God's grace, he would arrange for Mary to be enlisted in their company. Upon arrival at La Ramée he summoned the abbess aside and gave her a confidential and orderly account of his sister's peril; then with modest pleas and gentle warmth he broached his plan for her welfare, urging that she be received as a house sister.[69] With all promptitude, the abbess gave his petition a *favourable* hearing, and soon could assert it had also been favourably heard by the assembled sisters. In this was verified a revelation, shown him the previous night, while he lodged at the grange of Mellemont, a revelation assuring him his request would have results swifter than any would expect.[70] Thanking the abbess and community for their graciousness, he now conceived so sure a hope for his sister's conversion that he did not return to his monastery but, *gladsome and well pleased* (Isa. 35.2), directed his steps straight to the family home.[71]

(12c) His parents were greatly cheered by his arrival and started asking its motive, but he was too well aware of *times for being quiet and times for talking* (Eccles. 3.7) to give an immediate answer. Nonetheless, he beckoned his sister Mary aside and addressed her briefly with the following salutary instruction: 'It has been confided to me,[72] dearest sister, that the will of your heart and the will of your father are agreed and that you are lined up shortly to marry a certain young man. And what do I advise in this regard? Wedlock I praise, as a thing instituted by God; but what I notice in wedlock is the multiple danger it presents for the soul's salvation. You too could profitably take note of those dangers. Your father is fleshly and cares for you in a fleshly manner, aiming to marry you off to a fleshly husband, one who is *fleshly-*

---

[69] *Ut in sororem domus reciperetur:* literally, 'received so as to become a sister of the house'. From similar epithets with *domus* (*Arn* Pref. b, I.8a, 11b; II.21i) one might take this to mean that Mary became a lay sister; but from *Ab* 12cd it is clear that she became a nun (*monialis*).

[70] *Confestim [...] exaudiens [...] exauditam esse asseruit, ut revelatio vera esse probaretur [...] qua videlicet revelatione [...] celerem [...] consequeretur effectum:* the complex Latin sentence heightens the 'speed' of the events. One might ask if the abbess had been secretly forewarned by Abbot Walter, and had talked the case over with the nuns in advance.

[71] En route from La Ramée to Huy, did Abundus spend a second night at Mellemont? Either way, his final leg of the journey dwarfs the first day's thirteen kilometres hop from Villers to Mellemont. Why so short a first hop? I suggest it offered some practical advantage, such as a ride on an abbey vehicle, which may well have been Arnulf's own weekend bread run (*Arn* II.2, 3).

[72] *Insinuatum est mihi [...] quod [...] nubere debeas:* Goswin's terms of confidential communication deserve much study. *Insinuo* itself is also used in *Niv* 8c, *Arn* I.9b; II.9a, 14: title; *Ab* 4c, 12a and 15c. For *debeo* as used here, see *Niv* 15c, n. 62.

minded (Rom. 8.5), *earthly* (Phil. 3.19) and subject to death. I on the other hand care for you in Christ Jesus, with a charity at once brotherly and spiritual; and if I, find that you agree with my exhortation, I would like to dedicate you as a bride stably wedded to a heavenly groom, not subject to any death. And if you ask how that could be, let me inform you that I have already obtained for you a prebend and a living at the monastery of La Ramée, enabling you to take the nun's habit there, remaining a virgin and entering the service of Christ. The entire world would be closed out from your heart, and you would enclose Christ the Lord, your king and groom, within the embrace of your arms, the arms of a holy love, of a devoted obedience, even as he opens out his hands on the cross and surrenders himself totally into your embrace. Indeed, such is his unspeakable loving-kindness, and such his mercy, that he is forced to surrender himself thus to your embrace.[73] So open your mouth now to the Holy Spirit; let *his grace enlighten you* inwardly (Collect: Third Sunday of Advent) and enable you to weigh how much better it is to assent to this spiritual wedding than to that fleshly one. And note this: such a plan will far more please the holy Virgin Mother and her blessed Son.'[74] To this she replied with *compunction of heart* (*RB* 49.4): 'Dear brother, if the thing for me to do is to reject secular life and wed myself to Christ, to leave the world and enter the cloister, for the privilege of being *handmaid to the Lord*, then *be it done to me according to your word* and your promise' (Luke 1.38).

(12d) Hearing this, Abundus was gladdened indeed and, summoning their father, set about pleading his sister's case: 'Father dear, your daughter, my sister, has been inwardly instructed by a whispering of the Holy Spirit to disdain[75] the bond a fleshly wedding would bring her, and she desires instead to make her own a sisterly

---

[73] *Ut excluso a corde tuo [...] amplectaris quasi quibusdam ulnis [...], qui expansis [...] manibus in tuos se totum offert amplexus [...]:* a similar play on 'exclude/include' (or enclose) regarding recluses in *Niv* 1a: *excluso a se toto mundo, totas se incluserunt cum Deo.*

[74] A similarly Marian note will mark the girl's reply (next paragraph) and will next day be a major motive of the father's consent (*Ab* 12d). See also *Arn* II.20b, n. 174.

[75] *Vitam saecularem spernere [...] copulam carnalium contemnit nuptiarum et cohabitationem [...] desiderat adipisci.* How strong is this 'spurning' and 'contempt' of secular life and marriage? Goswin's only other use of *sperno* (*Arn* I.6e) is in a common sense choice between two options, 'rejecting' one and 'choosing' (*eligo*) the other. As for *contemno* (which Frenken transcribes as *contem-p-nit*), Goswin uses it four times: twice as a pejorative antonym to 'obedience' (*Niv* 9b and *Arn* II.4b) and twice as an admirable 'disdaining' of human wrongs or diabolic seduction (*Niv* 30b and *Arn* II.8a). Hence, my rather mild translation here as 'reject, disdain'. Also, the *copula* mentioned is not called *carnalis*, as if physical copulation were meant, but *copula carnalium nuptiarum*, meaning the interpersonal bond: 'a fleshly wedding'. The Latin table of contents has the synonymous, *maritali copulanda erat conjugio.* Also, the alternative to this *copula*, which is offered in the text, is equally interpersonal: 'sisterly cohabitation' *(cohabitationem sororum monasterii, Ab* 12d below).

companionship which I have recently engaged for her at the monastery of La Ramée, there to become a nun and *serve the Lord in reverence* (Ps. 2.11), on the alert as she looks forward to the goal[76] of her life.' On hearing this, the father was stricken inwardly with heartfelt chagrin and he replied to his son harshly. He asserted outright that he would in no way endure his daughter's departing, nor could he for a moment do without the sight of one so tenderly loved without being greatly disappointed. Abundus saw how his father was not yielding at all, and so he postponed any renewal of his request, putting his hope for a happy conclusion to his sister's case in *the God who was his helper* (Ps. 17.3) and in the blessed Virgin, his consoler.[77] On the other hand, a fear came upon the father that he might be impeding his daughter's welfare and that he might be punished by an avenging visitation from God. So next day, when his son began again to press his plea, he softened into a mood of loving-kindness and broke into tears with the words: 'My son, I do not wish, I do not dare, to oppose either you or my daughter. Then again, I am persuaded that my daughter's conversion would be pleasing to God and to the blessed Virgin. And so, *let it be done to you as you have requested*' (IV Kings 2.10).

(12e) This answer made Abundus doubly glad. It greatly gladdened the girl's mother as well, who, however many sons and daughters she might give birth to, wished, as far as she was able, to give them all over to God and bring them all up for him alone. On the other hand, among the populace, a surprising rumour went out, and many were astonished and in wonderment that a girl whose marriage had already been arranged should bid the world an eager farewell and enter a cloister. But other folk, better and more religious, praised Almighty God for the maid's conversion, naming it a wondrous *change* wrought *by the right hand of the most high* (Ps. 76.11); even as the worldlings and the uninstructed, in their love for this present age, could only scorn a maid thus settled in the fear of God. *Silly* themselves, such folk reckoned her a *silly, useless virgin*' (Matt. 25.2).

(12f) She herself, nevertheless, bade the relatives and friends farewell and made her way to the cloister of La Ramée, there to serve the Lord and to flee from that other cloister, the horrid cloister of hell. May heavenly grace strengthen her and may happy perseverance bring her through to yet another cloister, the glorious, delightful cloister of heaven.

---

[76] *Vigilanter praestolando terminum vitae suae:* of itself this would be just a chronological 'terminus of her life' (*Niv* 9c, 33a; *Arn* II.20d), but with *vigilanter praestolando* it becomes eschatological, and so I translate it as 'goal'.

[77] *Consolatrice sua:* used of our Lady in *Ab* 13c, 16g, 19c and *Arn* II.5c; but Goswin uses it of Ida herself in *Niv* 16d, 30e, 35ii.

13. Assumption Day and Jerome's Understatement

(13a) Once when *that resplendent festivity* came around, the one *beyond compare among all festivities of the saints* (Antiphon: Assumption), namely the Assumption of the perpetual Virgin, and when Abundus was with the rest of the brethren at vigils, he was deeply saddened as he listened to the reading taken from St Jerome.[78] At the outset of that sermon Jerome lacks assertiveness and speaks of the doctrine of the blessed Virgin's Assumption as if it were a mere matter of opinion. I imagine that, given a chance to discuss this with Jerome face to face and to point out the slighting of the Virgin Mother, Abundus could scarcely have kept calm. And little wonder if we note what Jerome says: namely, that she was buried in the valley of Jehosaphat and that later her tomb appeared empty. But why the surprise at the Church's believing her resuscitated and adorned with manifold well-deserved prerogatives? And why the surprise that she be even now glorying in a blessed immortality shared with her Son in heaven? Accordingly, Abundus longed to hear a definite statement on the matter, and from then on he took to praying frequently about it, begging that his desire on this score be fulfilled.

(13b) Thus, at prayer one day, he suddenly became *beside himself in mind* (Acts 11.5) and he beheld, confronting him, someone robed as a monk. This person bade him: *'Follow me'* (Acts 23.11). And follow him he did, or so it seemed in the vision, for the two of them now left the gate of the monastery, and Abundus, coming along behind, asked his leader: 'Where are you going to take me to, o servant of God?' The other turned and replied: 'Do not be afraid, just follow me with trust.' So *the pair of them together* (IV Kings 2. 7) forged ahead, and after a short distance they entered a garden, a wondrously delightful garden, like a true *paradise of the Lord* (Gen. 13.10), filled with trees fair and fruited. Forthwith his leader *was no more to be seen* (II Macc. 3.34).

(13c) The man of God was delighted at the beauty of the place, and, moving forward, came upon another man, *seated under a tree* (III Kings 19.4), a man elderly in years and venerable for the grey of his hair and the serenity of his countenance. In front of him he held a book in which he was writing at a lingering pace. The entire

---

[78] Transmitted among the works of Jerome as an address to Paula and Eustochium, *De assumptione sanctae Mariae virginis*, PL 30, 123–24; but in fact composed by Paschasius Radbertus (d. 860 AD), precisely to serve as readings for this feast; ed. by A. Ripberger, Corpus Christianorum Continuatio Mediaeualis, 56C (Turnhout: Brepols, 1985). Parts of it are translated and discussed by E. Wellens ('L'Ordre de Cîteaux et l'Assomption', *COCR*, 13 (1951), 30–51). One of Goswin's duties as cantor was to make sure the Patristic lectionary got to the refectory in time for a continuation of the vigils readings, and though we can be sure he took the option of skipping this, the fact remains that it was widely read in the refectory. It was in fact widely used at all three nocturns, and in the refectory. The malaise felt by Abundus was widespread. Wellens cites parallel objections in Caesarius (*DM* VIII.37) and in Thomas of Cantimpré (*BUA* II.29.10, pp. 537–39).

book was full of writing, except for the last four leaves, for these showed as yet no trace of the pen. So the man of God addressed the other and said: 'Please, venerable elder, tell me who you are and what this book is and why you are writing in it so lingeringly?' He replied: 'I am the prophet Elijah. As Scripture testifies, I was lifted up from earth in a *fiery chariot* (IV Kings 2.11), and this is the place to which, by God's will, I was brought. This book is called *the Book of Life* (Apoc. 3.5) and in it are written the names of the chosen, those who are going to be saved. As soon as any of the chosen migrate from the body, *the spirit of the Lord*, who *sees into everything* and knows everything (I Cor. 2.10), reveals to me their passing and also their names, which I then insert in this book. As for the lingering pace of my writing, you may understand from that *how few they are who are saved* (Luke 13.23). And as for these last four leaves of the book, seen to be still blank: when they too are duly filled, then will the world come to an end; then too will Christ the Lord come for the general judgment, to *render to all in accord with their works* (Matt. 16.27).

(13d) After Elijah had told him all this, our contemplative took leave of him and stepped into a basilica that stood there, not at all large but located by the garden's edge. Once inside, he fell to praying and suddenly beheld standing in front of him a bride-like person, indeed that fairest of the daughters of Jerusalem, the very one who used so faithfully to visit him, the Virgin Mary herself. She now accosted him by his own name: 'Brother Abundus, my beloved, draw near to me!' So he drew nearer and reverently greeted her. And she, loving-kind as ever, told him: 'You have, my dear, been suffering for my sake from a thing weighing on your heart. Hence have I thought to appear to you and bring joy and consolation to your heart. Granting that Jerome spoke of my Assumption as a matter of opinion, Augustine, on the other hand, came out with a definite statement. In a sermon of his[79] he clearly asserts my complete glorification, body and soul. But listen also to the reasoning that makes this so true and certain. My holy Son *was conceived of* my own clean flesh *through the Holy Spirit* (Apostles' Creed). If this be so, indeed, because it is so, how incongruous it would have been that he, as one part of my flesh, should be in heaven while the other part would be on earth!' Incongruous without a doubt, and unjust besides, for the body of the Son, and such a Son,[80] to be resuscitated and glorified in heaven, but the body of the mother, and such a mother, not to be resuscitated but to remain in the tomb until the universal resurrection of all bodies!

(13e) After hearing this, the man of vision *came back to himself* (Acts 12.11). He did not neglect to render the thanks he owed for all he had been shown, both to the Lord of all[81] and to her who had been his kindly consoler. And recalling the blessed Virgin's words about Augustine's definitely witnessing to her Assumption, Abundus

---

[79] I have no reference to suggest for this.

[80] *Corpus filii, et talis filii [...] matris, et talis matris:* similar reinforcing phrases are found in *Arn* I.4e (*ferulam et talem ferulam*) and in *Ab* 11d and *Arn* Pref. b.

[81] *Domino universorum:* the same divine title comes also in *Niv* 6b and *Arn* II.6e.

questioned a preacher of wide erudition. The preacher hesitated to assert what he himself had not read, but relayed the question to the masters in Paris, and from them he learned that Augustine, erudite as he was and most spiritual, had indeed preached that way in a sermon of his.

14. The Virgin Seen Solacing Monks at the Harvest

(14a) One day in harvest time, the monks were in a field, intent on *gathering in the crops,* as the Rule foresees (*RB* 48.7). Amid their dogged labour, the heat became excruciating, what with the fiery sun engulfing the earth with a heat as sweltering as that of a frying pan. The prior, therefore, gave a signal for all to take a rest, and Abundus took his a little apart from the others, where he could *pour out his heart like water before the Lord* his God (Lam. 2.19).

(14b) Suddenly he beheld two women, coming across the field towards the main body of monks at their rest. Simultaneously he beheld a man standing at his very side, one quite unknown to him. He nodded to the man, by way of asking who were these newly arrived women, and why had they come. The man answered that it was the mother of the Lord. Indeed, Mary herself had come along and was paying the community a visit. The other woman, her companion, said he, was the other Mary, the one known as the Magdalene (Luke 8.2). And what did that mother of loving-kindness, that mother of mercy,[82] then do? She took compassion on each of the monks, drew near to each of them,[83] and with the sleeve of her robe fanned each face with caressing, cooling strokes that chased away their sweat. And when she had finished doing this, she raised her right hand, made the sign of the cross and blessed the whole community, whereupon both women withdrew by the same route as they had come.

(14c) This vision is said not to have been seen by any of those present, except for Abundus, but from that moment to the end of the harvest, our harvesters were to enjoy during work time a coolness so gratifying that the very sun was felt to have tempered its ardour for them, and this, out of reverence for the mother of the Lord.[84]

---

[82] *Matrem esse Domini; Mariam causa visitandi [...] advenisse:* Frenken forces the punctuation of this text, which he acknowledges to be corrupt. It would not be like Goswin to separate the name *Maria* from the epithet *matrem Domini,* but, since the verb *(advenisse)* has slipped into the infinitive mood, and since no conjunction has been supplied, an editor's only option is to force the punctuation. But see also the rather strange word order in *haec mandat tibi mater Christi, Maria* (*Ab* 18d).

[83] *Compassa singulis [...] ad singulos [...] singulorum facies:* see *Ab* 11e, n. 64

[84] How does Goswin know that all the monks experienced relief and that all attributed it to our Lady? I suggest he is echoing some devout comment, private or public, which had echoed throughout the community. A heat wave can be quite a conversation piece in monasteries, especially in the abbot's remarks at daily chapter. If, for instance, this heat wave ended on a

15. Vision of Bernard of Villers and John of Nivelle

(15a) A monk of Villers named Bernard had run the course of his life in the Order and had reached the final stages. His immediate approach to death came at night, and so there was *an urgent rattling of the wooden gong* (*EO* 92.4, 116.18)[85] to awaken the brethren from sleep and to hasten them along to provide his soul with all due support as it took leave of his body. Once the soul had left and its *commendatio* was over (ibid.), the body was carried to church and the brethren went back to bed.

(15b) Abundus was thus half asleep and half awake, when suddenly there *stood before him* this same Brother Bernard (Acts 23.11), who seemed very pleased with himself, and who broke into speech saying: 'Oh, if I but wished it! Oh, if I but wished it, what great, what wondrous things I could tell of how divine is God Almighty![86] Oh, if I but wished it! Oh, if I but wished it, what sweet, what astounding things I could tell of the everlasting blissful glory the saints enjoy!' He went on to add: 'From the time I came to the Order and made profession as a monk, I lived out one long martyrdom, what with my head ever prone to aching, my body ever prone to illness, my heart ever prone to temptations. Yet, because I bore with these many inconveniences of heart and body, the good God, *bounteous giver of all good things* (Ritual: Meal Prayers), has prepared for me an everlasting repose as a colleague to the martyrs.' Having said this much, he slipped away from Abundus's eyes and *became invisible* (II *Macc.* 3.34)

(15c) Master John of Nivelle, a man of respectable *conversatio* and deserving of praise on many scores and *whose memory is in benediction* (Ecclus. 45.1), likewise appeared posthumously to Abundus, as to someone he loved.[87] Abundus asked how matters stood for him and he replied: 'All is well with me, sweet brother, dear friend! But if you wish to know more fully how things stand with me, let me tell you briefly and confidentially. While I was still dwelling in the mortal flesh, I was *God's helper* (I Cor. 3.9) in frequent dealings with religious women. I had a holy familiarity with them, while taking pains *to console the fainthearted* (Isa. 35.4; I Thess. 5.14) and

---

feast of our Lady, she would get public thanks, which would occasion citing of personal evidence of relief experienced as coming from her. Also, such a comment would have a worthy precedent in Herbert of Clairvaux (I.32) and in the *Exordium Magnum* (III.13).

[85] *Crebris ictibus tabulae:* in *EO* 92.4, 116.18, we are told how, on the verge of a death, the infirmarian comes to the cloister adjacent to the infirmary and gives this vigorous signal. For the wooden gong itself, see the note on *Arn* I 11c, n. 64.

[86] *O si vellem, o si vellem [...] de divinitate Dei omnipotentis dicerem:* A similar cry is accompanied by a smile in *Niv* 10c: *O quam bene! O quam bene!* Also, *divinitas* here has the same sense as in *Ab* 6a; *Arn* II.6f; and especially *Niv* 21d, 22b, 28f and 29b5. It means that transcendent aspect of God experienced only by persons far advanced in prayer.

[87] The three references in this chapter to mutual friendship between Master John of Nivelle and Abundus tell us much about Abundus's position within the Villers community, in that he was allowed to consort with the cream of the local clergy (see *Arn* II.13b).

hear the confessions of them all. During the confessions, sins would be laid bare in all their unclean aspects, apt to tickle the flesh to wanton revelry; but all this I converted into matter for virtue. Hence, though I stood amid this conflagration of the flesh, I was *never scorched by its flames* (Antiphon: Sext, St Lawrence); I held fast to my chastity, a chastity dedicated to God, and never did I fall in battle, nor did *my enemy ever gloat over me* (Ps. 40.12). Indeed, so broadly did I stretch my neighbourly charity, and so *keen a zeal* (III Kings 19.10, 14) did I practise for the salvation of souls, that I used to consider *myself a debtor both to the sophisticated and to the unsophisticated* (Rom. 1.14), conforming myself to all in everything. I longed for the good to move on to what was yet better, and the evil to *come to acknowledge the truth* (I Tim. 2.4). Such, therefore, were the two good things found in me: charity and chastity. Together they afforded me considerable standing with God and earned me great merit in his sight.' After saying these things, this godly man *vanished* from his beloved Abundus's sight (Luke 24.31).

(15d) That all might know how great a desire this blessed and godly man had for the saving of souls, I shall add a brief example. Master John's gaze once fell upon a woman who was a harlot; so he beckoned her and promised two shillings if she would desist from fornication for the one night. She agreed to the pact, but some bystanders remarked: 'What are you doing, good sir? Good master, what are you doing? Why waste such money?' He replied with cheery countenance: 'No, dear brothers, do not speak like that! There is more worth and merit with God in one night spent holding oneself back from sin than in all the passing things of this world!' Good evidence of how vehement a charity had inwardly *wounded* him (Cant. 4.9). A single night's hire he preferred to the wealth of all the world, if only it could lead to the saving of a soul!

16. Deathbed Conversion of a Nephew

(16a) Another Assumption day Abundus was anticipating that the blessed Virgin would be revealing something to him, as she did on her other feasts. Thus, at vigils that day he kept lifting the lucid gaze of his mind to contemplate that glorious looking-glass of the heavenly court, which is the Virgin herself.[88]

(16b) Suddenly he beheld her. Then he heard her tell him: 'Brother Abundus, at this moment a friend of yours is afflicted with troubles beyond measure. So I wish to alert you to implore my help for him.'[89] Straightway and wholeheartedly he gave

---

[88] *Ad contemplandum gloriosum illud spectaculum curiae coelestis:* Goswin also uses *spectaculum* at *Niv* 24c, to epitomize an episode seen in apparition, as in our English 'spectacle'. This meaning could apply here also, but I read it rather as synonymous with the *speculum* of *Ab* 8b, where our Lady is the 'looking-glass of all humility'.

[89] *Quapropter volo te esse admonitum ut pro illo meum implores auxilium:* there is a similar heavenly concern for earthly suffrages in *Niv* 9b.

himself over to interceding for the friend, for in his own inner spirit he knew well enough who the person was, none other than his sister's son, a citizen of Huy named John. But as for what John's anxious troubles might be, Abundus had no idea.[90] This John, young in years and bound by wedlock, had youth's typical nonchalance and *proneness to evil* (Gen. 8.21), ever ready with an ever-yearning mind to embrace this passing world's every variety of wanton revelry. It pleased God, however, to put a stop to his vagabond will by letting him fall ill, very soon to die. On the eve of the Assumption he was stricken with a severe insanity, which made his whole body shake so astonishingly that those around him could barely hold him down. From the fourth watch of the night until prime on the day itself, he kept wretchedly shouting: 'I am in hell! I am in hell!' [91]

(16d) This, then, was the trouble which the mother of God had mentioned to her loving[92] Abundus at vigils. When her vigils and lauds were over and it was time for the day's matutinal mass,[93] Abundus approached the altar and received communion from the hand of the priest. It was a Tuesday,[94] but, since he had not received the Lord's body on Sunday, he partook of that lifegiving banquet fare now. He had not yet swallowed the saving food when once again the blessed Virgin appeared to him and asserted that the frenzied youth had been freed, freed from the fierce fury that had come over him.

(16e) Indeed, when John had finally *come back to himself* (Acts 12.11), he had with serene countenance gazed on those sitting around him and said: 'Sign yourselves! Sign yourselves, my friends! Surely you saw it was the devil who held me so strongly chained all night and even till now, hoping to drag me down with him to hell! But *blessed be the Lord,* who has freed me and *has not given me as prey to those teeth* (Ps. 123.6)! Yes, I am convinced someone has taken compassion on my

---

[90] *Sed causam qua tribulatione angeretur penitus ignorabat:* similarly incomplete revelations come in the Letters of Thomas the Cantor. See Appendix IV, below.

[91] Alice the Leper similarly identified certain spasms as experiences of either hell or purgatory.

[92] *Amatori suo Abundo:* see *Ab* 10b, n. 54.

[93] *Hora missae matutinalis:* this was an additional community mass, celebrated after prime on Sundays and certain feasts (*EO* 34.1–3, 60.1–32; etc.).

[94] The illness can be dated by its context and thanks to mention of what day of the week a fixed feast fell on:

(i) The illness must have been later than 1213/14, when Abundus's visions began (*Ab* 6a), but (ii) before the end of 1237, when Goswin's literary patron, Abbot William, left office. Also, (iii) in a year when Assumption fell on Tuesday (1217, 1223, 1228 or 1234), and (iv) when the married sister of a monk born in 1189 would be old enough to have a married son. I favour the last possibility, 1234, when Abundus's reputation as an intercessor was well established and the memory of John's death was fresh enough in his mind to share with Goswin, who began his interviews about that time, or soon after.

sufferings, has prayerfully and powerfully come to my aid, so that the wicked old apostate stands cheated of his hope, forced to fall back in retreat. This whole *vexation has afforded me understanding,* (Isa. 28.19) and now I must acknowledge having all too often offended my creator. So please, quickly, call in a priest for me, a vicar of Christ,[95] that I may confess to him my sins.' A priest was duly called, and on his arrival the young man vomited from the bottom of his heart all the poison of sin he had imbibed throughout his life. Then, *putting off the old man* and *putting on the new* (Eph. 4.22–24; *EO* 102.41–43), he began to look forward with goodly confidence to the imminent day of his dying.

(16f) Meantime a messenger was sent to Villers to inform Brother Abundus of all that had happened to John. Abundus asked the messenger at what hour the malicious spirit had begun to weary him and *at what hour* it had abandoned him to his weariness (John 4.52).[96] In this way he learned, with full evidence, that all had happened at just the hours the mother of God had first revealed. When the messenger got home again, he found that the young man, who had been alive at his leaving, was now dead. The death, too, Abundus learned of by revelation. He was, however, still ignorant of what became of the soul; and so he prayed for a new divine revelation to learn which place it had gone to after laying down its baggage of flesh.

(16g) One night a short time later, after surrendering himself to repose, Abundus had *a vision of the night* (Dan. 7.13) and beheld a bridge, a very narrow bridge, across a wide, deep expanse of water. And there went John, there across that bridge! On reaching the midpoint, his footstep wavered, he slipped into the water and sank under completely. On seeing this, the merciful man Abundus called out to the mother of mercy and, with every fibre of his heart, begged that she swiftly snatch the poor wretch from those whirling waters. And she, consoler of the wretched, was on hand forthwith to fulfill her servant's plea: she heaved the lad from the water and set his drowned body high and dry. Abundus was shocked. The grief was too much for him. He mustered his most devout pleas and appealed to her again: 'Dear, gracious Lady, if ever I have done anything acceptable to you, let me plead with your loving-kindness. You, by your Son's grace, can give life even to the dead. Raise this dead man up!' He gave the command, and up the dead man rose! Her meek and humble servant *spoke further* (Isa. 7.10) to his Lady, asking for the meaning of the lad's thus drowning and thus being revived. She replied: 'In his drowning, understand that, while still in the mortal flesh, he was *bent headlong towards evil* (Gen. 8.21) and was drowned in a whirlpool of vices. *To the world,* he was reputed *alive,* but *to God he was really dead* (Rom. 6.10–11). And understand in his reviving that mercy came

---

[95] *Vicarium Christi:* used of confessors in *Niv* 13c, 29b–1; *Arn* I.1c. *Vicarius* is used in other contexts in *Ab* 7c; *Arn* II.16c.

[96] *Qua hora [...] fatigare coepit et qua hora fatigatum deseruit:* typical Goswinian tautology. *Fatigo* (usually in the passive) comes in *Niv* seventeen times, in *Arn* twelve times, but only three times in *Ab.*

his way from my Son, a mercy manifested in his repenting of his sins and confessing them all before he died. Indeed, if he had passed from the body still impenitent and without confessing, he would have been excluded from the fellowship of the *blessed* and assigned eternally to the punishments of hell.' When the vision was over and the man of vision had *returned to himself* (Acts 12.11), he rehearsed the memory of all he had seen. All he could then find suitable to do was to give due thanks to her who is the consoler of the desolate.

17. Freeing a Man from Fleshly Temptation

(17a) A certain devout man had a caring love for a girl living a dedicated religious life. In his best simplicity and the charity of Christ the Lord, he used to speak with her at times on quite familiar terms. It is the way with familiarity of a man to a woman, or of a woman to a man, that when it becomes excessive it can become quite a stumbling block and an occasion of sin for either party. This it clearly did for this man. The spiritual love he had been showing the girl turned into a fleshly love. *The spirit of fornication* (Litany), whose *breath brings the embers aglow* (Job 41.12), was stimulating him to evil. Fleshly thoughts were enticing and increasingly disquieting him. These thoughts he resisted as best he could, for he was aware that any such thought ripening in the heart has to be promptly resisted, lest any delay nurture and invigorate it. Fearful and with an eye to the future, lest the disease he was suffering *spread like a canker* (II Tim. 2.17) and sap the *vigour* and vitality of his soul,[97] he betook himself to Abundus and disclosed to him his temptation, asking him to pour out a prompt and efficacious prayer for himself to her who is the helper of the desolate and the queen of the world.

(17b) Abundus had no difficulty accommodating to the level[98] of this man in trouble, since he was always compassionate and nurtured kind feelings for the afflicted.[99] Thus with one loud whisper of his heart[100] he besought the mother of

---

[97] *Et vitalem animae ejus vigorem depasceret:* the same expression and same text from II Tim. is found also at *Niv* 6a.

[98] *Non fuit difficile viro Dei condescendere tribulato:* for *condescendo*, see *Niv* 1e, 6a. It never has a pejorative tone in Goswin.

[99] *Praesertim cum ipse esset valde compatiens et super afflictos pia gestans viscera:* the fancy order of words suggests a literary borrowing, though spontaneous uses of *viscera* are frequent in Goswin: *Niv* 9ac, 21d, 27e, 29b–5; *Arn* I.3b, II.1b, 7c, 16a.

[100] *Oravit itaque clamoso cordis susurrio:* this term s*usurrium* (whisper) is a favourite of Goswin's: it appears nine times in *Niv*, four times in *Arn* and two times in *Ab*. It is versatile enough to range from gossip going on behind Ida's back (*Niv* 1e) and from Arnulf's all-too-audible muttering as he prays in the dormitory (*Arn* I.9b) to the lofty two-way exchanges between Ida and the Trinity (*Niv* 28f). The term is largely avoided by Ida's editor, Henriquez, probably for its assonance with the pejorative term *murmurium*; but of itself it is neutral and

chastity and purity to hasten to the aid of this disconsolate man. His prayer was heard and a few days later the tempted man came back to his intercessor to thank him and tell him he had been freed from all temptation.

18. Saving the Vocation of a Tempted Novice

(18a) A young cleric had been coming often to Villers, trying to incline the *father of the monastery* to take him in (*RB* 33.5).[101] His importuning eventually won him what he sought and he was received as a novice. When his year of probation was partly over he began to tire of the rugged path and to be so pressed by temptations as even to wish to shrink from his undertaking back to the world from which he had come. Amid the bitter sadness of these temptations his heart was like a ship at sea, surrounded on every side by storms, until at last he saw what a good thing it would be to manifest his temptations to Abundus, whose suffrage and prayers would surely bring him some relief from the burden pressing upon him.

(18b) This he did, and Abundus, *like a prudent physician,* (*RB* 27.2, 28.2) applied a plaster of salutary exhortation to the wound of his heart and consoled him with gentle warmth. And what did the novice then do? Over and over again, he accepted a small measure of this consolation. For as long as Abundus was actually speaking to him, he would accept this little encouragement, but once out of his presence, he would slip back into a pit of temptation.

(18c) One day when his consoler was thus speaking with him, he answered that on the morrow he would head back to the world. On hearing this, the merciful man threw his whole self[102] into bringing aid *to the wavering brother* (*RB* 27.3). Indeed, he waylaid the blessed Virgin, *waylaid* that mother of mercy *face to face* (Ps. 94.2), for the need was greatly pressing. Thus, the following night, while Abundus was at leisure for prayer and contemplation, she, his most clement visitor, appeared to him

---

needs to borrow a tone from qualifying adjectives. Thus Goswin speaks four times of a *dulce susurrium,* twice of a *mellitum,* and once apiece of a *gratum, gratiosum, secretum, internum, familiare, clamosum* or *importunum susurrium.* The whisper can come from a heavenly person or an earthly, and can be a monologue or a dialogue, a *soliloquium* or a *colloquium.* These latter two terms Goswin qualifies with similar adjectives, including *devotum, sanctum* and *familiare.* He also uses the biblical verb *sermocinare,* though without adding emphasis or qualifiers.

[101] *Patris monasterii:* The same epithet comes in *Ab* 5a, 12b (*matris*). Goswin often adds this genitive, *monasterii,* when introducing a person or a locale, just as he adds *monasterium,* in the appropriate grammatical case, when introducing an abbey by name. The present phrase is too stereotyped to offer a clue as to which abbot of Villers is meant here.

[102] *Vir misericors totum se contulit ad ferendum opem.* For *vir misericors* see *Ab* 16h, 18c; *Arn* II.3d, 12a, 18a. I find no feminine equivalent used of Ida, though she is so often described as 'compassionate'. If not she, at least her 'eye' is 'merciful' in *Niv* 14a.

and *put a word into his mouth* (II Sam 14.3, 19) saying 'Tomorrow you must summon that novice and speak to him on my account and tell him thus and so.'

(18d) When daylight came, Abundus spoke to the novice secretly and as early as he could. He said: 'Peace with you, brother! *Take courage and be stouthearted!* (Deut. 31.7). Here is a message for you from Mary, the mother of Christ.[103] Back in the days when, for the sake of all your goodwill, you had finally obtained that the abbot accept you, there was an occasion when you were to have fornicated[104] with a woman, but the moment came and you thought the matter over again and again: how offensive to that mother it would be if you, so soon to be a monk, carried such a sin into effect before her very eyes. So, out of reverence and love for her, you brushed the woman aside and did not do the sinful deed. Such is the token the sweet Virgin is sending you: it should give you to understand how she wishes you manfully to resist temptation and *to share in the sufferings* of her Son (I Pet. 4.13), ever intent on happily persevering in good works. Indeed, unless *you persevere to the end, you cannot be saved'* (Matt. 10.22). When the novice heard this he was astounded. Acknowledging how true was what he had been told about himself, he learned from then on to bear with temptations as best he could. And when the year was over, he received the habit of a monk.[105]

19. Encouraging the Lay Brother Baldwin

(19a) Baldwin, a lay brother of Villers, who has since *gone the way of all flesh* (III Kings 2.2),[106] had, while still out in the world, not yet learned anything of the spiritual knighthood,[107] and so in the first year of his conversion, the year of probation, he had great difficulty keeping up with his confrères in its practice. He had a hard time bearing the discomforts *of the flesh* involved in the vigils, fasts and other outward observances of the Order, but on top of them came *stings* of temptation (II Cor. 12.7), such that in the end he was even thinking of return to the world, like *a dog going back to its vomit* (Prov. 26.11; II Pet. 2.22). *Amid* such a *predicament* (I Sam 22.2) he found *a man after his own heart* (I Sam. 13.14), Brother

---

[103] *Haec mandat tibi mater Christi, Maria.* See *Ab* 14b, n. 82.

[104] *Fornicari debuisti:* the verb *debeo* normally has the sense of a debt or a moral obligation, but often in Goswin it has the sense of 'being all lined up to do a thing'. I count five such uses in *Niv*, six in *Arn*, but only two in *Ab*, here and at *Ab* 12c.

[105] *Ac anno expleto, monachi habitum suscepit:* on what novices wore, see *EO* 102.13 and *Arn* I.7b.

[106] This is not the same Baldwin as in *Arn* I.9b, for that one was already at Villers when Arnulf was a novice, and so several years before Abundus himself had even entered.

[107] *Militiam spiritualem:* does Goswin have in mind that Baldwin had been a secular knight (*milit-*) before entering?

Abundus, who was to prove an apt consoler, one ready to share in bearing the burden of his temptations.

(19b) So he approached Abundus and told him what sufferings were bothering him. Abundus welcomed him warmly, and thereafter such familiarity grew up between them that Abundus took to confiding to him many of his heavenly revelations, though ever couching them in the third person, as if made to someone else. He also offered Baldwin kindly words, aimed at building his staying power in face of *the harsh and rugged things* (*RB* 58.8). And he offered his prayers too, aiming to equip Baldwin with a shield in face of the prolonged archery of the ancient foe, who shoots at us with deadly, impassioned arrowheads to make us desert the combat and retreat from the goal.[108] This is why, both before and after his profession, this humble recruit spoke more frequently and more familiarly with his loving helper, Abundus, than did the other lay brothers.

(19c) Baldwin well knew with what holy familiarity and special charity Abundus loved the Virgin Mother, second to only her Son; and so one day as they conversed together, he made this request: 'Dear friend, I beg you in the Lord's name: do what I am going to ask.'[109] He replied: *'What do you wish me to do for you?'* (Mark 10.35–36). And the answer: *'If I have found grace in your eyes,* (Gen. 47.29) please obtain for me from that warm and kindly consoler of yours that she deign to appear to me, deign for the sake of her unutterable sweetness and of your own good prayers. Yes, I am confident that if I were allowed but once to see her glorious face, the sight would be a remedy most efficacious for me, would rid my heart of its temptations and would enable me to bear with all that disturbs the flesh.' Abundus could refuse nothing to Baldwin, and in any case it was not difficult for him to plead in devout soliloquy; so he prayed and his *prayers rose up* like *the fumes of* fragrant *aromatic incense* (Apoc. 8.4) to the presence of the Virgin Mother from the thurible of his heart, a heart aglow with a fire divine.

(19d) And later on, indeed, when Baldwin was keeping a night time vigil, with *Ave Maria,* the angelic salutation, ever on his lips, the holy Virgin appeared to him, taking a visible form. He well knew it was God's mother and, since all he had asked had been that he see her, the mere sight of her now sufficed to console him. Indeed, it consoled him so much that, from now on he was more gladsome in adversity, and at times in his soliloquies he was even drenched with the tears of devotion.

(19e) Once too, he unquestionably wept in full view of many. His year of probation was over, and it was the Nativity of the blessed Virgin, and the customary sermon was being given at chapter. Baldwin was seated in view of the abbot,[110] with

---

[108] *A proposito resilire:* comparable expressions at *Ab* 16f, 18a; *Arn* II.8c.

[109] A vivid example of 'sending God', though without a countdown to a liturgical feast. However, see *Ab* 19e, below.

[110] *Sederet in ipso capitulo coram abbate, monachis circumsedentibus et conversis:* this implies that Baldwin, though a junior lay brother, sat inside the chapter room, not only for the brief profession ceremony but also for the subsequent sermon. See *UC* 13 and *Arn* II.7c n. 104.

monks and lay brothers seated around the room. At the opening of his sermon the abbot commended and magnificently extolled the superlative holiness of the Lord's *blessed* mother, and the bashful Baldwin was so touched to the quick *at these words of grace coming forth from* the abbot's *lips* (Luke 4.22) that he quickly covered his face with his hood, for *the tears were bursting* from his eyes and he could not *hold them back* (Gen. 43.30–31). Fittingly did one so given to saluting the mother of salvation now receive from heaven so sustaining a grace!

20. Assumption and St Bernard's Day; Death of Gerard

(20a) On Assumption day of a later year, at vigils, Abundus was intent on divine contemplation and suddenly passed over into *a totally other frame of mind* (II *Macc.* 5.17), wherein he beheld the blessed Virgin. She had with her the other Mary, the mother of the sons of Zebedee.[111] The Virgin herself had a thurible in her hands and was doing the circuit of the monks' twin choirs, incensing each of them in turn.[112] Those who were lazy and sleepy, she passed quickly by; but those wide awake and energetic in their singing, she honoured with more lingering pauses, reviving them with her incense and reinvigorating them. She eventually left the monks' choir and entered that of the lay brethren, incensing them in the same fashion. And when the incensing came to an end, the vision ended also.

(20b) A few days later, when Abundus was at vigils on the feast of the blessed Father Bernard, he began as usual to lift up the focus[113] of his mind to the contemplation of heavenly things. His senses were absorbed in a transport of contemplation, and suddenly he beheld the saving Lord himself, with his venerable mother and with the blessed Bernard. All three were standing up by the high altar, facing the community of monks and eagerly listening to the singing of the chant. And little wonder, inasmuch as the chant had so lively a wording, so agreeable a melody, as might have wafted down to earth from the very *paradise of God* (Ezek. 28.13). Anyone able and willing to attune the heart's ear to such sweetness with full attention, is forced[114] to melt away inwardly and dissolve into devout tears and

---

[111] Why is the companion not Mary Magdalene, as in *Ab* 14b, Conrad, *EM* 3.13, (4.11) and Caesarius, *DM* 7.15? And if not she, then why 'Mary, mother of the sons of Zebedee?' I suggest it was to honour Abundus's own beloved mother, who was likewise named Mary and who was likewise blessed with sons named James and John. These, like Abundus and his sister Mary, had become Cistercians (*Ab* 1ab).

[112] Such circuits were regularly made by superiors, to stir up the drowsy. See the notes on *Ab* 11e, 14c. See also many other Cistercian narratives, including Caesarius, *DM* 1.35 (p. 43); 4.54 (p. 222); 7.47 (p. 67). See also *EO* 103.8; 112.1; 113.1, 115.2.

[113] *Coepit more suo mentis aciem ad coelestia contemplanda sublevare:* on such active preparation for a vision, see the notes on *Niv* 2c; *Ab* 9a.

[114] *Jubilare cogatur [...] manipulos sunt messuri:* here, and in the paragraph that follows,

jubilant delight. There stood the Lord, with his loving-kind eyes intent on those serving him, and with his hand raised to bless those blessing him. Their good deeds, *sown as a crop of blessings,* are to yield for them sheaves of everlasting glory, as a *harvest of blessings* (II Cor. 9.6) bestowed by the Lord himself. And there stood the blessed Bernard, taking quite a delight in the chant, whose text he had himself composed.[115] There too stood the holy Virgin, joining in the singers' joy.[116] She turned to her beloved Abundus and in her familiar whisper said: 'Let me tell you this, my dear: everyone of stouthearted goodwill who spontaneously offers sincere service to my Son and myself, will have me for helper to reach everlasting bliss!'

(20c) To this she added: 'Go and visit Brother Gerard, the young monk lying ill in the infirmary, and give him this message from me: the octave day of my Assumption, after compline, is when he will migrate from this present wicked world. His dying on that day will betoken the fact that after death he will have but one day to endure in purgatory.[117] After this, Christ the Lord, his venerable mother and the holy abbot slipped away from Abundus's contemplating eyes.

(20d) Abundus, giving the credit for *what he had heard and seen* (Matt. 11.4) not to any merits of his but to the goodness of God, spent the rest of vigils, and the whole day that followed, very agreeably and in great exultation of spirit. That same day, after none, the aforesaid Brother Gerard was anointed by the abbot.[118] And so it

---

there are two sudden switches to the present tense, revealing that Cantor Goswin is not merely looking back to one occasion when the chant went well; his contentment is so habitual that he absentmindedly slips into the generic present tense.

[115] *Canto ipso, cujus litteram ipse composuit:* the Cistercian Office for St Bernard was then almost the same as in modern times (*GC* 1175.2, 1200.4). Its wording interweaves phrases from both the psalmody and the Bernardine biographies, and has a strongly Bernardine tone. But, apart from the readings, its 'letter' was scarcely 'composed' by Bernard himself.

[116] *Congratulans cantantibus:* see *Ab* 8b, where the phrase parallels *dulciter arridens* (sweetly smiling upon). See also *Niv* 14b, 20d.

[117] *His intersignis quod post obitum suum una tantum die poenam sustinebit purgatorii:* Goswin has a rich concept of 'sign', and two forms of the word: *signum* (*Niv* 15c; *Arn* II.13b, 17c, 18b; *Ab* 9c, 18d) and *intersignum* (*Niv* 4b, 28g, *Arn* II.18b, *Ab* 18 tit). In *Ab* 9c our Lady's frequent messages include 'signs' to confirm their credibility. Some signs lie in past events prophetically evoked from the client's conscience (*Arn* II.13b, 17c; *Ab* 18d). Other signs lie in the future, as here, and they are *intersigna*, sign and signified are interchangeable at the convenience of the interpreter. Just as smoke betokens fire, so fire betokens smoke, the more easily observable being the *intersignum* of the less. The message to Gerard could therefore be paraphrased: 'Approach the octave with confidence, since to die on it betokens but a single day in purgatory.'

[118] *Cujus superius mentio facta est [...] Die sequenti [...]* : I do not know why Goswin feels the need to remind us who Baldwin is. What is needed is an excuse for Abundus's failure to convey the message earlier. That is what the next sentence is all about: the logical time to convey it was on St Bernard's Day, in the interval after none (*EO* 33.1, 46.7). That time would normally have been free from work, but this particular year it was taken up with the anointing.

was only the following day that Abundus, bearer of good news, paid him his visit. Sitting down beside him, Abundus asked: 'How are things with you, dear Brother Gerard?' He answered: 'Things are going well with me, and I hope to recover from my illness.' Abundus retorted: 'No, not at all; it shall not be so. Recently it was revealed to someone,[119] by the blessed Virgin Mary that you are soon to depart the body. Tomorrow, the octave of her Assumption, after compline,[120] you will *go the way of all flesh* (III Kings 2.2), destined to receive from the Lord the good things of life perennial. Please do not doubt my words, for it is the holy Virgin who addresses the message to you.'[121] Of purgatory, however, he made no mention, lest the brother start presuming on his innocence and lest his heart be inwardly wounded by any trace of vainglory, which is the *arrow that flies by day* (Ps. 90.6). When Gerard heard the message, he gratefully blessed the Lord's mother, so *blessed among women* (Luke 1.42), whose devoted lover he had long been, rendering her devout and frequent service.

(20e) All that night, in sore straits from his illness and getting no sleep for his eyes, Gerard spent the time in such measure of holy meditation as his illness allowed. In the course of this, Christ the Lord appeared to him in visible form and *spoke to him face to face* (Num. 12.8). Gerard asked who he was. It was the Lord's wish that he realize his identity and so he answered that he *was Christ.*[122] Astounded, Gerard now found himself drenched in tears. He stretched out his hands as for a collect,[123] humbly adoring his Lord and Saviour with the words: 'Please, Lord Jesus Christ, my redeemer, You whose clemency is unspeakable, please *pour out on me*

---

[119] At this point the main manuscript breaks off, though its table of contents shows that this was its final chapter. The text is completed from the other surviving manuscripts. Note how Abundus here speaks of the seer in the third person, as mentioned in *Ab* 19b, above.

[120] In *EO* 115.44–45, a death occurring after compline is dated to the next day. Gerard does not die strictly 'on' the octave, but in the glow of its 'completion' at compline. The Latin for 'compline' is *completorium,* 'the service which brings the day to completion.'

[121] *Et ne de verbis meis dubites, hoc ipsum mandat tibi Virgo sanctissima:* the sentence ends abruptly. It had begun with what looked like a purpose clause, and so we would expect it to wind up with an explanation, such as mention of the *intersigna* about the one-day purgatory. We can, however, make sense of it as it stands if we read the *ne dubites,* not as introducing a purpose clause, but as a polite imperative: 'And please do not doubt that this is what the most holy Virgin commands you.'

[122] *Dominus agnosci se ab illo voluit et Christum se esse respondit:* in Goswin's few apparitions of Christ, the identity is usually clear enough from the insignia, or, as in *Niv* 7b, 22b, at least from the message. Rarely does a seer ask the identity of the person(s) appearing , though see Abundus's questioning of Elijah in *Ab* 13d. Compare the 'Messianic secret' in Mark's Gospel, first hinted at in Mark 1.25 and climaxing in Mark 14.61. Also, John's 'knowing' the identity of the risen Lord without daring to ask (John 21.12).

[123] *In modum orantis:* Goswin, the priest, sees in the bedridden monk's hands the posture used for a collect at mass.

your mercy' Ecclus. 18.9). So the Lord smiled on him and said: 'Be not disturbed, my son, and be not frightened in your heart: the mercy you are asking of me has already been prepared for you.' And, having said this, *he was wafted away* (IV Kings 2.3–10)[124] from the sight of his humble servant.

(20f) Reflecting that he had been graciously visited by the Lord, and also visited shortly before by a messenger from the blessed Virgin Mary, Gerard *rejoiced with exceeding great joy* (Matt. 2.10), well able to say with Patriarch Jacob: *'I have seen the Lord face to face, and my soul survives intact'* (Gen. 32.30). From then until his passing, he lingeringly gave thanks and trustfully looked forward to the mercy the Saviour had promised. Next day, on the octave of the Assumption, he was as one invited to a pleasurable banquet and unable to hide the devout emotion of his heart. At some moments it was suppliant prayer that he poured out to the Lord; at others, it was pleas and sighs addressed to the blessed Virgin. Oftentimes he was drenched in tears. And yet at moments, he relaxed into such outright laughter[125] that bystanders were amazed. There had been a freshness in Gerard's recruitment for Christ, for he had been quite religious since boyhood. Some say, he had even retained his virginity. His time within the Order, after profession, was some ten months. The word of the blessed Virgin Mary was to prove correct. That same day, after compline, Gerard laid down the baggage of the flesh. And then, as soon as his purgatorial satisfaction was complete, he came into his long-desired repose.

Appendices to the Life of Abundus

We here reproduce passages about Abundus in other early writings of Villers. The first of these is the account of his death in Jean d'Assignies' French edition of the Life. The Latin manuscript behind this has been lost, but the passage is reproduced in French by Frenken, as an appendix to his edition of the basic Latin text (p. 9). Our English imitates somewhat the elegant literalism of the French.

---

[124] *A conspectu servuli sui sublatus est.*

[125] *In risu etiam interdum perfundebatur lacrimis; aliquando etiam in risum solvebatur, ut [...]:* I omit the initial *in risu* as a copyist's error. Goswin's range of smiles and tears can overlap (*Niv* 29b–6; *Ab* 8b), but what here amazes the bystanders is just the rapid switch from outright tears to outright laughter.

Appendix I

An Account of Abundus's Death

Such then, in brief, are the prayers which the mother of mercy, the advocate of sinners, deigned to vouchsafe on behalf of her devout servant Abundus. Such too the greetings she offered him. And honoured though he was, with these and many other revelations from God and his blessed mother, Abundus was held nevertheless reverently and humbly in check by a variety of afflictions, which God was sending him to prove his patience. After he had long been afflicted by a severe and painful illness, Jesus Christ, ever the consoler of those who belong to him, appeared to him once more. Indeed, lest Abundus be in doubt about the vision, our Saviour took the shape that is his as the Crucified. Now the brother who had been serving Abundus in this long illness was that day thinking of leaving his bedside and returning to the cloister, but the Lord God gave him to understand that he would earn more profit by serving Abundus one day in the infirmary than by spending forty days in the cloister. This prompted him to serve the more eagerly from then on. This he did, throughout a whole long period in which Abundus was paralyzed, with all members so weak that he could neither turn over in bed nor lift his hand to his mouth. Despite all this, Abundus remained ever patient, until the time came for so great a patience to be repaid, namely, upon his departing from the miseries of this world to enjoy eternally the delights and consolations of the kingdom of paradise. This came about on the nineteenth of March 1239, which fell that year on the eve of Palm Sunday.[126]

---

[126] *Le lendemain de la Pasque fleurie:* literally, 'on the morrow of the Easter of flowers' meaning 'the Monday following Palm Sunday'. In fact, 19 March was a Saturday in 1239. I agree with Roisin and Frenken that Jean d'Assignies mistakenly read *postridie* for *pridie:* 'morrow' for 'eve'.

Appendix II

The Epitaph

This Epitaph comes down to us in several forms. The *Gesta* offer a five-line version (Martène and Durand, col. 1354; and MGH, p. 232) at the end of their abridged Life of Abundus, with the rubric: *est autem ejus epitaphium* (and his epitaph is this). The Bollandists, however, offer a five-line version at the end, not of Abundus's Life, but of Arnulf's (AASS, June, V, p. 606). Other discrepancies between these versions are a switch in the sequence of lines 2 and 3 in Martène and Durand, and a couple of changes of wording, most notably that the *Gesta* use *are* (or *a re*) where the Bollandists use *UT RE*.

To my mind, it is the Bollandists who give the correct wording, since it makes better sense, but it is the *Gesta* that point to the correct hero, since the allusions to songbirds and the musical scale befit a choir monk better than a wagoner. The fact that the same musical metaphor occurs in Ida's epitaph makes it all the more plausible that both were composed by Cantor Goswin.

In 1982,[127] N. Huyghebaert announced discovery of yet another version, from the Abbey of Sint Truiden. Its first four lines are identical with the first four of the Bollandist version, and its last line is identical with that of the *Gesta*. Unbeknown to Fr Huyghebaert, the six intervening lines of this Sint Truiden version are identical with six lines of another epitaph, which the Bollandists print, not at the beginning, but at the end of Arnulf's Life, and which I reproduce and translate as Arnulf's first appendix. These six lines are the two opening lines of that appendix, followed by the four which immediately precede the final line.

Fr Huyghebaert offers arguments based on rhyme and on Gregorian modes to support the *Gesta's* alternative reading for the end of the last line (*a re*, rather than *ut re*). Further light could well be shed by a study of the office Goswin composed for

---

[127] N. Huyghebaert, 'Arnould ou Abond? A propos d'une épitaphe de Villers-en-Brabant', *Cîteaux*, 33 (1982), 392–96.

Mary of Oignies.[128] Only its hymns[129] are currently available to me, and though I find them very worthy of Goswin, I find no echo of themes from these epitaph verses. Thus, for the meantime, I leave the riddle to be solved by those with more expertise than myself, or at a later date.

Pausat in hac tumba vir, simplicitate columba;
Qui leo virtute; jubilis simulatur alaudae;
Qui[130] turtur gemitu, visu, simulat atque volatu;
Par aquilae; salamandra, novo quia vixit in igne
Vis breviter justi laudes in fine probare?
Nunc canit inde LA-SOL, qui quondam flevit in UT-RE

In this tomb rests a man who resembles[131] a dove for simplicity;
a lion for strength of virtue,[132] a lark for jubilant cries,[133]
a turtledove for prayerful sighing, an eagle for keen sight
and lofty flight; a fabled salamander for surviving new fire.
Would you briefly give this just man's praise a final test?
He's now trilling on La-Sol, who once moaned on Do-Re![134]

---

[128] See the Select Bibliography above, under Misonne.

[129] Guido Maria Dreves: *Hymni inediti, Liturgische Hymnen des Mittelalters*, in *Analecta Hymnica Medii Aevi*, (Leipzig, 1892, volume 12, third series, nos 323–325), pp. 178–179.

[130] Martène and Durand switch this line with the preceding one, and so attach the extraordinary vision and flight to the dove rather than to the eagle.

[131] In successive lines the Latin uses different terms to express the resemblance, as needed for the syllable count: first an implicit verb 'to be', then the passive of *simulo*. (I liken), then its active, and finally the noun *par* (a peer of).

[132] The Latin *virtus* originally means 'manliness', and by extension, 'strength' In the Latin Bible it means 'miraculous power', and in ascetic circles, 'virtue'. Here, and in several expressions that follow, I paraphrase to catch all such shades of meaning.

[133] Both editions of the *Gesta* read *nobilis* instead of *jubilis*. Though *jubilis* certainly fits the context better, *nobilis* too could make sense, since *alauda*, besides its primary meaning of 'lark', was also a nickname for one of Caesar's most dignified legions, and for the men composing it. The line would then read: 'who was a noble legionnaire, likened to a lion in strength'.

[134] Here we have the same musical allusion as in Ida's Epitaph. The scribes of the *Gesta* read the *inde* as two words and did not understand the musical allusion, and so they wrote: *nunc canit in* de la sol *qui quondam flevit in* a re. In the Martène and Durand edition of the *Gesta*, the underlined particles are italicized, and in the MGH edition they are set in inverted commas. I leave it to the musical experts to explain how a melody in 'La-Sol' sounds joyful, while one in Ut-Re (or 'Do-Re' in our modern system) sounds sad.

Appendix III

Abundus's Role in the Vocation of Gobert of Aspremont

Mention is found of Abundus in the Life of Gobert, a devout knight who ends his career as a monk of Villers. The Life is given in full in AASS, August, IV, pp. 370–395. The episode involving Abundus is a vocational consultation typical of both Abundus and Arnulf, involving mutual recourse between a monk of Villers and a holy woman of the neighbourhood, with the solution coming from our Lady. The anecdote telling of this episode forms the opening of Book II of the Life. The author prefaces it with a skilful assembly of scriptural and patristic texts, honouring the knight's conversion.

A summary version of the Life is found in the Martène and Durand *Gesta* (col. 1318–1333) and in MGH (pp. 226–29). Here the episode itself is included (col. 1320E–1321B; p. 227), but the name of Abundus is dropped, even when it should be on the lips of the heroine of the incident, Emmeloth. In the original, when this holy woman bids Gobert go to Villers, she promises he will find the ideal man to consult, who is named Abundus *(virum perfectissimum, monachum nomine Abundum);* but in the the summary she simply names Villers as 'the suitable and congenial place you have so long been seeking' *(locum aptum et complacentem, quem tantopere quaesisti).* After that, the incident is abruptly closed with *quod et factum est* (the which also came to pass). The holy woman's name, incidentally, is given in MGH as 'Enymeloth' and in Martène and Durand as 'Evimeloch'. I translate very literally, to distinguish the style from Goswin's; but I also try to do justice to the drama and rhetoric.

II.1.37 Almighty God employed a threefold strategy with this valiant athlete of his (Gobert), to have him militarily defeat three distinct foes, *the world, the flesh and the devil.*[135] This triple strategy in the one soldier would be a service paid to the divine Trinity subsisting in the one substance. Gobert, like a good knight of Christ, longed to be more stably and more devotedly available for the duties of a spiritual, a clerical knighthood, and for that reason he wished to find his place within a fellowship of monks of the Cistercian regime. And for this, he was in search of a suitable monastic community. Having already toured many a province, many a monastic community, he now journeyed on as far as Nivelles, for he had heard good rumour about the religious women dwelling there, namely the beguines. Among others, he there came upon a virgin named Emmeloth,[136] who was indeed *acceptable to God* (I Pet. 2.5) on account of the *conversatio* of her honourable life.

II.1.38 To this virgin, the tenderly devout Gobert revealed the secrets he had in his heart about conversion. He also confessed to her that he had already toured many places in search of one where he could find some holy men and a spot for himself among them. He was putting his request to her as the most eager of recruits, asking her to pray to God over the matter, because if he did not find a suitable monastic community he was planning to find his way back to his native territory. The venerable Emmeloth, steeped in flame from on high, gave this reply: 'I would ask you, dear sir, and would beg of you with most serious pleading, that before turning back and leaving, you go on as far as Villers. Because there you are sure to come upon a monk by the name of Abundus, a man of real perfection. He it is who will *tell you what it behoves you to do* (Acts 9.6).

II.1.39 On hearing this, Gobert, with all his manly and tender warmth, *rejoiced with exceeding great joy* (Matt. 2.10). Full of God, therefore, he went off and *passed over as far as* Villers (*Luke* 2.15), where he came upon the lowly Abundus. Upon their meeting, Gobert uncovered to Abundus all his secrets and handed over to him his whole business, for him to take action upon it. Now Abundus was a *reverent and devout* monk (Gregory, *Dial* II 1.2), and so this is what he did. With much dedication he took up that business of the devout Gobert, of that venerable and dedicated knight. And taking it up, he first did homage to the blessed and glorious Mary, and then he consulted her upon the business, the one who is the Virgin Mother of God, and whom, after God himself, Abundus loved with the prerogative of an altogether *privileged love* (Antiphon: St John).

II.1.40 Thus did God's own Abundus do his consulting on this business. Thus too, by God's permission, did he soon have his answer from the blessed Virgin, from her who was alone such a friend to him. This is what he told Gobert: 'It is here that God

---

[135] Traditional triad; I do not know its origin.

[136] The etymology of the name, from *E,* meaning 'out of', and *melos,* meaning 'song', could amount to a 'song from out of this world'.

and the blessed Virgin wish you to stay; because this is for you something of a *land of promise* (Heb. 11.9), and from here you will be able to win through to the *fatherland of reward.*[137] Gobert was forthwith inwardly kindled with divine love, and put his whole reliance on this advice of the venerable Abundus. And we too, let us rejoice at this! Because what Ananias had been for the Apostle Paul, that the venerable Abundus would be for the devout Gobert. Ananias had taken Paul amid his atrocious fury against the Christians and had given him the rudiments of the Catholic faith. Abundus in turn would take the knight Gobert, so proud a lover of the world and so unequal a match for his foes, and he would teach him to despise that world, to break that pride with humility, to *love his enemy* for the sake of God and to observe the whole of monk-like religion.[138] Let the sheepfold rejoice at this, the sheepfold whose lamb became a teacher to the fierce wolf! Yes, let the sheepfold of Villers rejoice as she calls home her chosen ones and gathers them together from *regions far away* (Luke 15.13), just as *a hen gathers her chicks under her wings* (Matt. 23.37). Hence comes that song of the Church: *What has made one flock of us is the love Christ has for us. So let us reverence Christ our God and love him. For where charity and love are, there is God* (Antiphon: Foot-washing Ceremony).

II.1.41 Thus did Gobert, by God's providence and by use of the venerable Abundus's advice, make in advance choice of Cistercian Villers, there in Brabant, just as if there had been written in his heart that prophetic saying of the psalmist: *Here shall I dwell, for I have chosen it* (Ps. 131.14).

---

[137] *Quia haec est terra quasi repromissionis tuae; per quam ad patriam remunerationis poteris pervenire:* the striking parallel of the two similarly built and complementary genitives suggests a literary source, but I cannot identify it.

[138] *Et omnem monachalem religionem edocuit custodire.*

Appendix IV

Abundus in the First Letter of Thomas the Cantor

During the time of Abbot Walter (1214–21), a remarkable family from Leuven entered Cistercian life. While the father and three sons ended up at Villers, a daughter, named Alice, entered Parc-aux-Dames. The eldest son shared the father's name of Rainer, and both died early. The others lived on, and the son Thomas was cantor in the early 1260s (at least), and he used his writing skills to keep up a correspondence with the daughter. Two letters survive, the first from before the death of the other brother, Godfrey Pachomius, and the second from afterwards. Thomas also wrote a Life of Godfrey Pachomius, which survives (Roisin, p. 16).

Abundus is mentioned in the letter on account of a message he had for Godfrey, which Thomas uses to console Alice in her worries. This first letter dates from about 1260. Both are published with an excellent commentary by E. Mikkers in *COCR*, 10 (1948), 161–73. I translate also the passages before and after the mention of Abundus, to convey the tone and setting.

Line 33: Regarding your desire that I write you about our brother, there is nothing else for me to write beyond my usual message: that he is healthy in the measure usual for him. As for his decease, neither he nor I know anything, except for what our kinswoman, Lady Margaret of Meggelinis has said, namely that he will not be dying within those 'five years' (though more than three of them are already over). As far as I can tell, the watch he keeps on his conscience is neither lesser nor greater than he has kept from the beginning, and indeed, it is almost from the first that I have shared his *conversatio*.

Line 39: A certain lay brother, one who used to have more dealings with the choir monks than did the rest, once told a sacristan, who was an associate of his: 'One thing has me wondering. While some have really cooled off from the religious concern of their youth, there is still Dom Pachomius, whom I can gladly admire. I see he is as religious and as fervent as ever.'

Line 44: He always has confessed every day, and still does, anything his conscience is bothering him about. Likewise, on no account would he forego taking the major discipline every ferial day.[139] Inward tears he also has often enough. Indeed, his entire prayer consists in vehement weeping and in the imploring desire of his heart. But as for outward tears, these he complains of having all too seldom. He is intent on his psalmody day and night, and to that extent he is always at prayer and seems almost to bring force to bear on God, what with heart and body ever so fervent and his thoughts so settled upon what he is at.

Line 51: He claims to be ignorant of any loftier measure or manner of God's grace, by way of contemplations and meditations, let alone visions. Yet by no means does he despair; rather he perseveres with all alacrity in serving Christ in the same old way. But yourself, how fainthearted and sad you sound as you tell me that you have no inner sweetness. It is rather our brother who ought in a way to be despairing, for he has slaved away all these years so solicitously to earn his Rachel, and yet, for all his great toil, he is not yet allowed to have her.[140]

Line 57: But then too there is the virgin of virgins, lady of the angels, queen of the heavens, Mary the mother of the most high God! And there are those hours of hers,[141] that our brother ever chants with such reverence and devotion! She it was who once gave a message along these lines through the medium of Father Abundus,[142] while that servant of Christ was still with us in the flesh.

---

[139] *Quin omnibus privatis diebus magnam acciperet disciplinam:* I have not met elsewhere the expression *magnam disciplinam*, but I note that Thomas's family entered Villers about the time that its former Abbot Conrad was presiding over the General Chapter, which imposed the Friday discipline as a suffrage for public needs of the church (*GC* 1218.1). Individuals could substitute for it the seven penitential psalms. Perhaps 'the major discipline' means, not merely extending the suffrage from Fridays to all ferial days, but also giving its duration that of the seven psalms.

[140] Traditional theme in which the two sisters, Leah and Rachel, become wives of Jacob, each of them costing him seven years of slavery to their father. Rachel, fair but barren, stands for contemplation; Leah, plain but fruitful, stands for action. The theme parallels the better known dichotomy of the two New Testament sisters, Martha and Mary, and of the two disciples, Peter and John.

[141] *Cujus horas reverenter et devote semper decantat:* this means the famous 'little office of our Lady'. It was still optional in those days, and done privately. Moreover, a scene in Caesarius, *DM* suggests that it was done in silence, so that *decantat* would imply only a metaphorical 'chanting' (Caesarius, *DM* 7.51, p. 71).

[142] *Per nonnum Abundum:* the reverential title for addressing one's seniors, prescribed in *RB* 63.12. Elsewhere in the letter *frater* and *dominus* are used. Thomas uses the same courtesy even with his sister, addressing her in the polite second person plural. The deceased Rainer does the same when addressing Abundus, his monastic senior.

Line 60: She gave the message in three consecutive visions, in the first of which she said: 'Brother Abundus, my dear, do tell my beloved servant Godfrey not to wax so fainthearted and not to grow sad. Tell him to serve my beloved Son and myself in the way he has set out to do, and let him know beyond doubt that after the pilgrimage of this exile he will, in the fatherland, have the double of everything he complains of lacking along the way.'

Line 65: Our brother Godfrey's reply to this was: 'I am in doubt whether the "Godfrey" to whom she is sending this message is myself, for there are several Godfreys here. But please, my dear Dom Abundus, do ask the dearest Lady to deign once more to show you the presence of her most gracious countenance and to clarify for you to which Godfrey she is sending this message.'

Line 70: The devout man of God did not deny his fellow's request but gave his whole self over to prayer and obtained a renewed visit of the glorious Virgin. Whereupon she said: 'Tell him it is the Godfrey from Leuven.'

Line 72: But when our brother heard this, he replied that the message was not yet sufficiently clear, for he had still a scruple over there being two other Godfreys from Leuven, both of them taller than he. So he sent God's servant back a third time on the same matter.

Line 75: And the gentle Virgin, far from being weary of him or annoyed at his stubbornness, gave the message that it was the short Godfrey from Leuven. Along with that she sent him a message about cultivating humility and patience and about persevering in his accustomed service to God. Also that he was one of her chosen chaplains[143] and that he was going to reach through to the everlasting joys.

Line 81: Consonant with this account is what the same man of God, Abundus, once told us under oath: 'Our brother monk, Rainer,[144] has appeared to me, robed in such and such traits of heavenly glory, and this is what he said: 'Dom Abundus, please tell our brother Godfrey that my message to him is that he *take courage in the Lord and do manfully* what he is doing (Josh. 1.18),[145] assured that he is going to be allotted an everlasting reward of a glory equal to my own.'

---

[143] *Quod esset ejus capellanus et ad aeterna gaudia perventurus:* in Mexican literature of the 1600s, a cleric will sign his name to a letter to another with the epithet: 'ever a humble chaplain to your reverence'. I suggest that in Thomas's day this was a masculine equivalent for the feminine title 'bride of Christ'. See *Beat* I.10, 50, line 47, where Ida discerns that Beatrice will be awarded this latter dignity.

[144] From the context, Rainer junior is meant the son, not the father of the family.

[145] *Confortari in Domino et viriliter agere quod agit:* a scriptural phrase, combined with a classic slogan, *age quod agis* (do what you are doing).

Line 87: Dearest sister, I have written you these things about our brother so that you be not fainthearted, nor more or less in despair, over your resourcelessness and your aridity. Rather take his example of a pure confession and a holy *conversatio*. Yes, await the Lord's mercy, ever lifting your hope towards him in faith and alacrity. Yes, and ruminate with frequent mindfulness upon whatever message the Lord has for you in this letter of ours and in any of our previous writings.